Rogues, Rebels, and
Rubber Stamps

URBAN POLICY CHALLENGES

Terry Nichols Clark, Series Editor

Rogues, Rebels, and Rubber Stamps

The Politics of the Chicago City Council from 1863 to the Present

Dick Simpson

With a Preface by
Studs Terkel

A Member of the Perseus Books Group

Copyright © 2001 by Westview Press, A Member of the Perseus Books Group

Published in 2001 in the United States of America by Westview Press, 5500 Central Avenue, Boulder, Colorado 80301-2877, and in the United Kingdom by Westview Press, 12 Hid's Copse Road, Cumnor Hill, Oxford OX2 9JJ

Find us on the World Wide Web at www.westviewpress.com

Library of Congress Cataloging-in-Publication Data
Simpson, Dick W.
   Rogues, rebels, and rubber stamps : the politics of the Chicago City Council, 1863 to the present / by Dick Simpson.
      p.   cm. — (Urban policy challenges)
   Includes bibliographical references and index.
   ISBN 0-8133-9763-4 (pbk.)
   1. Chicago (Ill.). City Council—History.   2. Chicago (Ill.)—Politics and government.   I. Title.   II. Series.

JS715.S56   2000
320.9773'11—dc21

                                                                            00-049530

The paper used in this publication meets the requirements of the American National Standard for Permanence of Paper for Printed Library Materials Z39.48-1984.

10   9   8

PERSEUS
POD
ON DEMAND

For my father, Warren Weldon Simpson,
who taught me stubborn courage;
and for my mother, Ola Ela Felts,
who taught me idealistic compassion

Contents

Tables and Illustrations

Photos

Maps

Preface

STUDS TERKEL

Dick Simpson was one of those reform aldermen and political opponents who got under Boss Richard J. Daley's skin. In 1971, he got Daley so mad that the mayor-for-life almost had a stroke right on the podium. I remember that moment, as a choleric mayor aimed his roundhouse punches in the manner of W. C. Fields at that "college perfesser," Dick Simpson. Alderman Simpson was Daley's enemy because he represented the little people of Chicago and he organized a ragtag group of political opponents to challenge the omnipotent Daley and the Great Chicago Machine.

Now Simpson has given us the inside story of the Chicago City Council—those rogues, rebels, and rubber stamps who have ruled the city since it was swampland stolen from the Indians. He has recaptured a part of our history that has been lost. It turns out that this is important, too. The battles on the stage of the city council are, as Simpson tells us, about defeats and sometimes surprising victories in the struggle for democracy and justice.

We are taken back to the great battles of the Civil War, the reform struggles of now forgotten mayors like Edward Dunne, the surprising defeat of big business by rogues like Bathhouse John Couglin and Hinky Dink Kenna, the battle over nepotism in Richard J. Daley's council, right up to the aldermanic scandals in son-of-boss Richard M. Daley's rubber stamp city council of today. This is a story we need to take to heart as we begin a new millennium. It is a guidebook for future rebels and reformers, not only in Chicago but throughout America.

Having tried most of my working life to give voice to the voiceless, I am delighted to discover new and previously unknown tales from the Chicago City Council, which everyone in Chicago thinks they know. It makes me wonder what other stories lie hidden in the musty vaults of city halls in other towns and cities. Hopefully, journalists, historians, and political scientists will follow Simpson's lead—and even more hopefully, maybe someday the little people will retake and reshape their own local governments. The struggle for democracy and justice is too important to be left in the hands of politicians.

Prologue:
The Clash in the Council

On July 21, 1971, as a young, newly elected alderman, I rose in the Chicago City Council to question Mayor Richard J. Daley's proposed appointment of Thomas Keane Jr. to the Zoning Board of Appeals. Keane was both the son of Daley's city council floor leader and the vice president of Arthur Rubloff Co., the largest real estate firm in Chicago.

I was hesitant to oppose his appointment because his father, Alderman Thomas E. Keane, was Daley's powerful ally. I knew that opposing his son's appointment would be seen as a personal insult to Alderman Keane and that my future legislative proposals could be thwarted. Nonetheless, this appointment of Tom Keane Jr. was not only a case of nepotism but also favored the city's largest real estate firm on a board that directly controlled zoning.[1] Since zoning determined the value of his firm's real estate properties, the younger Keane's membership on the Zoning Board of Appeals was fraught with conflicts of interest.

In questioning Keane's appointment, I made a very short speech: "This appointment poses the problem of the faith of our citizenry in our city government. Why is it that members of the same family get appointments in several sections of government and only large firms seem to get representation on boards dealing with zoning and construction?" Interrupting my speech, Mayor Daley challenged, "Who's going to ask those questions and make those charges?" I replied, "My students will." Daley countered, "And you'll encourage them."[2]

After other aldermen had spoken at length in Tom Keane Jr.'s defense, Daley read a sentimental poem by Grace Noll Crowell entitled "Sons." He then launched into the longest and most emotional tirade of his colorful career:

> I hope the halls of all the great educational institutions will stop being places for agitation and hatred against this society. And talk about the young people! With their cynical smiles and their fakery and polluted minds, and the idea that I made this appointment because a man's name was Keane and he was the son of a famous member of this council!

I made this appointment because I have known Tommy Keane, the boy I appointed, since he's been a baby. And I know his mother, Adeline Keane, one of the greatest women I know, not only in this city but in any city in the United States . . . a fine Polish-American woman, who raised a fine boy. And should that boy be told by any professor or faker that he shouldn't hold office because his name is Keane and she's his mother?

Where are we going with this kind of society? Where are we going with these kind of educators? You are doing this to the young people of our country! . . . A teacher is supposed to be dedicated to tell the truth. What kind of truth is that? . . .

Let's look at the record of the universities and what they are doing to the minds. Is that what's being told to them? I made the appointment because he is the son of the Chairman of the Finance Committee? . . . That is what we have too much of in education today—hypocrites and fakers—afraid to face the truth, afraid to let the young people to go into the combat of election contests.

They want to stand behind the cloak of a great university and tell us how wrong our country is, how wrong our society is, and they know nothing about it and they refuse to take any steps to correct it. They haven't got the guts to tell what's wrong.

That what's being taught today. And [Simpson] is not the only one. He's typical of the large numbers in universities polluting the minds of the young people. . . . and if this is the society in which we live, that we're afraid to appoint our sons, or our nephews or our relatives or are afraid to appoint any member of our family because of what? Of fear of what might be said? Not the truth. But the fear.

Who creates fear? Who creates these phony issues The very people we're talking about. Let me say to you very frankly, if you're a teacher, God help the students that are in your class, if this is what is being taught.[3]

It seems strange that my simple challenge to a minor government appointment should provoke such a great outcry from the mayor and his allies. When the vote came, Tom Keane Jr.'s appointment was approved by an overwhelming vote of 44–2 with only 43rd Ward alderman William Singer joining me in opposing the appointment.

Commentators described Daley's speech as "ungrammatical, illogical, [and] embarrassingly maudlin," and as a gross overreaction.[4] It was his wildest tirade in his mayoral career. His face was purple with rage and his aides feared he would have a stroke. Longtime Republican alderman John Hoellen called Daley's speech "the most outrageous display of mayoral intemperance I've seen in 24 years in the City Council."[5] A one-hour recess had to be called after Daley's tirade and the rest of the council meeting was chaired by Alderman Claude Holman, the president pro tem, in order to give the mayor an opportunity to recover his composure.

This floor debate on nepotism and favoritism captures the clash of cultures, philosophies, and generations in Chicago in the 1970s. The Democratic Party machine mentality that favored the status quo society with its attendant racism, favoritism, and nepotism was being seriously challenged by a diverse and growing reform movement. The machine had provided a ladder to political power for the ethnic groups of Chicago by appointing supporters to government jobs, delivering city services, and keeping the peace in a multiethnic, multiracial, multicultural city. Favoritism and nepotism were side effects of this system of political patronage. Reformers decried what they viewed as wasteful, tyrannical machine politics and demanded more efficient, honest, and open government that gave citizens a voice in the decisions that most affected their lives. For them, favoritism had no place in efficient, effective, and open government. The two philosophies clashed dramatically. By the 1970s, Daley had been mayor for two decades. Year by year his power and arrogance had grown. He and his government were not about to change their ways without a fight.

Since Daley had read the maudlin poem "Sons" in defense of nepotism, I countered at a press conference the next day with W. H. Auden's poem "Epithet on a Tyrant," which reads in part:

> *He knew human folly like*
> *the back of his hand*
>
> *. . .*
>
> *When he laughed,*
> *respectable senators burst with laughter,*
> *and when he cried*
> *the little children died in the streets.*[6]

[handwritten margin note: Simpson's rebuttal to "poem" to Daley's "Sons"]

In his poem Auden compared elected representatives applauding Hitler's and Mussolini's every whim with Roman senators crazily applauding the mad caesars of their time. I used the poem to imply that machine aldermen similarly applauded, flattered, and blindly voted with "Da Mayor," Richard J. Daley. By this time Daley had been elevated from mayor to the unchallenged position of "Boss" of all Chicago. But as our dueling poems indicate, by the 1970s there was a serious challenge from a younger generation that would not be dismissed easily.

Revising Regime Studies

This vignette exemplifies the clashes that have occurred in the Chicago City Council. The council's debates and votes provide an extreme example of American politics. Since social science has a long tradition of using extreme cases to illuminate political structures and institutions, I use the

story of the city council to illuminate American politics.[7] Chicago and its
city council express aspects of American society in a visible and stark
form not seen in other parts of the country. In its 150 years, the council
has been a small stage on which men and women have struggled with
fundamental challenges. The battles enacted here reveal facets of the
American political struggle in unvarnished relief.

Urban historians and some social scientists have begun to examine the
growth of American cities and the evolution of urban politics, studying
individual cities and particular historical eras such as the Civil War and
comparing cities in particular regions of the country.[8] From these studies
we have learned that urban histories are varied despite similarities, that
economic development has a profound effect on a city's politics, and that
other historical events and forces, like wars, depressions, and popular
ideologies, also shape the political processes.

For four decades urban scholars concerned with urban politics have focused on power structures in urban settings.[9] Their research has charted
informal patterns of influence and explored key decisions in city politics
that characterize particular urban regimes. Although the mayor and a
few powerful city council members have been included as part of the in-
ner circle of these governing regimes, research frequently has down-
played the role of city elections and city councils in urban governance.
On the other hand, the few political scientists studying city councils have
focused narrowly on formal government structures, the racial and ethnic
makeup of councils, or the political careers of aldermen.[10] Only a few
have looked at city council roll call votes for what they can reveal about
the city's power structure and decisionmaking.[11] Although regime studies have mostly overlooked the importance of the city council, direct
studies of councils have failed to account for their importance in the governance of cities, their role in the regime, and the practical effect that their
laws have on the lives of their residents.

The starting point for my book is the current ruling paradigm in the
study of urban politics—the urban regime. Clarence Stone in *Regime Politics*, his influential book on American cities, defined an urban regime as
"the informal arrangements by which public and private interests function together in order to be able to make and carry out governing decisions."[12] A regime in Stone's formulation is thus a stable informal group
with access to institutional resources that enable it to have a sustained
role in making government decisions over different city administrations.
Each regime is composed at least of business and some government
members. Each regime has distinctive policy agendas and a history of
collaboration over time.[13]

Stone also developed a general typology of regimes and power structures in cities. He suggested categories such as caretaker, redevelopment, middle-class progressive, and lower-class opportunity expansion regimes. Other scholars have suggested regime typologies such as maintenance, developmental, average, progressive, and lower-class regimes and, alternatively, machine politics, progressive politics, and management regimes.[14] However, these regime typologies have been less effective because 65 percent of the urban regimes studied in the United States have been developmental regimes while progressive regimes have accounted for another 30 percent.[15] Thus there is very little variation between urban regimes in the United States. Furthermore, scholars attempting to apply the typology in cities abroad have had to develop entirely different categories such as organic, instrumental, and symbolic regimes based on motivations for regime participation.[16]

The concept of urban arenas has been developed to describe further the institutional framework, political culture, and spheres of activities that provide the primary arena in which different regimes operate.[17] Despite all of these elaborations, neither community power studies nor the current regime literature has created a completely satisfactory way of measuring and categorizing regimes. Moreover, these studies seldom relate different regimes to political phenomena like elections, government decisionmaking, city council voting, and policy outcomes. Regardless of these weaknesses, the regime concept is powerful and therefore I describe six different regimes at different points in Chicago history to frame the narrative of this book.

In this book, however, I extend previous "power study" and "regime" literature by exploring the power struggles that take place in elections and on the floor of the council. I explore election outcomes and the interaction between mayors and council members, as revealed in council voting behavior, to characterize the political patterns within Chicago. By restoring electoral data and city council roll call voting to the study of urban politics, I provide a more accurate picture of the regimes that have governed Chicago, as well as some of the most telling events in Chicago's history. If we are to understand this city and its history, we need to know the platforms on which politicians campaigned, the coalitions of voters that supported them, and the reasons for the fierce council battles that made the city's laws and spent the public's money. Understanding the regime that governs a city requires not only identifying the individuals and institutional leaders who have influence but studying the public conflicts that occur in elections and council struggles. These particulars must inform any general conclusions about community power structures and regimes.

I begin my analysis with a simple model of urban politics that looks like this:

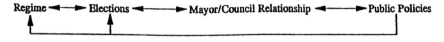

FIGURE P.1   Urban Politics Model

This model, which follows the simple input-output models frequently used in political science, suggests that the coalition which makes the fundamental governmental and business decisions for a city affects and is affected by elections for public office, which in turn determine the nature of the city council, which finally produces public policies.[18] For instance, in earlier historical periods in Chicago, a "growth machine" composed of developers, chief executives of large businesses and institutions, and major political and governmental officials supported a machine politics of mostly uncontested elections. These uncontested elections led to rubber stamp city councils that followed directions given by a mayor or a political boss. The mayor's rubber stamp council then passed legislation and levied taxes in a manner that contributed to progrowth, unfettered business development, along with policies that favored patronage, corruption, and waste in government needed to maintain the machine. These governmental policies thus strengthened all the major members of the growth machine during much of Chicago's history. More recently in Chicago, changes in regime composition, electoral coalitions, types of councils, and policy outcomes created a "progressive regime" under Mayor Harold Washington that later dissolved into an entirely New Chicago Machine under Richard M. Daley.

There are thus alternative patterns of government to the growth machine. Yet in each regime the same four elements shape the polity. Previous community power and regime studies were important because they uncovered some important aspects of the overall pattern. However, they did not uncover the pattern of mayor/council interactions in a way that facilitated comparisons between cities or between different historical eras in the same city.[19] In this book I extend regime studies to make that possible.

A study of history reveals that the story of the Chicago City Council, as well as American politics generally, is not simply a reflection of a particular regime or power structure. It is more fundamentally the story of the struggle for justice and democracy. Thus an ideal philosophical model of what urban politics should be needs to be considered, not just an empirical urban politics model. It may well be that this ideal is never achieved, that it is a useful myth taught in high school civic classes and college political science courses. Yet we need an image of the ideal to which we can compare the empirical reality of cities like Chicago. If the American civic

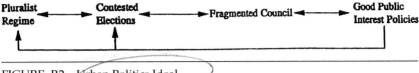

FIGURE P.2   Urban Politics Ideal

ideal were put in the same form as our model of urban politics, it would look something like the above.

This ideal model suggests that many competing interests and social groups should make up the regime. A polyarchy is defined as multiple groups (such as business groups, neighborhood groups, public interest groups, and political parties) struggling for and sharing power. This multiplicity of interests naturally leads to competitive elections and a frequent turnover in public officials. In such a system, candidates are forced to present their qualifications and issue positions to voters who then choose between real alternatives. Competitive elections in turn lead to a deliberative city council. It is our American democratic faith that debate by representatives of different points of view, which necessitates persuading various aldermen to join temporary majority coalitions in order to pass particular legislation, inevitably creates more just public policies.

Of course, it can be maintained that this type of representative democracy is beyond our ability and is even less likely to be achieved if we also demand a high level of informed citizen participation across racial, ethnic, and class divisions. It may also be true that although America's civic culture may articulate such an ideal, in practice the leaders or elites do most of the governing. It is also true that even democracies have sometimes chosen to support unjust policies. Nonetheless, this ideal provides a standard against which to measure the Chicago City Council and indeed our entire American political experiment. Reformers have held to such ideals when they have proposed changes to "improve" the political system. When we measure the Chicago City Council and Chicago politics generally by these ideal standards, they fail to measure up as fully democratic, and consequently the laws that the council enacts fail to provide full justice for all city residents.

Studying the Chicago City Council

Crooks and saints, hacks and reformers, ordinary and extraordinary elected officials have fought their political battles in the Chicago City Council. Near riots and grand ceremonial events have occurred within these chambers. Throughout the history of this council, the struggle for grand ideals such as democracy and justice have been coupled with backroom deals, bribery, intrigue, small successes, and great failures. Wars and depressions, protests and riots have all been reflected in these council chambers. And in this clash of cultures, ideals, ambitions, and power the story of America is writ large.

Chicago is an extreme example of American culture, and its city hall struggles are an extreme example of American politics. As a city of clout, Chicago reveals an often hidden side of our country. Just as Chicago is a window on our larger American civilization, its city council is a unique window on Chicago. The council's story demonstrates the limitations of American democracy and justice during different eras of our history.

In telling this story of the Chicago City Council, I employ historical narratives taken from news stories, the official record set forth in the *Journal of Proceedings of the Chicago City Council*, memoirs of important political figures, interviews with participants in the fray, quantitative council voting statistics, and my own observations from eight years as a Chicago alderman. From these sources emerges a history of this city within the larger development of the nation. I provide a detailed analysis of council votes that goes beyond individual characters and controversial confrontations in order to uncover underlying patterns in the political life of the city. This history reflects the weaknesses of representative democracy as practiced in this most American city. Using both quantitative and qualitative techniques, as well as philosophical questions and empirical evidence, provides the clearest understanding of Chicago and American politics.

I begin each chapter on a particular city council with a brief overview of the council's place in the broader history; then I introduce the principal political leaders and provide a narrative of crucial elections as well as the votes and battles in the council. Some readers will be satisfied with the historical and narrative accounts. Scholars and political scientists will want to consider the quantitative data of aldermanic voting portrayed in histograms and factor analyses in Chapter 10. This quantitative data provides a snapshot of the council and an X ray of the health of the body politic.

Ultimately, the purpose of this book is to tell the story of the different political regimes that have held sway historically and are in power today. It is the story of one city's struggle to achieve democracy and justice. It is a story in which reformers have repeatedly urged change and have assembled a political following supporting those changes, only to be repulsed. Succeeding reformers have arisen with a slightly different vision under new political circumstances and, like ocean waves, have crashed once more against the flood wall of Chicago politics.

In Chapter 1, I report the colorful history of the Chicago City Council from the Civil War until the Great Chicago Fire. In Chapter 2, I tell of the council under the control of the "Gray Wolves" from the Chicago Fire until the Great Depression. In Chapters 3–9, I cover the history of Chicago from Bosses Ed Kelly in 1933 and Richard J. Daley in 1955 to his son, Mayor Richard M. Daley, who governs at the beginning of the third millennium. In Chapter 10, I provide a quantitative and statistical analysis of city council voting. In Chapter 11, I summarize my findings and speculate on what this history means for American public life in the twenty-first century.

Notes

1. Mike Royko, *Boss: Richard J. Daley of Chicago* (New York: Dutton, 1971), p. 73. In his book Royko raised the charge of nepotism and put it in colorful biblical terms: "There was Otto Kerner, confidante and a federal judge, and he begat Otto Kerner, governor, federal judge, and husband of Cermak's daughter; John Clark, ward boss and assessor, begat William Clark, attorney general and 1968 U.S. Senate candidate; Adlai Stevenson, governor and presidential candidate, begat Adlai Stevenson, U.S. Senator; Dan Ryan, ward boss and County Board president, begat Dan Ryan, ward boss and County Board president; . . . Joe Rostenkowski ward boss, begat Daniel Rostenkowski, congressman; Thomas Keane, ward boss and alderman begat Thomas Keane, ward boss and alderman; Joe Burke, ward boss and alderman, begat Edward Burke, ward boss and alderman."

Over the years in his newspaper column, especially after the fight over the Keane appointment, Royko updated the list with the names of the newest sons, brothers, sisters, and cousins to get major government appointments. Even today, there are many Richard M. Daley relatives and friends with everything from local government jobs to million-dollar city contracts.

2. Harry Golden Jr., "Daley Assails Colleges for 'Agitation and Hate,'" *Chicago Sun-Times*, July 22, 1971, pp. 1, 4.

3. This text was pieced together from the quotations cited by Golden, "Daley Assails Colleges," p. 4; and Bill Boyarsky and Nancy Boyarsky, *Backroom Politics* (Los Angeles: J. P. Tarsher, 1974), pp. 21–22. They took their quotations from an audiotape of Daley's speech recorded by radio station WMAQ.

4. Boyarsky and Boyarsky, *Backroom Politics*, p. 22.

5. The descriptions of Daley and Alderman Hoellen's quotation are from Jay McMullen, "What Got into Mayor Daley?" *Chicago Daily News*, July 21, 1971, pp. 5–6.

6. Reported in a newspaper article entitled "Simpson Rhymes in Rebuttal." The source has been lost, but a copy of the article and the poem is in the Dick Simpson Papers, Special Collections, Main Library, University of Illinois at Chicago.

7. See, for example, Robert Michels, *Political Parties* (London: Hearst's International Library, 1915). Later editions have been published by the Free Press. In this classic study Michels demonstrates that the European political parties in the early twentieth century having the most democratic ideology, namely, socialist parties, were oligarchic. Therefore, more conservative parties that did not even espouse

democratic ideals were also oligarchic, and Michels is able to pronounce his famous "Iron Law of Oligarchy" covering all political parties even though he had studied only the extreme cases in Europe in a particular period.

8. Examples of books on individual cities include Sam Bass Warner Jr., *The Private City: Philadelphia in Three Periods of Its Growth* (Philadelphia: University of Pennsylvania Press, 1968); Anthony Orum, *City-Building in America* (Boulder: Westview, 1995), which covers primarily the history of Milwaukee but also Cleveland, Austin, and Minneapolis-St. Paul; and Robert G. Spinney, *City of Big Shoulders: A History of Chicago* (DeKalb: Northern Illinois University Press, 2000). An example of an urban history on a particular period is Mary Ryan, *Civic Wars: Democracy and Public Life in the American City during the Nineteenth Century* (Berkeley: University of California Press, 1997). Examples of general urban histories with a clear point of view are Sam Bass Warner Jr., *The Urban Wilderness: A History of the American City* (Berkeley: University of California Press, 1972); and Stephen Elkin, *City and Regime in the American Republic* (Chicago: University of Chicago Press, 1987). For an example of a study that compares cities in a region, see Amy Bridges, *Morning Glories: Municipal Reform in the Southwest* (Princeton: Princeton University Press, 1997).

9. Among the best known of the community power studies are Floyd Hunter, *Community Power Structure* (Chapel Hill: University of North Carolina Press, 1953); Robert Dahl, *Who Governs?* (New Haven: Yale University Press, 1961); and Clarence Stone, *Regime Politics: Governing Atlanta, 1946–1988* (Lawrence: University of Kansas Press, 1989).

10. See, for instance, R. P. Browning, D. R. Marshall, and D. H. Tabb, *Protest Is Not Enough* (Berkeley: University of California Press, 1984); Susan Welch and Timothy Bledsoe, *Urban Reform and Its Consequences* (Chicago: University of Chicago Press, 1988); and Timothy Bledsoe, *Careers in City Politics* (Pittsburgh: University of Pittsburgh Press, 1993). Of thirty-two articles written on city councils between 1988 and 1993 that appear in the *Social Sciences Index*, published by H. W. Wilson, 50 percent focused on structural characteristics and most of the others on the ethnic and racial makeup of city councils or struggles between city councils and city managers. A search of articles from 1993 to 2000 shows that the general pattern of city council studies continues.

11. Earlier descriptive and structural studies of the Chicago City Council are found in William Slayton, "Chicago's House of Lords: A Study of the Functions of the Finance Committee of the Chicago City Council" (M.A. thesis, University of Chicago, 1943); and William Russell Gable, "The Chicago City Council" (Ph.D. diss., University of Chicago, 1953). A study of roll call voting in the Chicago City Council has been done by Jeff Slovak, "Urban Political Organization: The City Council As a Structural Component of Community Decision-Making" (M.A. thesis, University of Chicago, 1974). A study of the effects of single-member district elections on roll call voting in six northeastern and southern cities has been done by Rory Austin, "Electoral Rules and Race: The Effects of Local Electoral Structures on Racial Polarization in City Councils" (paper presented at the Midwest Political Science Association in Chicago, April 1999). The roll call voting of the Richard M. Daley city council has been published from time to time in *Illinois Pol-*

itics. I know of no other studies of city council roll call voting other than my own earlier publications.

12. Stone, *Regime Politics,* p. 6.

13. Stone, *Regime Politics,* p. 4; and Karen Mossberger and Gerry Stoker, "The Evolution of Urban Regime Theory: The Challenge of Conceptualization" (paper presented at the Urban Affairs Association Meeting, Los Angeles, May 3–6, 2000).

14. Stone, *Regime Politics*; Barbara Ferman, *Challenging the Growth Machine: Neighborhood Politics in Chicago and Pittsburgh* (Lawrence: University Press of Kansas, 1996), p. 136; A. Works and M. Yasuoka, "Exploring Urban Regime Types: Putting Some Names to the Faces" (paper presented Midwest Political Science Association, Chicago, 1997); K. DeBell, "Greening the City Explaining Chicago's Environmental Policy, 1970–1996" (paper presented at the Midwest Political Science Association, Chicago, 1997).

15. Whitt Kilburn, "Structural Variation and Agency in Urban Regimes" (paper presented at the Midwest Political Science Association Meeting, Chicago, April 2000), p. 19.

16. Gerry Stoker and Karen Mossberger, "Urban Regime Theory in Comparative Perspective," *Environment and Planning C: Government Policy* 12 (1994): 195–212; and Stoker and Mossberger, "The Evolution of Urban Regime Theory: The Challenge of Conceptualization" (paper presented at the Urban Affairs Association Meeting, Los Angeles, May 2000), p. 12.

17. Ferman, *Challenging the Growth Machine,* pp. 3–8.

18. Among the earlier political scientists to use such models was David Easton, *The Political System* (New York: Knopf, 1952). Such models were applied to cities by various contributors in Terry Nichols Clark, ed., *Community Structure and Decision-Making* (New York: Chandler/Wiley-Interscience, 1968).

19. This is not to claim that there have been no comparative studies of urban politics. The most extensive has been the study of 7,000 cities by the Fiscal Austerity and Urban Innovation (FAUI) Project. Its latest book-length publication is Terry Nichols Clark and Vincent Hoffmann-Martinot, eds., *The New Political Culture* (Boulder: Westview, 1998).

PART I

Divided Councils

Aldermen Bathhouse John Couglin and Hinky Dink Kenna of the notorious 1st Ward in 1924. (Used by special permission of the Chicago Historical Society, Photo ICHI–10927.)

1

Nineteenth-Century and Civil War Councils, 1833–1871

The apocryphal story is told that when Chicagoans met in a saloon to elect their first city officials and the votes were counted, there were more votes cast than there were residents. This tale typifies the corrupt Chicago politics that characterized much of the nineteenth and twentieth centuries. The official story, however, is that in 1833 citizens incorporated Chicago as a town and elected T. J. V. Owen as president and E. M. Kimberly as clerk by a completely legal vote of 12–1. Later that year, five town trustees were elected by twenty-eight qualified voters at one of the hotel taverns that served as the only public meeting places before City Hall was built.

Chicago's beginnings date even earlier from 1779 at the end of the American Revolution, nearly sixty years before its official incorporation as a town. It was then that a French Canadian mulatto, John Baptiste du Sable, started the first trading post on the Chicago River at the base of Lake Michigan. In 1803, Fort Dearborn was built on the bank opposite the trading post to provide an army base for attacks and negotiations with the Indians. By 1818, enough people had settled in Illinois for it to become a state and by then Chicago had begun to attract permanent settlers in addition to fur traders and soldiers. By the time it became a town in 1833, the Treaty of Chicago had been signed, which guaranteed Indian resettlement west of the Mississippi River by 1835. New settlers and land speculators back East fueled the escalation of Chicago land prices, when they were assured that the new city would not have to fear any future attacks from the Indians who had previously burned Fort Dearborn to the ground. Also in 1833 the first newspaper, the *Chicago Democrat*, started publishing. With 200 wagon loads of settlers coming through each week and some deciding to stay, Chicago grew rapidly, reaching a population of 4,000 in 1836. As a result, there was an enormous land boom with real estate prices growing at very inflated rates.

Chicago incorporated as a city in 1837 with William Ogden, a real estate speculator and developer, as its first mayor. Ten aldermen, including future mayor Francis Sherman, were elected to serve on the city council.[1] In the spring of 1837, during Chicago's first official year as a city, the land boom collapsed and the notes of the Illinois Bank, its principal financial institution, became worthless. Mayor Ogden persuaded the city council to issue script as local paper money to keep business going and to pay taxes.[2] Business soon recovered and Chicago began to grow once more. By the 1840s, Chicago was finally beginning to look like a city—even if a wild and muddy one.

Chicago originally developed as a nexus of transportation from its position on the Chicago River at the base of Lake Michigan. It became the crossroads of trails across the Midwest to western settlements. In 1848, the Lake Michigan–Illinois River Canal opened to improve commercial transportation between midwestern farmlands and the Great Lakes, and by the 1860s, the railroad connection through Chicago to the East and West Coasts made Chicago the capital of the Midwest.

In 1854, another national economic panic occurred and many banknotes again became worthless. But such economic turndowns, however serious for individuals, did not prevent Chicago's continued growth. Chicago had been built on very swampy land between the river and the lake, so in 1855, in its first major civic project, the entire business district, with its streets, buildings, and sidewalks, was raised as much as ten feet higher so that at least the business district was mostly above the mud. Chicago remade itself, as it would in the future, most notably after the Chicago Fire of 1871.

From Chicago's incorporation as a village in 1833 until at least 1847, it had what historians have called "the booster system of city government."[3] Throughout much of the nineteenth century, businessmen, especially those involved in real estate, and lawyers, who depended on the future development of the city to keep and enlarge their fortunes, were often chosen as governors, mayors, and aldermen. Seven of eight mayors between 1837 and 1848 were wealthy, and only two of the first nineteen mayors before the Civil War were not prominent businessmen.[4] A study of Chicago aldermen from 1837 to 1860 found that "70 percent of them had predominantly booster-business interests." During this period, this "booster elite made [public] policy directly" and continued to influence public policy in Chicago throughout its history.[5] Thus in Chicago's earliest political regime the leading businessmen and politicians were the same, and they followed a natural progrowth policy that benefited not only the city but their own real estate holdings. In this regard Chicago was similar to other American cities. Sam Bass Warner in his study of Philadelphia found an enduring tradition of privatism in which the "wealthy presided over a municipal regime of little government" that died out around the Civil War.[6]

A study of New York City (which was founded and developed much earlier than Chicago) showed that the pattern of direct business control of government prevailed there as well. Gabriel Almond found that in the period between 1789 and 1835, 60 percent of the city's political officers were lawyers and another 20 percent were merchants. Among aldermen, merchants made up the largest occupational group, composing at least 56 percent of all council members. Altogether, a full 61 percent of all politicians came from wealthy and well-to-do origins.[7] After the Civil War, however, the number of business leaders in policymaking offices began to decrease steadily. Wealthy businessmen began to avoid politics after democratization and the enfranchisement of immigrants. They could do so because their positions of power and prestige in the economy were never seriously endangered, and they could influence the governing regime to obtain favorable laws and contracts without engaging in the political struggle directly.[8]

In Milwaukee, Chicago's neighboring midwestern competitor, the story is much the same. From 1818 to 1870, Milwaukee "had taken on the character of a private city, in which the ideology of privatism, or, more plainly capitalism clothed both private and public affairs" and businessmen ruled directly. However, the industrialization of Milwaukee after 1870 "unleashed the energies of city government" to provide for more public services and to secure public order. As in Chicago, Philadelphia, and New York, the backgrounds and ideologies of the politicians also changed profoundly after the Civil War.[9]

As with other American cities, the first progrowth booster regime in Chicago did not last. Local politics at the end of the booster period became highly partisan, with Democrats running against Whigs, Republicans, and short-term parties such as the abolitionist Liberty Party. Partisan differences on issues such as slavery led to the bloody Civil War, in which Chicago would be very much a participant. Despite their partisan differences, even at the height of the war, aldermen and mayors frequently agreed on decisions relating to the practical development of the new city, especially its continuing physical and economic growth. This partisan, fractured regime united sufficiently to keep Chicago government delivering basic services to its citizens and support to the national war effort.

There is no doubt that the Civil War changed Chicago politics permanently. The period of simple boosterism ended. The progrowth regime of businessmen/politicians came to an end as the forces that had created the war made partisanship the hallmark of this new political era. Historian Mary Ryan characterizes this shift from "civic wars" to new "civil wars" in American cities as bringing "violent disputes about the legitimacy of public authority," just as the Civil War raged over the legitimacy of the national government.[10] Ethnic clashes gave way to racial clashes, local problems gave way to the national conflict, and local politics became entrenched in partisanship, not only between Republicans and Democrats but also in splits within parties, such as the division between Peace Democrats and War Democrats. In Chicago all of these conflicts were reflected in voting at the ballot box, in city council battles, and in demonstrations in the streets. The issues of slavery and saving the Union became the focal point of local politics, although some local decisionmaking about city services, budgets, and public works remained outside the new political fault lines.

Another development that helped transform the older political system was the elimination of property restrictions and the admission of religious and ethnic minorities into political life. Opening up the political process in this way transformed urban politics of the later half of the nineteenth century into a scene of "vigorous confrontations and bloodless civic wars."[11] Aldermen in Chicago came more and more to represent ethnic groups such as Germans and the Irish rather than the Yankee entrepreneurs who had governed the city during the booster era. As a result, power at City Hall was fragmented, divided, and contentious. Businessmen could no longer dictate policies without considering the wishes of the general population represented by ethnic aldermen in the council and, by the turn of the century, by ethnic mayors.

If Chicago, which has been called "the concentrated essence of Americanism" and the most "characteristically American of America's largest cities," was a city of contrasts and conflicts in the nineteenth century, it was also a city of great vitality and energy.

The great theme of Chicago's nineteenth-century history is the battle between growth and control, restraint and opportunity, privatism and the public good. Chaotic Chicago seemed to have sprung up spontaneously, without planning or social foresight, a pure product of ungoverned capitalism. Yet the city that was a spiraling spectacle of smoke and disorder had a magnificent chain of parks and boulevards, one of the best sewage and water supply systems in the world, a Sanitary and Ship Canal that was one of the engineering marvels of the century, and a splendid complex of cultural and civic buildings, along its downtown lakefront. The city that critics compared to a gigantic real estate lottery, where everything was for sale, even its streets, undertook some of the most ambitious public improvement projects of the age.[12]

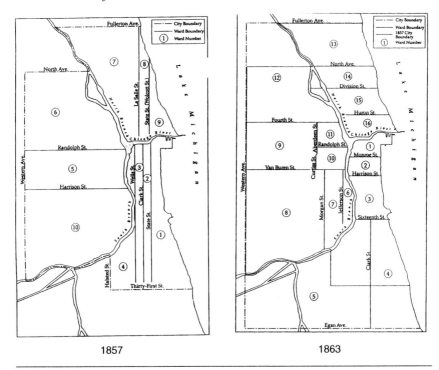

1857   1863

FIGURE 1.1   Chicago Ward Maps, 1857 and 1863

The midpoint in Chicago's extraordinary development from a frontier town to a modern city was the Civil War, which threatened to destroy the city as well as the Union.

By 1860, Chicago had grown from a population of 4,000 to 110,000. It was now a center of commerce as well as transportation. It was nationally, not just regionally, important. In 1860, the Republican Party held its national convention at Chicago's Wigwam (the convention center especially built for the occasion) and nominated Illinois favorite son Abraham Lincoln as president of the United States. Lincoln won the subsequent election, but the battle of Fort Sumter a year later in 1861 began the Civil War. Throughout 1861 and 1862, Chicago mobilized effectively in support of the Union cause, supplying both men and goods to the war effort. At the same time, Chicago entered another economic boom. Chicago businesses provided not only meat but many of the supplies used by an ever growing army. As the war continued, however, the number of wounded and dead mounted. Workers in Chicago's industries were paid in unsecured "greenbacks" printed in ever greater numbers (and diminishing value) by the Union government. Soon the immigrant workers and former Southerners who opposed the war were joined by some of Chicago's leading citizens, such as Cyrus McCormick, the owner of the large farm equipment factory, and Wilbur Storey, the publisher of the *Chicago Times*, who began to criticize the war publicly.[13]

Although Chicago had supported the war in 1861 and 1862, despite some vocal local opposition, tensions now heightened. The war was not going well, and even some former supporters doubted the wisdom of continuing the fight. Partisanship reached such critical proportions that the city council was even prevented from meeting. Before 1863 was over, a newspaper was closed by martial law and there was near rioting in the streets of this Northern stronghold.

By studying the critical years of 1862–1863, we can see how the regime in Chicago evolved from the booster years and how city government weathered the greatest crisis in its history until at least the Great Depression some seventy years later. Chicago's booster regime was transformed into a divided partisan regime, which by the Chicago Fire of 1871 had evolved into a different business/political machine regime from the partisan one of the Civil War era. Chicago government during this partisan period ran on two tracks. On the one track there was a partisan stalemate that gradually resolved into a majority consensus in support of Lincoln's continued prosecution of the war, despite strong reservations about some actions of the national government and continuing tensions between Washington and Chicago. On the other track, the aldermen and the mayor, despite major partisan differences and local disagreements, continued the essential functions of local government during wartime. They even undertook major public works to solve some of the city's pressing health problems.

By the end of the Civil War in 1865, Chicago had become the undisputed capital of the Midwest, bypassing rivals like St. Louis, Detroit, and Milwaukee. Chicago emerged from the war as an industrial giant in America's heartland. The years 1862–1863 were pivotal to Chicago's social, economic, and political transformation, although many of the trends, such as industrialization and the incorporation of a growing immigrant population, had begun before the war.

By 1862–1863, the mayor's executive authority was greater than it was in the previous booster era. The city council over which the mayor presided in 1863 had grown from twenty members from ten wards to thirty-two members representing sixteen wards, as shown in the Chicago ward map (Fig. 1.1). The mayor was a Democrat and the council, during most Civil War years, had a slight Democratic majority despite Chicago's support for a Republican president and, often, Republican congressmen. Democrats, however, were themselves divided into War Democrats, who supported the Union war effort, and Peace Democrats, who thought it was time to end the bloody Civil War. Although most major businessmen and newspapers such as the *Chicago Tribune* supported the war, industrialists like Cyrus McCormick and equally popular newspapers such as the *Chicago Times* had come to oppose the war. Thus Chicago and its leaders were divided. And as the human costs and sacrifices grew, it was not certain how Chicago would fare, or even if it could hold together. In this, Chicago reflected a nation torn apart by a Civil War.

Mayor and Party Leaders
in the Civil War City Council

Although Chicago in 1861–1862 was controlled by the Republicans, the state legislature was in the hands of the Democrats. In March 1862, the Democrats in the legislature redistricted Chicago wards to their advantage. Then Chicago Republicans made a major blunder at their municipal convention in April 1862. The supporters of former alderman Charles N. Holden defeated efforts to nominate popular former congressman and mayor Long John Wentworth as their mayoral candidate. Some of Long John's outraged adherents then threw their support to the Democratic nominee, businessman and former mayor Francis C. Sherman, who was elected by a majority of 1,188 votes.[14] As one historian of the period recounts, "The Republicans had dominated all recent campaigning, but the [1862] election found them divided and dispirited. . . . Turnout was slight on the cold, rainy election day. . . . For one year from Fort Sumter in April 1861 to Shiloh in April 1862, the elan inspired by Lincoln's call to arms and Douglas' call for unity had sustained Chicago's war effort. Defeats and the high price of victory eroded that spirit."[15]

The pro-Republican *Chicago Tribune* was so displeased with the outcome that it pronounced the election a triumph of Democrats "and the conservative citizens over Abolitionism. . . . If this be the voice of Chicago, [Southerners] may well reason that Abolitionism has culminated as a power in the North."[16] Such charged rhetoric was the hallmark of the politics of the Civil War era.

Francis C. Sherman, Chicago's mayor during most of this turbulent period, was born in Newtown, Connecticut, on September 18, 1805. He moved to Chicago on April 7, 1834, when he was twenty-nine. At the time Chicago was still a small muddy town, not much more than an Indian trading post and fort. He put up a small frame boardinghouse and with the profits from that venture bought a wagon and began a stage line from Chicago to Joliet, Galena, Peoria, and other Illinois towns. In 1835 he began to manufacture bricks, which went into many of the early homes and commercial buildings in Chicago, and thus made his fortune.

He was elected alderman after Chicago became a city in 1837 and served as mayor from 1841 to 1842. The Whigs, who were dominant nationally in the 1840s, presented no candidate for mayor in the March 1841 election because Whig president William Henry Harrison was ill and the party was in disarray. Mayor Sherman was thus elected without opposition and eight of the twelve aldermen elected in 1841 were also Democrats. Since there were few controversial and pressing issues in 1841–1842 and Chicago's population still numbered only about 5,500, governing during his first term was easy for Mayor Sherman.

After his first term, Sherman served as city treasurer, county commissioner and then as president of the county board, building the courthouse as the seat of local government. He went on to serve in the state legislature from 1843 to 1847. After fourteen years in brickmaking, Sherman retired in 1850 and devoted himself to public affairs and the development of his properties. Sherman had built the three-story City Hotel in 1843. He added another two stories and renamed it the Sherman House in 1850. Along with the Tremont, the Sherman House became one of the city's grand hotels when it was again remodeled and opened once more in 1861. His business dealings made Sherman wealthy and one of Chicago's leading citizens.

In 1862 Sherman, a pro-Union War Democrat, defeated former Republican alderman C. N. Holden and was elected mayor on a nonpartisan ticket under the slogan "for the Union and the Constitution." Since Mayor Sherman's son, Francis T. Sherman, fought under the Union army throughout the Civil War and was promoted to the rank of general, there was no doubt as to Sherman's loyalties, but there was considerable opposition to his policies and even more to his Democratic Party allies. As a result, despite his election as mayor the previous spring, Sherman narrowly lost an election to Congress when he ran against Republican Isaac Arnold in October 1862. The *Chicago Tribune* wrote in opposing Sherman's congressional election that "he never read politics in his life. He is profoundly ignorant of parliamentary tactics. He knows no more of statesmanship or the profound questions to be submitted to him than he does of Choctaw."[17]

As mayor in 1862, Sherman's most influential act may have been to appoint a committee that recommended a new city charter, bringing the communities of Bridgeport and Holstein into the city and lengthening the terms of office of the mayor, treasurer, collector, city attorney, and clerk of police court from one to two years. Bringing the Irish-American and German-American communities within the city boundaries and adding these new ethnic wards to the voting rolls assured victory for the Democrats in 1863.

With the help of the new ethnic voters, Mayor Sherman was narrowly reelected in 1863 and presided over a city council that was divided between nineteen Democrats and twelve Republicans. Although he ran for reelection for the last time in 1865, Sherman withdrew from the mayor's race after Lincoln's assassination. Republican John Rice won on a pro-Lincoln, pro–Civil War platform, arguing that his election would "be an endorsement of the acts and administration of our [national] Government."[18] The *Tribune* again opposed Sherman in 1865: "He has made what should be a government of the people a government of a faction. It is well known that His Honor is weak and vacillating. Mayor Sherman is not the man for the time." But Sherman would probably have been re-elected despite Republican and *Tribune* opposition had not the president's assassination created such a patriotic fever and a voter backlash against all Democrats in the North.

When Francis Sherman died on November 8, 1870, the *Tribune* in its obituary gave a more balanced assessment of his life and contributions than it had during his campaigns: "Although frequently accused of a lack of polish and a deficiency of education, the public had confidence in his strongly marked practical sense, and personal integrity overruled the defect; and the wealth which enabled him in later years to render life more enjoyable was the honest result of persevering industry."[19] Historians such as John Moses and Joseph Kirkland have rendered even more positive judgments: "Mr. Sherman was a plain man, of substantial and practical parts, and administered the city government during this trying and difficult period in a spirit of loyalty, uprightness, and economy as far as that was consistent with liberal appropriations for bounties and other war measures."[20] In retrospect, Francis Sherman was a practical, self-made businessman who guided the city during the Civil War without falling prey to more extreme Democratic Party members who wanted to give in to Southern demands and without letting extreme Republican Party members tilt Chicago government to mob action or martial law. Sherman, like many Chicago mayors to follow him, was not learned, but he surrounded himself with lawyers and newspaper editors who helped to draft his speeches and official documents. Sherman steered a difficult middle course in this highly partisan period without the brilliance or oratory of an Abraham Lincoln. Yet, despite some personal defects, he was able to keep Chicago moving forward in one of the most trying periods of its history. He was both a holdover from the booster regime of earlier Chicago and a forerunner of the practical politicians/mayors who would guide the city during most of the twentieth century.

Other leaders besides the mayor played critical roles in the Civil War period. One of them was the Democratic Party's floor leader and head of the council's Finance Committee during Mayor Sherman's terms of office, Irishman John Comisky. (The spelling of the Comisky family name was later changed to Comiskey.) Unlike Yankee leaders such as Sherman, Alderman Comisky was born in County Cavan, Ireland, in 1826 and immigrated to Chicago in 1852 where he worked in banking. In the 1850s, he served as clerk of the Cook County Board and as deputy county treasurer. Comisky was feisty, short-tempered, and sensitive to perceived slights. In 1859, he was first elected alderman, a position which he held, except for two years, until 1870. Like Sherman, Comisky was a loyal Union supporter. On April 20, 1861, Aldermen John Comisky and Malcolm McDonald organized the famous "Irish Brigade," the Twenty-Third Illinois Infantry, to fight in the Civil War. They signed up 325 recruits at the meeting and 1,200 within a week. Alderman Comisky later introduced the Civil War bounties ordinance and directed the bounty process to recruit soldiers for the war effort from Chicago.

Alderman Comisky lived close to where the Chicago Fire broke out on Chicago's South Side. Although he had retired from the council, in 1871 he played "a leading part with other citizens in the work of relief and in the reorganization of the city" after the fire.[21] His son, Charles Albert Comiskey, owned the Chicago White Sox from the founding of the American League in 1900 until his death at the end of the season in 1931. It is Charles Comiskey for whom the current White Sox stadium, Comiskey Park, is named. The Comiskys have played an important role in Chicago's history.

On the opposite side of the aisle in the city council, Republicans were led by Alderman Charles C.P. Holden. Alderman Holden, another resettled Yankee, was born in Groton, New Hampshire, on August 9, 1827, and came to Chicago on June 30, 1836, when the town included only 4,000 residents. He first worked in a grocery on North Water Street and later in a bookstore on Lake Street. When war was declared against Mexico in 1846, he enlisted in the Fifth Regiment of the Illinois Volunteers. After the Mexican-American War, he stayed in California for four years and returned to Chicago in 1854. In 1855, he began eighteen years service with the new Illinois Central Railroad as an examiner of lands. The company had received a grant of 2,595,000 acres from the federal government along the railroad tracks from Chicago to Cairo at the southern tip of Illinois. It was Holden's job to sell these railroad lands to early settlers and speculators.

In 1861, Charles Holden was elected to the Chicago City Council and served as an alderman until 1872. He was thus alderman when the new water system was inaugurated, the first lake tunnel was begun, the Civil War was fought, and the city began its recovery after the Chicago Fire. During the Civil War period, he was active in introducing the "patriotic resolutions" in support of the national administration and its prosecution of the war, in increasing the bounties paid to army volunteers, and in generally supporting the war effort. He led the bloc of Republican aldermen in their opposition to Mayor Sherman and Alderman Comisky. He was tenacious, contentious, and stiff-necked in his judgments and his politics. After the Chicago Fire, Alderman Holden, as president of the city council, helped the city rebuild and conducted the investigation to determine when the fire reached different parts of the city. After retiring from the council in 1872, he continued his public service as a member of the County Board of Commissioners and West Park Board of Commissioners until his death on February 9, 1905.[22]

These three men, Sherman, Comisky, and Holden, of such different temperaments and backgrounds, played leading roles in the city government during this crucial period. Although they led the partisan factions during the Civil War, they were able to support the Union and govern the city in the time of its greatest crisis.

Civil War Clashes

At the height of the Civil War, partisan antagonisms brought Chicago government to a total standstill. During 1862 and early 1863, the city council was deadlocked, although Mayor Sherman was a Democrat and there was a slight Democratic majority in the council. The deadlock was so serious that between December 22, 1862, and March 23, 1863, no council meetings could be held because the Republicans refused to attend to make a quorum. The *Chicago Tribune* argued that the continuing deadlock in the city was a "dastardly attempt while Union members were absent from the city to throw the political power into the hands of an unscrupulous Copperhead faction" (i.e., Southern sympathizers). To prevent the Democrats from taking actions that might undermine the Union war effort, the Republicans refused to make a quorum, and thus no laws could be passed in the council during this four-month period.[23]

The city council of 1862–1863 had been evenly divided between ten Republicans and ten Democrats at the April 1862 election. However, Democratic mayor Francis Sherman was able to cast the deciding vote in tied council votes. The death of one Republican alderman and the fact that Republican alderman Edward Solomon was away from Chicago fighting with the Union Army's Eighty-Second Illinois Regiment further reduced Republican strength to eight members. According to the *Chicago Evening News*, "by and by Ald. [Peter] Shimp (Dem.), ashamed of the company he had been dragged into, announced himself to be a War Democrat and the enemy and antagonist of Copperheads [Southern sympathizers] everywhere. That reduced Copperheads to nine votes in the Council, and gave the Republicans nine. Still the Mayor had the [deciding] vote."[24]

At the March 23, 1863, council meeting, the logjam broke in a most dramatic fashion. The meeting began with the Democratic majority present when the Republicans suddenly marched in and took their seats. When the opening roll was called and the preliminaries disposed of, Alderman

Major Edward Solomon took his seat unannounced and completely changed the balance in the council. Major Solomon was on leave from the war front. The Democrats had been tricked. With Alderman Solomon present and Alderman Shimp voting against them, the Democrats were outnumbered. The debate became fiery and the meeting full of drama. The meeting's main agenda was to select election judges for the 1863 city elections. Early in the meeting, Democratic alderman Peter Shimp moved that the Democrats be given a majority of election judges in eight wards and the Republicans a majority in eight, as "a matter of fairness, justice and equality." Democratic floor leader John Comisky argued that since the Democrats had a majority of aldermen in the council, they should have more judges than the Republicans. He angrily attacked Alderman Shimp's integrity: "Alderman Shimp, did you not sell out yourself and your constituents to the Republicans for a consideration?" Alderman Shimp angrily replied, "I pronounce that a base falsehood. The gentleman hasn't got money enough to buy me."[25] Mayor Sherman had to call for order from the chair after which Alderman Shimp's proposal was defeated by a party line vote.

Democratic alderman Charles Woodman then tried to amend Alderman Shimp's motion to give the Democrats control of election judges in twelve wards and the Republicans in four. His amendment failed by a vote of 10–9. Alderman Comisky tried to adjourn the meeting and lost by the same 10–9 vote. Democratic alderman Baragwanath proposed a formula of Republican judges in seven wards, Democrats in eight, with the mayor to select the judges in one ward. His proposed amendment also failed. After Alderman Baragwanath's amendment was laid on the table, Democratic floor leader Comisky dejectedly conceded defeat, charging, "We have been sold out by Alderman Shimp."

However, the political battles at this dramatic council meeting continued to consider broader and more symbolic issues. At 2 A.M. in this long and stormy meeting, Republican floor leader Charles Holden offered a series of what he called "patriotic resolutions." Holden cleverly used his Republican majority this night to shape the coming election to his party's advantage. The controversial resolutions urged that all "partisan divisions and contests be suspended . . . that every citizen owes allegiance to the [national] Government, and he who denies its authority or fails in his duty to uphold the honor of its flag, is an abettor of treason and should suffer the penalty due to his crime. . . . [We are] pledged to an unconditional support of the Government in all its Constitutional efforts to suppress rebellion, and an uncompromising opposition to treason in whatever form it appears." The resolutions called for a mass public meeting at Bryan Hall on April 9, 1863, to ratify these resolutions and ended, "That we, the [City] Council, equally divided as Democrats and Republicans

enter into this movement with the utmost good faith and pledge our-
selves to give it our aid, countenance and support, as individuals."[26]

The Republicans and Alderman Shimp voted in favor of the resolutions and the other Democrats opposed them. The final vote was 10–3,
with one Democratic alderman refusing to declare his vote and five Democratic aldermen absent because they left the meeting before the resolutions were introduced. According to the newspaper accounts, they left so
they could avoid voting on the controversial resolutions. For his support
of these resolutions, Alderman Shimp was voted out of the Invincible
Club, a Democratic Party club, and there were calls for his expulsion
from the Democratic Party. Alderman Shimp answered these complaints
in a letter to the newspapers: "Patriotism to my country and honesty to
my constituents are alike distasteful to the Invincible Club, and I am
therefore excommunicated."[27] Despite the internal party split, Shimp
continued in the city council as a Democrat, although voting with the Republicans more frequently. He was vindicated in his controversial stand,
however, by his reelection in 1863.

The *Chicago Evening News* declared that these Republican resolutions
embodied "the right sentiment and we hail the action of the [City] Council with the heartiest approval. They have struck the right chord and the
loyal people of the city will respond cordially. Let party nominations and
party excitements be done away with for the present."[28] But Mayor Sherman vetoed the resolutions as a partisan Republican attempt to commit
the Democrats in the city council to uncritical support of Lincoln's war
efforts:

> [The resolutions] urge, in the name of the Mayor and Aldermen . . . that the
> people of this city shall at this particular juncture, on the eve of an election
> for city officers, suspend all party divisions and contest, and lay aside all
> party names and platforms; that said people of all parties shall assemble at
> Bryan Hall, on the evening of the 9th of April . . . to then and there organize
> a political party, hostile and adverse to the organization known as the Dem-
> ocratic party. To such resolutions, no matter how patriotic may be the lan-
> guage in which they are expressed, I cannot as Mayor, nor as a citizen, nor as
> a member of the Democratic Party, give my approval. . . .
>
>   [The national administration] has made personal rights, personal free-
> dom, the laws, and even the Constitution itself, subordinate to the demands
> and exactions, not only of a party, but of the most fanatical and radical por-
> tion of that party. Act after act, order after order, proclamation after procla-
> mation have been issued, as if with the purpose of dividing the people and
> forcing them into political parties. That such policy should compel the Dem-
> ocratic party to take issue with the Administration as to its general and par-
> ticular management and conduct of the war, and of the civil affairs of the na-

COL. WOOD'S MUSEUM IN 1865

FIGURE 1.2 Downtown Chicago, 1865

tion, ought not be a matter of surprise. . . . It is an insult to the Intelligence of the Democratic party to suppose that they can be induced to join a new party having for its object the election of Republican officers, under the flimsy guise of "a Union League."[29]

The Chicago *Evening News* was horrified that Mayor Sherman vetoed the "patriotic resolutions." Both it and the *Chicago Tribune* endorsed the entire Republican slate of city officials in the upcoming city elections. The *Evening News* wrote, "From our hearts we pity Mayor Sherman. Himself an unlettered, unscheming and honest-minded man, he has suffered himself to be led and controlled by a squad of cheap and disloyal attorneys, until he is a mere machine in the hand of the operating wirepullers."[30] The *Chicago Tribune* further argued that Mayor Sherman was "in bad company when he affiliated with the *Times* [the Democratic paper] and the Copperhead element."[31] At this stage the Democratic Party supported the war but condemned the management of it. Over the next few years, the party would become even more hostile to the management of the war, would support peace and disarmament, and would oppose President Lincoln more vocally.

1863 Elections

The 1863 municipal election was the first in which the mayor was elected to two-year terms and the number of wards increased from ten to sixteen under the new city charter. Mayor Francis Sherman was running against Republican businessman Thomas B. Bryan, owner of Bryan Hall, one of Chicago's largest auditoriums. In Bryan's first campaign speech, he declared that he had not sought the nomination, but he accepted it because of the great issue of union or disunion. "The Union men I conceive to stand pledged to a hearty support of the Government in its efforts to suppress the accursed rebellion. Their platform, as I have more than once claimed, is simply *a loving devotion and an inflexible fidelity to the Union*."[32]

The rhetoric of patriotism expressed in the patriotic resolutions and in Republican campaign rallies almost won the election for the Republicans. However, the new Bridgeport and Holstein neighborhoods brought within the city boundaries by the Charter of 1863 helped reelect Mayor Sherman by the closest mayoral vote in Chicago's history: 10,252 to 10,095. More impressively, nineteen Democratic aldermen were elected to twelve Republicans with one vacancy in the council.

The *Chicago Tribune*'s analysis of the election was that the opposition Democrats misrepresented themselves as "the real and only friends of the prosecution of the war," used the widespread opposition to the new conscription law "distorted by false representations . . . as an autocratic measure, by which the 'rich and well born' hoped to force the laborer to the fighting while they stayed at home and reaped the spoils of victory." The Democrats spent enormous sums of money on the campaign and, according to the *Tribune*, won by the vote of the immigrant Irish. In a saying later unknowingly echoed by Richard J. Daley, the *Tribune* mourned that "we had not enough votes to win a victory."[33] The *Tribune* further declared,

> All the majority claimed for Sherman by his Copperhead friends is found in the vote of the additions made to the city by the last Legislature. Four hundred and ninety-five majority in *Bridgeport!* . . . It is a satisfaction to know that in Chicago as it was before the Legislature glued these additions on, Mr. Sherman, elected last year by about twelve hundred majority is beaten and well beaten. And it is a further satisfaction to be able to say that, in the wards where intelligence and refinement, education, religion, temperance, and all the attributes of virtuous citizenship, do most abound, there Mr. Bryan found his strongest support and largest majorities.[34]

Routine City Services

Despite partisan divisions, the city council was still able to support the war effort, retain the city's fiscal health, and deliver routine services. After this closely fought election, the council reassembled on May 5, 1863, to hear Mayor Sherman deliver his inaugural address in which he described the state of the city and the issues it would confront over the next two years:

> Not withstanding the derangement in the general business of the country caused by the rebellion, it has been our good fortune thus far to have escaped many of the embarrassments which have so seriously affected most of the larger cities; the business avocations of our citizens have been pursued with undiminished profit and safety; and our city has continued to increase steadily in growth and all the elements of permanent prosperity. . . Our commercial and manufacturing interests have advanced to an extent at least commensurate with the increase of population [of 80,000 people since 1860] . . . and the blessings of good order and tranquility have been enjoyed without interruption or disturbance. . . . During my past term of office, it has been my constant endeavor to inculcate the strictest economy in municipal expenditures. . . . The flourishing condition of the city and of its finances, ought not to stimulate us to indulge in lavish and extravagant expenditures. . . .
>
> I am a Democrat, devoted to the success of Democratic principles because those principles make the Constitution the sole and unchangeable test of all

political operations. While the [Democrats] do not favor every measure that may be strictly constitutional, they are opposed always to everything that is not constitutional. . . . The devotion to law as the only arbiter of public rights, necessarily requires that the Democratic party should give their undivided support to the Government, no matter by whom administered, in every effort to maintain the Constitution. . . . While [Democrats] are lavish in all things needed or asked by Government to put down the rebellion against the laws and Constitution, they are not the less opposed to, and by all lawful means will resist, the employment of the power and means placed by the people in the hands of the Executive to put down those engaged in rebellion, for the illegal and wanton oppression and destruction of the true and faithful people of the Northern States who are not engaged in rebellion.[35]

The divisions between Democrats and Republicans, War Democrats and Peace Democrats, shaped the city council and public policy throughout the Civil War period. City councils from 1837 until the Chicago Fire in 1871 headed a small city government with restricted governing powers. Aldermanic functions were entirely different from those in the stronger councils of the twentieth century. City governments of the mid-1800s also differed from later municipal governments in that they were not intended to be run as democracies. Most taxing and spending decisions were isolated by law from the control of elected representatives. Financial decisionmaking was not primarily a matter of "politics" but of "administration," and city council decisions focused on administrative disputes such as the number of police to hire and the salaries of particular city officials. In general, city governments in the early and mid-nineteenth century did not make their "administrative" decisions by determining public opinion. Rather, like managers of small businesses, they decided on the basis of their own judgment.

Chicago was no exception to these general trends of local government in the nineteenth century. Chicago government made financial decisions about public works and city services based on the desires of those who had "direct personal and pecuniary interests" in the outcomes. "Interest" was not interpreted as a democratic ideal. Citizens believed "that the distribution of services was equitable when each city dweller *got what he paid for,* no more no less."[36] Chicago's city government for most of the nineteenth century segmented its policies and based its decisions on what was best for the groups whose financial interests would be affected directly and who would have to pay for the city services, not on what was best for all citizens.

Thus city governments in the nineteenth century "were designed to minimize the redistributive effects of local government by removing as many of their services as possible from the general funding process." The goal was to keep property taxes low and the portion of the city budget funded by those property taxes as small as possible. As a result, U.S. cities delivered higher services at lower costs except in the maintenance of law and order.[37]

In general, nineteenth-century city governments strove to serve the needs of property owners, not the general public. As Mayor Sherman said in his inaugural address, a basic purpose of city government was "to inculcate the strictest economy in municipal expenditures" and to avoid "lavish and extravagant expenditures." Chicago followed this model of limited city government. The most important policies were the financing of physical infrastructure through special assessment. To have a voice in the decisionmaking process required ownership of property directly affected by the decision. Costs of infrastructure improvements were paid by special assessment payments by property owners to defray the cost of a specific public works project, not from general taxes or city funds. Those who would have to pay had a say in the decision commensurate with the percentage of the cost they were to pay. New public works projects like paving streets or sidewalks, which constituted the greatest number of pieces of legislation passed by the city council during this period, were undertaken by petition of the property owners. The aldermen simply shepherded property owners' petitions and ensured that projects were done by the city as cheaply as possible. According to the index for the city council's *Journal of Proceedings*, there were 167 petitions, ordinances, and vetoes of special assessments during the 1863–1864 council year for improvements such as street paving, street repairs, lampposts, and sidewalks. This was far greater than the number of ordinances introduced by the mayor or the aldermen for any other purpose. Improvement and repairs by special assessment remained the most common item on the city council agenda even during this volatile Civil War era, and they were generally administrative and apolitical decisions.

In Chicago, the assessment system and relatively limited general powers of city government had the effect of partially depoliticizing government and preventing the government from redistributing wealth. Since the use of public funds was an administrative decision directed by interested property owners, politicians on the city council had little control over city money. Since money raised by property taxes for the city's general fund was low, politicians on the council did not have the power of public patronage. There were very few city jobs to award. Similarly, aldermen could not court constituencies with the promises of general government services because, for the most part, they could only create new government programs by directly charging those who benefited. This was "a period in Chicago's history when its government was clean enough to satisfy even the most fastidious of urban reformers."[38] However, by the 1860s this was beginning to change as more city employees were hired, city services, including large public works projects, were increased, and city budgets grew dramatically. Corruption had been limited up to the Civil War because there was little politicians could do to favor friends or hinder enemies, but by the later 1860s corruption was beginning to emerge in the council and in local government more broadly.

On the one hand, since aldermen did not have to appease constituencies on many mundane decisions of local government, council votes on routine city services depended on the independent judgment of the aldermen as to what was best for the city; thus there were no permanent voting alliances on these issues. On the other hand, controversial Civil War and party power issues resulted in close votes along party and ideological lines as had the vote on the so-called patriotic resolutions sponsored by Alderman Holden. Substantive issues of conscripts and volunteers for the Civil War, election district judges, and the patriotic resolutions reflected the narrow partisan divisions and often ended in evenly divided votes in the council. The mayor was unable to overcome these partisan divisions or to force his own party members to support him on routine city service issues. Because he lacked the clout of later Chicago political bosses, Mayor Sherman was unable to exercise the type of control over aldermen that would characterize the rubber stamp councils of the twentieth century.

Ironically, by removing the populist control of funding decisions and by limiting the range of government services, the council became free to vote for or against the mayor and the Democratic Party floor leader on all but partisan Civil War issues. This pattern of independent voting and temporary coalitions on routine city services contrasts with the many closely divided roll call votes in the Civil War councils caused by extreme partisanship. Aldermen in later, more powerful, activist city councils would use their ability to redistribute wealth and to provide more government services and patronage jobs to buy support. After the Great Chicago Fire they created personal political machines, and after the Great Depression party bosses created a monolithic political machine to keep themselves in office. Mayor Sherman's council, in contrast to these later city councils, was divided by partisanship but unrestrained in routine city government decisions by either a party machine or a politically powerful mayor.

As Mayor Sherman indicated in his inaugural address, Chicago was blessed in this period with rapid population growth, a permanent increase in prosperity, and a civic order undisturbed by riots or the devastation of war that had occurred in other American cities. The difficult task for Chicago government and its political leaders was to support the national government in its prosecution of the Civil War despite the partisan differences over the conduct of that war. At the same time, Chicago local government needed to solve persistent problems of a growing city.

Public Works

One issue that transcended partisan boundaries was public works. In the *History of Cook County* the editors list twelve "Labors of Hercules, 1855–1870":

1. raised street grades and buildings, two to six feet
2. paved seventy-five miles of streets with wood
3. built eight-five miles of horse street railways
4. straightened the Chicago river channel
5. tapped a vast territory with railways
6. established sewerage and special assessment systems
7. established the Union Stock Yards
8. built and regulated a chamber of commerce
9. constructed the lake tunnel and secured good water
10. reversed the flow of the Chicago River
11. built tunnels under the river
12. raised nearly 27,000 volunteers for the Union army[39]

Of all these feats, creating the lake tunnel, deepening the canal, and reversing the flow of the river are recognized as the most astonishing physical changes to benefit Chicago during the Civil War era. All were organized by the city government.

Long before the Civil War, there had been cholera outbreaks caused by contaminated water. "Smelling committees" from the city council confirmed the terrible state of the Chicago River, worsened by the meatpacking plants, which simply disposed of animal waste directly into the river. The *Chicago Tribune* wrote that "the Chicago River is a bed of filth" and that "the public waxed indignantly loud in its clamors, and the Common Council found themselves *compelled* to take action of some description. ... [so] that measures of a permanent nature be devised both for thoroughly cleaning the river and securing also an undiminished supply of wholesome water."[40] Aldermen described a particularly loathsome area of the river, Healy's Slough, as "a nuisance 'of the vilest and most dangerous kind, which any civilized people ever had to contend with . . . a rank compound of villainous smells.' . . . On an inspection tour, [the aldermen] saw Healy's water 'colored crimson' from the blood that was pouring undiluted off the Milward company's packing floor."[41]

The first plan, diverting the flow of the Chicago River into the Lake Michigan–Illinois River Canal, did not work because the canal was too shallow. Finally, in 1864, the state legislature approved reversing the flow of the river so that polluted river water would flow to Illinois farmland instead of backing into the lake, which supplied the city's drinking water. This engineering wonder was completed in 1871 at a cost of over $3 million, with $2.5 million of the cost paid by the state. However, the work of cleaning the river was hampered by the limited jurisdiction of the city government despite loud citizen complaints. As late as 1866, Mayor John B. Rice vetoed an ordinance that would have ordered the city's Board of Public Works to dredge Healy's Slough and to bill the cost to the owners of the adjacent real estate. Mayor Rice believed that the city did not have the authority for such general public works to be billed to adjacent property owners without their agreement. Clearing the Chicago River of waste by reversing the flow of the river took the city and state government a decade to complete, and keeping Chicago's drinking water pure continued to be a problem throughout the nineteenth century. Chicago did not begin chlorinating its drinking water until 1912; both filtering and chlorinating did not come until 1947, despite the fact that the city had successfully experimented with filtering water at its famous Columbian Exhibition in 1893.[42]

In 1863, Mayor Sherman and the council agreed to create a lake tunnel to draw Chicago's drinking water from two miles out in the lake in order to guarantee citizens clean, safe drinking water. At the October 5, 1863, city council meeting city engineer Ellis Chesbrough recommended acceptance of the bid by Dull and McGowen to construct a lake tunnel at a cost of $361,539, with Dull and McGowen assuming all risks, as opposed to a bid by Will, McBean, and Company, which would not accept the risks. Despite his role as Democratic Party floor leader, Alderman Comisky opposed the Dull and McGowen bid, arguing that it was actually higher than the bid by Will, McBean. Other aldermen opposed the ordinance because they thought the lake tunnel project unnecessary, since they believed that the various projects flushing out the river would be sufficient to provide clean drinking water.[43]

After considerable debate, the lake tunnel project was approved by a vote of 18–11. The vote on the lake tunnel differed from votes on partisan Civil War issues in that Democrats and Republicans were on both sides of the issue. All Republicans but one supported the mayor and the city engineer, but the Democrats split evenly with the Democratic floor leader Alderman Comisky leading the opposition. Moreover, different arguments entered the debate: (1) which bid was cheaper, (2) which contractor had the best credentials to do the work, (3) what protections and guarantees were provided against extra costs, (4) how the bonds should be let, (5) whether other methods of cleaning the river might be cheaper and more effective, and (6) would the tunnel structure last over time? Aldermen of different political persuasions had different reasons for voting for and against the proposal and the bids.

The ground was broken for the lake tunnel project while Francis Sherman was still mayor on March 17, 1864. His successor, Mayor John Rice, laid the last brick in a grand ceremony in the tunnel on December 6, 1866, which he called "the wonder of America and the world."[44] The dual projects of reversing the river's flow and building the lake tunnel secured Chicago's fresh water supply for the next decade and would be the basis for a clean water system, after additions of water treatment plants to remove bacteria, that provides water for the city up to the present day.[45] The lake tunnel project and reversing the flow of the Chicago River demonstrate that the council of the Civil War period could, with mayoral and executive branch leadership, cope with the major issues facing the city beyond the war itself.

Martial Law

Not all local political events of the Civil War period occurred within the council chambers. The mayor and aldermen frequently were drawn into broader Civil War issues. The *Chicago Times*, owned and edited by Wilbur Storey, was the primary newspaper for the Democrats, and the *Chicago Tribune* was the primary newspaper for the Republicans. The *Chicago Times*, by partisan and controversial city council votes, became the official publication of record for the city government during Mayor Sherman's administration. However, Wilbur Storey and the *Times*, who had originally supported the war, became increasingly hostile to President Lincoln and his management of that war. Because of its strongly worded editorials, the *Times* had been banned from the Chicago Board of Trade and several Chicago clubs, and its commercial reporter was banned from the floor of the Board of Trade. The *Times* had argued, many thought treasonously, that the Civil War was "a war of a political party . . . [and that] the man who does not wash his hands of all participation in such a war shares the guilt of those by whom it is prosecuted. Support of this war and hostility to it show the dividing line between the friends and enemies of the Union. . . . The professed Democrat, therefore, who has his senses about him and is deliberately for the war is not a Democrat in fact, but an Abolitionist of the most radical and destructive kind."[46] This went much further than Mayor Sherman's inaugural address in which he declared that the Democratic Party would support the war but would oppose any attempts by the national government to curb civil liberties in the North.

Because of its inflammatory editorials, General Ambrose Burnside, who was the commanding general for the military district that included Illinois, on June 1, 1863, ordered suppression of publication of the *Times*. His order nearly caused a riot in Chicago. On June 4, after the military occupied the *Times* building, more than 20,000 people gathered at Courthouse Square in front of city hall. Despite speakers who urged moderation, the crowd vowed that if the *Times* were suppressed, they would stop the *Tribune* from publishing as well. Private armed guards under Colonel Charles Jennison were put on the roof of the *Tribune* building to protect it. Thus the struggle for freedom of speech clashed with the need for unified support of the war effort. This clash was on the verge of erupting violently on the streets of Chicago.

Leading politicians from both political parties gathered at City Hall to deal with the crisis. The meeting was called by Judge Van Higgins, chaired by Mayor Francis Sherman, and included Republican congressman Isaac Arnold. Chicago's first mayor, W. B. Ogden, offered a resolution at this meeting, which concluded that "the peace of this city and state, if not the general welfare of the country is likely to be promoted by suspension or rescinding of the recent order of General Burnside for the suppression of the *Chicago Times*." The city's leaders joined in a petition to President Lincoln asking him to rescind General Burnside's order and a telegram of the resolution was immediately sent to President Lincoln. President Lincoln wisely revoked "the order suppressing the circulation of the Times" and ordered Burnside to "take no further action in the matter."[47]

The *Times* resumed publishing and the riot was averted. Mayor Sherman and leaders of both political parties had managed to act in unison to avert a great crisis. One result of the bipartisan action of the city's leaders, however, was that Congressman Isaac Arnold was defeated in the next election. The *Tribune* and the Republicans could not forgive his act of bipartisan leadership. The lesson of his defeat and Alderman Peter Shimp's repudiation by the Democrats for his attempt to end the partisan stalemate over election judges was not lost on the other Republican and Democratic politicians. Partisan lines in the council became more rigid and partisan issues generally were not compromised.

Partisanship Lessens over Some War Issues

An important issue that bedeviled the council in 1863–1864 was raising the funds to encourage volunteers for the Union army to avoid conscription. On this issue, party factions in the council were able to find compromise solutions despite often heated rhetoric. Alderman Charles Holden, the Republican leader who had created such a furor with his patriotic resolutions before the 1863 election, proposed on June 25, 1863, an additional property tax to raise funds to pay a bounty for volunteers and to help equip their regiments. It passed unanimously. Previously, wealthy individuals and the Chicago Board of Trade had helped equip Chicago regiments, and some wealthy Chicagoans paid volunteers to serve in the army in their place. But the demand for more and more troops was overwhelming private recruitment efforts. By 1863, volunteers were paid a bounty to enlist so that Chicago could avoid a draft. Because of the city council's efforts, Chicago was able to avoid the "draft riots" that occurred in New York City in July 1863, killing at least 106 persons.

At a special city council meeting on July 20, Alderman John Comisky, the Democratic floor leader, proposed an ordinance for organizing volunteer companies to take the place of conscripts in the service of the United States. The ordinance allocated a sum not exceeding $120,000 as a war fund from the proceeds of the special property tax. The fund was to be "specially appropriated and set apart for the purpose of paying bounties to members of volunteer companies, organized to take the place of men . . . drafted as conscripts." It would contribute to bounties of up to $300 for each volunteer. The drafted men intended to be relieved by this ordinance were less wealthy married men or heads of families whose income was less than $700 or single men whose income was less than $500 a year. The ordinance came up for a vote at the August 10th council meeting and the debate was quite partisan. Alderman Comisky, for instance, deplored the national administration for perverting the original purpose of the war and "conducting it for the purpose of securing the perpetuation of the Abolition party."[48] But after all the debate, and fairly close votes on various proposed amendments, the ordinance carried nearly unanimously, by a vote of 29–1, with only Alderman Tolcott voting no.

Like nearly all the acts of the council in 1863, this issue was not finished with the vote on August 10. On August 24, Mayor Sherman, on behalf of the council, wrote directly to President Abraham Lincoln and Governor Yates of Illinois deploring the possibility of a draft, despite the $120,000 raised for volunteers and the large number of troops raised from Cook County and Chicago. He pointed out that the draft rolls contained over 28,000 names, when the entire list of registered voters in Chicago was only 20,347. The council subcommittee on volunteers and conscription believed that the draft list contained 8,000 more names than could have been legally entered.[49] President Lincoln responded that the federal government would be overwhelmed if it attempted to work out these matters with each city and that it would instead work with the states to get draft lists corrected and to handle appeals from the draft. The mayor and the council continued to work together to avoid the draft in Chicago. The draft enrollment list and conscription process was one Civil War issue on which Democratic and Republican aldermen agreed.

On December 11, 1863, the city council decided to raise the city's portion of the proposed bounty for individual recruits from $50 to $75 in an attempt to recruit more volunteers.[50] The county board followed the example of the city council and raised property taxes to provide a bounty of $112 for every volunteer from outside Chicago and added a $28 bounty to the city's $75 for every volunteer from Chicago. By February 1, 1864, bounties had been paid to 1,372 volunteers in the latest call for soldiers. From 1861 to 1863 Cook County (including Chicago) had supplied 10,455 volunteers, but it still had an official deficit of 3,717, which was to be made up by volunteers recruited by bounties or through a draft.[51] Over the entire course of the war, Cook County sent 22,436 men to fight, 15,000 of whom were from Chicago, which at the time had a population of only 110,000. About 4,000 of these soldiers from Cook County died in the war.

At the beginning the wealthy were able to buy their way out of the draft by paying a commutation fee of $300, but Congress repealed that provision in July 1864. Up until 1864 a substitute could be enrolled for any wealthy person who was drafted and chose not to serve for as little as a few hundred dollars, but by the summer of 1864 the price was as high as $1,200, even though the average salary for the working class was less than $1,000 a year.[52]

Conscription was a vexatious problem until the war ended in 1865. On February 23, 1865, a delegation of three prominent Chicago leaders met with President Abraham Lincoln. They were Samuel Hayes, a Chicago attorney, Roselle Hough, a former soldier and wealthy meat packer, and Joseph Medill, the proud and sometimes overbearing publisher and editor of the *Chicago Tribune*. Two were Democrats and Medill was a leading Republican. A month earlier, President Lincoln had issued another call for 300,000 additional soldiers, of which Cook County's share was to be 5,200 men. Only weeks after Chicago's first draft of 1864 had ended, the city was faced now with another conscription crisis. The delegation requested that the draft enrollment be revised. On February 27, 1865, the delegation met with Edwin Stanton, the secretary of war, and President Lincoln. After Stanton turned them down, President Lincoln lost his temper.

"Gentlemen," he said in a voice full of bitterness, "after Boston, Chicago has been the chief instrument in bringing this war on the country. The Northwest had opposed the South as the Northeast has opposed the South. It is you who are largely responsible for making blood flow as it has. You called for war until we had it. You called for emancipation and I have given it to

you. Whatever you have asked for you have had. Now you come here begging to be let off from the call for men which I have made to carry out the
war you have demanded. You ought to be ashamed of yourselves. I have a
right to expect better of you. Go home and raise your 6,000 men.

"And Medill, you are acting like a coward. You and your *Tribune* have had
more influence than any other paper in the Northwest, in making this war.
You can influence great masses and yet you cry to be spared at a moment
when your cause is suffering. Go home and send us those men."[53]

So the delegation returned home and Chicago once again used bounties
to gather the men needed to fight until the end of the war.

The Powers of Local Government

During the Civil War local government changed. From the 1830s until the
1860s, the state legislature retained considerable control and local politics
followed the booster system of city government. The mayor and the city
council were, of course, central to that system. "Under the 1837 [city]
charter, the mayor was an elective official, but his executive powers were
limited, and he was in many respects subordinate to the council." By the
consolidating act of 1851, the mayor's powers were increased. "The responsibility for the enforcement of laws and ordinances, the obligation to
give information and make recommendations to the council, the right to
appoint the council committees, and perhaps most important of all, the . .
. veto power made the mayor a [more powerful] figure." In 1857, the
mayor gained the further right to appoint, with council approval key administrative officials, and a two-thirds vote was now required to override
his veto.[54]

By the 1860s, the city council had become a purely legislative body, and
the mayor and his appointees took over the administrative functions of
government. Instead of a booster system of government, it had become a
more partisan government. By 1860, the council had evolved twenty
committees with mostly three members each to supervise various municipal functions. "Gradually the influence of these committees grew to the
point that their recommendation of a measure was tantamount to its . . .
enactment as an ordinance. After 1857, the council, except by unanimous
consent, could not act on matters of ordinances . . . until a report had
been made by the appropriate committee."[55] The council's rules of procedure also granted that the mayor, as presiding officer, was to decide all
points of order "subject to an appeal to the [City] Council" and gave him
the deciding vote on "all questions upon which the Council is equally divided." Unlike later city councils, the council committees in the Civil War
era were appointed by the mayor, not the council. Since the councils from
the Civil War until the Great Depression were fragmented and divided,

there was a balance of power between the mayor and the council that changed from administration to administration.

Individual aldermen retained control over most city services and improvements in their wards, provided that property owners were willing to pay for the improvements by special assessment. The city, for administrative purposes, was divided into three sections or divisions. Issues relating exclusively to streets and alleys in any division of the city were referred to the committee of that division, which included all aldermen whose wards fell within it. When only individual wards were involved, proposed ordinances were directed to the ward's aldermen and the senior alderman from the ward (since two aldermen represented each ward) became the subcommittee chairman to hold hearings on the ordinances.[56]

During the Civil War years in particular, there was a great multiplication of government activities. Expenditures by city government grew from $45,000 in 1848 to $2.9 million in 1865, of which $200,000 was spent paying off bonds, $1,400,000 was spent by the board of public works, and $900,000 was paid for all other city services including schools, police, lighting, streets, and sanitation.

During the Civil War, Chicago government was transformed from the era of boosterism to a highly partisan, activist government that could undertake broad public projects like building the lake tunnel and reversing the Chicago River. From a sleepy small town, Chicago had developed into a major city. However, this transformation had its negative aspects. Conflicts of interest, graft, and corruption among members of the city council greatly increased. In 1869, a "people's ticket" headed by Roswell Mason was elected to overthrow the ring of corrupt officials and "to restore Chicago to decent government," but corruption continued. In the late 1860s, the *Tribune* characterized the majority of aldermen, known as McCauley's Nineteen, "as dishonest and corrupt as any that has ever disgraced any municipal government." These aldermen solicited and accepted bribes, and the Cook County Board was similarly corrupt. Corruption became so flagrant that a grand jury was impaneled to investigate the bulging contents of strong boxes in a local bank. Six aldermen and six former aldermen were indicted and four were convicted and sentenced to six months in jail for their graft and corruption.[57] This period after the Civil War set a standard of corruption that aldermen would follow for more than a century.

The End of the War, 1863–1865

On June 18, 1863, the Democratic Party finally came out in clear opposition to "a further prosecution of the war and demanded that a convention be named to secure peace upon a Union basis."[58] Local elections in

November 1863 brought a shift to Republican dominance. The Republicans nominated Joseph E. Gary for superior judge and the Democrats, Buckner S. Morris. Gary was elected by a margin of 3,000 votes in the city and nearly 5,000 votes in the county. The Republican Party's other candidates for county offices were elected by similar margins. At the aldermanic elections in 1864, Republicans carried the contests by a little more than 300 votes, so the balance of council changed back from nineteen Democrats to eleven Republicans to an even sixteen-sixteen partisan split. "In order to secure a quorum [in 1864] Mayor Sherman was more than once obliged to arrest and bring into the room a reluctant Republican. At this time Alderman Valentine Ruh, a War Democrat, came out for the Republicans and thereafter in the City Council voted with that party."[59] He joined fellow War Democrat Alderman Shimp in voting with the Republicans on most party issues after 1864 so the Republican/War Democrat faction held the majority during Mayor Sherman's last year in office. Divided, partisan government reigned as Republican dominance continued to grow.

In the November 1864 election, former Republican Mayor John Wentworth easily defeated the Peace Democrat candidate, industrialist Cyrus McCormick, and returned to Congress to represent Chicago. Lincoln was reelected president over General George McClelland and carried Cook County by a vote of 18,667 to 14,351.

When President Lincoln was assassinated just before the 1865 municipal elections, the entire city turned out to pay tribute to him as his body lay in state at City Hall. Mayor Francis Sherman, who had been running for his third consecutive term as mayor, withdrew his candidacy "because he could not stand with the Copperheads who had murdered the President."[60] As a pragmatic politician, he also knew that running as a Democrat, he could not win given the immense Republican sentiment engendered by the assassination. Without opposition, the Republican mayoral candidate, John B. Rice, a local theater owner, was swept into office.

Some historians have concluded that democracy failed in American cities during this period.[61] Yet Chicago and its city council managed to govern fairly well even in the face of great tensions and partisan differences in a divided city. Despite some months in which the council could not meet for lack of a quorum and some partisan issues on which aldermen would not compromise, Chicago's city government was able to carry out its duties even during the war. After 1865, city government would be dominated by Republicans and too many officials of both parties would become corrupt. Nevertheless, Chicago and the Union survived the Civil War and the greatest political and social divisions in U.S. history. Chicago had gone from a booster system of government to a divided partisan regime. It would evolve again into a progrowth regime of businessmen and machine politicians in the post–Civil War period.

Notes

1. A very valuable listing of all aldermen and mayors with brief biographies of the mayors is Frederick Rex, *Centennial List of Mayors, Aldermen, and Other Elected Officials of the City of Chicago* (City of Chicago, 1937). It was reprinted by Chicago Historical Bookworks (n.d.).

2. Finis Farr, *Chicago: A Personal History of America's Most American City* (New Rochelle, N.Y.: Arlington House, 1973), p. 42.

3. Robin Einhorn, *Property Rules: Political Economy in Chicago, 1833–1872* (Chicago: University of Chicago Press, 1991), p. 28 n. 1.

4. Donald Miller, *City of the Century: The Epic of Chicago and the Making of America* (New York: Simon & Schuster, 1997), p. 77.

5. Einhorn, *Property Rules,* pp. 28, 40. Einhorn quotes the study of Chicago aldermen's business backgrounds by Rima Shultz, "The Businessman's Role in Western Settlement: The Entrepreneurial Frontier, Chicago 1833–1872" (Ph.D. diss., Boston University, 1985), p. 402.

6. Sam Bass Warner Jr., *The Private City: Philadelphia in Three Periods of Its Growth* (Philadelphia: University of Pennsylvania Press, 1968), pp. x–xi, 9–10, 82.

7. Gabriel Almond, *Plutocracy and Politics in New York City* (Boulder: Westview, 1998), pp. 15–16.

8. Almond, *Plutocracy,* pp. 68–71.

9. Anthony Orum, *City-Building in America* (Boulder: Westview, 1995), pp. 39, 62–71.

10. Mary P. Ryan, *Civic Wars: Democracy and Public Life in the American City During the Nineteenth Century* (Berkeley: University of California Press, 1997), p. 308.

11. Ryan, *Civic Wars,* pp. 307, 315.

12. Miller, *City of the Century,* p. 19.

13. Farr, *Chicago,* pp. 81–84.

14. Don Fehrenbacher, *Chicago Giant: A Biography of "Long John" Wentworth* (Madison, Wis.: American History Research Center, 1957), p. 194.

15. Theodore J. Karamanski, *Rally 'Round the Flag: Chicago and the Civil War* (Chicago: Nelson-Hall, 1993), p. 92.

16. *Chicago Tribune,* April 1862, as quoted in Weston Goodspeed and Daniel Healy, eds., *History of Cook County, Illinois* (Chicago: Goodspeed Historical Association, 1909), 1:394.

17. Biography of Francis Cornwall Sherman, Chicago Historical Society Files, p. 7.

18. Biography of Francis Cornwall Sherman, p. 8.

19. Biography of Francis Cornwall Sherman, pp. 10–11.

20. John Moses and Joseph Kirkland, *The History of Chicago,* vol. 1, *Aboriginal to Metropolitan Chicago* (Chicago: Munsell, 1895), p. 138.

21. Edward F. Dunne, *Illinois: The Heart of the Nation* (Chicago: Lewis, 1930).

22. Biography of Charles C.P. Holden, Chicago Historical Society Files.

23. *Chicago Tribune*, March 25, 1862, as quoted in Goodspeed and Healy, *History of Cook County, Illinois*, 1:396–397.

24. "Meeting of Common Council: A Tenth Ward Snake Strangled by a Union Soldier," *Chicago Evening News*, March 24, 1863.

25. "A Field Night in the Council: [Democrats] Fall into Their Own Trap," *Chicago Tribune*, March 24, 1863; and "The Common Council Meeting: The Defeat of the Copperheads," *Chicago Tribune*, March 25, 1863.

26. "The Union Movement in Chicago: The Common Council on Record," *Chicago Tribune*, March 25, 1863.

27. "A Broadside on the Copperheads from Ald. Shimp: He Refuses to Be Read Out of the Democratic Party," *Chicago Tribune*, March 26, 1863.

28. "The Union Movement in Chicago," *Chicago Evening News*, March 24, 1863.

29. "A Disgrace to Chicago: Mayor Francis C. Sherman Vetoes the Patriotic Revolutions," *Chicago Tribune*, April 3, 1863.

30. "The Loyal Resolutions of the Common Council Vetoed by the Mayor. 'Hove-in' Sherman Being a Candidate for Re-Election Defines His Platform," *Chicago Evening News*, April 2, 1863.

31. Goodspeed and Healy, *History of Cook County, Illinois*, 1:397.

32. "Great Union Ratification Meeting," *Chicago Tribune*, April 17, 1863.

33. "The Election," *Chicago Tribune*, April 23, 1863.

34. "Where the Majorities Were Found," *Chicago Tribune*, April 2, 1863.

35. "Special Meeting of the New Common Council: Inaugural Message of Mayor Sherman," *Chicago Tribune*, May 5, 1863.

36. Einhorn, *Property Rules*, p. 14.

37. Einhorn, *Property Rules*, pp. 6–15. On the delivery of city services, Einhorn cites Jon C. Teaford, *The Unheralded Triumph: City Government in America, 1870–1900* (Baltimore: Johns Hopkins University Press, 1984).

38. Einhorn, *Property Rules*, p. xv.

39. Goodspeed and Healy, *History of Cook County, Illinois*, 2:55.

40. "The Water Question: A Plan for Cleansing the River," *Chicago Tribune*, January 16, 1863.

41. Einhorn, *Property Rules*, p. 1. The statements from the aldermen are quoted from Chicago City Council Proceedings Files, 1865/66:458, at the Illinois Regional Archives (IRAD) at Northeastern Illinois University library.

42. Miller, *City of the Century*, pp. 429–430, 492.

43. *Chicago Tribune*, October 6, 1863.

44. A. T. Andreas, *History of Chicago from the Earliest Period to the Present Time* (Chicago: A. T. Andreas, 1885), 2:71.

45. By 1997, problems with some of the lake tunnels constructed since the Civil War developed. As Peter Kendall and Gary Washburn report in "Water System Shows Its Age Again," *Chicago Tribune*, August 31, 1997, one of the tunnels dug through the blue-clay bottom of the lake gave way during construction work and had to be sealed off. Lake Shore Drive had to be partially closed to traffic while repairs were made over a seven-month period.

46. Goodspeed and Healy, *History of Cook County, Illinois*, 1:472.

47. Goodspeed and Healy, *History of Cook County, Illinois*, 1:492.

48. "The Common Council. The Anti-Conscription Ordinance. Its Passage with Trifling Amendments," *Chicago Tribune*, August 11, 1863.

49. "The Common Council. Regular Meeting. Bounties to Recruits," *Chicago Tribune*, December 22, 1863.

50. "The Common Council. Special Meeting. Bounties to Volunteers—Seventy-Five Dollars Voted to Recruits," *Chicago Tribune*, December 11, 1863. Also see "Special Meeting of the Common Council. Bounty Offered to Recruits. The Council Has Redeemed Itself," *Chicago Evening News*, December 11, 1863.

51. Goodspeed and Healy, *History of Cook County, Illinois,* 1:479

52. Karamanski, *Rally 'Round the Flag*, pp. 198–199, 235.

53. Karamanski, *Rally 'Round the Flag*, p. 226.

54. Bessie Louise Pierce, *A History of Chicago*, vol. 2 (Chicago: University of Chicago Press, 1940).

55. Pierce, *History of Chicago*, p. 306.

56. *Rules and Order of Business of the Common Council of the City of Chicago,* March 27, 1860, pp. 2, 6. This document is available at the Chicago Historical Association and the Illinois Regional Archives.

57. Pierce, *History of Chicago*, pp. 297, 299.

58. Goodspeed and Healy, *History of Cook County, Illinois*, 1:398.

59. Goodspeed and Healy, *History of Cook County, Illinois*, 1:398. City election results in November 1863 from "Chicago Election," *Chicago Tribune*, November 4, 1863.

60. Karamanski, *Rally 'Round the Flag*, p. 246.

61. Ryan, *Civic Wars*, p. 308.

2

The Councils of the Gray Wolves, 1871–1931

Politically, three great transformations occurred in Chicago between its founding and the Great Depression. In the early "booster" years of the city, businessmen, lawyers, and realtors governed directly, serving as mayors and aldermen. By the Civil War partisanship and political party loyalties were much more important, and ethnic leaders like John Comisky came to leadership positions in the city council—boosterism was replaced by a divided partisan regime. After the Chicago Fire, these ethnic leaders formed stronger political machines and the city council became fragmented and corrupt. Machine aldermen in the council prevailed over reformers, even when reformers were mayors for brief terms. Although businessmen no longer governed directly after the Chicago Fire, the government continued progrowth policies, and businessmen occasionally rallied to directly run grand projects such as the 1893 World's Fair or to promote the 1907 Burnham Plan for future development of Chicago. After the Chicago Fire, however, politicians and aldermen had, for the most part, taken the power from business leaders to control the government directly. During the post–Civil War and post–Chicago Fire period, a regime of businessmen and politicians ruled over a fragmented power structure and government.

Local government from the Chicago Fire in 1871 until the Great Depression in 1929 was characterized by corruption, "boodle," and fragmented power. In the city council, power was split between powerful committee chairmen, and in the political system, it was split between competing party bosses in the wards. It was a political system that favored big business interests and undermined the authority of the mayors. The city council was at the center of a corrupt political system in which aldermen and judges could be bribed; the laws and the police favored the businessman, not the workingman; and public officials were often motivated by ambition and lust for money. The period comprising the late nineteenth and early twentieth centuries saw clashes between reformers and those businessmen and political "bosses" who supported the corrupt, machine-controlled government. The battle between machine and reform was the great civic war that replaced the partisanship of the Civil War period.

From the Chicago Fire until the 1930s, Chicago had a fragmented political system in which party membership was a less powerful organizing factor than it had been in the Civil War. As alderman and University of Chicago professor Charles Merriam observed of this period, "Chicago has never had an effective boss of the New York or Philadelphia type, with a well-organized machine capable of holding out against public opinion for any length of time. But a series of petty feudal chieftains of spoils have wrought havoc with economy, order, justice."[1] No single ethnic group, interest group, or political party completely dominated. Ward elections of aldermen in different ethnic areas, a plethora of separate units of local government, and numerous elected offices encouraged decentralization.

In this era, Chicago had a strong council–weak mayor form of government. The city council controlled public policy, determined the city budget, and forced department heads to answer to council committees. Because of fragmentation in the council, however, "aldermen had to form alliances with their colleagues to find enough votes to pass legislation. The system of independent leaders helped foster informal means to organize legislation. Logrolling . . . was common with 'boodle' aldermen and reform aldermen alike."[2]

Chicago's rapid development at the turn of the century brought new problems that the political system based on ward bosses and political fiefdoms had difficulty solving. "Chicago entered the new century with no comprehensive building and sanitary code, and the few building codes actually enacted were freely violated. . . . the streets themselves were often unpaved, unrepaired, and seldom cleaned. . . . The public school system did not have the resources to cope with an influx of new [immigrant] pupils, most of whom did not speak English. . . . During the depression years of the late nineteenth century, the city had neither the financial nor legal means to help this great pool of unskilled industrial laborers and their families."[3]

The Birth of Chicago Machine Politics, 1871–1905

A turning point in Chicago history came when the Great Chicago Fire of October 8, 1871, destroyed 18,000 downtown buildings across four square miles, including all the hotels, theaters, and commercial structures in the business district. More than 250 people died and the Board of Trade estimated the value of the lost property at $200,000,000. Yet Chicago quickly rallied under the leadership of Mayor Joseph Medill to rebuild a grander and more fireproof city.[4]

The city council had an active role in providing relief for those who suffered from the fire. Alderman Charles C.P. Holden, the city council president who had served as alderman since 1861, established a temporary city headquarters at the First Congregational Church on the West Side of Chicago and soon gathered the mayor and enough aldermen for an emergency session. The city council remained in continuous session at the church from October 9 until October 17, 1871, when the permanent Aid and Relief Society took over the relief effort. It was later estimated that "the Council helped 75,000 people and maintained control of the city during a crisis that easily could have dissolved into chaos."[5]

The first real political machine was also born after the Chicago Fire. A gambler–saloon keeper named Michael Cassius McDonald "was the first to detect the common bonds of interests of the criminal element and politicians and introduce one group to the other" after the fire of 1871. The *Chicago News* gave McDonald, who was the first party boss of Chicago, credit "for electing aldermen who lorded it in the city council and county commissioners who stole everything in sight, and for providing contracts for public works that had thievery written between the lines."[6] McDonald used his political clout to prevent the police from raiding his several gambling houses and those of his allies. "After becoming boss of the city, [he] assigned locations for houses of prostitution, granted licenses for gambling, and distributed money from criminals and brothel-keepers to police officials, court employees and judges."[7] When he refused to fix a political case for his former allies, several aldermen went to jail for a crooked city contract of $128,500 to paint the courthouse, which served as City Hall, with a useless mixture of chalk and water.

When reform mayor John Roche was elected in 1887, McDonald went into semiretirement, only to return to power when Carter Harrison was reelected mayor in 1893. Both Carter Harrison I and his son, Carter Harrison II, were tolerant of the ward bosses who helped elected them. Meanwhile, the city continued to grow and expand. A chief symbol of Chicago's new status was the Columbian Exposition of 1893, which was magnificent. The dazzling exposition ran from May to October 1893 during a depression that saw 8,000 businesses go bankrupt in the United States. Yet 27 million people visited the fair, nearly half the population of the country, despite money being scarce, jobs few, and wages low.

In the last week of the Columbian Exposition, Mayor Harrison was assassinated by Eugene Prendergast, a disgruntled job seeker. Harrison

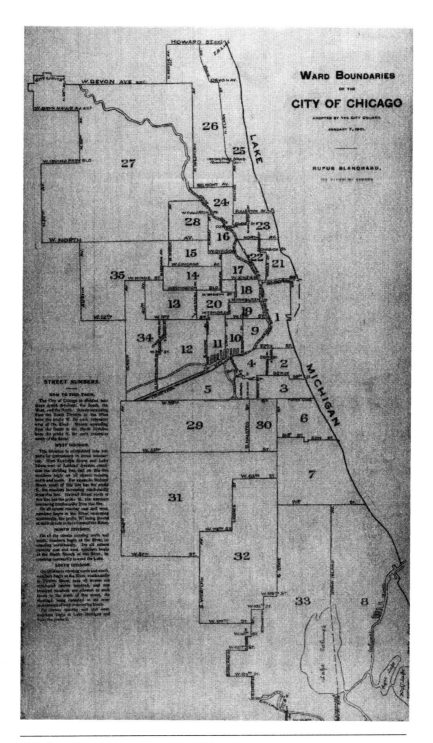

FIGURE 2.1   Chicago Ward Map, 1901

served five terms as mayor between 1879 and 1893 and his son, Carter Harrison II, served from 1897 to 1905 and from 1911 to 1915. They were the longest serving father and son mayors in Chicago until the current Richard Daleys. During the reign of the Harrisons, the city council continued to be ruled by local party ward bosses.

At the turn of the century, "the unwieldy body of the Chicago City Council offered a vision of political fragmentation and a patchwork of competing fiefdoms. Political corruption was wide-open [at the end of] nineteenth century Chicago, and it merely changed its form as the twentieth century took shape."[8] Lincoln Steffens, a reporter for *McClure's Magazine*, named the Chicago aldermen "'the gray wolves' for the color of their hair and the rapacious cunning and greed of their natures." He described the systematized graft in the city as "boodling" and council grafters as mostly "a lot of good natured honest thieves."[9] According to historians, the years between the Columbian Exposition in 1893 and the creation of the unified Democratic Party machine by Anton Cermak in 1931 were "the most disreputable in the city's history."[10] Mayor Carter Harrison II described the council in this period as "a low-browed, dull-witted, base-minded gang of plug uglies with no outstanding characteristic beyond an unquenchable lust for money."[11]

At the turn of the twentieth century there were seventy aldermen from thirty-five wards, as shown in figure 2.1, with two aldermen representing each of them, a Chicago tradition since 1837. Aldermen served a single year in office from 1837 to 1847 and two-year terms from 1847 to 1935. In 1935 their terms were lengthened to four years, as they are today.

Two of the most colorful aldermen of this era of Gray Wolves were Bathhouse John Couglin and Hinky Dink (Mike) Kenna, both of whom represented the notorious 1st Ward on the Levee along the South Branch of the Chicago River. Bathhouse John Couglin, whose nickname came from the string of bathhouses he owned, was first elected to the city council in 1892 by a margin of 1,603 to 768 with the blessing and support of party boss Mike McDonald. His sidekick and fellow 1st Ward boss, Mike Kenna, got his nickname, Hinky Dink, from *Chicago Tribune* editor Joseph Medill while he was still a newsboy; Medill said he was "such a little fellow." Kenna grew up to become a saloon keeper, successful precinct captain, and, later, the ward boss who provided the organizational skill to run the 1st Ward "machine." Kenna was elected as the second 1st Ward alderman in 1897 in the same election that made Carter Harrison II mayor. Bathhouse John and Hinky Dink would remain on the city council forty years, from the 1890s until the 1930s, and were apt symbols of the color and corruption of this period.

The leading economic groups of the 1st Ward were legitimate businessmen on the one hand and saloon and brothel keepers on the other. The illegitimate businesses far outnumbered the legitimate businessmen in their fancy homes on the east side of the ward. A vice commission appointed by Mayor Busse in 1910 found in the notorious 1st Ward "over 1,000 brothels, 1,800 madams and pimps and 4,000 prostitutes . . . bringing in an annual revenue of sixty million dollars, on which the profits were fifteen million."[12] Neither the wealthy living along the lakefront nor the poor living in the slums were too concerned with their aldermen. "It was the saloon men, the keepers of brothels, the gamblers and the numerous denizens of the underworld who took the most practical interest in the ward's politics for they were at the constant mercy of the police and they had to elect, buy and hire politicians to protect them."[13] Rogues like Bathhouse John Couglin and Hinky Dink Kenna were the perfect aldermen to represent them.

An English editor named William T. Stead in his book, *If Christ Came to Chicago*, decried the corruption he found at the time of the Columbian Exposition, especially in wards like the First, and launched a political reform movement under the umbrella of a new organization, the Civic Federation. Stead described how the party precinct captains won elections—through hard work, personal contact, and vote buying. The "boodling" and corruption in the city council during this era he described in the following way:

> If it is a very small matter [requiring city legislation], a trifle [in the way of payment] will suffice, for your Alderman is not above small pickings by the way. It is a very different matter, however, when the question is one involving a railway franchise or a new gas ordinance. Then much more elaborate machinery is employed. The Council is sometimes divided and redivided into various rings. In the present Council one Alderman, who can usually be found in the neighborhood of Powers & O'Brien's saloon, can control forty others. The head of the big ring is the boss. There is also a smaller ring of ten subsidiary to the greater ring and working together with it. The support of both rings is necessary when an ordinance is to be passed over the Mayor's veto.[14]

At the turn of the century, aldermen were paid stipends of less than $200 a year for their service in the council. In comparison, the *Record* declared, "In a fruitful year the average crooked Alderman has made $15,000 to $20,000."[15] Thus most aldermen were on the take. Stead concluded that no more than ten of the seventy aldermen in the council "have not sold their votes or received any corrupt consideration for voting away the patrimony of the people."[16] The leading Democratic paper of the time, the *Chicago Herald*, said that aldermen are "in nine cases out of ten a bummer and a disreputable who can be bought and sold as hogs are bought and sold at the stockyards."[17] The council's character was summed up colorfully by 9th Ward alderman Nathan T. Brenner, who said that of the members of the council, perhaps only three were not "able and willing to steal a red-hot stove."[18]

In 1896, the reform elements in Chicago who had followed William Stead's lead in founding the Civic Federation formed a new political organization, the Municipal Voters' League, under the leadership of businessman George E. Cole. Its mission was to rid the city council of corrupt aldermen. In the spring 1896 election, the Municipal Voters' League was able to defeat eighteen of the twenty-three aldermen it had targeted. However, it was unable to defeat Bathhouse John Couglin or the chief leader of the boodlers, 19th Ward alderman Johnny Powers. From 1907 to 1921 the Municipal Voters' League endorsed candidates who won 59.4 percent of their aldermanic races, but it was unable to achieve more extensive governmental reforms or to eliminate either machine politics or corruption.[19]

In 1904 journalist Lincoln Steffens found Chicago criminally wide-open, its political parties controlled by bosses and open corruption centered in the city council. Still he viewed Chicago as a reform city because of the electoral successes of the Municipal Voters' League.[20] His hope that reform forces would soon triumph completely proved too optimistic. Even as reform groups organized, machine politics was changing. Roger Sullivan, who led one of the two major factions in the Democratic Party at the turn of the century, became Chicago's major political boss after Mike McDonald retired. Sullivan made political corruption into a big business. He personally became a millionaire with a fake gas company, which obtained a city council franchise. The Sullivan machine followed new principles: "The old politician, an independent operator, was content to knock down a little graft to allow businessmen to make monopolies and fortunes. The new Machine politician, using the disciplined approach to government, became both politician and businessman. He was the city and he did business with the city."[21] Sullivan and his associates, George Brennan and Adolph Sabath, provided bonding for enterprises doing business with the city and gained ownership stakes in construction companies, which were then richly rewarded with city contracts. Despite the success of the Sullivan machine, as the twentieth century began, there remained many small, ward-based political organizations rather than one grand machine with total control.

The council remained the focus for boodle, and the most famous boodle schemes granted franchises for the street railways and utilities. Ironically, 1st Ward aldermen Couglin and Kenna joined Mayor Carter Harrison II in foiling the plans of businessman Charles Yerkes. In 1896, aldermen in the pay of streetcar baron Yerkes sought a fifty-year extension of his streetcar franchise with little compensation to the city government and no improvement in services to riders. Yerkes offered a small fortune of $150,000 to Aldermen Couglin and Kenna for their support.

When Mayor Carter Harrison II met with the two aldermen to appeal for their help in defeating Yerkes, Bathhouse John told the Mayor, "Mr. Maar, I was talkin' a while back with Senator Billy Mason and he told me, 'Keep clear of th' big stuff, John, it's dangerous. You and Mike stick to th' small stuff; there's little risk and in the long run it pays a damned sight more.' Mr. Maar, we're with you. And we'll do what we can to swing some of the other boys over." With their backing, the Yerkes ordinance was defeated 32–31, marking "the end of the era in which the word or threat or the purse of Charles Tyson Yerkes would control an aldermanic vote."[22] It is a great irony that Yerkes and his powerful city council ally, Alderman Johnny "Da Pow" Powers, were ultimately defeated by the vote of the two admittedly corrupt aldermen from the 1st Ward, Bathhouse John and Hinky Dink. They were afraid to take too big a bribe and they owed their political loyalties to Mayor Carter Harrison I and his son, Carter Harrison II.

After the Harrisons, the reigns of three particular mayors in various years from 1905 to 1931 illustrate the Gray Wolves era: Mayors Edward Dunne, Fred Busse, and Big Bill Thompson. These mayors were vastly different in temperament, style, beliefs, and political support. Yet the council of the Gray Wolves continued unabated under each of them. Some of the key political battles in Chicago's colorful history occurred during their terms of office and provide a window into the regime which governed during the Council of the Gray Wolves.

Edward Dunne's Council, 1905–1907

This corrupt council of the Gray Wolves continued from the nineteenth into the twentieth century. However, there was a chance of substantial change during reformer Edward Dunne's term as mayor from 1905 to 1907. It was a heady time in Chicago. Both the Cubs and Sox were in the World Series and Upton Sinclair published his famous book, *The Jungle*, on the Chicago stockyards. Dunne's election marked the most serious challenge to the existing order in Chicago politics until Harold Washington's election in 1983 nearly eighty years later. The main focus of Dunne's reform efforts was to establish immediate municipal ownership of the public transit system. Dunne's failure demonstrates the limits of reforms initiated by a mayor in a strong council–weak mayor system. Dunne's reform attempts failed because he had no way to influence aldermen who opposed him. He was constrained by a two-year term and limited patronage. Because he was not a party boss, Dunne could not overcome the entrenched power of established ward bosses and city power brokers who felt threatened by his reforms. Thus he failed to achieve either municipal ownership of the transit system or reelection as mayor.

Dunne was born in Waterville, Connecticut, on October 12, 1853. His family moved to Peoria, Illinois, when he was two, and he graduated from Peoria High School in 1870. He spent three years at Trinity College at the University of Dublin, Ireland. In 1876, five years after the Chicago Fire, he began to study law in Chicago and was admitted to the bar in 1878. He married Elizabeth Kelly in 1882, and they had thirteen children. He was elected circuit court judge of Cook County at the age of thirty-eight in 1891 and reelected in 1897 and 1903. In those years, he lived in River Forest, a town adjacent to Chicago.

Judge Dunne's most famous case was a First Amendment battle in which Judge Hanecy had cited publisher William Randolph Hearst, along with editors and cartoonists of the *Chicago American,* on charges of contempt of court for publishing negative opinions about a case that Judge Hanecy had just decided. In his decision, Judge Dunne wrote: "I held that no contempt had been committed [because Judge Hanecy had issued a final order in the case] and it being a final order . . . the press had a right to comment upon and criticize that decision, even to the extent of libeling the honored and respected judge who had rendered the opinion without exposing themselves to prosecution for contempt of court."[23] Upholding the freedom of the press in this controversial case brought Judge Dunne a national reputation.

Dunne moved into the city from River Forest in 1903 and announced his mayoral candidacy in January 1905. He maintained that he moved to Chicago because his home in River Forest was too small for his large family when his eleventh and twelfth children were born as twins in 1901. He said that when he moved he had not the slightest idea of becoming a candidate for mayor. Other political observers believed, however, that this was a calculated political move in order to run.[24] In any case, Mayor Carter Harrison II declined to run for reelection in 1905 because he figured that Republican candidate, John M. Harlan, was invincible. Former Judge William Prentice of the Chicago Federation of Labor then threatened to run as an Independent candidate on the platform of municipal ownership of public utilities and the transit systems if Dunne was not slated as the Democratic candidate. The entry of Judge Prentice into the race would probably have doomed any other Democratic nominee in the general election. So the Democrats agreed to make Judge Dunne their standard bearer.

Not long before the mayoral election, Judge Dunne returned from a European trip. While in Switzerland, he had sent a telegram for only eight cents. The same telegram would have cost fifty cents to send in Chicago. He inquired about state-owned enterprises such as the telegraph services during the rest of his European trip and became convinced that the cost of all public utilities would be greatly reduced by public ownership. When he returned, the Iroquois Club, of which he was a member, gave a dinner in his honor at which he spoke about the value of public ownership in a speech that was widely reported in the Chicago newspapers.[25]

On January 15, 1905, Judge Murray Tuley (who had been in the audience at the Iroquois Club speech) in an open letter to the people of Chicago declared that "the only hope of victory [in the battle for municipal ownership of utilities] was for the Democrats to nominate a mayoral candidate 'who would inspire confidence throughout the city in his determination and ability to carry out the municipal ownership policy.'"[26] Judge Tuley went on to write, "I have no hesitation in suggesting to the people of Chicago, opposed to the impending corporate domination, that in this emergency they themselves call Judge Dunne from the judicial bench to the mayoral chair."[27] His letter inspired delegations from thirty-three of the city's thirty-five wards to urge Dunne to run for mayor. Dunne had the backing of the William Jennings Bryan, Governor Peter Altgeld, and Randolph Hearst faction of the Democratic Party and encountered no overt opposition from the either the Roger Sullivan–Mayor John Hopkins faction or from powerful ward bosses like Bathhouse John Couglin and Hinky Dink Kenna. Judge Dunne was popular because he combined personal urban liberalism with an Irish Catholic heritage, and the Irish were still one of the larger voter blocs in the city.

The Democratic Party politicians' point of view was summed up by a city employee quoted in the *Chronicle*: "I care nothing for municipal ownership. I'm for Judge Dunne. I have a good job in city hall and I'd be a fool to oppose him. Another reason I'm for him, I'm for a [wide] open [drinking] town, I want to see North Clark Street like it was in the old days."[28]

The Republicans nominated John M. Harlan, who had run on a municipal ownership platform in 1897 but now hedged his support of immediate municipal ownership. He was backed by the regular Republican organization as well as the business and financial community, which opposed municipal ownership. Many "reform" and "civic" leaders of Chicago supported Harlan because they had a different conception of reform. "The middle-class and largely Protestant 'good government' reformers opposed [Dunne because] their views on what constituted reform differed from his. They were interested in efficiency in government, civil service reform, better law enforcement and the like. Dunne was concerned mainly with social reforms designed to help the common man: municipal ownership of utilities and transportation systems, higher real estate taxes for corporations, and better salaries for government workers."[29]

In his campaign, Dunne held Democratic Party rallies in every ward of the city but refrained from endorsing or opposing aldermanic candidates unless they endorsed his platform of immediate municipal ownership. In the 1st Ward, where Alderman Kenna "urged his supporters to vote for the judge because he was going to give the streetcars to the people, Dunne responded with an effusive endorsement of one of the most notorious Gray Wolves." In return, the 1st Ward voters gave Dunne a plurality of 3,800 votes. Dunne won his election because he added to this regular Democratic Party vote by mobilizing a series of volunteer political action clubs organized by occupation, sex, ethnic group, and geography.[30]

In the April 4, 1905, election, Dunne defeated Harlan by a vote of 163,189 to 138,671. In traditional Democratic wards his political affiliation and ethnocultural ties were most important, but in other wards his clear stand on municipal ownership was key to winning Republican and Independent votes. According to newspaper accounts, Dunne was also helped because John Harlan "was about the most hopeless candidate who ever ran for office in Chicago. . . . Running against Harlan, [Dunne] could have been elected on any kind of platform. He was victorious in spite of his platform and not on account of it."[31] Mayor Dunne, however, interpreted his election as a mandate for immediate municipal ownership of street railways and utilities.

One of Mayor Dunne's first notable acts in office was to appoint the most radical leaders of his Bryan–Altgeld faction of the Democratic Party, along with social workers and labor leaders, to the top positions in his administration. For instance, famous defense lawyer Clarence Darrow was made corporation counsel and well-known social worker Jane Addams was appointed to the school board. "[Dunne's appointees] vigorously enforced public health and building codes; went to court to force corporations to pay higher real estate taxes; increased the salaries for teachers; cracked down on some of the more serious violations of the drinking, gambling and vice laws; and effected moderate reforms in the police department."[32] However, Mayor Dunne never gained control over the fragmented council of Gray Wolves, which was still run by the ward bosses and their allies. As a result of his own indecisiveness in pushing the municipal ownership program and aldermanic opposition to his proposed ownership plans, the main platform on which he had been elected was not enacted.

The Battle for Immediate Municipal Ownership of Street Railways

The battle over the street railways and public ownership of utilities was not new to the city council. The first street railway franchise had been granted on March 4, 1856, for a period of twenty-five years "until the city should elect to purchase it." Even this original legislation provided for ultimate purchase and public ownership of the railways by the city.[33] Furthermore, street railway franchise issues and the location of the railways on particular streets had been on the agenda frequently at council meetings during the Civil War. The original administrative division of the city into north, south, and west divisions was responsible for the creation of three different street railway systems in the different divisions and the lack of free transfers between the different systems. These separate private railway systems continued to plague the transportation (or traction) system into the twentieth century.

Chicago was not alone in its struggle with the traction companies. Hazen Pingree, mayor of Detroit from 1890 to 1897, was one of the first mayors of a major city to successfully fight the traction companies. He became involved because of a streetcar strike in Detroit in 1891, followed by the Depression of 1893. In his third term of office in 1895, Mayor Pingree, by vetoing "countless franchise renewals," forced the company to replace its antiquated horsecar system with electrically powered cars and won "a low-cost three cent workingman's fare from the system." In a similar way, Mayor Samuel "Golden Rule" Jones of Toledo, Ohio, fought for similar workingman's fares from 1897 to 1904. His successor, Toledo mayor Brad Whitlock, secured a three-cent fare during workingmen's hours in 1913.[34]

In contrast to Detroit and Toledo, the streetcar battle in Illinois was mostly won by the traction companies. For example, the Illinois legislature in 1865 extended the length of the franchises to ninety-nine years over the veto of Governor Oglesby. However, there were occasional victories for the reform forces. For instance, in 1896, when Carter Harrison II was in office, Charles Yerkes had failed to unify the traction system under his control on terms most unfavorable to the city. Later, when Edward Dunne became mayor, the city was able to obtain a decision from the U.S. Supreme Court that the Ninety-Nine Year Act of 1865 was unconstitutional. With this victory, the public transportation battles began again.

On April 1, 1901, citizens voted on a referendum in favor of public ownership by an overwhelming margin of 142,826 to 27,998. When Mayor Dunne was elected mayor on a platform of immediate municipal ownership on April 5, 1905, citizens reaffirmed their desires by a similar referendum vote of 153,223 to 30,279.[35] However, Mayor Dunne delayed for three months after his inauguration before submitting his proposals for municipal ownership to the city council and its committee on local transportation. Finally, he offered two proposals: one plan called for Chicago to construct and operate its own system, and another contract plan would have created a private corporation headed by five prominent citizens to build and operate a single traction system. Unfortunately, the Committee on Local Transportation did not favor either plan. As Mayor Dunne later wrote, "I was not long in finding out that the committee on local transportation was hopelessly hostile to the principle of municipal ownership. . . . The committee decided by a vote of 8 to 5 on September 11, 1905, to defer its consideration, and instead to invite proposals for an extension of their franchises from the traction companies."[36]

When Dunne's special traction counsel, Walter Fisher of the Municipal Voters' League, finally negotiated an agreement to purchase the transit system and convinced both the companies and the city council committee to agree on "compromise" or "settlement" ordinances, Mayor Dunne found so many problems in the agreement that he vetoed the ordinances that focused on better regulation of the existing traction system. In the mayor's view, fatal flaws in the ordinances drafted by Fisher and the committee "would practically prevent the consummation of the people's desire for municipal ownership."[37]

On January 7, 1907, Mayor Dunne proposed that the council put the issue of municipal ownership of the street railways to a voter referendum. The Committee on Local Transportation proposed instead to regulate the existing "traction" system without another referendum. The mayor's referendum proposal was defeated by a council vote of 40–26 because the majority of the aldermen believed "that the people prefer a speedy rehabilitation of street car services [and] went on record as unwilling to obstruct in any way the universal public desire."[38]

In his veto letter to the council, the mayor reminded aldermen that they had passed an earlier resolution unanimously declaring it to be "the sense of the council that the procedure in dealing with any ordinance or ordinances for the settlement of the Chicago street railway question should provide for a referendum."[39]

The council floor leader from 1907 to 1909 was Republican alderman Frank Bennett, who represented Hyde Park, where he had served as assessor when it was still a separate town in 1888. Although he served in the Chicago City Council only from 1907 to 1909, he was the floor leader during this period. Later he served as the city's commissioner of public works under Mayor "Big Bill" Thompson, as state of Illinois director of public works, and as vice chairman of the Chicago Plan Commission. Alderman Bennett on January 7, 1907, moved that the mayor's resolution be published and considered concurrently with the traction ordinances, even though this would not leave enough time to prepare petitions for the referendum if the council did not vote to put the issue on the ballot.

Leading the mayor's forces in the immediate municipal ownership battles was Democratic alderman William E. Dever, who would later serve as a reform mayor from 1923 to 1927. Dever had been born in Wobrun, Massachusetts, in 1862, the oldest boy in a family of eight children. His father had owned one of the largest tanneries in Massachusetts. So when Dever moved to Chicago in 1887, he worked at a tannery on Goose Island until he completed his legal studies at the Chicago College of Law in 1890 and was admitted to the bar. He became involved in politics through the Chicago Commons settlement house, was a part of the reform movement and a member of the Municipal Voters' League, and served as alderman from 1902 to 1910.[40]

When Alderman Bennett moved that the mayor's referendum resolution be considered concurrently with the traction ordinances, Aldermen Dever moved that the rules be suspended and the mayor's referendum resolution adopted immediately. In defense of the mayor's proposal, Alderman Dever argued that deferring the mayor's resolution would provide insufficient time to get the petition signatures to put the referendum on the traction settlement on the ballot. Both "conservative and radicals ought to unite in the agreement to submit the settlement to the people. The only honest objection to the referendum proposal is that it will delay the settlement and prolong the bad service. Why gentlemen, it is humiliating that this council should say to the street car companies: 'You have punished us with bad service so long that we now throw up our hands and give in to you.' The companies have driven the people into desperation so that they could exact ordinances to their liking." Democratic aldermen Nicholas Finn and Michael Zimmer joined Dever in arguing that "the people had been pledged by the aldermen that no traction settlement would be made without a referendum vote."

Republican alderman Foreman, who had offered the original resolution for a referendum the previous year, argued that last year there would have been "ample time for a referendum without unnecessarily delaying the settlement." A year earlier there had been two large blocs in the community and in the city with different positions on the ordinance. Since then, however, according to Alderman Foreman, "Compromises have been made all around and all the [council committee] members are satisfied. . . . There is a practical unanimity in this community on these ordinances. The council, I assume, is practically unanimous. Then why delay further the regeneration of our street car service? If we wait until there is no objection at all to the ordinances we shall never get a settlement."[41]

Democratic alderman Charles Werno, who chaired the Committee on Local Transportation, concurred with Foreman that "'the people of Chicago want the traction question settled and they want it settled now.' This expression was greeted with applause from the strap hangers in the gallery. 'I believe that if the committee brings in the ordinances within a week or two we shall begin to see an improvement in street car service at once. . . . The council must act without delay. . . . The only thing to do is to go ahead and act—act like men. The people who sent us here expect results.'"[42]

The mayor remained firmly committed to the referendum despite the council's opposition. He told the press at the end of the January 7 meeting, "I believe I am right. The referendum fight is not over. It has just begun."[43] On January 8, Mayor Dunne wrote an address to the people of Chicago asking them to help by passing referendum petitions on the proposed traction ordinances within the twenty-four days left before referendum petitions were due to be filed. Citizens mobilized and petitions were passed and signed in large numbers. The Committee on Local Transportation, seeing the massive public response to the mayor's appeal, reversed itself and passed a resolution to place the referendum on the ballot at the April city elections.

The *Tribune*, along with many business groups, continued to press for passage of the compromise traction ordinances and to oppose municipal ownership. On January 2, before the dramatic January 7 council meeting, the *Tribune* wrote, "The men and women who have to use the street cars are firmly opposed to [an amendment for a referendum], for it spells delay. They wish the passage of the ordinance to be followed by the immediate commencement of the work of reconstruction. . . . They want an immediate settlement for that will mean the taking of immediate steps to renovate the *worst street car system in the world*"[44] (emphasis added). On January 8, 1907, the day after the council had voted down the referendum amendment, the *Tribune* published the results of its "traction vote" public opinion poll among employees of State Street businesses. This *Tribune* poll found that 6,403 respondents favored settlement now, whereas 833 favored a referendum in the spring. The highest ratio in favor of immediate settlement in one store was 18 to 1, and the mean ratio on State Street was 7 to 1.

The same news story quoted employees at Mandel Brothers Store who were in favor of immediate settlement, such as M. Garbiner, who said, "Miserable transportation. Never get a seat. The sooner the better." A. Rahm complained, "This thing has been delayed long enough." Of course, the *Tribune* quoted none of those who favored holding the referendum.[45]

On January 16, 1907, Mayor Dunne publicly announced that he would run for reelection "upon my known record as mayor."[46] A few weeks later at the February 4, 1907, council meeting, the city railway and union traction ordinances were adopted by a vote of 56–13. Some thirty-eight amendments proposed by the mayor's supporters on the council were defeated by similar votes. Debate began at 8:00 P.M. and lasted until 3:45

A.M. in the longest city council meeting until then. The *Tribune* called it "a record breaking session."

At the beginning of this marathon session, the galleries were filled with folks waiting in the halls to get in when any observers tired. The gallery included employees of the street railways, advocates of immediate municipal ownership, partisans of the Independence League, the Referendum League, city employees, former aldermen, lawyers for the traction companies, a dozen women students from a University of Chicago sociology class, and the wife of alderman and future mayor William Dever.

Two particularly important amendments offered by Alderman Dever and supported by Mayor Dunne at the council meeting provided that the city receive at least 8 percent of the income from the transit companies and that a new licensee not be required to pay the required 20 percent bonus in buying out a traction line if it granted a lower four-cent fare for passengers. The first amendment to guarantee the city a larger share of the money collected by the street railway companies was defeated, 50–13. The second amendment to make the purchase price of a traction company cheaper if a new licensee offered cheaper four-cent fares lost, 48–9.[47]

At this long council meeting the mayor's forces, led by Alderman Dever, offered thirty-eight amendments and made dozens of speeches, but they were unable to change the outcome. The minds of the aldermen were already made up, as is often the case in the city council battles. Alderman Dever began the debate with a motion to have the matter deferred for one week, which he lost, 55–14. That vote set the pattern for the evening. The mayor, his aldermanic supporters, labor unions, and many citizens wanted public ownership of the streetcar lines. On the other side, the aldermen on the Committee on Local Transportation wanted to regulate the traction systems but leave them in private hands. After all proposed amendments were defeated, the committee's ordinances were finally adopted by an exhausted city council at 3:45 A.M.

As expected, Mayor Edward Dunne vetoed the traction ordinances on February 15, 1907. He concluded that these ordinances "failed to protect the property rights of the city and that while masquerading as municipal ownership ordinances, they would utterly fail to accomplish that purpose." In his veto message he argued that "these ordinances are not municipal ownership measures, but ordinances masking under the guise of municipal ownership while really and in fact giving the present companies a franchise for twenty years, if not longer. . . . The people [in previous referendums] have demanded that any ordinances which may be passed dealing with this traction question must preserve the right of the people to municipalize at the earliest possible moment, and they have a right to have their repeated demands carried out in spirit and in letter."[48]

In the February 15 council meeting, at which aldermen mostly restated the same arguments on both sides, the mayor's veto was overridden by a vote of 57–12, with Alderman Adolph Larson, who had voted with the mayor at the previous session, changing sides in the final roll call vote. Alderman Larson said that his vote against the ordinances the previous week was simply a protest against their passage without careful consideration of the proposed amendments. But he opposed municipal ownership and thus now voted to override the mayor's veto. In defending the mayor's veto, Alderman Dever said that traction companies had been "bribing aldermen and legislatures and generally corrupting the body politic." In his view, municipal ownership was a necessity because traction companies would continue to corrupt future city councils with bribes unless there was municipal ownership. In support of the compromise settlement ordinances, Alderman Milton Foreman argued in favor of overriding the mayor's veto, saying that "the one urgent and sovereign need of the city of Chicago is good street railway service, not passable street railway service, but the street railway service that is perfect and up to date in all particulars." He argued that passage of these ordinances was the only way good street railway service could be obtained.

The ordinances were put before the voters at the April 2, 1907, election. Business organizations such as the Commerce Association and the Real Estate Board began to mobilize and work for their passage immediately after the February 15 meeting. Citizens were so dissatisfied with street railway service that they reversed their earlier referendum votes and now approved the compromise ordinances. As a result, the transportation system would remain privately owned and a larger, unified public transportation system would not be created for another forty years.

Why weren't the amendments to the traction ordinances adopted? Because the mayor had lost the backing of the machine aldermen like Bathhouse John Couglin and Hinky Dink Kenna. The Republicans, who for the most part backed businesses, held that ordinances simply regulating the street railways were the best policy. When the Democratic Party boss aldermen added their support to that of the probusiness Republicans, they were a majority in the council.

One reason that Mayor Dunne lost support from the "Gray Wolves" in the crucial municipal ownership votes is that he had begun to enforce the city's liquor laws, in response to considerable public pressure. Pushed by the Law and Order and Anti-Saloon Leagues, the council in March 1906 had doubled saloon license fees to $1,000 to force disreputable saloons out of business, and the mayor had gotten the council to stop issuing the special bar permits that allowed clubs and dance halls to serve liquor after 1:00 A.M. Enforcing the liquor laws lost Dunne support among some ethnic groups and many of the ward bosses in the council who depended

on bars and brothels for election support and on the bribes from bar owners to enrich themselves.[49]

Although Mayor Dunne was defeated in his reelection effort in 1907,
he went on to be elected governor of Illinois, serving from 1913 to 1917.
The *Chicago Tribune*, which had opposed him throughout his term as
mayor, later credited him with getting improved ordinances governing
street railways and with getting state legislation and city ordinances that
set cheaper prices on gas and electricity. But the *Tribune* continued to
fault Mayor Dunne for trying "to revolutionize" the school board with
"radical appointments" and with interfering with the effective operations of the Fire Department.[50]

Charles N. Wheeler, long-time reporter at the *Inter-Ocean, Tribune,* and
Herald-Examiner, wrote a more favorable analysis of Dunne's career:

> First . . . he was an honest man. And in those hectic days, honesty in public
> service was a quality that shone forth brilliantly, if lonely. Second . . . his pri-
> vate morals were unassailable. . . . He was almost boyish, always witty,
> never supercilious, and ever enjoyed a good story. . . . In sheer courage, he
> represented the absolute. So much so that the epithets "bull-headed," "stub-
> born" and "obstinate" were not altogether undeserved. . . . The record of his
> two-year struggle to achieve municipal ownership would fill volumes of
> highly dramatic narrative. While he failed of this purpose, the fineness of his
> character, his unimpeachable forthrightness and exemplary private life were
> impressed on the whole community, and indeed, on the nation. . . . The im-
> pious, the mendacious and the shameless resented him.[51]

Fred Busse's Council, 1907–1908

Dunne was followed as mayor by U.S. Postmaster Fred Busse, whose
election in 1907 resulted from a compromise between reformers and machine politicians in the Republican Party. Busse was a machine politician
who supported some municipal reforms. He declared his candidacy on
the same day that the city council overrode Mayor Dunne's veto of the
traction settlement ordinances. In his speech to 100 Republican politicians who had urged him to run, Fred Busse said, "I know that while a
member of the legislature, while state treasurer, and as postmaster of
Chicago, I may have made some mistakes, but these mistakes were honest ones, and if I become mayor of Chicago I probably will make more,
but they will be honest mistakes. I do not expect to set the world afire if I
become mayor, but I am confident that the end of each year will show
some progress in the betterment of municipal conditions in Chicago."[52]
Whereas Republicans were united in their support of the uncontroversial
and rather lackluster Busse, Democrats were split between support for

Mayor Dunne and for former Mayor Carter Harrison II, who had returned from Santa Fe to enter the race. Dunne was able to win the Democratic nomination against Harrison, but he lost the general election because some Democratic ward committeemen supported Busse.

Fred Busse, unlike mayors in the nineteenth century, was born in
Chicago just after the Civil War, in 1866. His father, a German immigrant,
owned a hardware store. After working in his father's store, Busse went
into the coal business. He became president of the Busse-Reynolds Coal
Company and then of his own Busse Coal Company. He was elected
town clerk of North Chicago in 1891. In 1894 and 1896, he was elected to
the Illinois House of Representatives and later served as state senator
and state treasurer. President Theodore Roosevelt appointed him postmaster of Chicago in 1906. "During his tenure in these public offices,
Fred Busse did little to draw attention to himself as anything other than a
competent officeholder, a man who made himself available to his constituents, and one who had made few enemies." Although he was head
of the Republican Party on the North Side of Chicago, unlike many party
bosses of the era, he was not tainted with corruption.

Unlike Mayor Dunne, who traveled the length and breadth of the city
campaigning, Busse gave no speeches and made no campaign appearances. While returning to Chicago from Washington, Busse was injured
in a train wreck and confined to bed under doctor's orders. "One gets the
impression from reading the newspapers that the accident was a rather
fortuitous event: had he really wanted to, or if the Republican party had
wanted him to, he might have risen from his bed of pain and gone
speechmaking a few times. However, as one observer of the campaign
cogently remarked of the accident, 'this relieved him from the necessity
of a speechmaking campaign, which would not have been at all to his liking. He rarely talks in public.'"[53]

Mayor Dunne in a letter to voters listed reasons to reelect him: he "had
reduced the water and gas rates, thrown safeguards around the sale of
foods, started the negotiations for lower telephone rates, and done other
praiseworthy things. [However, he failed] to call attention to the fact that
under his administration the saloon license was raised from $500 to
$1000, although this single measure doubled the income of the city from
this source and permitted the addition of 1,000 policemen to the force
that was so unsuccessfully coping with crime up to that time."[54]

Mayor Dunne later told of a private meeting with Busse before the
mayoral election: "Now," said [Busse], "I can't make a public speech. I
never did, and I won't now. I am not going to make a spectacle of myself
on the public platform. I am going to leave Chicago and keep off the platform. You can go to it with your speeches and go to the limit, but treat me
personally as decent as you can." Dunne told Busse the he never resorted
"to personal abuse in any public speech and that [Busse] would be the

last man towards whom [he] would resort to that character of a speech." However, the train accident placed Dunne in a difficult position. Busse "was injured in a railway accident. It turned out afterwards that he was not seriously hurt. Nonetheless, he was hurt. I felt it would be unmanly to tell the public then that he had told me he would leave the city and make no campaign. It would look like kicking a man when he was down. The result was that the accident made him many sympathizers and lost me many votes."[55]

To make matters more difficult, the popular President Teddy Roosevelt endorsed Busse in reply to a false statement in Hearst's *Chicago American* that the "President was going to remove Mr. Busse because of scandals in the post office." In his endorsement, the president wrote, "I can wish Chicago no better fortune than to have Mr. Busse as mayor, because he has shown by what he has done as postmaster that he would make one of the best and most efficient executives any city could possibly have." The *Tribune*, of course, endorsed Busse's election because Mayor Dunne had failed to support the compromise traction ordinances, whereas "Mr. Busse stands for the enforcement of these [settlement] ordinances and for the carrying out of the contracts which they propose with the traction companies." The *Tribune* opined further that Busse "stands also for a progressive civic polity—for a 'Greater Chicago'—and his candidacy promises a business administration."[56]

Mayor Dunne agreed that "the traction question became the outstanding issue" in the campaign. However, it was his final break with the ward bosses that made his reelection impossible:

A few days before the mayoralty election, William Loeffler called upon me in the mayor's office. He previously had been city clerk and was a power in politics in certain wards of the city. He also wielded a considerable amount of influence among certain politicians. He said to me, "Mr. Mayor, you are going to be beaten next Tuesday unless you make certain promises to some of the leaders of the party in the three river wards about police inspection in those wards. Why don't you promise them what they want, then you will be elected for four years and after election you can then tell them to go to hell." But I told him that while I appreciated his courtesy in calling upon me, I could not comply with his suggestion or make any promises to the bosses about police inspectors who would have charge where gambling or prostitution might be carried on and that I would make no promises that I did not intend to keep. "All right, then," [Loeffler] said, "your goose is cooked next Tuesday."[57]

Busse was elected by a vote of 164,839 to 151,823. A Socialist candidate received 13,469 votes and a Prohibition candidate, 5,876. Dunne, who had won the last election by a margin of 24,518, was defeated by 13,016 out of the 336,000 votes cast. The 1st Ward, which had given Mayor Dunne a plurality of 3,795 votes in 1905, now gave him a much smaller margin of only 851. The same dropoff occurred in most of boss-controlled Democratic wards. The *Chicago American* wrote, "The chief surprise of the election . . . was the remarkable falling off in the vote polled by Mayor Dunne in the 'gray wolf' wards. Although nearly 85 per cent of the registered vote in the city was polled, Mayor Dunne was so unmercifully 'knifed' in these wards that he ran far behind."[58] At the same election, the traction ordinances the mayor opposed were approved by the voters, 165,846 to 132,720, with twenty-five wards voting in favor and only ten wards voting against the ordinances. Despite Democratic mayor Edward Dunne's defeat and the election of twenty-one Republican aldermen, the election of fifteen Democratic aldermen still gave the Democrats a two-vote majority in the seventy-member city council. Although the Municipal Voters' League was able to defeat "gray wolf" alderman Charles Martin, most of the other gray wolves like Aldermen Hinky Dink Kenna and Johnny "Da Pow" Powers were reelected so the council remained under their control.

Mayor Busse's regime was characterized by an ineffective administration and an inability to articulate and implement his desired reforms. After the election, the city council under Mayor Busse began easily enough on April 15, 1907, with the unanimous adoption of the *Rules and Order of Business of the City Council.* The rules set the regular council meetings on every Monday evening at 7:30 P.M. Lobbying on the floor of the council was forbidden. Debate was limited to five-minute speeches, except by consent of the council. Every member present was required to vote unless "he is directly interested in the question, in which case he shall not vote." As with previous councils, there were twenty-three standing committees, including three on streets and alleys for each of the three administrative divisions of the city (North, South, and West). The appointment of membership on the committees was also nearly unanimous, passing by a vote of 67–2.[59]

Chicago Charter Reform

The most important issue after municipal ownership of the transportation system was the proposed adoption of a new municipal charter giving greater powers to the city government. Municipalities in Illinois were controlled by state government. A separate charter would have given the city government greater powers to tax and to provide the services that a growing metropolis needed. Mayor Busse's failure to pass the proposed city charter left him with no clout in the council for other measures he favored.

The process began on October 28, 1902, when "seventy-four men from the city's leading business and social clubs, civic organizations, political groups, and a few delegates-at-large assembled as the Chicago New Charter Convention. . . . The overwhelming majority of these men were successful businessmen and professionals; the Chicago Federation of Labor sent two delegates, but except for three men from Jewish business clubs, the city's ethnic population was underrepresented."[60] The unbalanced and unrepresentative nature of the charter convention membership set the stage for the charter's eventual failure to gain voter support. However, this first convention succeeded in drafting an enabling constitutional amendment to create a city charter, which was approved by the legislature and then by the voters in a referendum in November 1904.

In May 1905 the city council appointed an official charter convention. Since Republicans had the majority in the city council in 1905, they voted for an appointment plan offered by Republican alderman Milton Foreman. There were to be seventy-four delegates, fifteen selected by the council, fifteen state legislators selected by the presiding officers of each house, fifteen by Republican governor Deneen, fifteen by Democratic mayor Dunne, and two each from the board of Cook County commissioners, sanitary district, board of education, library board, and the three park boards of Chicago. The resulting convention was again unrepresentative of the population of Chicago. "Of the sixty-two delegates whose political affiliation are identifiable, thirty-nine were Republicans, twenty-two were Democrats, and one was an Independent. . . . By occupation, there were twenty-six lawyers, thirty-two businessmen, two social workers, one professor, and one minister."[61] As a result, this convention, like the earlier Chicago New Charter Convention, also turned out to be unrepresentative of the majority opinion in the city, much to the surprise of the delegates.

According to historian Maureen Flanagan, charter reform failed for four reasons: (1) antipathy between Chicago and the rest of the state made getting a good charter proposal through the state legislature difficult; (2) ongoing labor strife in the city divided businessmen and labor unions so that most businessmen supported the charter while most labor unions opposed it; (3) the battle over temperance, which influenced all major decisions of the time, caused many ethnic groups to oppose the charter; and (4) the struggle over who should shape the reforms divided reformers so that "radical" or social reformers like former mayor Dunne opposed the charter when it came to referendum.[62]

The charter produced by the charter convention was a weak home rule charter. It proposed merging some units of government and improving the revenue system but specified "that the city did not intend to assume any home-rule powers that would conflict with general state laws. . . .

The convention moved even further away from attempting to secure home rule by passing a provision acknowledging the superior legal position of the state in regard to all municipal affairs." However, the proposed charter did provide for the city to raise more tax revenue, which was a very important new authority. The city's bonding power under the charter would automatically increase to 5 percent of full property valuation and its tax levy to 5 percent of assessed valuation. Previously, the city had been restricted to only 2 percent of assessed property valuation with other local governments dividing the remaining 3 percent. Under the proposed charter, the city council annually would allot the property tax revenue for all local governments, including the parks, schools, and libraries. On the other hand, the proposed charter was less popular than it might have been because it failed to provide for an elected school board, women's suffrage, or liquor regulation, although the delegates at the convention did attempt to write a separate bill on the regulation of liquor in Chicago, which the legislature overwhelmingly rejected.[63]

When the charter was submitted to the state legislature, legislators further undermined the charter's support by rejecting a direct primary to nominate municipal candidates, adopting a change from the existing system of thirty-five wards with two aldermen to fifty wards with one alderman each while gerrymandering ward boundaries to favor Republicans, as well as killing the bill to regulate liquor in Chicago. Each of these changes created a different bloc of opposition voters. In the referendum campaign, various political machine factions, progressive reformers like former mayor Dunne, ethnic groups opposed to prohibition, and taxpayers who feared higher property taxes joined to defeat charter reform. When Mayor Busse came out strongly for charter reform, he guaranteed aldermanic opposition to his other proposed reforms in public transit and the school system because the charter threatened the power of the ward bosses. As a result, Mayor Busse, even more than Mayor Dunne, was unable to control the city council during his term of office.

The final referendum vote on the proposed city charter came on September 17, 1907. The charter was supported by good government forces with a business orientation and opposed by more "radical" reformers concerned with social reforms. Politicians were split in their support, with most of the aldermen supporting the charter. But ethnic groups, which feared that prohibition forces would use the new charter to outlaw drinking in Chicago, opposed it. The referendum was defeated by a 2 to 1 margin, to the surprise of its supporters. The Sunday before the election at an unprecedented anticharter demonstration of 50,000 voters, the former deputy chief of the Board of Local Improvement's Law Department charged that "victory of the charter would be followed by a 40 per cent increase in rents in Chicago." As public opinion galvanized in opposition to the charter, party precinct captains served notice on their ward bosses that they could no longer support the charter. The *Chicago American* quoted one as saying, "To the devil with the charter. . . . It will be political suicide for me to go along farther. My people are against the charter almost to a man. I don't propose to beat my brains against a stone wall."[64]

So the charter was defeated by a vote of 121,479 to 50,581. The *Chicago Tribune* concluded that "the opposition of the United Societies [of Chicago ethnic groups] with their false idea that their personal liberty [to drink] was endangered, and of the small property owners who feared that their taxes would be raised, aided by the efforts of certain corporate interests which had reasons for disliking the act, proved too hard to be overcome."[65] Mayor Busse concluded that "this indifference on the part of the general public [indicated by the low voter turnout] has been a mistake. While the charter contained some provisions that were disagreeable to this, that, or the other special interest or element in the community, yet on the whole it was a good thing for Chicago. Its adoption would have enabled the administration to do many things in the way of public improvements which would have been of lasting benefit to the city and its people." As the mayor predicted, major projects were not begun in his administration, both because of the finance restrictions of the old constitution and state laws and because he could not gain sufficient control of the council to undertake great projects. As Busse lamented, "We need a new sewer system, a rehabilitated water service, more and better pavements, a high pressure water system for fighting fires downtown, and a subway. But now that the charter is beaten it will be hard for the city to find the money for any one of these great improvements. Some of them will have to wait indefinitely if ever they are accomplished in this generation."[66]

Big Bill Thompson's Councils, 1915–1923 and 1927–1931

William "Big Bill" Thompson was one of the most colorful mayors in Chicago's history, serving a total of three terms. He was a theatrical, larger-than-life demagogue who changed his image and his position on issues several times. He was first elected mayor in 1915 and easily won his reelection in 1919. But he had a more difficult time winning in 1927 and lost his reelection in 1931. In both the 1915 and 1919 city councils Democrats were the majority; in 1915 Democrats held thirty-two of the fifty aldermanic seats, but Republican Thompson had no difficulty in gaining support across party lines. He was a strong, charismatic leader. His immense personal popularity, flamboyant style, and dramatic political oratory gained him the support of Chicago's ethnic groups (especially blacks), religious groups, organized labor, and organized crime.[67]

William Hale Thompson was born in Boston on May 14, 1869, and was brought to Chicago eight days later by his family. His father successfully sold Chicago real estate and the family became wealthy. Thompson had a good early education at Fessenden Prep School for Boys and traveled with his mother to Europe at an early age. Although Thompson's father wanted him to go to Yale, he fled west at age fourteen and drifted for a decade before coming back to Chicago and going into politics. He achieved success in the cattle business and ranching before, at age twenty-three, he was called back to manage the family estate (valued at $2 million) after his father's death.

While in the West he adopted the cowboy hat, western boots, and "the cowboy code" which he used for his later public appearances. He returned to Chicago a husky, muscular young man of 225 pounds, joined the Chicago Athletic Club's football team, and was made its captain. It became the premier championship football team in the United States.

Thompson was first elected 2nd Ward alderman to represent the mostly black South Side from 1900 to 1902. Although he came from a wealthy family and didn't need to go into politics, he became allied with Republican boss William Lorimer. John M. Smyth, a Republican Party official, introduced them saying, "Billie, [Thompson] is quite a young fellow! I've had my eyes on him, he'll go far. He has the right idea, good administration and liberality of policy without excesses. That's what we need, Billie. Locally us Republicans always pay too much court to the church element and to reformers. The people want liberality. Let's find a young chap like this one, Billie, an American of good connections and a believer in personal liberty."[68]

In his first election "Big Bill" defeated a popular incumbent, Alderman Charles Gunther. The 2nd Ward, like the 1st Ward, was economically diverse, with a millionaires' row on one end and a red-light district of bars and prostitution on the other. Although Thompson's contacts, wealth, and charm helped him win his election, his aldermanic career was not particularly distinguished. He was both praised and condemned by the Municipal Voters' League. Although he supported some reform measures, he also cooperated with the Gray Wolves who ran the council. About his only accomplishment as alderman was that he got an appropriation for the first of the municipal playgrounds for his ward. He was simply overshadowed in the council by more colorful and powerful aldermen like Bathhouse John Couglin. In 1902, he moved on to the county board for two years but was no more outstanding there.

Former alderman and Thompson opponent Charles Merriam described "Big Bill" as "heavy and not unhandsome in earlier days, with an engaging smile and the air of a *bon vivant*. . . . Thompson has . . . a flare for showmanship. He soon learned to value political dramatics and to like them. A very indifferent speaker at the outset, he acquired the arts of the stumper, and became an effective haranguer of audiences, who flocked to hear his unbridled attacks upon his foes. . . . Whatever he [promises to do] will be vivid, colorful, exaggerated and difficult if desirable, but it will be entertaining and will relieve the tedium of the time. And the absurdity and irrelevance of one slogan will melt into another without the change attracting attention. He is not interested in statesmanship, but in showmanship; not in logic but in votes. . . . he plays the role of orator and mob master . . . [while] the details of city government are dry and uninteresting [so] they [are] turned over to willing hands, relieving the Master, until another hour of showmanship comes."[69]

Thompson won his first mayoral campaign in 1915 under the guidance of his mentor, Fred Lundin, a Swedish party boss who served as his campaign manager. He defeated municipal judge Harry Olson in the Republican primary. "Rather than a Lorimer protégé, voters saw a candidate who was physically attractive, spoke well, and knew the value of a good campaign song. . . . In contrast, Olson came off as a drab reformer."[70] Thompson's 2,325-vote margin of victory was more than provided from the 2nd Ward black community that he had served as alderman. He won the 2nd Ward by 6,800 votes. After the primary, the Republican Party united behind his candidacy to defeat County Clerk Robert Weitzer, who had beaten Carter Harrison II in a Democratic Party primary that had left the Democratic Party divided. Thus Thompson won the general election in 1915 by 148,000 votes, one of the largest pluralities in mayoral elections up until that time.

Thompson's first mayoral campaign was composed of two ingredients: good organizing and good showmanship. For eight months before the primaries Thompson supporters met weekly at the Sherman Hotel. Under Fred Lundin's leadership the core group of twenty grew to hundreds, and they created a pledge card campaign of support for Thompson. During the Christmas holidays of 1914, Thompson rented the Auditorium Theater to announce his candidacy. "After speeches had been made a curtain was pulled aside and there stood a Christmas tree laden with great bundles of signed pledge cards. The announcement was made that more than 140,000 voters had signed cards pledging support to Thompson for mayor." He ran on a platform of pure populist rhetoric: "Drive the crooks out of town" and "Improve the street car service." On the basis of Lundin's organizing and Thompson's rhetoric, he was elected.[71]

During his first eight years in the mayor's office, Thompson controlled a powerful Republican machine that extended beyond Chicago's borders to the county, state, and national levels. Mayor Thompson became known as the "Big Builder" during these years because of his control of the city council and his massive public works projects. Numerous pieces of legislation were passed in the early Thompson councils to build bridges and buildings and to widen streets in ways that predecessors like Mayor Fred Busse had not achieved. However, the city council was still essentially the Council of the Gray Wolves, even though most of the old-time machine aldermen other than Bathhouse John Couglin retired before Thompson's last term in 1927. The aldermen who replaced them were from the same mold, and corrupt party bosses from both political parties always made up at least one-third of the city council.

Thompson easily won reelection in 1919 by organization and demagoguery and he continued to court the Black vote. As Thompson biographer Douglas Bukowski put it, "Thompson . . . learned to use words the way most politicians depended on organization. The detail work of politics mostly bored him. Where other mayors sought ways to control the city council, Thompson simply tried to overwhelm it—and all opposition—through his demagogy." Thompson won election in 1919 on the generally popular platform of "home rule, lower utility rates, and free speech."[72]

Toward the end of his second term, citizen discontent was growing, however, and reformers appealed to citizens who were fed up with crime and government. Writers on the period claim that Al Capone and his gang contributed more than $260,000 to Thompson's campaign.[73] This is reporter Mike Royko's description of Thompson's alliance with the crime syndicate: "[Thompson] made the gangsters happy by giving them the run of the town, and they made the Police Department happy by giving them a piece of the profit. Everyone was happy except the people being shot and the citizens who thought things were getting a bit outlandish, even for Chicago."[74] By this time, Thompson had given up his earlier good government image and turned to patronage and favors as the way to control Chicago government.

In 1923, Thompson chose not to run for reelection and publicly announced his retirement from politics. William E. Dever, a reform Democrat who had served as alderman from 1902 to 1910 and led the campaign for immediate municipal ownership of the traction system, won the election. Despite the fact that Mayor Dever was personally tolerant of alcohol, during his term in office he attempted to make Chicago "as dry as the driest small town." He declared, "I am not a prohibitionist, but I do believe in law and order."[75] This made Dever very unpopular and ruled out his reelection. Persuaded by those who opposed Dever's strict enforcement of prohibition laws, Thompson ran again in 1927. Thompson campaigned this time for a "wide-open city," the nonenforcement of Prohibition laws, and the slogan "America First," aimed at King George V of England. He claimed that England's influence was too great and needed to be reversed. His slogan gained national appeal to such an extent that

Thompson later became obsessed with forming a national America First Party. His efforts to create an isolationist national political party failed and destroyed much of his political power in Chicago the year after his mayoral reelection. More importantly, in his 1927 election campaign Thompson was a "wet," whereas reform mayor William Dever was a "dry" who enforced the unpopular Prohibition laws. Thompson allowed "for police surveillance and periodic raids of [drinking] establishments that flagrantly violated any of the city ordinances governing their operation, while leaving the majority of clubs alone . . . [and he] retained a special mayoral prerogative to issue licenses to any club he wished, regardless of contrary political pressures in City Council."[76] In short, under Mayor Thompson, Chicago was to be a wide-open "wet" city.

Thompson's political machine was in full swing during the 1927 mayoral election. Some Thompson voters got city jobs, some special privileges, and some Christmas baskets from the precinct captains. Once again Thompson had pledge cards signed by 433,000 voters pledging their support. He ran on promises to oppose the League of Nations and World Court, to put "America First," and to run Scottish school superintendent William McAndrew out of town. If King George of England ever dared to set foot in Chicago, he would "punch him in the snout." These later themes were particularly popular among Irish voters. Thompson's flamboyant election style is exemplified by his performance at the Cort Theater in the Republican Primary campaign of 1927.

Thompson crossed to stage center with a cage in each hand. Each cage contained a large, gray rat.

He put the cages on a table and then addressed the rats before the stunned crowd.

He called the animal to his left "Doc" [after Dr. John Dill Robertson, his primary opponent]. The other one was "Fred" [after Fred Lundin, who had been his mentor and was now supporting Robertson in the primary].

The place exploded into applause.

Thompson waited for the hubbub to die down and then delivered his lines: "Don't hang your head, Fred. That's better now—" Here he prodded the rat with a stick. "Always active, Fred, didn't you send me that cable to Honolulu, and didn't I come back and save you from the penitentiary? [Lundin had been indicted for his part in a school board corruption scandal.] Didn't I get the best lawyer in town (Clarence Darrow) to keep you outta jail?"

"I knew a year before that you were double-crossing me, but I wanted to live up to the letter of the cowboy code. Don't you think, Fred, in view of all that has happened, that you have earned the name of rat?"

Now he turned to the second rodent.

"Doc, didn't the medical profession and others protest against my plan to appoint you health commissioner? Didn't I stand by you in the face of all opposition, and give you that position? You have circulated the story that I am in bad health and will die soon. Well, Doc, I am not going to die just to please you and Fred."[77]

By demagoguery and vote fraud, and with the support of some ward bosses, Thompson emerged as the victor in the 1927 election. As Will Rogers observed at the time, Mayor Dever tried "to beat Bill [Thompson] with the better element vote. The trouble with Chicago is that there ain't much better element."[78] Despite his victory in the 1927 election and his continuing popularity, Thompson was unable to exert the power he had in his previous terms as mayor. Democratic supporters of former Mayor Dever still possessed a significant number of seats in the council and the Republican machine had begun to crumble as it divided into Senator Deneen and Mayor Thompson factions.

It was the beginning of the end of Thompsonism. In 1928, Thompson placed the final straw on the back of an already weak Cook County Republican Party. Joining forces with a former rival, then Cook County state's attorney Robert Crowe, the Thompson machine backed a candidate slate in the 1928 elections that included Small for governor, Smith for U.S. senator, and Crowe for state's attorney. When Republican U.S. Senator Charles Deenen sponsored an opposing ticket, two rival factions (Thompson versus Deneen) were created within the Republican party. Republican aldermen were forced to choose sides and thus divided an already weak Republican city council.

The primary election of 1928 was known as the "Pineapple Primary." During State's Attorney Crowe's administration, murder, corruption, and intimidation increased. In a single year over 100 "pineapple" hand grenades (which looked like small pineapples) were set off with no prosecutions. Three bombs exploded in February, including one aimed at Judge John Sbarbaro. Just two weeks before the 1928 primary election, the homes of U.S. Senator Charles Deneen and his candidate for state's attorney, Judge John Swanson, were bombed. State's Attorney Crowe responded that the bombs were "a trick [that] they had bombed their own houses, to gain sympathy!"[79] The public, revolted at the blatant political violence, overwhelmingly elected Deneen's slate of candidates.

Thompson, who had threatened to resign if his candidates were not elected, was politically and personally devastated by the loss of his candidates in 1928. The man who had controlled one of Chicago's most formidable machines up until the 1930s was banished from the Cook County Republican convention, and his American First Party experienced massive defeats at the national level. Thompsonism had received the final blow from which it never recovered. But the day after the election Mayor Thompson changed his mind about resigning. However, he soon suffered a nervous breakdown and became known as Chicago's "absentee mayor."[80] His absence following his nervous breakdown prevented him from exerting influence over the city council in the last months of 1928 and allowed organized groups such as ethnic coalitions and organized labor to exercise more power. Although Thompson had bounced back by 1930, Anton J. Cermak, a Democrat, easily won the 1931 mayoral election and quickly replaced Thompson appointees and supporters with his own loyal Democrats. Cermak went on to create a more centralized and powerful political machine than any before in Chicago history.

Thompson's Last Term

Thompson had been a strong, charismatic mayor and a great campaigner in his first terms. His early terms of office helped to establish the tradition of builder mayors in Chicago. Even his last term (1927–1931) affected Chicago politics for decades. Thompson's long rule and his defeat of reform mayor William Dever caused Chicago's political reform movement to atrophy. Unable to gain mayoral support or influence in the firmly entrenched, machine-controlled city council, reformers mostly gave up on reforming Chicago politics and turned their energies to working with the national government in which, after the election of President Franklin Roosevelt, they had much more influence.

Since race and ethnicity were major factors in city politics since the Civil War, Thompson became a master of coalition politics as well as political showmanship. This helped him win elections, but it made his control of the city council more difficult when his coalition splintered. Despite Thompson's immense personal popularity, he lost political power from the crushing defeats of his attempts to influence national politics with his American First Party. Like the fragmented city councils of 1907, the Thompson Council from 1927 to 1931 was divided even though it was smaller. In 1923, a redistricting act had enlarged the number of wards from thirty-five to fifty and cut the number of aldermen to one per ward, as the Charter Commission had originally recommended, but this structural change could not eliminate the political fragmentation in the council. (See Chicago Ward map on p. 76.)

Mayor Thompson's third term started with great fanfare at his colorful inauguration on April 17, 1927, when he reorganized the council to his liking, appointed the members of his cabinet to great applause and unanimous votes of the council, and offered a resolution directing Chicago school superintendent McAndrew to appear for questioning before the

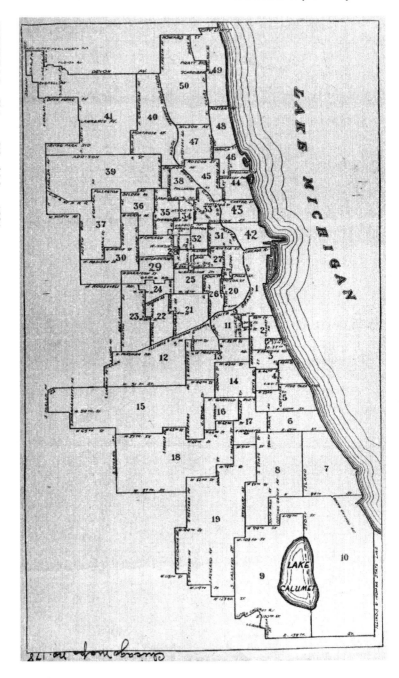

FIGURE 2.2   Chicago Ward Map, 1921

city council's Schools Committee to answer charges of pro-British teaching in the schools. He also introduced an ordinance on this occasion drafted by his corporation counsel to repeal the Dever ordinance requiring water meters at businesses and homes. Overall, the mayor characterized his inauguration as "a happy family party."[81]

A week earlier, aldermen from each of the ten-ward groups (1st through 10th, 11th through 20th, etc.) met in caucus and selected one alderman to serve on the five-person Committee of Organization as they traditionally do. The committee then retired to a resort in Miami, Florida, to make up the lists of committee assignments and to negotiate the committee chairmanships. The mayor had considerable voice in the council reorganization and at the inauguration the committee's work was revealed. Forty-Sixth Ward alderman Oscar Nelson, vice president of the Federation of Labor and a Democrat who had backed Thompson's election over Mayor Dever, was made the mayor's floor leader, although the chairmanship of the Finance Committee was given to 30th Ward alderman and Democratic committeeman John S. Clark. After some dissent, the council voted 46–4 to approve the new plan for its organization. In his inaugural address the mayor made his usual extravagant promises "to proceed vigorously in ousting Superintendent of Schools McAndrew, drive crooks out of the city in thirty days, make the Mississippi waterway a reality, solve the traction problem, erase the city's predicted financial deficit for 1927, speed up the river straightening project, and push street widening improvement to quick completion."[82] Other than ousting the school superintendent, Thompson's promised projects were not completed in his term of office.

For instance, no progress was made on solving the traction problem, which Mayor Dunne had attempted to resolve by creating a single public transportation system under municipal ownership. Early in 1928, 24th Ward alderman Jacob Arvey, who had been Mayor Dever's floor leader and who would head the Democratic Party after World War II, offered proposed state legislation in a council transportation subcommittee that would give unlimited power to the city to grant a transit franchise without a time limitation. Three days after Arvey's proposal was introduced, however, the subcommittee voted to suspend work on the proposed legislation until after the April 10, 1928, election for fear that it would harm Governor Len Small's chances of reelection. Alderman James Bowler argued at the subcommittee meeting that "we cannot get anywhere while the traction question is being made a political football. It is useless for us to continue. The members of this committee are being put in a bad light and the public is getting a wrong impression of what is happening. If we proceed, under such conditions, we will create a breach that we cannot later bridge. I move we discontinue hearings until after the April primaries."[83] Unfortunately, with Governor Small's defeat in the 1928 election, no special session of the legislature was called as Thompson and Small had planned to provide general home rule for Chicago and a solution to the continuing problem of public transportation. Whereas Thompson had been able to get Governor Small's help in the past, he did not have the same access to Governor Small's successor, whose election he had opposed. Thus, like previous city councils, the 1928 council failed to resolve the public transportation problem.

Mayor Thompson had also made plans for the Board of Local Improvements to build the first Chicago subway, which would then be leased to Samuel Insull's Chicago Rapid Transit Company to run. Insull was reported to have told the Dever administration that he would be willing to lease a subway if the city built it. It would have to be built by special assessments of property owners in the area where it was to be constructed and there was considerable opposition by the affected taxpayers. Although Boston had created the first subway in America in 1897 and New York had opened its first subway in 1904, Chicago lagged behind. Public transportation on street railways, elevated lines, and the creation of a new subway system were not the only transportation issues confronting the city council in 1928. Also at stake was the condition of the streets and the need to build new "superhighways" into the city. Mayor Thompson, with the help of Governor Small, had succeeded in doubling the city's bonding authority. The Chicago Plan Commission proposed a comprehensive plan for new bonds to improve the streets of Chicago. However, on February 28, 1928, those plans hit a major setback in part because of Thompson's inability to control factional conflict in the council. In what the *Tribune* called a "dramatic session" of the Finance Committee, bond issues for $59 million were amended to eliminate a proposed superhighway on Avondale Road and a proposed high-speed traffic artery from the Loop west along Monroe or Congress streets. Both West Side and North Side aldermen were upset with the new list of bond projects. So at the Finance Committee meeting on March 3, 1928, the committee reversed its previous decision and added $5 million for the Avondale superhighway, raising the proposed bond issue to $66 million. Just before adjournment of a stormy six-hour session, a strong Democratic bloc of aldermen demanded the addition to the bond issue of several million dollars for street lights, playgrounds, and refuse dumps. Finance Committee chairman 30th Ward alderman John Clark was then delegated to meet with the mayor to resolve the aldermanic disputes over the bond issue.[84]

On March 5, 1928, the Finance Committee again reversed itself, disapproving three of the four bond issue projects proposed by the Chicago Plan Commission. It discarded the projects for Avondale Avenue, South

Park Avenue, Wacker Drive, and a proposed new West Side boulevard. This reduced the proposed bond issue to be put on the ballot to $56 million. However, this aroused a new set of aldermanic opponents. The Avondale project was now attacked by the very aldermen on the Northwest Side who had previously supported it. Alderman Max Adamoswki complained that "45 percent of the cost will come from special assessments [of the property owners along the route of the roadways]. My people won't stand for it. To hell with the subdividers [developers who want to develop new homes in the suburbs], I say."[85]

On March 7, Mayor Thompson, working with Plan Commission chairman James Simpson and Finance Committee chairman John Clark, put together a final package of proposals now amounting to $78 million to go before the city council at its March 10 meeting. There were to be a total of thirty-one projects, including the controversial Avondale highway, South Park Avenue, and a Michigan Avenue subway from Sixty-Third to Sixty-Seventh Streets. At the council meeting the bond issue was passed with opposition to only two proposals: the Avondale highway and the proposal to widen Madison Street. There were twelve votes cast against the Avondale highway and three against the Madison project.

The fight over street repairs and superhighways was a classic case of legislative logrolling. "Every nook and corner of the city has been taken care of," Finance Committee chairman John Clark said after the meeting. "I believe there will be an overwhelming vote in favor of the entire program. As a result, we will get started on work that will give thousands of men employment and make all the rest of the country sit up and take notice."[86] However, Mayor Thompson and his aldermanic supporters grossly underestimated the voters, even in the affluent flapper era of 1928. At the spring municipal elections, when the entire Thompson slate went down to defeat, all thirty-one of the city bond issues were defeated by a 2 to 1 margin.

The aldermen opposing the large bond issues were right about the views of the voters. Again in the fall election of 1928, a scaled-down bond issue of $26 million, including municipal airport improvements, street lights, and street widening projects, went down to a similar 2 to 1 defeat. The voters thought even these improvements would raise their taxes too much. Thus Thompson, "the builder mayor," failed to obtain support for big new public works projects at the end of his reign. The Great Depression of 1929 would put off these improvements for more than a decade.

Fragmented City Councils

In general, during his last term, Thompson was detached in his relations with the city council. "Thompson had long ago given up trying to dominate it; he had neither the patience nor the resources to subdue the various factions."[87] Although he was a great demagogue, Thompson did not become a strong political boss. Economic conditions, governmental decentralization, and Thompson's temperament prevented him from building an even stronger party machine and ruling in the style of later "boss" mayors like Cermak and Daley. "Thompson held parts of a machine that he was incapable of assembling." He built a "prototype machine based on class, ethnicity, and race" but could not build the strong single political machine of the future.[88]

In the city councils between the Chicago Fire and the Great Depression neither a dynamic reform mayor like Mayor Dunne nor a go-along businessman–politician mayor like Mayor Busse could control the council, which was fragmented and out of their political control. Although machine-oriented "builder mayor" Thompson could usually get the support of aldermen for public works in his earlier terms of office, even he failed when he proposed to raise taxes too high or if major projects required a referendum of the voters. Grand plans for immediate municipal ownership of the traction system, a controversial city charter, and huge bond issues were beyond these mayors' abilities. The power of the mayors was further weakened in the Council of the Gray Wolves because many of the aldermen were corrupt ward bosses whom the mayors could not control. These mayors were weakened most of all if they lost major battles, for example, Mayor Dunne's unsuccessful attempt to achieve municipal ownership of the traction system, Mayor Busse's failure to gain adoption of a new city charter, and Mayor Thompson's failure to establish his America First Party. Once a mayor lost these battles, the aldermen knew they could again take control of the city government from a mayor who had lost public support. Rather than move the city forward, however, the aldermen were content to divide the spoils.

Alderman Charles Merriam described the usual factional divisions in the city councils of the early twentieth century this way:

> There are many lines of cleavage in the Council. There is first the old line division between Republicans and Democrats, with an occasional sprinkling of Socialists; and each party is divided into two or more factions, often more hostile to each other than the parties themselves. Then there is a group made up of those, on the whole favorable to the claims of the public utility corporations, and those more disposed to protect the public interest. There is a division between the wets and the drys. Sometimes, geographical lines are drawn between the North Side, the South Side, and the West Side. Occasionally lines were drawn between the Catholics and the Protestants. There was a division between the purchasable and the non-purchasable vote. . . . These various lines crossed and recrossed in various ways.[89]

So the city councils of this era had no permanent divisions or voting blocs but only various factions that aligned and realigned according to the issues being voted on and the political power of the authors of the legislation.

Alderman Merriam also reported to his constituents in 1915 that "the chief difficulties in the City Hall are, first, the amount of dishonesty, commonly known as 'graft,' found in municipal relations; second, the extent to which incompetency is found as a result of the habit of treating office and contracts as political spoils; third, the lack of broad vision and constructive ability."[90]

The Council of the Gray Wolves, which had dominated city government to a large extent since the Chicago Fire, would end with Thompson's third term as mayor. The Great Depression of 1929 swept away not only the good times but Republican rule. Thompson would be the last Republican mayor of Chicago in the twentieth century. The fragmented Thompson council was replaced by rubber stamp councils under Democratic machine control.

Mayor Thompson's place in Chicago's history remains ambiguous. Historian Douglas Bukowski argues that "the image of mayor as big builder may be Thompson's most enduring legacy to Chicago politics."[91] The streets, bridges, and municipal buildings built during his terms and the continuing public expectation that, above all, the mayor of Chicago should be a builder are a part of Thompson's legacy. Reformers of the time, of course, saw the mayor quite differently. Harold Ickes, who along with Alderman Merriam opposed Thompson, wrote that he "was the Huey Long of his time and locale—without Huey's brains, however."[92] Merriam concluded, "It is difficult to discover in the Thompson policies any central thread except the perpetuation of power. . . . It is obvious that no line of continuity runs through [his] policies except that of opportunism, availing itself of whatever comes, with a keen eye to observing what will probably go."[93] To reformers, Thompson was a dangerous demagogue who helped destroy the progressive reform movement in Chicago. Yet "Thompson's audience and the source of his power were the urban public itself. . . . Big Bill was a nightmare [for reformers like Merriam] because the city he appealed to was closer to reality than the city they were trying to build."[94] Thompson gave the people what they wanted.

The consensus of historians, journalists, and political scientists is that Mayor Thompson was the worst mayor of a major American city in the nineteenth and twentieth centuries. Of sixty-nine experts who ranked the best and worst mayors in a survey, forty-five put Thompson in the "mayoral hall of shame" for his corruption and demagoguery.[95]

After the Great Depression and World War II, the political system would change again. The new centralized Democratic machine would reduce the Council of the Gray Wolves to more pliable rubber stamp councils under the domination of boss mayors who had the power to carry out the developments supported by the downtown businessmen who dominated the Chicago economy. This new progrowth regime would be led by mayors who controlled the party, the council, and the government bureaucracy; business leaders who controlled the private sector; and leaders of large institutions like hospitals, universities, and labor unions. Businessmen would deal with strong boss mayors on major projects and aldermen simply would obey orders. No longer would "rings" of aldermen have to be bought to get an ordinance passed after the Council of the Gray Wolves disappeared.

Notes

1. Charles Merriam, *Chicago: A More Intimate View of Urban Politics* (New York: Macmillan, 1929), p. 18. Also quoted in Loomis Mayfield, "The Reorganization of Urban Politics: The Chicago Growth Machine After World War II" (Ph.D. diss., University of Pittsburgh, 1996), chap. 2., p. 1.

2. Mayfield, "Reorganization of Urban Politics," chap. 2, p. 3.

3. Maureen Flanagan, *Charter Reform in Chicago* (Carbondale: Southern Illinois University Press, 1987), pp. 17–20.

4. Finis Farr, *Chicago: A Personal History of America's Most American City* (New Rochelle, N.Y.: Arlington House, 1973), p. 108.

5. *Chicago: Its City Halls and Its City Council* (an eight-page pamphlet produced by the City Council Committee on Finance, the Chicago Historical Society, the *Chicago Sun-Times*, and the *Chicago Tribune*, 1987), p. 3.

6. Len O'Connor, *Clout: Mayor Daley and His City* (Chicago: Regnery, 1975), p. 9.

7. Farr, *Chicago*, p. 130.

8. Bill Granger and Lori Granger, *Lords of the Last Machine: The Story of Politics in Chicago* (New York: Random House, 1987), p. 33.

9. Lincoln Steffens, *The Shame of the Cities* (New York: Hill & Wang, 1957), p. 165. First published by McClure, Phillips in 1904.

10. *Chicago: Its City Halls*, p. 3.

11. Quoted by Alderman Edward Burke in a talk at the University of Illinois on February 25, 1999. A copy of the audio tape from that talk is in Dick Simpson's papers in the Special Collections, Main Library, University of Illinois at Chicago.

12. Richard Lindberg, *Chicago by Gaslight: A History of Chicago's Netherworld, 1880–1920* (Chicago: Academy Chicago Publishers, 1996), p. 136.

13. Lloyd Wendt and Herman Kogan, *Bosses in Lusty Chicago: The Story of Bathhouse John and Hinky Dink* (Bloomington: Indiana University Press, 1967), pp. 26–27. Originally published by Bobbs-Merrill in 1943.

14. William Stead, *If Christ Came to Chicago!* (Chicago: Laird & Lee, 1894). Reprinted by Chicago Historical Bookworks, 1990, pp. 175–178.

15. Stead, *If Christ Came*, p. 182.

16. Stead, *If Christ Came,* p. 183. Steffens estimated at the turn of the century that fifty-seven of the sixty-eight aldermen were crooked, based on studies done by the Municipal Voters League. Steffens, *Shame of the Cities,* p. 169.

17. Quoted in Stead, *If Christ Came,* p. 183.

18. *Chicago: Its City Halls,* p. 3.

19. Mayfield, "Reorganization of Urban Politics," chap. 2, p. 13.

20. Steffens, *Shame of the Cities,* p. 164.

21. Granger and Granger, *Lords of the Last Machine,* p. 43.

22. Wendt and Kogan, *Bosses in Lusty Chicago,* pp. 187–199.

23. Edward F. Dunne, *Illinois: The Heart of the Nation* (Chicago: Lewis, 1933), 2:193.

24. Dunne, *Illinois,* 1:265.

25. Charles N. Wheeler, "Hon. Edward Fitzsimons Dunne," in Dunne, *Illinois,* 2:494–495.

26. John Buenker, "Edward F. Dunnes: The Limits of Municipal Reform," in Paul Green and Melvin Holli, eds., *The Mayors: The Chicago Political Tradition* (Carbondale: Southern Illinois University Press, 1987), p. 36.

27. Quoted in Dunne, *Illinois,* 1:249.

28. Buenker, *Mayors,* p. 37, quoting James Quinn, a city employee whose comments were recorded in the *Chicago Chronicle,* February 26, 1905.

29. Michael Funchion, "Political and Nationalist Dimensions," in Lawrence McCaffrey et al., *The Irish in Chicago* (Champaign: University of Illinois Press, 1987), p. 66.

30. Bruenker, *Mayors,* p. 38.

31. Charles Powers, "Edward Dunne," *Chicago Tribune,* January 8, 1911. A typed copy is in the Edward F. Dunne Biography File at the Chicago Historical Society, pp. 3–4.

32. Funchion, *Irish in Chicago,* p. 66.

33. Dunne, *Illinois,* 1:195.

34. Melvin Holli, *The American Mayor: The Best and the Worst Big-City Leaders* (University Park: Pennsylvania State University Press, 1999), p. 51.

35. Dunne, *Illinois,* 1:225, 246.

36. Dunne, *Illinois,* 1:271.

37. Dunne, *Illinois,* 1:279.

38. "Council Refuses Traction Delay: Turns Down Mayor's Plan to Take Steps for Referendum at Spring Election," *Chicago Tribune,* January 8, 1907, p. 1.

39. "Council Refuses Traction Delay," p. 2.

40. The biographical facts are taken from John R. Schmidt, "William E. Dever: A Chicago Political Fable," in *Mayors,* pp. 82–83.

41. "Council Refuses Traction Delay," p. 2.

42. "Council Refuses Traction Delay," p. 2.

43. "Council Refuses Traction Delay," p. 2.

44. "Speed the Ordinance," *Chicago Tribune,* January 2, 1907.

45. "Traction Change Chorus Swelled," *Chicago Tribune,* January 8, 1907, p. 2.

46. Dunne, *Illinois,* 1:280.

47. "Extra. 4:00 a.m.: Aldermen Adopt Car Settlement," *Chicago Tribune,* February 5, 1907, p. 1.

48. "Mayor Dunne Presents Message Vetoing Traction Ordinances," *Chicago Tribune*, February 15, 1907, p. 2.

49. Flanagan, *Charter Reform*, pp. 33–34.

50. Powers, "Edward Dunne," pp. 3–4.

51. Charles Wheeler in *Illinois*, 2:492–496.

52. "Leaders in Plan to Elect Busse: Republicans Begin Campaign to Put Postmaster in the Mayor's Chair," *Chicago Tribune*, February 11, 1907, p. 1.

53. Maureen Flanagan, "Fred A. Busse: A Silent Mayor in Turbulent Times," in *Mayors*, p. 50.

54. "Leaders in Plan to Elect Busse," p. 1.

55. Dunne, *Illinois*, 2:306–307.

56. "Roosevelt Out for Busse," "Failure of Dunne Presages Defeat," and "Great Campaign Finish at Hand," *Chicago Tribune*, April 1, 1907, pp. 1–2.

57. Dunne, *Illinois*, 2:294–295.

58. "Dunne Is Knifed in Gray Wolf Wards," *Chicago American*, April 3, 1907, p. 1.

59. *City Council Journal of Proceedings*, April 15, 1907, p. 56.

60. Flanagan, *Charter Reform*, p. 50.

61. Flanagan, *Charter Reform*, p. 61.

62. Flanagan, *Charter Reform*, pp. 3–4.

63. Flanagan, *Charter Reform*, p. 77.

64. "Measure Denounced by 50,000 Voters" and "Infamous Referendum Doomed Tomorrow," *Chicago American*, September 9, 1907, pp. 1, 4.

65. "Charter Beaten: Vote Two to One," *Chicago Tribune*, September 18, 1907, p. 1.

66. "Charter Beaten," p. 2.

67. Much of the general historical background on the Thompson era comes from research in a paper by Constance Mixon: "The 1928–1929 Chicago City Council: The Beginning of the End of Thompsonism" (independent study paper, University of Illinois at Chicago, 1995).

68. Carter H. Harrison, *Growing Up with Chicago* (Chicago: Ralph Fletcher Seymour, 1944), pp. 210–211. Quoted in Mayfield, "Reorganization of Urban Politics," p. 10.

69. Merriam, *Chicago*, pp. 186–188.

70. Douglas Bukowski, "Big Bill Thompson: The 'Model' Politician," in *Mayors*, p. 62.

71. Philip Kinsley, "Tribune Obituary Notice of William Hale Thompson," in *A Tragedy with a Laugh* (pamphlet on file at the Chicago Historical Society, January 1931 [presumed]), pp. 12–13.

72. Bukowski, *Mayors*, p. 78.

73. C. Johnson and C. Sautter, *Wicked City Chicago: From Kenna to Capone* (Highland Park, Ill.: December Press, 1994).

74. Mike Royko, *Boss* (New York: Dutton, 1971), p. 40.

75. J. P. Yoder, "Dry Chicago Is Aim of Mayor," *Duluth Herald*, 1923. Article in the Dever scrapbooks at the Chicago Historical Society.

76. William Kenney, "Chicago's 'Black-and-Tans,'" *Chicago History* 26, no. 3 (Fall 1997): 24.

77. Granger and Granger, *Lords of the Last Machine*, pp. 69–70.

78. Douglas Bukowski, *Big Bill Thomopson, Chicago, and the Politics of Image* (Urbana: University of Illinois Press, 1998), p. 185.

79. "Pineapples and Boomerangs," *World Book*, June 1928, p. 126.

80. S. J. Duncan–Clark, "Future of 'Big Bill' Puzzles Chicagoans," *New York Times*, November 18, 1928, sec. 3, p. 1.

81. Philip Kinsley, "Throng Sees Mayor Seated," *Chicago Tribune,* April 18, 1927, pp. 1–2.

82. "Mayor Outlines Civic Program; Wins Aldermen: Promises to Make Good Campaign Pledges," *Chicago Tribune,* April 18, 1927, p. 2.

83. Oscar Hewitt, "Aldermen Quit Car Bills Till After Primary," *Chicago Tribune*, February 24, 1928, p. 5.

84. "Avondale Road Backers Push Bond Demands: Will Urge Aldermen to Reconsider Tomorrow," *Chicago Tribune*, March 2, 1928.

85. "Council Group Rejects Bonds for Avondale," *Chicago Tribune,* March 6, 1928, p. 1.

86. "Voters to Pass on $77,959,000 Bond Projects," *Chicago Tribune,* March 11, 1928, p. 12.

87. Bukowski, *Big Bill*, p. 228.

88. Bukowski, *Big Bill*, pp. 134, 247.

89. Merriam, *Chicago,* p. 225.

90. Alderman Charles E. Merriam, "Report to the Voters of the Seventh Ward," 1915, p. 7. Copy in Leon Despres Papers at the Chicago Historical Society, box 8, folder 3.

91. Bukowski, *Mayors*, p. 80.

92. Harold Ickes, *Autobiography of a Curmudgeon* (New York: Reynal & Hitchcock, 1943), p. 173. Quoted in Bukowski, *Mayors*, p. 81.

93. Merriam, *Chicago,* pp. 189–190. Quoted in Mayfield, "Reorganization of Urban Politics," p. 10.

94. Barry Karl, *Charles E. Merriam and the Study of Politics* (Chicago: University of Chicago Press, 1974), p. 82.

95. Holli, *American Mayor*, pp. 3–4, 12–13.

PART II

Rubber Stamp Councils

Alderman Dick Simpson in 1971 with his microphone being turned off by the sergeant at arms and the police.
From the author's collection (photographer unknown).

3

Kelly-Nash Machine Council, 1933–1947

In the booster era in the early nineteenth century, lawyers, land speculators, and successful merchants took the positions of mayor and aldermen and governed the city directly. They provided for limited or segmented government, supported a progrowth policy, and promoted public safety in a rapidly growing city. In the partisan era during the Civil War and immediately afterward, business leaders and politicians, now including ethnic leaders particularly in the city council, managed to keep the civic wars from causing a total breakdown of local government. The city government in this crisis period managed to undertake major public works projects like reversing the flow of the Chicago River and building the Lake Tunnel to secure pure drinking water. The private sector was able to supply the material the Union troops needed to win the war, and the city government through its use of bounties was able to provide thousands of volunteers for the army and to provide relief for widows and orphans created by the war.

The Gray Wolves period that followed cemented an alliance of some businessmen, aldermen, and mayors through campaign contributions and corruption. The result was a city government that would support industrial and capitalist developments from the Chicago Fire until the Great Depression. Chicago continued to grow and expand, with its population frequently doubling every decade. Other business leaders were allied with good government reformers who sought to make city government more honest, efficient, and effective. These business and civic leaders undertook some projects on their own, such as the 1893 World's Fair and the 1909 Burnham Plan. They also supported efforts like the City Charter referendums, since they had a major hand in drafting the proposed city charter. Business leaders, for the most part, however, did not support social reforms to strengthen government and curb business excesses such as Mayor Dunne's proposals for immediate municipal own-ership of the traction system and utilities.

The Great Depression and World War II once again transformed the governing regime of Chicago in ways that would permanently alter Chicago politics. The scattered political machines and factions in both political parties that had been the norm in the late nineteenth and early twentieth centuries were replaced by a single all-powerful political party machine. The balance of power between the political parties also shifted. Republicans, who had been dominant since the Civil War (with occa-sional interruptions of Democratic mayors and city council majorities), would be replaced by the Democratic Party machine for the rest of the century. The business community, which naturally had supported Re-publicans and reformers, gradually made an accommodation with this party—tolerating and cooperating with Mayor Ed Kelly and finally join-ing Mayor Richard J. Daley to form a "growth machine." The election of Anton Cermak in 1931 and the subsequent reign of the Kelly-Nash ma-chine from 1933 to 1947 began this political transformation.

In 1929, during the reign of Mayor Big Bill Thompson, the Great De-pression hit Chicago hard. So Mayor Thompson, like Republican presi-dent Herbert Hoover, was defeated by a massive margin in 1931. Thomp-son once again tried in his campaign to use political rhetoric and rallies to bring victory, but his underlying political base had eroded. In one ap-peal to voters Thompson railed against his opponent, Democrat Anton Cermak:

> Tony, Tony, where's your pushcart at? Can you imagine a World's Fair Mayor with a name like that?
>
> I won't take a back seat from that Bohunk—Chairmock, Chermack or whatever his name is.
>
> Calls himself a "Master Executive" . . . you Negroes know what a master is . . . who kicked all the Negro caddies off the golf courses?
>
> The Master clubbed the Irish . . . the Poles . . . off the ticket. . . . Vote for me . . . jobs for Poles . . . jobs for Negroes . . . jobs for the Irish.[1]

Anton Cermak in response put together a campaign to "salvage Chicago's reputation." Thompson was successfully portrayed to the vot-ers by Cermak's supporters as "a buffoon, irresponsible, incapable, sur-rounded by grafters and gangsters." And Thompson's attempt to drive a wedge among Cermak's ethnic supporters with his campaign speeches backfired. Cermak's reply to Thompson's attack in the last week of the campaign was dignified:

> [Mayor Thompson] finds fault with my name. That's the same name I've al-ways had, it has been honored by the people of Chicago and Cook County

during my public career [as ward committeeman, alderman, and president of the Cook County Board] and I say I wouldn't trade it for all the mayor's jobs in the world.

Of course we couldn't all come over on the Mayflower—or maybe the boat would have sunk. But I got here as soon as I could, and I never wanted to go back, because to me it is a great privilege to be an American citizen.[2]

Perhaps no Republican could have won the mayoral election in 1931, when one-third of the nation was unemployed. The years immediately following the Crash of 1929 were particularly severe in Chicago. Unemployment reached 40 percent and, despite city relief expenditures in excess of $35 million in 1932, misery increased. The school board paid public school teachers in script and many police officers and firemen were fired for lack of funds. The building boom in Chicago, which had averaged over $95 million a year in new buildings from 1909 to 1916, slowed to $2.4 million a year in 1931 and 1932. Even in the late 1930s only $14.2 million was spent on the construction of new buildings each year.[3]

With the Depression, all major Republican political leaders lost their elections. First, U.S. Senator Charles Deneen was defeated in the primary of 1930, Big Bill Thompson lost his reelection as mayor to Cermak in 1931, and Herbert Hoover lost the presidency to Franklin Roosevelt in 1932. Cermak defeated Thompson by 671,189 to 476,922, with a large voter registration and an amazing 82 percent of the registered voters actually casting their votes in this key Chicago election. Not only had the immigrant population continued to grow in Chicago since the Civil War, but Republican programs had clearly been insufficient to stem the terrible Depression.

Mayor Cermak, only two years after taking office, was assassinated in what is usually thought of as an attempt to murder President Roosevelt in Miami in 1933. After being elected mayor, Cermak had installed his ally, 29th Ward alderman Patrick Nash, as the boss of the Democratic Party. Behind closed doors, the Democratic ward committeemen under Nash's leadership now selected Edward J. Kelly to succeed Mayor Cermak and then orchestrated a unanimous 47–0 vote in the city council confirming his selection. This decision to select Kelly, who was not an alderman, required a change in state law so that the council could pick the interim mayor from outside its own members, a practice that was not continued after Mayor Kelly's selection.

Cermak in his brief term as mayor had begun to eliminate waste in city government and to make it more efficient. Nevertheless, Ed Kelly inherited a nearly bankrupt city in 1933. "In his first official act, [Mayor Kelly] signed tax warrants worth $1.7 million and dispatched paychecks to the city's teachers. The city also sent checks to the other municipal payrollers, most of whom had not been paid in months. . . . In the first few months of his administration, Ed Kelly scored a number of triumphs including meeting municipal payrolls, wiping out a significant portion of the city debt, establishing good relations with the state legislature, and keeping the schools open."[4]

This is Mayor Kelly's own account: "I started with nothing except the love of my home town and—more important—the support of a City Council solemnly pledged to follow me. The banks and bond-buyers of the land refused [in the beginning] to have anything to do with us. More shocking, thousands of Chicagoans had stopped paying taxes. . . . I was confronted with three very tough tasks: 1) I had to raise a lot of money in a hurry; 2) I had to find jobs by the thousands for Chicago's unemployed, and 3) I had to jar the spirit of Chicago out of its despond."[5]

Mayor Kelly was successful and soon enjoyed the support of the business community because the city's finances were improving and city services were restored to the downtown business district. Mayor Kelly also courted the black community, which had been loyal to Republican mayor Big Bill Thompson. Blacks slowly switched their allegiance to the Democratic Party because of the New Deal programs of President Roosevelt. Mayor Kelly gained their support, particularly in his reelections, because he appointed blacks to municipal posts and supported them in their campaigns for elective office. Most surprisingly for Chicago, Mayor Kelly supported the principles of desegregated housing and desegregated education. Of the blacks whom Kelly supported in appointments and elections, the most important was former Republican alderman William Dawson, who represented the 2nd Ward and later became the Democratic boss of the black submachine covering all the black South Side wards. By 1939, one-fourth of Chicago's more than 3 million people were still foreign born, many more were second-generation ethnics, and African Americans now numbered 234,000.[6]

The Great Depression marked a major regime change in Chicago politics. First, and most obviously, the nature of fragmented Chicago political machines were permanently changed. The Democratic Party machine put together by Anton Cermak and strengthened by Kelly-Nash was different from the older machines that had developed in Chicago since the Chicago Fire. The Democratic Party after 1931 was centralized into a single political party. Over the next several decades it was to gain dominance as the Chicago machine and, by the 1960s, Chicago had become for practical purposes a one-party town. There were still factions within the party, but through the party's central committee, Democrats came up with a single slate of candidates and forced party precinct captains to support the entire ticket. Individual ward bosses remained to give out patronage jobs and to make sure that the precinct captains delivered the party vote on election day, but the top party "boss" gained more and more power.

Businessmen still supported Republicans and reformers with contributions and sponsored various civic groups like the Civic Federation and the Better Government Association to provide a check on the excess of machine politics. But business leaders found dealing directly with the mayor to get the projects and laws they needed to promote development and make profits an easy way to cement their relations with the new regime. Essentially, business leaders had to collaborate only with the mayor and sometimes with the governor to get things done.

> While many of the city's wealthiest and most influential families shared a generations-old affiliation with the Republican party, they reached a comfortable arrangement with the Kelly-Nash organization. Bankers tolerated Kelly because he kept city finances in order, guaranteeing a profitable market for city bonds and tax anticipation warrants. Moreover, Kelly's dramatic success in keeping Chicago solvent between 1933 and 1935 earned him the gratitude of the LaSalle Street bankers. The mayor courted the Loop merchants by providing services for the downtown area. First-rate police and fire protection, along with prompt maintenance work on streets and sidewalks, provided everyday reminders of city hall's beneficence. Most noteworthy was the construction of the state street subway, a boon to Loop merchants. . . . And finally, Kelly earned the plaudits of the business community through his sustained opposition to personal property and state income taxes.[7]

Some changes in this period were not as great as they appeared. For instance, Harold Gosnell in his classic book, *Machine Politics*, found that during this period that "Democrats were substituted for Republicans in practically all of the local offices. But these Democrats were not New Deal Democrats at heart. They were just like their Republican predecessors—spoils politicians." The social and economic discontent created by the Depression failed to bring more fundamental political change in Gosnell's view because "the city lacked the kind of leadership which was necessary to guide the inarticulate demands of the masses."[8] In hindsight, however, it is hard to see what kind of reform leadership would have been adequate to make a more radical transformation of Chicago politics. Perhaps a leader like Franklin Roosevelt at the head of a radical mass-based political party in Chicago would have been sufficient, but none of the leaders or local political parties of the time could pull off the change for which reformers yearned.

The Democratic machine created under Cermak, Nash, and Kelly differed from all earlier party machines. The new Democratic Party united very different ethnic groups and grew stronger than any previous political organization in Chicago. Despite the change from Republican to Democratic loyalty among the majority of voters, at the bottom of the party hierarchy there was little change in either party. Gosnell found in a study of 500 ward committeemen elections between 1928 and 1936, only thirteen incumbents were defeated. He concluded, "Their superiors [in higher political office] might change, but the ward bosses [in both parties] clung to their posts in spite of economic and political storms." Of course, the change in general political fortunes did have some effect. In 1928, before the Depression, three-quarters of the Republican ward committeemen held elected or appointed positions in government. By 1936, only one-sixth did. Conversely, by 1936, all but seven Democratic ward committeemen held government office, and three of those who did not hold government positions had occupations that allowed them to profit from their government connections by contracts and clients.[9]

Like Anton Cermak, Mayor Edward J. Kelly was a natural choice for the ethnics of Chicago. He was second-generation Irish, having been born in Chicago in 1876. He grew up near the Southwest Side stockyards on West 38th Street. His father, who came from Galway, Ireland, had worked as a teamster and, by the time Ed was born, was a Chicago fireman. Later he would become a Chicago policeman. At age twelve, Ed began work as a "cash boy" at Marshall Field's. Later he was an office boy for a whisky brokerage and a worker at Armour's cannery. His formal education stopped at eighth grade, although later he went to night school. In 1895, Kelly went to work for the Chicago Sanitary District and worked his way up various positions in the sanitary district to chief engineer over the next thirty-eight years despite having no formal education beyond high school.

Kelly was a strong mayor in the Chicago tradition. As he himself said, "These people look to me for leadership. To be a real mayor you've got to have control of the party. You've got to be a potent political factor. You've gotta be a boss!"[10]

Critics of the Kelly-Nash machine called it the "Nelly Cash Machine" and claimed that it was really just an organization that served to make the party bosses rich. Yet it "worked itself quickly into the fabric of Chicago life in the 1930s because it could provide jobs no one else could. . . . The struggle to survive made people appreciate the favors of the Machine, which were delivered by the precinct worker . . . [who] gave valuable favors and expected votes in return."[11]

Even opponents like Harold Gosnell admitted that the Kelly-Nash machine softened class conflict and served as a buffer for governmental agencies that dealt with distressed citizens during the Depression. It helped poorer citizens and new immigrants cope with the society in which they found themselves and provided direct social welfare services as well as a connection to government agencies. For party supporters, it also provided jobs, the possibility of advancement, and a chance to make money. Moreover, it provided stability. "Businessmen, journalists, under-world leaders, bankers, and labor chiefs knew that they could count upon the local machine to do business in the old way in spite of the changes that had taken place in the role of the national government."[12]

Although machines in other cities like New York and Philadelphia were defeated during the Depression, the economic deprivations did not destroy the new Democratic machine of Chicago. Gosnell believed that was because of "an unfavorable press situation [for reformers], a lack of leadership [among reformers] and the character of party division [especially in the Republican Party] at the beginning of the depression."[13] However, the Chicago Democratic machine was strengthened by its association with President Roosevelt, who became immensely popular. Mayor Kelly maintained close ties to the president in spite of opposition from Chicago reformers who served in Roosevelt's cabinet. Mayor Kelly's ties to the president enabled him to obtain federal funds to help Chicagoans and to build public works during the Depression. In return, Kelly provided Roosevelt the votes to win reelection.

The City Council, 1939–1940

Mayor Kelly was reelected in 1935, 1939, and 1943 against sometimes strong candidates. He had such complete control over the city council that at least one historian has recorded that "until the last year of his tenure, never more than ten of the fifty aldermen ever dared to oppose a measure he favored."[14] This is not strictly true, as eighteen aldermen voted against Kelly's position on rules governing the sale of liquor at a June 16, 1939, meeting. Nonetheless, Kelly won all important city council votes by overwhelming majorities throughout his tenure.

Kelly, like most of Chicago's political leaders, was not servile. As he wrote in his autobiography, "In 1908 my life and the lives of other working on the North Shore Channel [of the sanitary district] were made miserable by the slave-driving tactics of a fellow who had been made a straw boss because he was the son-in-law of a Republican leader. One day I could stand no more. I knocked him down with a punch and walked off the job, figuring that my days in the Sanitary District were done. But Robert R. McCormick, then president of the Sanitary District, and as vigorous a proponent of the Republican Party then as he is today, put me back to work. He said that any man who punched another who had greater political power, and punched him justly was a good man."[15]

The first major challenger to Mayor Kelly was Dwight Green, the Republican nominee in 1939. Green was born in Ligonier, Indiana, in 1897 and attended Wabash College at Crawfordsville, Indiana. After serving as a flight instructor in World War I, he received his law degree from the

University of Chicago in 1922 and became a special attorney for the Bureau of Internal Revenue. Green gained his greatest fame in 1931 as the trial attorney on the legal team that convicted Al Capone. Although he lost the mayoral election in 1939, he served as governor of Illinois from 1940 to 1948.[16]

In the 1939 campaign, Green launched verbal attacks against Kelly and the Kelly-Nash machine for four months. On the weekend before the election at ward rallies and in a radio talk he maintained, "This is the people's fight against the payrollers. Next Tuesday the Kelly payroll army will be out full force. The machine spent $2,500,000 to get Mr. Kelly nominated. It is spending another $2,500,000 trying to elect him so all the payrollers can go on stuffing taxpayers' money into their pockets."[17]

Green charged that the Democrats also controlled the public schools and relief agencies, and he blamed the Kelly organization for unemployment and high taxes. But his attacks brought nothing but silence. Kelly did not mention Green's name during the campaign. The Democratic organization was united (despite a bitter primary), but the Republican party was badly split in 1939. Even progressive forces were divided. For instance, organized labor endorsed Kelly. African Americans had mostly switched their allegiance from the Republican to the Democratic Party by 1939 and Kelly got at least half of their votes. Other supporters and beneficiaries of the New Deal policies voted for Kelly. Even former U.S. district attorney George Johnson, in a radio address on the eve of the election, declared that Chicago was no longer a crime capital; rather, the city led the nation in crime prevention, for which he gave Mayor Kelly and his police commissioner much of the credit.

Thus the results of the 1939 election were not surprising. In a record election of nearly 1.5 million votes, Dwight Green lost by 183,000. Mayor Kelly in his election night victory speech promised $7 million in new housing, new recreation centers for children who didn't live near the big parks, a new immense convention hall on Navy Pier, and a final settlement to public transportation problems that had dogged the city for decades. The city council elected with Kelly was also a sweep for the Democrats. Forty-four Democrats and only six Republicans would form the council from 1939 to 1943. Thirty-four aldermen had been reelected to four year terms of office. Only fourteen incumbents had been defeated, and there were only two open seats in this election that had been vacated through death.[18]

At his inauguration on April 12, Mayor Kelly spoke of the need to "Pull Together for Progress" and outlined six major goals for this term in office: (1) relief for the unemployed, (2) safe highways to improve automobile transportation, (3) a unified traction ordinance for a single public transportation system, (4) a new plan commission and better city planning, (5) new building codes, parks, and playgrounds, and (6) a new council committee on labor and industrial relations to ensure peaceful negotiations between labor and business.[19]

The only difference in the composition of the city council itself was that there were more Democrats, fewer Republicans, and some new faces. One of these new aldermen was 5th Ward alderman Paul Douglas, another University of Chicago professor in the tradition of Charles Merriam. He had come to Chicago in 1919 to teach economics at the university and was forty-seven years old when he ran for alderman. Although Douglas entered the race as an Independent, Mayor Kelly arranged for him to be endorsed by the Democratic Party as well. In a meeting in the mayor's office with Independents and Democratic Party officials, Douglas agreed to run "provided that it was understood that if elected, [he] would take orders from no one. At this, [Mayor] Kelly brought his fist down on the table, shouting, 'That is what I want!' He said the council was too one-sided and needed someone to stir it up."[20] Douglas was unique on the city council because he was "a scholar, a humanist, a conservationist, an economist, [later] a Marine, a Quaker, a reformer, a rebel, a liberal, and [after he returned from World War II] for eighteen years [would be] widely recognized as the 'conscience of the U.S. Senate'" as he had been of the Chicago City Council from 1939 to 1942.[21]

By Paul Douglas's assessment, "the ablest member of the council was Alderman Jacob M. Arvey, of the 24th Ward, chairman of the all-powerful Finance Committee and Kelly's floor leader."[22] Alderman Arvey, who later succeeded Pat Nash as the Democratic Party's boss, began his political career in 1914 when he worked for the election of an Independent, William J. Lindsay, who ran unsuccessfully for judge of the municipal court. Later, when Arvey was more powerful within the Democratic Party, he would make Lindsay a judge.

Jake Arvey was short, only five feet four and a half inches tall, and weighed only 152 pounds, but he was smart, hard-working, and tough. His father, a milkman, died when Jake was thirteen. Arvey worked first as a shipping clerk and then as a delivery boy for a custom tailor in the Loop. He finished high school in the evenings and later graduated from John Marshall Law School. After being admitted to the bar, he became an assistant state's attorney in 1918 and was elected 24th Ward alderman in 1923 at the age of twenty-eight. He was Democratic ward committeeman of the nearly all-Jewish 24th Ward on the West Side of Chicago in the North Lawndale and Douglas Park neighborhoods from 1923 to 1941. During the New Deal era, President Roosevelt called the 24th the "best Democratic Ward in America." In one key election under Arvey's leadership the ward voted 29,000 for Roosevelt and only 700 votes for his opponent.[23]

Despite his major role in the city council, Arvey, like Paul Douglas, went to fight in World War II with his National Guard unit, the Thirty-Third Infantry Division. He was his division's legal and civil affairs officer with a rank of lieutenant colonel, and he received the Legion of Merit and two Bronze Stars for his war service. After he returned from the war, he was elected chairman of the Cook County Democratic Party. After several years as party boss and council floor leader, he retired to private life as a lawyer and philanthropist.[24]

Arvey ran the 24th Ward well. His precinct captains passed out matzoh, noodles, and chickens at Passover and Christmas. Arvey fixed fifty to sixty parking tickets a week by taking them to Mayor Kelly, who had them voided. As Arvey later said, "People wonder why we won. It was because we were active almost every day of the year. [Because of that] in that period [from the 1920s until the 1940s] we always received over 90 per cent of the total vote."[25] A study of the council's Finance Committee under Jake Arvey's chairmanship concluded that Arvey was second in power and importance only to the mayor.[26] As with other Finance Committee chairmen and floor leaders, it was Alderman Arvey's job to see that the mayor's ordinances and resolutions passed, to keep the other aldermen in line politically, and to determine which Workman's Compensation claims were paid. In earlier years the Finance Committee chairmen also controlled all patronage appointments, but that power had mostly gone to the mayor and the party chairman by 1939. However, the Finance Committee chairman still coordinated the hearings on the city budget and, with the input of the mayor and city department heads, determined the operating budget of the city.

During the 1939 council period, the Republican council minority was unorganized and posed little threat to the mayor's programs. By sharing influential positions such as committee chairmanships with Republican aldermen, however, Mayor Kelly and Alderman Arvey gained their support for the mayor's legislation. There was also a small Independent group in the council during this period led by Alderman Douglas. At its peak the Independent bloc included Aldermen John Boyle, Earl Dickerson, Frank Hilburn, Roy Olin, and Richard Walsh.[27] By Douglas's own account, this was not much of a voting bloc: "During the first year [1939–1940], I stood alone in the council and the votes were usually 49 to 1. As the second year opened, [Alderman] John Boyle, a Courtney man [who had backed State's Attorney Tom Courtney for mayor in the 1939 Democratic primary] from the Sixteenth Ward, joined me. We formed an alliance on economy measures and on the traction and bus franchises. . . . A few others occasionally joined us, and once our count rose to nine. The council was again becoming a deliberative body."[28]

Even this level of opposition was not as great as it appears. In 1939, Paul Douglas himself voted with the mayor's floor leader, Jacob Arvey, on divided roll call votes 94 percent of the time. Of the bloc that Douglas identified as Independents, only Alderman Boyle voted less often than Douglas with the floor leader and he supported the administration 80 percent of the time. In one anomaly, Alderman Dorsey Crowe of the 42nd Ward voted in stubborn opposition at two meetings. If all sixty of those divided roll call votes are counted, he voted with the Democratic administration only 17 percent of the time. A more accurate measure, excluding those two meetings, has Alderman Crowe voting with the administration 50 percent of the time.

Alderman Crowe was a typical ward boss. He had been elected alderman of the 42nd Ward in 1919 and won ten successive elections in the Gold Coast–Rush Street neighborhood north of the Chicago River. He eventually became the dean of the city council and presided as president pro tem under Mayor Richard J. Daley. He served in the council until his death from a heart attack at the age of seventy in 1962. When a woman once accosted him saying that he only won his last election against two Independent candidates in 1959 because he paid fifty cents to each one who voted for him, he replied in blunt, typical machine alderman fashion: "Madame, you can't get that done for 50 cents. It costs $5."[29]

Many of the aldermen in 1939, of course, continued in the style of their predecessors. First Ward alderman Bathhouse John Couglin had died by 1939 but he had been replaced in the council by his old ally, Hinky Dink Kenna. Paul Douglas in his memoirs recounts: "Kenna never liked me, and one day when I was speaking about ghetto conditions and inadequate relief, he rose to his feet with a scornful grunt. 'Housing relief! Tain't seemly,' he snorted. Clapping his ever-present derby on his head and with an ice-cold eye, he stalked out of the council chamber, never to return. Time had passed him by. He died a few months later."[30] But when the last of the so-called Gray Wolves died, he was more than adequately replaced by another saloon keeper, 43rd Ward alderman Paddy Bauler. A few years later, after Mayor Richard Daley's 1955 election, Paddy remarked memorably, "Chicago ain't ready for reform." Certainly from the 1930s to 1980s Chicago wasn't ready. Corrupt ward committeemen and alderman remain a Chicago tradition that continues to this day.

In spite of ward bosses such as Arvey, Crowe, and Kenna, who had their own fiefdoms, Mayor Kelly strengthened his control from the time he became mayor in 1933 until he was ousted by the party as a liability in 1947. By then, various corruption scandals had grown, the Kelly administration was failing to deliver basic city services effectively, and civic leaders were calling for Boss Kelly's removal. The last straw, however, was Kelly's support of open housing for Negroes. It persuaded the white ethnic party bosses to dump Kelly and replace him on the ticket with businessman Martin Kennelly.[31]

In general, Kelly, especially in the early years of his reign, solidified the

Democratic Party and the party's control over city government. The Democratic Party balance in the city council increased during his reign. Under Dever in 1923 Democrats had 72 percent of the council seats, under Thompson in 1927 they declined to 57 percent, under Cermak they again increased to 74 percent of the city council, and by 1939, under Mayor Kelly Democrats had increased to a phenomenal 88 percent, a level they wouldn't surpass until 1959.[32] So there was a Democratic majority that neither the Republican minority nor the Independents could effectively block in the council of 1939. Whether Kelly could tame the Gray Wolves was the issue. Would the aldermen or the mayor rule the city and divide the spoils? In elections, factional politics and local party bosses would continue to be the norm, but in the city council Kelly gained the support he needed to govern with only token dissent. The era of the Gray Wolves was over, although aldermanic graft and corruption continued.

Mayor Kelly also increased his power in the party, especially after the death of Patrick Nash, but he couldn't completely control the factional groups. Powerful local ward bosses and multiple power centers continued to exist. Kelly argued that it was necessary to be a boss because of the circumstances of the time, but he worked with the city council in a different way than most bosses. He wrote, "I worked perpetually with the City Council sitting down with every dissident clique that arose and ironing away differences which could have wrecked all of us. And because of such sessions, we found such harmony that I was never forced to veto a single measure during my 14 years in office."[33]

Public Transportation, Superhighways, and the City Budget

The issues of 1939 included the creation of a new Chicago Plan Commission to plan future city development and the continuing struggle over how the sale of alcohol should be regulated. But the major issues facing the major and the city council were big transportation and public works projects for 1939 and battles over the city budget at the end of the Depression. At the end of April 1939, the city council was set to begin negotiations again with the private traction transit firms. The problems of public transportation had vexed the city council since the Civil War and had been a dominant council issue during the Gray Wolves period. Now, with help from the New Deal administration in Washington, Mayor Kelly's firm control of the city council, and support from the downtown business community, great strides forward would be made.

The council's Transportation Committee was headed by Alderman James R. Quinn. Negotiations had begun the preceding year, but the value of the transit companies to be purchased and the compensation that they would pay the city for their franchises were critical issues still to be resolved. Under court order, a new committee to represent the elevated and surface transit lines had been selected. The city was hoping to use federal Public Works Administration (PWA) funds to purchase the transit lines and consolidate them into a single public transportation system.

In 1937, under Mayor Ed Kelly, the city had successfully applied to Roosevelt's Works Progress Administration for a grant and a loan to begin Chicago's subway system, and on December 17, 1938, the city broke ground for its first subway. At its August 8, 1939, meeting the city council Finance Committee approved the first of what was expected to be $1 million in payments for the right-of-way to build the city's first subway system beneath sixty-five parcels of private property. At its August 30, 1939, meeting the council approved by a vote of 35–6 an appropriation of $6 million, in addition to the $40 million that had been approved in November 1938, to cover the cost of building the subway system. At the same meeting the city council by a vote of 32–6 granted authority to the corporation counsel to acquire the easements for building the subway. This was not without significant debate however.

At the council's Finance Committee meeting, 14th Ward alderman James McDermott asserted that the construction of the subway system would cost "untold millions of dollars and add greatly to the already heavy municipal burden of debt."[34] Alderman McDermott charged that in addition to the $46 million in building costs, the city might be held liable for damages of up to $6 million to private utilities and untold millions for damages to private buildings along the route of the subway. The city administration maintained that the individual property owners would have to pay for any changes in utilities or any structural changes to buildings made necessary by the subway construction. However, these liability issues would have to be decided by the courts and had not been authoritatively resolved by the time the committee and the city council had to vote on whether or not to proceed with construction of Chicago's first subway. Alderman McDermott also maintained that the city would have to pay another $9 million to equip the subway because the transit companies wanted to take the money for equipment for the new subway from the city's traction fund which had been appropriated by the council to create a unified public transportation system.

Despite these additional costs, the federal Public Works Administration had agreed only to pay $18 million, 45 percent of the original estimate for building the subway. The city would have to pay the rest. The problem of building and paying for the subway would continue to dog the city council for several years, but it opened on October 17, 1943, in the middle of World War II. Finally, in 1947, two years after the end of the war, the Chicago Transit Authority took over the operations of the various private companies and a public transportation system finally existed in Chicago. Mayors and city councils had struggled with these transportation issues from the time of Chicago's first horse-drawn street railway in 1859. It had taken nearly ninety years for Chicago to develop a unified public transportation system, including the new subways, which the city government had been seeking to build since the turn of the century.[35]

Just as public transportation was moving forward in Chicago, Mayor Kelly proposed a $100 million superhighway program to be financed through the sale of bonds that were to be paid off by revenue from a state motor fuel tax over the next twenty years. At its August 30 meeting, the city council approved two resolutions and an ordinance to begin the process: (1) a resolution asking the state Finance Department to sell the first $100,000 worth of superhighway bonds; (2) a resolution setting up a joint engineering committee representing the city, state, and county to make preliminary plans; and (3) an ordinance creating a department of superhighways to coordinate the work.[36] There was some opposition from various aldermen to the hurried passage of these superhighway proposals. "Ald. James B. Bowler, however, won the committee's unanimous consent when he reminded the aldermen that Chicago [had] fallen behind other large cities in traffic facilities."[37] The superhighways that had been so controversial in the 1920s under Mayor Thompson were approved unanimously by Mayor Kelly's council in 1939.

The final set of disputed issues was the 1940 city budget. One of Paul Douglas's first fights in the city council was to prevent cuts to the food budget for families receiving relief from the city government:

> With hundreds of thousands of Chicagoans badly underfed and, indeed, not far from starvation, the city, facing a shortage of funds, cut the [relief] food budget by 40 per cent. Deciding to fight this, I took a market basket into the council chamber with a week's food ration for a family of five. This was scanty enough, but when I took away 40 per cent of the bread, milk, eggs, and pork, I showed that what was left was less than a starvation diet. Two fat aldermen tried to prove that this was the diet for a day rather than a week. . . . a corpulent joker, having taken some of the food, gaily passed it around. This was treated as a joke by one of the reporters, who continued to refer to it as such for many years. Word sped up to the Mayor's office on the fifth floor. In a few minutes Kelly came hurrying in to announce that he had found a million dollars in the budget, which would be used to increase the food allowed relief clients.[38]

There are several lessons in this council story. First, Alderman Douglas did a superb job in dramatizing the effects of a budgetary decision. Second, the aldermanic majority ignored his arguments and demonstration, as did at least one member of the press, but Douglas was heeded by Mayor Kelly. It was the mayor, not the aldermen, who responded to Douglas's attack by providing new relief funds. Alderman Douglas was able to use the opportunity of the city council meeting to get action, but not by rational persuasion of the council members. The council of 1939 was a rubber stamp council that approved the mayor's proposals and voted his wishes but did not, on the whole, take much initiative. Kelly, however, was sensitive to Douglas's criticisms. He paid attention because he knew Douglas both represented and might further mobilize public opinion.

In 1939, Alderman Douglas also sought to amend and improve the city budget in other ways. One of his proposals was to save money by changing the way in which the city utilized bridge tenders. There were some twenty bridges over the Chicago River, each of which had six bridge tenders, one at each end of the bridge for three eight-hour shifts. Alderman Douglas proposed saving the city money by using roving bridge tenders (particularly since the river and the lake are frozen and impassible by boats for at least three months of the year).[39] Alderman Douglas's amendment was not accepted in 1939. Over the years that followed, Mayor Kelly would partially implement this budget reform, but it would be almost fifty years before this reform would be fully implemented. Yet had Alderman Douglas not made the proposal in 1939 and had the Independent aldermen not pushed the proposal again in the 1970s, the change would never been made.

The Chicago Machine

Because it was a rubber stamp council, Mayor Kelly lost no votes in the council of 1939–1940. Other than the speeches and floor battles of Alderman Douglas, there was not even a clear articulation of alternative policies and programs for the city. For this reason Kelly had particularly wanted Douglas to provide at least some progressive, New Deal alternatives in the council.

In Chicago during the 1930s and 1940s, Mayor Kelly's political interests, those of the aldermen, and the business community "coincided with using federal money for infrastructure developments. The city gained physical improvements to help commerce and Kelly [and the aldermen] got more patronage jobs."[40] Kelly convinced President Roosevelt's Public Works Administration to provide funds to refurbish Midway Airport, to speed roadway construction on streets like Lake Shore Drive, and eventually to pay for three-quarters of the cost of the new State Street Subway. Like the national government, Chicago, under strong executive leadership, gradually worked itself out of the Depression. As a result, Chicago contributed mightily to World War II and slowly began to prosper, especially during the postwar period, when Mayor Kelly's administration completed major public works—new roads, superhighways, and the subway. He solved public problems that had bedeviled city government for up to ninety years. He created a new unified public transportation system under the C.T.A., uniform liquor laws in the post-Prohibition era, and a smaller, more effective Chicago Plan Commission. Yet the same kind of rogues, scoundrels, and reformers continued to fight over the spoils and the future of the city. The old Gray Wolves certainly would have recognized the council and the issues that they had fought over and profited from decades earlier.

After the Great Depression, political power centralized in a single Democratic Party, which became ever more dominant in future decades. Governmental power centralized in the hands of the mayor. Unlike the fragmented city council controlled by the Gray Wolves, the council was under the control of the mayor and his floor leader. It had become a rubber stamp council. When Mayor Richard J. Daley came to power, he simply strengthened and further centralized the party machine and the mayor's control of the council. As Kelly had said, "you've gotta be a boss." It is a lesson that Daley would take to heart.

Notes

1. From the stenographic notes of campaign speeches quoted in Carroll Wooddy, "Jubilee in Chicago," *National Municipal Review*, June 1931, p. 321; and Alex Gottfried, *Boss Cermak of Chicago: A Study in Political Leadership* (Seattle: University of Washington Press, 1962), p. 205.

2. Edward L. Gorey, *Chicago Evening American*, March 31, 1931, quoted in Gottfried, *Boss Cermak*, p. 226.

3. Loomis Mayfield, "The Reorganization of Urban Politics: The Chicago Growth Machine After World War II" (Ph.D. diss., University of Pittsburgh, 1996), pp. 86–88.

4. Roger Biles, "Edward J. Kelly: New Deal Machine Builder," in Paul Green and Melvin Holli, eds., *The Mayors: The Chicago Political Tradition* (Carbondale: Southern Illinois University Press, 1987), p. 113.

5. Edward J. Kelly, "Started with Nothing but Love of Chicago; Needed $200,000," *Herald-American*, May 9, 1947. A series of copyrighted newspaper articles included in the Edward J. Kelly biography, Chicago Historical Society Biography Collection.

6. WPA Federal Writers' Project, *Chicago and Suburbs: 1939* (Evanston: Chicago Historical Bookworks Reprint, 1991), pp. 5–6.

7. Biles, *Mayors*, p. 115; "Mayor Kelly's Chicago," *Life*, July 17, 1944, p. 75; and "The Kelly-Nash Political Machine," *Fortune* 14, August 1936, pp. 126–139.

8. Harold Gosnell, *Machine Politics: Chicago Model*, 2d ed. (Chicago: University of Chicago Press, 1968), p. 26. Originally published in 1937.

9. Gosnell, *Machine Politics*, pp. 27, 39–40.

10. The Kelly quote is taken from Victor Rubin, "You've Gotta Be a Boss," *Collier's*, September 25, 1945, p. 36. It is quoted in Biles, *Mayors*, p. 125.

11. Bill Granger and Lori Granger, *Lords of the Last Machine: The Story of Politics in Chicago* (New York: Random House, 1987), p. 103.

12. Gosnell, *Machine Politics*, p. 184.

13. Gosnell, *Machine Politics*, p. 186.

14. Biles, *Mayors*, p. 125.

15. Ed Kelly biography, Chicago Historical Society Biography Collection.

16. "Picture-Story of Green's Career," *Chicago American*, February 21, 1958, Ed Kelly biography, Kelly folder, Chicago Historical Society Biography Collection. See also David Camelon, "Nation's Eyes Focused on Green's Rise," *Herald Examiner*, October 9, 1940.

17. "Green, Kelly Begin Final Vote Drive: Plead for Big Ballot; Each Claim Victory," *Chicago Tribune*, April 1, 1939, p. 1.

18. From 1837 to 1847 aldermen served one-year terms. From 1837 to 1935 aldermen served two-year terms. From 1935 to the present aldermen have served four-year terms. *Chicago: Its City Halls and Its City Council* (an eight-page pamphlet produced by the City Council Committee on Finance, the Chicago Historical Society, the *Chicago Sun-Times*, and the *Chicago Tribune*, 1987), p. 1.

19. Philip Kinsley, "Pull Together! Kelly Urges in Inaugural Talk," *Chicago Tribune*, April 13, 1939, p. 1.

20. Paul Douglas, *In the Fullness of Time: The Memoirs of Paul H. Douglas* (New York: Harcourt Brace Jovanovich, 1971), p. 87.

21. F. Richard Ciccone, "The Conscience: Paul Douglas," in *Chicago and the American Century: The 100 Most Significant Chicagoans of the Twentieth Century* (Chicago: Contemporary Books, 1999), pp. 26–27.

22. Douglas, *Fullness of Time*, p. 91.

23. *Chicago Sun-Times*, August 26, 1977.

24. The biographical data is mostly taken from Joe Matthewson, "Jacob Arvey, Boss Emeritus," *Chicago Tribune*, March 18, 1973. See also Donald Schwartz, "Jack Arvey: The Man Behind the Name," *Chicago Sun-Times*, December 13, 1964.

25. Quoted in Matthewson, "Jacob Arvey."

26. William Slayton, "Chicago's House of Lords: A Study of the Functions of the Finance Committee of the Chicago City Council" (M.A. thesis, University of Chicago, 1943).

27. Slayton, "Chicago's House of Lords," p. 28 nn. 1–2.

28. Douglas, *Fullness of Time*, p. 99.

29. "Ald. Dorsey R. Crowe Dies, Dean of the City Council," *Chicago Sun-Times*, July 2, 1962. Crowe biography in the Chicago Historical Society Collection.

30. Douglas, *Fullness of Time*, p. 91.

31. Biles, *Mayors*, pp. 124–125.

32. Mayfield, "Reorganization of Urban Politics," pp. 466, 470, figs. 6, 8.

33. Ed Kelly biography, Chicago Historical Society Biography Collection.

34. "Aldermen Fear Untold Millions in Subway Costs," *Chicago Tribune*, August 31, 1939, p. 15.

35. Brian Cudahy, *Destination Loop: The Story of Rapid Transit Railroading in and around Chicago* (Lexington, Mass.: Stephen Greene, 1982), pp. 54–60.

36. "Council Creates Bureau to Build Superhighways," *Chicago Tribune*, August 31, 1939, p. 11.

37. "Council Creates Bureau to Build Superhighways," p. 11.

38. Douglas, *Fullness of Time*, p. 97.

39. This budget amendment on roving bridge tenders would be proposed again during the eight years I served as alderman (1971–1979). It would not be fully implemented until after Harold Washington became mayor and the Reagan era cutbacks in federal government grants to cities necessitated more efficient and effective use of public funds. It is illustrative of the way change frequently comes to Chicago, slowly through the repeated efforts of reformers.

40. Mayfield, "Reorganization of Urban Politics," p. 91.

4

Richard J. Daley's Rubber Stamp, 1955–1976

The post–World War II period ushered in a time of prosperity, growth, and affluence for Chicago. In 1950, the city reached its largest population, 3.6 million people, while the percentage of first- and second-generation immigrants declined from 77 percent at the turn of the century to 45 percent. The black population, on the other hand, increased to 492,000, or 14 percent, in 1950 and continued to expand. The city was growing and changing. Chicago politics solidified into a new pattern that would last for decades. Its electoral politics would come increasingly under the control of the Democratic machine under Boss Richard J. Daley. The old Council of the Gray Wolves, which had existed before Mayor Kelly, was replaced by the rubber stamp council. Planning, development, and government policies would be directed by a private/public partnership or developmental regime of big business, Mayor Daley, and leaders of major institutions such as hospitals, universities, and labor unions known in later social science literature as the growth machine.[1]

In 1947, Mayor Kelly was replaced by businessman and would-be reformer Martin H. Kennelly, who left most of the city's business in the hands of the city council and his department heads. He was a weak mayor, although he strengthened the civil service system during his tenure. He said at the beginning of his term, "Chicago is a council-governed city. The aldermen are elected by the people of their districts. I don't think it's a function of the mayor to boss the aldermen." In the council during the Kennelly years, the powerful aldermen "made committee assignments, controlled the awarding of franchises, and regulated city business in the best interest of the Democratic party." During Kennelly's reign, the council regained much of the control that it had enjoyed during the era of the Gray Wolves. As a result, corruption and scandal were again the order of the day.[2]

Jake Arvey, who had been Democratic Party boss, was also replaced after electoral disasters in 1950 by sixty-six-year-old municipal court clerk
and ward committeeman Joe Gill. After the 1952 elections, however, Gill
resigned as head of the Democratic Party Central Committee. Both Arvey
and Gill then lobbied for the election of County Clerk Richard J. Daley as
the new head of the party. He was blocked at first by a South Side Irish
clique headed by city council Finance Committee chairman Clarence
Wagner. However, during the selection process, Wagner was killed in a
car wreck. On July 21, 1953, with the leader of the opposition faction out
of the picture, Daley was easily elected as head of the party.

Richard J. Daley was a first-generation Irish American and grew up in
the Southwest Side's Bridgeport neighborhood. His father was a sheet
metal worker and union man. Daley attended De La Salle High School.
At the same time, he joined the Hamburg Social and Athletic Club (which
included elements of both a street gang and a social organization) and
served as the club's president for fifteen years. From this base, he began
his political career as a secretary to 11th Ward alderman Joseph McDo-
nough. He obtained a DePaul University law degree as he moved up
through various elected and appointed positions in city, county, and state
government. He won his first election on a write-in ballot as a Republican
state representative after an incumbent died in office, but he switched
back to the Democratic side of the aisle as soon as he arrived in Springfield. At the end of his slow and methodical rise to power, he became
both chairman of the Democratic Party and mayor of the City of
Chicago.[3]

One of Daley's most sympathetic biographers, Eugene Kennedy, wrote
of the mayor:

> To understand the man Richard J. Daley, one must appreciate the steady ap-
> prenticeship of his political career and how his fascination with and achieve-
> ment of power were linked at every step with his capacity for bureaucratic
> activity, for discovering sustaining delight in balance sheets, patronage lists,
> the dusty inner springs and levers of legislation, and the endless round of
> social engagements—weddings, wakes, and funerals—dutifully kept. His
> great political power was built on his own personal power to live the minor
> city and state politician's life and to wait, with hardly an expression on his
> face, but with all the patience of the hardened bureaucratic-beast, for the
> moment to strike.[4]

On December 1, 1954, Kennelly announced his candidacy for reelection
as mayor. On December 15, he appeared before dissatisfied party slate
makers to present his candidacy. On December 20, the Central Committee voted 49–1 for Daley over Kennelly as their nominee. After that,

Mayor Kennelly portrayed this election as a contest of "the people against the bosses." He attempted to lead "an old-fashioned crusade of the city's best elements against the benighted forces of bossism and corruption while defending the achievements of his eight years in office against the ravenous designs of the boodlers and spoilers primed to raid the public till."[5] Kennelly in his speeches linked the Democratic machine, organized crime, and the African-American community, and he blamed a black political leader, Congressman William Dawson, for his failure to receive the Democratic mayoral nomination. Unfortunately for Kennelly, once again there were not enough votes among the "best elements" in the electorate to reelect him.

Many of the newspapers in 1955 echoed Kennelly's themes. The *Chicago Tribune* wrote: "Mr. Daley is . . . the candidate of the hoodlum element. He will also be the candidate of those who wish to load the city's offices once again with political payrollers and thus undo the great work of Mayor Kennelly in giving the City a real merit system of appointments and promotions. Mr. Daley will also be the candidate of those who want to see the city purchase of supplies and contacts let in the good old-fashioned way, with a nice percentage for the politicians."[6]

Although Kennelly was the incumbent, had plenty of money, was a far better orator than Daley, and used the new television media to good effect, Daley had the unions and the party precinct workers on his side. Daley campaigned as the candidate of the people in the neighborhoods: "My opponent says, 'I took politics out of the schools, I took politics out of this and I took politics out of that.' I say to you: There's nothin' wrong with politics. There's nothin' wrong with good politics. Good politics is good government. . . . Let them be the State Street candidate [supported by the commercial businesses]. Let others be the LaSalle Street candidate [supported by lawyers and stockbrokers]. I'm proud and happy to be your candidate. . . . I'm a kid from the stockyards and I say to all of you, I'll stand with you."[7] His precinct captains won the primary election for Daley with a margin of 100,064 votes out of 764,015 cast.

Then in the general election Daley faced 5th Ward alderman Robert Merriam, son of University of Chicago professor, alderman, and former mayoral candidate Charles Merriam. Robert Merriam was a hero of the Battle of the Bulge and a captain in the infantry, earning four battle stars and a Bronze Star for bravery. After returning from the war, he had been elected to the city council in 1947 from the liberal 5th Ward, which his father had served. He was backed by both the regular Democratic ward organization and Republicans in both his aldermanic elections. He soon became a leader of the "economy bloc" in the Chicago City Council which, in the tradition of his father and Alderman Paul Douglas, sought to curb waste and corruption in city government. Merriam also chaired the emergency crime committee of the council, which with Republican support attempted to expose the link between crime and politics.

On the Sunday after the primary, Alderman Merriam attacked Daley as "the machine candidate and presented what he described as 'evidence of the link between Chicago crime—Syndicate crime—and machine politics.'" Merriam also focused attention on vote fraud. He produced evidence that a precinct captain, "Short Pencil" Sidney Lewis, had erased votes legally cast for Kennelly. However, when the Democratic-dominated Board of Election Commissioners held hearings, they censured Merriam, not Lewis. Merriam then sent letters to voters in sixty-five of the strongest Democratic precincts, only to have 2,982 returned as undeliverable. Based on his projections from that sample, he claimed that there had been as many as 100,000 "ghost voters" in the primary election, from which Daley emerged as the Democratic nominee for mayor.[8]

Merriam's campaign was furthered when the Chicago Bar Association accused Democratic Party candidate for city clerk, Alderman Ben Becker, of accepting payoffs and kickbacks. Daley resolved that political problem by replacing Becker with John Marcin, who had been slated as city treasurer, as the Democratic candidate for city clerk. He then made popular businessman Morris B. Sachs, who had been defeated on Kennelly's ticket, the Democratic Party's candidate for city treasurer So he ended with a better slate of city candidates.

In the meantime, Merriam gained the backing of three of the city's four major newspapers and most civic reform organizations, but it was not enough. On April 5, 1955, he lost by a vote of 708,222 to 581,555 with a hard core of eleven white ethnic and black machine-controlled wards giving Daley a plurality of 125,179. That election night Alderman Paddy Bauler of the 43rd Ward made his immortal declaration: "Chicago ain't ready for reform." And certainly, in 1955, Alderman Bauler was right. Now that Daley was both mayor and head of the Central Committee of the Cook County Democratic Party, Bauler in his vulgar but accurate way also predicted: "Keane and them fellas—Jake Arvey, Joe Gill—they think they are gonna run things. . . . They're gonna run nothin'. They ain't found it out yet, but Daley's the dog with the big nuts, now that we got him elected. You wait and see, that's how it is going to be."[9]

In the crisis-filled years of the Depression and World War II Chicagoans opted for a strong mayor and a rubber stamp council under Cermak and Kelly. However, the 1950s were the beginning of years of affluence. General Eisenhower had been elected president in 1952 and reelected in 1956. The social movements that would burst upon the scene in the 1960s were submerged in the Beat Generation. Americans were free of the sacrifices that World War II demanded, and the economy was booming. With more government funds, Chicago was able to provide better city services than it had since the Great Depression. And in Mayor Daley, the city once again had a "builder mayor" to push public work projects and private developments. There was an ebullience and a sense that anything was possible for the America that had won the war and become one of the two great superpowers. For most Americans, it was time to buy a car and a home, and to live the good life. Having a builder mayor like Daley fit the mood of the times. Opposition aldermen in the council could not create sustained criticism and alternative programs that were as attractive to Chicagoans as what Daley and his machine could offer. Chicagoans, as always, were willing to put up with a little graft and corruption as long as city services were provided.

The years 1955–1956 were a time of centralizing power and rebuilding parts of the city, especially the downtown. It set a pattern that Richard J. Daley was to follow for the next twenty years. Historian Roger Biles characterized this period as follows:

> Seizing power from the disreputable city council whose defalcations had earned its members the ignominious nickname "the gray wolves," Daley muted the prevailing image of venality, assumed control of the budget process, and centralized all patronage matters. . . . Because he also ruled the Democratic machine autocratically, the mayor centralized power in the city in a manner reminiscent of the Kelly-Nash era. Businessmen, government officials, labor union leaders, and national politicians knew that one man possessed the authority to speak and to act for Chicago.[10]

However, if one man possessed "the authority to speak and act for Chicago," then neither the people's representatives in the city council nor the people themselves possessed that power. At first, there was relief that the Council of Gray Wolves, which had reemerged in Mayor Kennelly's reign, was now under the control of a "boss" mayor once again. The business community and the newspapers that had opposed Daley's election in 1955 quickly backed Daley as the man who could "get things done." Mayor Daley's first administration boasted of dozens of completed public works, 475 new garbage trucks, 174 miles of new sewers, 69,600 new street and alley lights, 72 downtown parking facilities, 2,000 new policemen, and 400 new firemen.[11]

Aldermanic Elections of 1955

The April 5, 1955, general elections ended with the Democrats winning thirty-nine seats in the city council, up five from the thirty-four seats they controlled before the election. In one of the closest elections, Republican Jack Sperling beat far North Side incumbent 50th Ward Democratic alderman Robert Bremer by thirty-one votes, 17,200 to 17,169. But, in general, the Democrats strengthened their control over the council of 1955.[12] One of the most important aldermanic elections was in the 5th Ward, in which a successor to Alderman Robert Merriam was to be chosen. There were four candidates for the seat in this officially nonpartisan election: Leon Despres, a prominent lawyer, state chairman of the Independent Voters of Illinois (IVI), and an active member of the American Civil Liberties Union, ran with the endorsement of both IVI and the Republican Party; Hugh Matchett, a Republican lawyer ran as an Independent; Dorothy O'Brien Morgensten ran with the endorsement of Mayor Kennelly; and George Uretz, a lawyer and former assistant corporation counsel, ran as the 5th Ward regular Democratic organization under the leadership of Democratic committeeman Barnet Hodes.

It appeared, at first, that Dorothy Morgensten would be a strong candidate in Hyde Park because she was on Mayor Kennelly's "blue ribbon" ticket and was the wife of William Morgensten, director of public relations at the University of Chicago. She said that she ran for two reasons: "The first reason I'm in this is that I'm for Mayor Kennelly. . . . The second reason is my intense interest in the conservation for the Hyde Park area, and in extending the conservation movement throughout the city."[13]

It also might have been expected that Hugh Matchett, who was the only registered Republican in the race, would have received the Republican Party nomination and would have been a strong candidate. However, his father, Judge Matchett, had been a political foe of Republican ward committeeman "Bunny" East. Disavowing political motives, East maintained that "the alderman's office belonged to the people, not the politicians and that his organization had always observed the nonpartisan aspect of the aldermanic race." Hugh Matchett argued instead that "Bunny" East had carried factional politics too far when the 5th Ward Republican organization endorsed Despres, a Democrat affiliated the with IVI, which Matchett called "a left wing Democratic organization bordering on socialism."[14]

In the primary, Despres received 6,913 and Uretz, 5,985 votes. Morgenstern came in third with 2,944 votes while Matchett trailed with 1,031. Despres and Uretz, having received the most votes in the primary, were thrown into a runoff election to decide the outcome. Soon after the primary, Mrs. Morgenstern, her supporters, and the backers of Mayor Kennelly in the 5th Ward threw their support to Despres at a tea at the Quadrangle Club of the University of Chicago. With the votes of Independents and Republicans, as well as Kennelly and Merriam supporters, Despres won the runoff election handily. In the final election, while Daley easily defeated Merriam in the mayoral race, Despres won his aldermanic seat with 11,437 votes to Uretz's 7,483.

The Council of 1955

On April 7, when the election results were known, the *Chicago Sun-Times* moaned that the city council would be made up "of many veteran members of the wrecking crew that worked at cross purposes with Mayor Kennelly. Even more distressing is the fact that the minority forces of economy and reform no longer will have the skillful, dedicated leadership of Bob Merriam." The *Sun-Times* feared that with the enlarged Democratic Party majority in the council some reform aldermen would sell out. Its editorial ended: "A vigilant, courageous and fighting reform-economy bloc, such as Merriam once led, would be indispensable in helping the new mayor achieve worth-while ends—and in helping to defeat measures which are dear to the hearts of the council boodlers."[15]

When the new council assembled, a revised economy bloc caucused under the leadership of Republican aldermen Freemen and Geisler, issued a press statement, and demanded four committee chairmanships in the council. However, only Republicans, neither reform Democrats nor Alderman Despres, attended the caucus. Maverick Democrats such as Alderman Seymour Simon did not trust the Republican members of the bloc, and Independent alderman Despres was not yet sure of the effect of the committee assignments and rules, although he voted with the economy bloc frequently after the first council meeting.[16]

In their statement after their caucus members of the economy bloc said, "We shall not be obstructionist. We are not in any way prejudging the mayor's program or the issues to be raised in the new city council. . . . [We pledge to support Mayor Daley in all matters] in the best interests of the people including those in which he may be opposed by elements in his own party."[17] For his part, Mayor Daley replied through a spokesman that he appreciated the "cooperative action" expressed by the Republican aldermen, but whether they should get the four committee chairmanships they requested was "a council matter." Meanwhile, the council's Rules Committee voted to eliminate four committees and to cut the number of aldermen who served on committees.

When the council held its organizing meeting on April 21, 1955, the aldermen approved the proposal by the Rules Committee by a vote of 42–6, with Republicans Geisler, Buckley, Burmeister, Hoellen, Freeman, and Sperling voting against the committee assignments. The Democrats as a bloc, some Republicans, and Alderman Despres voted for the Rules Committee report. The only Republican who had served on the Rules Committee, Alderman Nicholas Bohling, was made chairman of the Committee on Judiciary and State Legislation. However, his committee's authority over aldermanic elections was transferred to the Rules Committee. All of the other committees were chaired by loyal, regular Democrats. The council rules were also changed to create a Finance Committee of thirty-one members instead of all aldermen, as in most previous councils. This meant that only six of the Republicans, including only three economy bloc members, would serve on the most important council committee that handled the most critical legislation. The practice of allowing only aldermen who had served at least one term in the council to serve on the Finance Committee was a 1955 innovation that continues today.

Alderman Bohling, with the support of the other Republican members of the council, attempted to propose an amendment that would make committee assignments effective for only one year instead of the entire four-year term. However, his amendment was defeated by a 38–10 vote along straight party lines, except that Republican Alderman DuBois voted with the Democrats. After that, Bohling gave up, saying, "I have more proposed [rules] amendments, but it looks like introducing them would be a waste of time."[18]

In the new council under Mayor Daley, five aldermen represented the leadership of the council factions and thus it is worthwhile to detail their backgrounds, roles, and perspectives. The five are Aldermen Cullerton, Keane, Depres, Simon, and Hoellen. Alderman P. J. "Parky" Cullerton remained head of the crucial Finance Committee while Alderman Thomas Keane, who would soon take over as Daley's floor leader, headed the Committee on Traffic and Public Safety. Parky Cullerton was born into politics. His granduncle, Edward F. Cullerton, was an alderman for forty-eight years, longer than anyone else. But Parky Cullerton was also politically savvy. It is said that he never introduced an ordinance that failed to pass, although in later years as the mayor's floor leader he found it much easier to pass his legislation. He made it a rule "to listen more than he spoke," so he left most of the floor debate to others such as Keane.

Parky Cullerton was elected 38th Ward Democratic committeeman during the Depression in 1932 and then 38th Ward alderman in 1935. He was later involved in various scandals. In the early 1950s the Building and Zoning Committee, which he chaired, spent $160,000 preparing a new zoning ordinance that accusers argued should have cost about $7,000. The extra money, of course, went to relatives and friends of the politicians on the committee.[19]

Like many aldermen, Cullerton had limited formal education. He had attended Crane Technical High School and then studied electrical engineering two years at Lewis Institute, which later merged into the Illinois Institute of Technology. After returning from the service in World War I, he went to work for his father, who was a building contractor. He next became an electrical engineer in the city's fire alarm office and then was named to the Board of Local Improvements. He served as alderman from the 38th Ward from 1935 until 1958. In those twenty-three years he never missed a council meeting. He was a crusty, blunt-speaking Chicago politician who became head of the city council Finance Committee when Daley became head of the Central Committee of the Democratic Party and for a similar reason, the death of former alderman Clarence Wagner in a car crash. However, his election as Finance Committee chairman came with a struggle.

There was a battle of epic proportions between Alderman Tom Keane's former law partner, William Lancaster, and Cullerton for Finance Committee chairmanship. "Votes among aldermen were being solicited at a high bid of $5,000 a crack for the coveted post, which was then a sure ticket to fame and riches and gave its holder the position of administration floor leader."[20] In this battle, Cullerton simply had more votes than Lancaster and Keane could buy.

After serving twenty-three years in the city council, Cullerton was appointed county assessor and then reelected in four-year intervals from 1958 to 1974. As assessor he was plagued by scandals. He was investigated by a state senate committee for giving tax breaks to wealthy owners of downtown high-rises in return for large campaign contributions. Finally, eighteen of his employees were convicted of bribery and corruption. Even though he wasn't indicted or convicted, he was convinced by the party not to seek reelection as assessor because he had become a liability to the entire party ticket.[21]

In 1958, when Cullerton was appointed assessor, Alderman Thomas E. Keane replaced him as chairman of the Finance Committee and as floor leader for Mayor Daley. Tom Keane was also born into politics. His father, Thomas P. Keane, had served as alderman from 1931 until his death in 1945. His son, Thomas E. Keane, then took over the 31st Ward seat from 1945 to 1974. When Tom Keane was sent to jail for corruption, mail fraud, and conspiracy, his wife, Adeline Keane, held the seat from 1974 to 1979. Then the Keane political dynasty ended.

Keane, a lawyer, was first elected to the state senate in 1938 and served until he replaced his father in the city council in 1945. "Keane was confident and sometimes ruthless. His brilliance was unquestioned. He grabbed for power in the city council and played a key role in dumping . . . Martin H. Kennelly as mayor in 1955, clearing the way for . . . Richard J. Daley to win the office. Keane and Daley worked well together—the mayor interested in amassing great local and national political power and Keane in becoming chairman of the important Finance Committee and floor leader of the council."[22] As he would later tell journalist Mike Royko, "Daley wanted power and I wanted money; we both got what we wanted."[23] "Keane was . . . the master mechanic in City Hall at the peak gearing of the Machine. He was a brilliant, sarcastic born-politician."[24] Jay McMullen, a long-time journalist who later married Mayor Jane Byrne, described Alderman Keane's methods of operating this way:

Keane is the mayor's chief City Council confidante and hatchetman. . . . As the Mayor's floor leader, Keane must push administration measures through the Council, easy work considering the lopsided 38 to 12 majority the administration can command on a party-line vote. . . . Keane conducts Council debates like a symphony director, often with an accompanying cacophony of discordant sound that leaves television viewers aghast. He confers with his cronies before each meeting at which controversial measures are coming up. They marshal their arguments and Keane parcels out little batches of them to the men he wants to back him up in floor debate.

When the voting starts, he looks over to Ald. Fred Roti (1st Ward) and gives the signal—sometimes a mere nod of his head—on how to vote. The others follow Roti. When it is a particularly obnoxious measure presented by a Republican or independent, Keane might turn thumbs down to Roti, like some Caesar dispatching a fallen gladiator.[25]

At an aldermanic Christmas party in 1972 Mayor Daley affirmed, "I couldn't have done what I've done without Ald. Keane."[26] But in October 1974, Keane's career ended ignobly with a conviction in federal court for conspiracy to defraud and mail fraud. He was sentenced to five years in a federal penitentiary and a $27,000 fine for acts like making lush profits on a 148-acre tract of prime Chicago-owned land in suburbia after he pushed the sale through the city council; getting an associate an assessment cut of $229,248; selling off a city street so that the Sears Tower could be built; and gaining a $2.7 million assessment reduction for the Hyatt Regency O'Hare Hotel based on a misleading complaint submitted on behalf of the hotel's owners. Many similar conflicts of interest would be unveiled at Keane's trial in 1974, but in the council of 1955 he was just moving up in power. Only after Cullerton was promoted to assessor in 1958 would Keane become the most powerful political figure next to Richard J. Daley for the two decades before his fall.

No account of the council of 1955 would be complete without a description of Alderman Despres, who led the opposition to Mayor Daley for the next twenty years. Many have claimed that he is the greatest alderman in Chicago's history, and he certainly stands with his Hyde Park predecessors Charles Merriam and Paul Douglas as a great Chicago reformer. Reporter Lois Wille, writing about Despres in 1970, opined:

This week's City Council meeting was worse than usual. A number of administration alderman called [Despres] "liar" and "distorter" and "hypocrite" and "prophet of doom," as they normally do. Then Mayor Richard J. Daley himself left the rostrum to denounce Despres from the council floor.

Never before has the mayor been moved to step from the rostrum to debate. . . . And then Alderman Kenneth Campbell (20th) got up and called

[Despres] "consistently illogical and consistently a dissenter." . . . No sooner does floor leader, Thomas E. Keane (31st) produce an administration proposal than Despres is on his feet, dissecting it, heading straight for the nerve center . . . pouring out a dazzling array of statistics and studies and sociology and sheer guts. . . . What keeps him going is that every so often, usually after years of fighting, one of his proposals finally makes it through the council. . . . "You just have to push, squeeze, cajole, pressure, and keep pressuring, maneuvering," he said. Then with an aroused press and public, "the administration finally introduces the proposal as its own."[27]

Despres grew up in Hyde Park. He had a successful career as a labor lawyer as well as an outstanding tenure as a Chicago alderman for twenty years. He was the lone Independent alderman in the council from 1955 to 1959, although he often joined with Republicans from the economy bloc on budget measures and administrative reforms. He often found them to be unreliable supporters of the measures he proposed, however.

Jay McMullen, at the time of Despres's retirement in 1974, described his council role this way:

Leon Despres combined the preaching fervor of a country parson, the intellectual power of a Hyde Park egghead, and the wrath of a Lucifer when he mounted one of his frequent attacks on the policies of Mayor Richard J. Daley.

He never feared to stand alone on an issue—even when his fellow liberals ran out on him. He presented an unforgettable scene, standing there railing at the gods of City Hall and, as it were, daring them.

His tirades are legendary. There was no oratorical weapon of which he was not the master. He used satire, cold reason, sentiment, biting wit and humor, his own lofty idealism and morality, just plain good sense and an amazing physical endurance in his appeals to change the course of city government.

Despres often stood on his feet all day at council sessions, displaying an awesome grasp of legislative issues equalled only by Ald. Thomas E. Keane (31st), the mayor's council floor leader. Their legislative duels were brilliant episodes of erudite conflict in otherwise agonizing marathons of tedium.[28]

It was clear from Despres's first day in the city council that he was going to be an outsider clashing with the mayor and the regular Democratic aldermen. At that meeting Daley told him, "We're going to put you down just as we put [Robert] Merriam down."[29] But the party was never able to defeat Despres in elections, even though he lost vote after vote in the council.

In 1956, Despres had an important success with behind-the-scenes support from Mayor Daley and Alderman Keane. He actually passed an ordinance under his own name that took control of driveway permits from the aldermen and made these permits an administrative decision by the Department of Streets and Sanitation. It eliminated a major source of aldermanic corruption and further weakened the power of the aldermen. But over the years, most of Despres's proposals fared differently. He fought for seven years before the administration moved to outlaw racial discrimination by real estate brokers, and he fought to control lead poisoning for three years before the majority voted to restrict the lead content of paint.

Contrary to the myth that machine aldermen got better services than Independent aldermen such as Despres, he actually got very good city services for his constituents. But in the end Despres was to leave behind a greater and very special legacy from his work in the city council. As reporter David Axelrod noted, "Despres' tribute is, fittingly, not a material one. It comes every time an independent alderman rises in the City Council to expose corruption and discrimination in the municipal government. He was their mentor, and now they carry on in his tradition. And in the long run, this will be a greater honor to Despres, and more beneficial to the people of Chicago, than a bridge, or a road, or a school in his name."[30]

Although his role in the 1955 city council was less central than that of Cullerton, Keane, or Despres, 40th Ward alderman Seymour Simon, who also was first elected in 1955, played a unique role. In the 1955–1956 city council he voted 85 percent of the time with Alderman Cullerton, Daley's floor leader. But this meant that he opposed the administration 15 percent of the time on key divided roll call votes, which was a lot for a Democratic alderman. As his career continued, he became more and more of an enigma to the regular machine aldermen. Alderman Simon said, "I'm not trying to prove anything. I'm just trying to represent the people who elected me." He would later say about his more controversial decisions on the state supreme court, "I think I've always been one to stand up and speak my own mind and march to my own drumbeat." Alderman Simon's independence is a good example of why Daley's control over the city council was not complete when he became mayor in 1955.[31]

Simon was born in Chicago in 1915 and lived in Lawndale with his family, who later moved to Albany Park on the North Side in 1924. He attended Northwestern University and Northwestern University Law School. Since his father was a lawyer and Seymour liked to debate, he followed in his father's footsteps and became a lawyer. After law school he worked in the Justice Department in Washington, D.C., and returned to

Chicago after World War II. Wanting to run for public office some day, in 1952 he became a precinct captain in the 40th Ward.

Simon was elected 40th Ward alderman because Alderman Benjamin Becker, who was supposed to seek reelection, was added to the Democratic Party slate when the slate makers needed a Jew to run against Morris Sachs for city clerk. When Becker moved up, Seymour Simon was slated for 40th Ward alderman and continued on the ballot as the Democratic nominee, even after Becker was dropped from the slate by Daley when he was accused of splitting legal fees with another attorney in cases involving city matters.

This is Alderman Simon's recollection of the council meetings in 1955:

> I used to love to go to those meetings. You'd go down that back hallway. I used to feel this was like a baseball player must feel going out through the tunnel to the dugout to get in the ball game. The council had a lot more arguments and differences of opinion and debates in those first six years [I served in the council] than it had when I came back to it in 1967. It was a much more open body. Daley did not like being opposed in any way. He would show his dislike, particularly for Democrats who opposed him. I did on several occasions, but he made no effort to cut down speeches and clamp down on the debate the way he did later on.[32]

From 1955 to 1961 Simon was sometimes a "backup man" who helped Tom Keane defend city proposals against attack. In 1961 he was chosen to replace Sidney Deutsch, who had died, as finance chairman on the Cook County Board of Commissioners. Following the death of another alderman, Simon advanced to become Cook County Board president from 1962 to 1966. But Democratic Party leaders became disenchanted when Simon failed to agree to their deals and patronage, and he was purged from the 1966 party slate. Consequently, Republican Richard Ogilvie was elected county board president and went on to become a distinguished Republican governor of Illinois. Seymour Simon, even after the purge, continued to have strong support in the 40th Ward, where he remained Democratic ward committeeman. In 1967, he was reelected 40th Ward alderman and served in that capacity until 1980. During his second city council era, he was a thorn in the side of Mayor Daley and his floor leader, Alderman Keane. He recalled these as

> the years of my greatest fun in politics. I realized I wasn't going to become governor or United States senator. I didn't have to watch my number and I figured I'd just have a good time in council. I'd say what I had to say, I'd do what I wanted to do, and I just would be my own man completely. When I

look back at those years, when I think of times when I was up there shaking my fists at this great and mighty leader, and the great and mighty leader was screaming back at me through the microphone, and the tussles I had with him, the number of times I stood up to him, belly to belly, and several of those times he backed away. I enjoyed it. Not many people had the opportunity or the courage to stand belly to belly with him. It was a frightening thing, particularly when he'd start yelling up there from the microphone.[33]

Finally in 1980, the Democratic Party slate makers agreed to slate Alderman Simon for the state supreme court in return for his promise to support the entire party ticket. He served as Illinois Supreme Court justice until his retirement in 1988.

On the Republican side of the aisle from 1947 to 1975 was 47th Ward alderman John Hoellen, who was born in 1914 and lived in the North Side German neighborhood called Ravenswood. His father had been born of German parents in Chicago and had served in the city council from 1925 to 1933. Hoellen declared that his father "was crucified by the machine" and died of a heart attack in 1936, just forty-nine years old. Hoellen "always felt that the machine was evil because of all the evil they wreaked upon my father." Like Alderman Simon, Hoellen had gone to Northwestern University and Northwestern University Law School.

He was elected to the council as a Republican in 1947 and reelected six times. He later ran against Daley as a Republican candidate for mayor in 1975. Hoellen describes his early years in the council this way:

It was a sickening and terrifying experience to be involved in the city council during that period. Graft was rampant. I was shot at on January 21, 1947, by a hoodlum. He had been told that if he killed [me], he would be able to take over gambling in the 47th ward. . . . Each gambling joint (there were three of them operating when I first became alderman) had a daily gross of $45,000, of which $15,000 was net profit. If you tried to cut in on $15,000 a day, you were dealing with some very big numbers, and the syndicate in Chicago was a very rough and tough organization, but I stayed in [government] and tried to change the system."[34]

Hoellen would later say, "Mayor Daley always looked at [opposition] as a kind of cancer and he struggled to eliminate all of his opposition to stifle it. He brooked no quarter. . . . Daley as a politician is as smart as an alley rat. He is vindictive, knows nothing but raw power, and the sharp fang, and he will use it wherever he can in order to obtain his goals."[35] Alderman Hoellen, from Daley's first election as mayor in 1955, was a leader of the Republican opposition. However, the number of Republican aldermen continued to dwindle and they became less and less a force in the council until 1977, when there would be no Republican aldermen left. Even today there is only one Republican among the fifty aldermen.

The City Budget in 1955–1956

Immediately after the 1955 election, Mayor Daley adopted a more active and cooperative role with the city council than Mayor Kennelly had. Mayor Daley at his inauguration in April 1955 vowed: "I have no intention of interfering in any way with the proper function of the City Council. But, as mayor of Chicago, it is my duty to provide leadership for those measures which are essential to the interests of all the people—and, if necessary, to exercise the power of veto against any measures that would be harmful to the people."[36] As his first year in office advanced, however, he gained dominance over the council and shaped it to his will. At first he was deferential to aldermen and hesitant in the legislation he presented to the council. But as he gained confidence, he became stronger and more willing to act. In later years, he would become sterner, more dogmatic, and less willing to tolerate any opposition that questioned his absolute authority.

In the first week after he became mayor, Daley's Bridgeport friend and administrative aide Matthew Danaher, who would later become involved in corruption scandals, served as traffic director for a stream of aldermanic visitors. Early visitors included regular Democrats such as Aldermen Bieszczat, Marzullo, and Holman. But they also included Independent alderman Len Despres, who said of his meeting: "The mayor asked me to support him when I thought he was right and to oppose if I thought he was wrong." In the press and in these meetings Daley indicated that he intended "to work closely with aldermen rather than adopt a hands-off attitude toward the City Council as Kennelly did."[37]

The most important battles in Daley's first term were budget and tax issues. They included tough votes on sales taxes, aldermanic expense accounts, utility taxes, and the first city budget of the Daley administration. The first financial battle in the council was a half cent increase in the sales tax presented by Mayor Daley on July 7, 1955. It was adopted by a vote of 42–3 after a wild floor fight in which Mayor Daley verbally attacked Southeast Side Republican alderman Nicholas J. Bohling. The proposed Daley ordinance raised the sales tax from two and a half cents to three cents, providing the city of Chicago an additional $21,648,000 a year. Alderman Bohling made a motion to defer action on the sales tax, which Alderman Einar Johnson seconded. When he renewed his motion just before the final votes on the tax, however, it died for lack of a second. He then moved that the sales tax increase be repealed if the revenue article of the state constitution were revised to permit broader municipal taxing powers. This amendment failed 37–9, with voting along strict party lines and only Republicans backing Alderman Bohling. Then Alderman Johnson moved to make the tax effective only until December 31, 1957, as demanded by the retail stores in the city. Alderman Johnson's amendment was defeated 35–10, with only Democratic alderman Seymour Simon joining the Republicans.

When Bohling then asked Daley to make a formal statement in the council's *Journal of Proceedings* that the increase would be removed as soon as the state revenue article was revised, Daley exploded. "Daley arose in his seat on the rostrum and took the floor. He started out in a firm, quiet voice, but soon his voice rose, his face grew red, and he waved his arms. He accused Bohling of doubting his word, and added: 'In 25 years of political life it has never been necessary for anyone to have the written word back up the oral word of the man in this chair. I have said to the members of the legislature, to the people, to the members of the City Council that the sales tax will end as soon as other sources of revenue are available.'"[38] After all amendments failed and after Daley's outburst and tirade against Bohling, only three aldermen voted against the sales tax: Bohling, Johnson, and Despres.[39]

Along with the new sales tax, a supplemental 1955 budget was submitted for $6.8 million from the additional sales tax revenue that year to be used to hire 1,000 new policemen and 500 firemen, and to expand refuse collection and street cleaning. Since the city did not get home rule taxing powers to create new taxes until the new state constitution was ratified in 1970, the city's sales tax only grew larger and the 1955 increase was never repealed. By 1999, the combined state, city, and county sales taxes had grown from 3.0 percent to 8.75 percent. The additional policemen, firemen, and city services paid for by the sales tax increase had an important political effect, helping solidify Daley's position as mayor, increasing citizen satisfaction with city services, and causing voters to reelect him in his critical first reelection in 1959. He had followed the advice of Alderman Joseph Rostenkowski (the father of later Congressman Dan Rostenkowski) to "put the money where [citizens] can see it." The sales tax increase was used "to buy better government" and to secure Daley's reelection.[40]

Following the recommendations of the Chicago Home Rule Commission, Mayor Daley had convinced the state legislature to change state law to give the mayor the right to draft the city budget. In the months before he was elected, his ally state senator William Lynch steered the bill through the legislature, which transferred authority for presenting the budget from the council to the mayor's office. During the long period of the Gray Wolves and all previous city administrations, the city council drafted the city budget, although the city departments and the mayor might issue reports and make recommendations on various budget line items. From 1955 on, the mayor would propose a line-item budget for every penny to be spent and the aldermen could only revise or ratify it. This had the profound effect of changing Chicago government from a strong council–weak mayor form of government to a strong mayor–weak council government in practice. And this trend was only accelerated as Daley's councils were reduced more and more into the mold of rubber stamps.[41]

In November 1955, Mayor Daley introduced his first city budget under the new state law. But instead of examining the overall massive city budget, the aldermen and the public focused on one small budget item. Aldermen were prevented by state law from raising their own salaries of $5,000 a year. However, they did propose to raise their expense accounts from $1,800 to $3,000 a year, which raised their overall payments of salaries and expenses by 16 percent. In addition to their salaries and expense accounts, they also received a $55 per month car allowance for travel and a salary for one secretary. The aldermen argued that their parking fees were greater than their $55 car allowance and that they "are clouted for all kinds of tickets for benefits, advertising programs and local school, church and parish functions . . . evenings at bingo games and other functions. . . . Every summer there are picnics you can't avoid. . . . Aldermen have a good deal more coming [than just a $1,200 raise in their expense accounts]."[42]

Alderman Despres revealed that his aldermanic service office was budgeted to spend $10,541 in 1956, much more than his aldermanic expense account. The 5th Ward aldermanic budget is shown in Table 4.1. Despres maintained that "a conscientious alderman needs two assistants, one for ward work and one for municipal legislative and administrative work." In addition to his important legislative work, Alderman Despres determined that each year his aldermanic office handled nearly 4,000 citizen inquiries, requests for city services, and complaints.[43]

The media and the public were not persuaded, however. In the words of the *Chicago Sun-Times*:

> Under ideal conditions a good argument could be made for raising the salaries of Chicago's aldermen. For example, if even a bare majority of the City Council members were conscientious, hard-working public servants, the voters probably would not begrudge a pay boost for all of them. But twice in recent years—in 1953 and 1946—the voters emphatically turned down proposals to increase aldermanic salaries. The voters just aren't convinced that the aldermen are worth more than $5,000 a year in terms of services rendered, character, competence or reliability.[44]

TABLE 4.1   Fifth Ward Budget, 1956

Expense	Costs in Dollars
Salaries, 2 secretaries & cleaning man	1,800
Social Security	4,200
Telephone	900
Lighting	140
Office supplies, stationery	150
Maintenance & scavenger	300
Accounting	125
Postage	150
Newsletters	900
Contribution drive expenses	300
Miscellaneous	1538
Insurance	38
TOTAL	10,541

After all the public and newspaper debate, when the vote on the budget was taken in December 1955, the aldermen got their expense account raise. Alderman Despres was allowed by the mayor to move this amendment to the budget. He spoke briefly, repeating the argument that the "expense of aldermanic offices run between $10,000 and $11,000 a year" and that even with the $1,200 expense account increase, aldermen would "run a considerable deficit." The increase was then adopted by voice vote, with only North Side Democratic alderman Hartigan voting against the proposal.[45]

In addition to the aldermanic expense accounts, a number of other issues came up in the budget hearings. An example of the range of issues debated as departments defended their budgets was Alderman Despres's attempt to eliminate $70,000 for the police censorship board. Until the 1980s, the police censored films shown in Chicago, and the proposed 1956 city budget included salaries for thirteen individuals needed to censor movies and to guarantee that the censored sections of the films were not shown to the public. In the conservative, Democrat-controlled city council of the 1950s, and for several decades afterward, the Despres amendment was defeated in the Finance Committee hearings. The censorship board remained, but the budget hearings provided an opportunity to debate ending local movie censorship.[46]

Before the overall city budget was adopted, the mayor moved to create a "gross receipts tax" on utility companies, including the gas, electric, and telephone monopolies in Chicago. The three ordinances to tax each company's gross earnings at 5 percent passed by identical 38–9 votes on

December 1, 1955. The debate on the measures lasted two hours. Mayor Daley's backers supported the new tax on the grounds it was needed to carry out "a vast program of improvements, including better street cleaning and more police and fire protection." The new taxes would bring the city approximately $21,500,000 annually.

> During the debate on the three ordinances, [Republican Alderman] Allen A. Freeman (48th) charged [that] he [had] supported the recently adopted 2 cent city sales tax because he felt it would be sufficient to help the city improve its facilities. "This is no time to kill the goose that laid the golden egg," Freeman argued. "Passing the utility tax in addition to the sales tax is nothing more than increasing the sales tax. This utility tax will be passed on to consumers for services they buy from the companies." . . .
>
> [Alderman Dubois (9th) said he would support the proposal but would demand a reduction in the tax rate on real estate next year. Mayor Daley later said that he would "lead the fight next year for a reduction in the tax rate on real estate." In the end, however, there was no comparable property tax reduction in 1956.]
>
> Defending the mayor's request for the utility tax, [regular Democratic] Ald. Mathew W. Bieszczat (26th) . . . said Chicago's neighborhoods have been neglected too long because the city fathers feared to impose new taxes. "This town has been asleep for many years because we oppose taxes for new revenue," he said. "No wonder people are moving to the suburbs where they're willing to pay higher taxes as long as they get the services they need."[47]

Daley won the new utility taxes, which were primarily opposed by members of the economy bloc. However, aldermanic voting on this controversial tax increase was not strictly by political party. Voting against were Aldermen Despres, Johnson, Laskowski, Buckley, Immel, Burmeister, Hoellen, Freeman, and Sperling. The council's lone Independent, some Democrats, and some Republicans opposed the tax increases.

All of these maneuvers over new taxes and aldermanic expense accounts finally led to the vote on the budget itself. On December 12, 1955, the aldermen unanimously approved Mayor Daley's first city budget of $562,462,214. "The unanimous vote was the first in the memory of veteran observers. Mayor Daley had tears in his eyes as he thanked aldermen for their display of confidence in his administration. He vowed: 'With the help of God, I hope I will be able to do for my family and you what you have a right to expect.'" This unanimous approval, however, came only after the economy bloc had offered fifty amendments that would have saved nearly $2 million in a very long ten-hour council meeting. Some of the proposed budget amendments called for the following:

1. raising the pay of ranking police and fire officers
2. reducing appropriations of city council committees by $181,000
3. eliminating fifty jobs in the municipal court bailiff's office for a savings of $218,000
4. reducing the cost of maintaining the police and fire telegraph system by $190,500
5. eliminating the Bureau of Sewers to save $547,114[48]

Eight separate packages of budget amendments received roll call vote support ranging from a low vote of eight in favor to a high vote of fourteen in favor and thirty-six opposed. In the end, however, all budget amendments were defeated. After ten hours of debate, four of the economy bloc aldermen who had voted against the budget in the original roll call changed their votes. Alderman Bohling said although he was not in favor of what he termed "across the board [pay] raises [for city employees]," he thought the new executive budget should be passed. Aldermen Sperling thought that "this was a hopeful administration" and Freeman said, "in all fairness to the Mayor he should change his vote." Even Alderman Hoellen, who had led the filibuster, voted for the new budget, though he still believed that the budget should have provided for "700 new policemen and should get rid of the payrollers."[49] Alderman Despres said, when the budget passed, "in voting for the budget I do not mean to indicate any change or weakening of position. I favored all the amendments we voted on, and I think this budget would be a better document if they had been adopted. But we now have the responsibility of passing a budget for the city of Chicago for 1956. It would be a better budget with the amendments. But here it is. In city government there are always two basic problems—what do you get and what do you pay for it. We know now how much money we have to pay for it. Let us hope that in 1956 we will all work to get our money's worth to make and keep Chicago a good place to live in."[50]

Consolidating Daley's Power

The general trend in the city council in the Daley years was ever greater mayoral control and less powerful aldermen. One of the most important pieces of legislation in the 1956 council brought another shift of power away from aldermen. Driveway permits had long been a principal source of corruption for aldermen and an embarrassment for the city administration. At its January 18, 1956, meeting the council focused on a major fight over a Crime Commission report. While they did, Alderman Despres quietly introduced a reform proposed by the Chicago Home Rule

Commission that had failed in the previous council. Permits for driveways to homes and businesses were granted until 1956 by city council ordinance. As the newspapers put it: "It has long been charged that some aldermen receive payoffs for obtaining council approval for driveways. By 'aldermanic courtesy,' if the local alderman fails to approve, the permit is not issued."[51]

Alderman Keane was the "guiding hand" behind the ordinance, and support from Daley and Keane was key to the ordinance's passage. Despite their support, however, the newspapers declared, "a rough fight is expected when the ordinance is up for study before the committee on local industries, streets and alleys, headed by [regular Democratic] Ald. Harry Sain (27th)." Then to the surprise of political observers, Alderman Harry Sain announced that he favored divesting the council of the power to issue driveway permits.[52]

To build public support for the ordinance, Alderman Despres wrote an op-ed piece in the *Chicago Daily News* to make the case for reform.

> At present, an owner can obtain a driveway permit only if the City Counci passes a specific driveway ordinance. The practical effect of this procedure is to give the alderman of the ward complete legislative discretion on whether or not there will be driveways, and, if there are any, their width, location and number. Therefore, we necessarily have 50 separate standards, one for each ward. . . .
>
> In a great modern city, however, driveway permits should be governed by uniform, fair and ascertainable rules, with proper right of appeal against injustices. The Chicago Home Rule Commission, which was a distinguished body of municipal experts and included Alderman Bohling, Cullerton and Keane, unanimously recommended that the City Council delegate its driveway permit power.[53]

An existing civic organization, Citizens of Greater Chicago, followed a week later with a letter to the editor revealing that since April 1955 some 4,187 driveway permits had been introduced by the aldermen and that the large number of permits and the aldermen's other duties make it "exceedingly difficult to make an objective evaluation of each driveway proposal." They also reminded voters that the Home Rule Commission had maintained that "the City Council is unnecessarily engaging in administrative matters that can be much better and more promptly performed by the regular administrative agencies."[54]

The Committee on Local Industries held a hearing on the ordinance on March 13, 1956, and voted against the ordinance, 8–2. Alderman Despres was able to get ten civic organizations, including the Chicago Bar Association, to testify in favor of the ordinance, but they were not enough to sway the committee. Alderman Simon then produced four witnesses from his Northwest Side ward

> who testified that unpleasant motels or skating rinks were next door to them or that Alderman Simon had prevented them by withholding driveway permits. They said they favored . . . leaving . . . the power with the alderman who would use his judgment to protect the neighborhood. [One of Alderman Simon's witnesses] told of six motel sites and one factory site which are zoned under the present and prospective zoning ordinance [in and around the 40th Ward], where refusal of driveway permits would protect the neighborhood. [This community leader] said that with a petition bearing 2,000 signatures he felt able to sway any alderman and he did not feel able to sway a commissioner of streets and sanitation.

At the end of the hearing, however, Alderman Despres concluded that the presentations of the witnesses for and against the ordinance, as usual in council hearings, did not change the opinion of any of the aldermen.[55]

Since Despres did not feel that the ordinance would pass at the March 14 council meeting, he had the committee report deferred and published. The newspapers were uniformly pessimistic about the ordinance's chances of passing after the negative committee vote.[56] However, on March 28 the council voted 28–20 to give up their power over driveway permits. The debate took two hours and the opposition, sensing impending defeat, put the ordinance with routine legislation in the omnibus vote at the end of the meeting so that they would not be on record as opposing it. However, that approach didn't work because Republican alderman Patrick Petrone moved that the ordinance be sent back to the corporation counsel and the committee for further study. Alderman Hoellen moved to table Petrone's motion. The aldermen, after Mayor Daley spoke of giving his endorsement to the Despres proposal, voted for Alderman Hoellen's motion, 28–20.

In opposing the driveway permit ordinance, Alderman Simon argued that "the measure is theoretically appealing, but practically unsound" because the issuance of permits will become "virtually automatic. . . . This thing has been represented as a reform measure. I'm in favor of reform. But I, for the life of me, can't see how this is a reform measure. Reform is not surrender and submission to big business and gas companies." In his flip answer to Alderman Simon, Alderman Keane remarked, "This isn't reform: it's progress."[57]

The turning point, however, came after Alderman Petrone made his motion to send the ordinance back to the corporation counsel and the Committee on Local Industries, Streets, and Alleys for further study.

Mayor Daley at that point in the debate assured the council that he would not allow any law to go into effect without having standards spelled out. "The requirements for the permits will be spelled out step by step. . . . Henceforth permits will be issued strictly on a basis of good zoning and good traffic engineering." Then Alderman Hoellen, in speaking for his proposal to table Alderman Petrone's motion, said, "Too long has the city council been regarded as a bunch of grafters and boodling politicians." To which machine Democrat African-American alderman Kenneth Campbell replied angrily, "I had made up my mind to vote for the ordinance despite the sensible arguments by Ald. Simon." But Alderman Hoellen was about to convince him otherwise.[58]

In the face of strong opposition and the fact that even a number of the aldermen who voted for the Despres ordinance and against the Petrone amendments actually favored aldermanic control of driveway permits, why did the ordinance pass? The newspapers offered a series of reasons. First, a referendum on the ballot on April 10 would raise aldermanic pay from $5,000 to $8,000 a year. Although aldermen in the 1956 city budget had enlarged their expense accounts, the referendum was their only hope of raising their pay. So aldermen were reluctant to alienate reform-minded voters who might vote to defeat their pay raises. Second, Mayor Daley clearly supported the Despres ordinance and a vote for the Petrone motion would openly defy his leadership. Aldermen Keane and Cullerton had already passed the word that this was an "administration measure." Third, Alderman Deutsch voted with the majority because he was a candidate for sanitary district trustee in the April primary, just as Aldermen Prusinski and Laskowski voted with the majority because they were both involved in hot fights for ward committeemen in the upcoming election. Finally, as support for the ordinance grew, some aldermen who had opposed it earlier "climbed on the bandwagon."[59]

The key to passing "reform" measures such as the driveway ban or the first Chicago Ethics Ordinance in 1987 was to get the ordinance to the floor of the city council for an official roll call vote before an election in order to put aldermen on the record. Aldermen are afraid to vote against reform measures on the floor if their vote might hurt them in upcoming elections, whereas they are perfectly willing to keep measures bottled up forever in the Rules Committee or vote for other parliamentary ploys that keep reform measures off the floor and prevent an official vote. With the help of Alderman Keane, committee chairman Harry Sain, and Mayor Daley, as well as the threat of the upcoming salary referendum, Despres was able to curb this source of aldermanic corruption and power in 1956. The referendum raising aldermanic salaries to $8,000, which also had Mayor Daley's backing, then passed in the April 10, 1956, referendum. Before 1921, aldermen had been paid $3,500 a year. In 1921, their salary was raised to $5,000. Despite the best efforts of the aldermen over the next thirty-five years, their salaries remained at $5,000 until the referendum of 1956. Salaries remained at $8,000 until 1979 and then increased rapidly. Of course, being an alderman was officially a part-time job with full-time benefits, which made the $8,000 salary in 1956 pretty good. It was less attractive by the 1970s.

The council of 1955–1956, Daley's first year in office, was clearly a rubber stamp council and it stayed that way throughout Daley's reign. Needless to say, the white ethnic aldermen strongly backed Daley, who protected their wards from integration and provided spoils and favors. But during the 1950s and 1960s the black aldermen, with the exception of an occasional Independent, were called the "Silent Six" because they also supported the Daley administration on all votes, even the ones opposing civil rights legislation. They almost never spoke up in council for improved race relations, integration, or even better services for the black community. The economy bloc and Republican aldermen who had provided the primary opposition bloc to Mayor Daley's proposals slowly disappeared from the council. Thus the bloc of all Daley opponents shrunk from twelve in 1955 to as few as three in the 1970s.

Reporter Mike Royko provided the classic description of these Richard J. Daley councils:

> It is his council and in all the years it has never once defied him as a body. Keane manages it for him, and most of its members do what they are told. In other eras, the aldermen ran the city and plundered it. . . . They were known as "the Gray Wolves." His council is known as "the Rubber Stamp."
>
> He looks down at them, bestowing a nod or a benign smile on a few favorites, and they smile back gratefully. He seldom nods at the small minority of white and black independents. They anger him more than the Republicans do, because they accuse him of racism, fascism, and of being a dictator. The Republicans bluster about loafing payrollers, crumbling gutters, inflated budgets—traditional comfortable accusations that don't stir the blood. . . . Sometimes Keane and his trained orators can't shout down the minority so Daley has to do it himself. If provoked, he'll break into a rambling, ranting speech, waving his arms, shaking his fists, defending his judgment, defending his administration, always with the familiar "It is easy to criticize . . . to find fault . . . but where are your programs . . . where are your ideas?" [Or as he would say after the 1968 Democratic National Convention about the protestors: "What trees do they plant?"]
>
> If that doesn't shut off the critics, he will declare them to be out of order.
> . . .
>
> All else failing, he will look toward a glass booth above the spectator's balcony and make a gesture known only to the man in the booth who oper-

ates the sound system that controls the microphones on each alderman's desk. The man in the booth will touch a switch and the offending critic's microphone will go dead and will stay dead until he sinks into his chair and closes his mouth.[60]

Richard J. Daley's Last Years

Because of Daley's successful first term in office, in 1959 Chicagoans reelected him over Republican Tim Sheehan by a vote of 778,612 to 311,940, a landslide margin of 71 percent. But in the 1960s he encountered the civil rights movement and began to lose support in the African-American community because of his staunch support for continued segregation in Chicago.

By the end of Boss Daley's reign in the 1970s the city council was a battleground for cultural and political values, which had emerged with clarity, force, and passion in the 1960s. When Martin Luther King was assassinated in Memphis in 1968, the West Side of Chicago exploded in the largest race riot in Chicago since 1919. During the riots, Mayor Daley gave his infamous "Shoot to Kill" order. After flying over the West Side, where stores had been looted and fires set, Daley said at his City Hall press conference:

> I have conferred with the superintendent of police this morning and I gave him the following instructions, which I thought were instructions on the night of the fifth [the first day of the riots] that were not carried out. I said to him very emphatically and very definitely that an order be issued by him immediately and under his signature to shoot to kill any arsonist or anyone with a Molotov cocktail in his hand in Chicago because they're potential murderers, and to issue a police order to shoot to maim or cripple anyone looting any store in our city.

Daley claimed that he had been misunderstood, but two days later at a council meeting he read a statement drafted by his press secretary and corporation counsel in which he reaffirmed:

> It is the established policy of the Chicago Police Department—fully supported by the administration—that only minimum force necessary be used by policemen in carrying out their duties. But this established policy was never intended to support permissive violence, destruction, and a complete denial of that respect for law which is vital to our democratic way of life. . . . We cannot resign ourselves to the proposition that civil protest must lead to death and devastation—to the abandonment of the law that is fundamental for the preservation of the rights of all people and their freedom.

The council, with the exception of his usual aldermanic critics like Despres, applauded and supported the Boss in 1968. Whatever their personal feelings, if Daley told the police to "shoot to kill," his aldermen would vote the same way. Most aldermen continued to praise the mayor and decry the riots and the rioters. Because of the council's consistent support of racial discrimination, blacks and liberal whites came to understand that the mayor and the council majority were opposed to the civil rights struggle. Continuing confrontation over racial change would shape Chicago politics for decades.[61]

On the heels of the race riots came the clash between anti–Vietnam War forces and supporters of President Johnson and Mayor Daley in August 1968 at the Democratic National Convention. Parallel clashes occurred in the convention hall and in the parks and streets of Chicago. More than 5,000 antiwar protestors and an even larger number of police and national guardsmen sparked a "police riot" that the nation watched on television.[62] The protestors demanded an end to the Vietnam War, less hierarchical control, and an individualism that allowed everyone to "do their own thing." The forces of status quo, symbolized by Mayor Daley, supported hierarchical control, publicly encouraging the president to continue the war, supporting law and order, conforming to social norms, and maintaining private control of property. This became a clash of ideologies about the future of the country as well as a challenge to Mayor Daley's continued control of Chicago.

By the 1970s these clashes, made so graphic by civil rights marches and by protests at the 1968 convention, would recur in city council meetings. What was at stake fundamentally in the various floor fights of the 1970s were two different concepts of democracy—the machine's version of party democracy and the reformers' dream of participatory democracy. Just as pitched battles had surrounded King's march on Cicero or in the streets, parks, and convention hall at the Democratic National Convention, these same conflicts now broke out as legislative clashes within Daley's rubber stamp council.

By the 1970s, most of the Republicans who had made up the economic bloc, providing balance in the 1955 council, had died, retired, been coopted, or been voted out of office. For many years, Despres had been the principal voice of opposition and the "conscience of the council." From time to time he had been joined by black Independent aldermen like A. A. "Sammy" Ranner and William Cousins. After 1968, however, the tide of reform began to rise. In 1969, Bill Singer was elected from the North Side—the first Independent Democrat to break the machine barrier there. In 1971 Despres, Cousins, and Singer were joined by myself and black Independent Anna Langford. We became a hard core of opposition joined often by Father Lawlor (a conservative Catholic priest from the Southwest Side) and Republican John Hoellen. Our group was occasionally enlarged by other Republicans and by Seymour Simon. On rare occasions, we could gather as many as fourteen votes in opposition to the mayor's proposals. In addition to reaching a critical mass in numbers, we had discipline, coordination, commitment, and competence, which made us a force larger than our numbers, much like an opposition party in a parliamentary system. We were supported by social movements, civic and political organizations, volunteers, and money. We could not be bought or corrupted, and we were not easily defeated in elections.

Daley's opposition to the civil rights and peace movements and the "police riot" of 1968 radicalized many liberals, moderates, and civic leaders in Chicago. This changed Daley's treatment in the media. In the past, City Hall reporters and newspaper editors only praised the mayor and blamed corruption and mistakes on government underlings. But then national and international reporters and photographers were beaten up by the Chicago police in 1968. Television cameras recorded live the Chicago police beating young college students. In the eyes of the national media the police were little better than Gestapo troops and Daley little more than a petty dictator.

In 1968 even Hugh Hefner, the hedonistic owner of the *Playboy* magazine empire who lived in the penthouse at the Playboy Building a block off Lincoln Park, was radicalized. He saw cops beat up the kids, and tear gas from the park wafted through his windows. As a result, this most apolitical of businessmen, who made his millions from a slick sex magazine, funded and encouraged a Town Hall meeting in the Old Town neighborhood next to the park. When the Town Hall meeting structure fell apart, we recruited its participants and leaders into the fledgling Independent Precinct Organization, which I founded from volunteers backing Eugene McCarthy for president in 1969. Hugh Hefner's desertion of the Daley regime was duplicated by thousands of other people who saw the clash at the Democratic National Convention firsthand or on television.

Now news stories critical not only of aldermen or city bureaucrats but also of the mayor himself appeared in newspapers and on television and radio. Civic leaders began to publicly oppose the mayor's more foolish schemes like building a third airport in Lake Michigan. More Chicagoans were unwilling to give unqualified support to Mayor Daley's machine in return for providing petty political favors. Public opinion had not swung completely against the mayor. Public opinion polls taken immediately after the 1968 Democratic Convention found that 71 percent of the public supported the Police Department's handling of the demonstrations and 61 percent said that Mayor Daley was doing a good job.[63] The mayor's apologists have taken this as a sign of the correctness of his policies, but this neglects the 40 percent of the public who now opposed the mayor. To successfully run his kind of machine, Daley needed the support of a majority of people, the acquiescence of most citizens, and a small, discredited opposition. Daley now confronted significant public opposition. The job of the opposition bloc in the council was to expand the number of people who opposed the mayor until a majority would be willing to vote against machine candidates for both alderman and mayor.

Our job in the city council opposition was to point out government waste, corruption, and errors, to give voice to previously smothered doubts about the government, to demonstrate mistaken policies Daley and his aldermen adopted, and to hold up an alternative ideal of democracy and justice. Formal democratic rules of the council, despite the tyranny of the majority, made it possible to act out these conflicts on a stage that had the public's attention. Television cameras and radio mikes from the council chambers fed the drama directly to the watching public with little journalistic commentary. Thus I was able to question whether or not the appointment of Tom Keane Jr. was a blatant case of nepotism and corporate favoritism. Daley's raving in response only confirmed that this was indeed the nature of machine politics. It was one thing for Mike Royko to write in his newspaper columns that nepotism existed, but in appointing Keane and in giving his own sons the city's insurance and court receivership business, Daley caused more Chicagoans to question their city government. Only a few Chicagoans were sons or relatives of political bosses who could expect favored treatment, jobs, money, and political spoils. The other 3 million Chicagoans, despite their ability, skills, knowledge, character, or determination, could not get equal treatment from the government they elected and to which they paid taxes. Eventually, citizens would revolt at the ballot box.

By 1971, Mayor Daley was beginning his fifth four-year term of office. Since 1953, as chairman of the Central Committee of the Cook County Democratic Party, he had been the party boss. Since 1955, he had been mayor of Chicago. He had used the power of the two offices to strengthen his control over the party, city council, and Chicago government. Daley loved the city and tried to do what he thought best for it, but he did not brook dissent, nor did he adjust to the social changes sweeping the country. As a "builder mayor," he was able to launch public works projects and encourage private investment, so he had been good for Chicago during the 1950s. By the 1970s, however, he was unable to cope with the city's racial problems, the loss of the city's industrial base, and the demand for greater citizen participation in local government. These weaknesses set the stage for his greatest failures.

Alderman Thomas E. Keane served as Daley's floor leader from 1958 to 1974, coordinating the forty or so machine aldermen who loyally supported Mayor Daley. When Keane was sent to prison, he was replaced as floor leader by Mayor Daley's own 11th Ward alderman, Michael Bilandic. The opposition to Daley, Keane, and Bilandic in the council was still led by Alderman Leon Despres who had served since Daley had first become mayor in 1955. In 1971, Despres was joined by more Independent and opposition aldermen than had served in the council for many years and went from being a lone voice of dissent to a leader of a true opposition bloc.

One of Despres's newfound allies and a sometimes competitor was a new rising star in the Independent Democratic movement, 43rd Ward alderman William Singer, who had grown up on the South Side of Chicago when it was still heavily Jewish. Singer had gone east for his education, first to Brandeis University and later to Columbia University's law school. He was a young, smart, liberal, ambitious lawyer who worked as an intern for U.S. Senator and former alderman Paul Douglas and, later, on Robert Kennedy's campaign for president in 1968. Singer as a reformer scored an upset victory in a special aldermanic election in the then 44th Ward on the North Side of Chicago in 1969. He was redistricted and became 43rd Ward alderman in 1971, when I was elected alderman of the new 44th Ward. Singer loved being an alderman. As he later said:

> You do two different things if you are a full-time, conscientious alderman. One of them is being a legislator. I don't want to be overly critical of my colleagues, but most of them are not legislators. They vote, but they don't draft legislation. They don't think of bills to introduce. They'll put in an order to commend a church for a hundredth anniversary or something, but not real legislation or in spending time on the budget. I made that my special area of interest. I spent hours with Tom Keane learning about that. There weren't more than four or five major pieces of legislation that I eventually got through. But there were a number of pieces of legislation that I did sponsor that were defeated when I sponsored them, but later [were] picked up by the machine. I voted with the machine, or the majority, ninety-five percent of the time, because most of the matters are routine, things that you want to support—motor fuel tax appropriations for street cleaning and snow removal, the sidewalk appropriation increased, things like that. I really liked being a legislator. I liked knowing how to run the city.[64]

Singer was not one to quietly wait his turn in the style of the machine Aldermen. Instead, Singer and Rev. Jesse Jackson of Operation PUSH led an alternate delegation that successfully unseated the Daley-led delegation at the 1972 Democratic National Convention. He was a brash, liberal politician who opposed Mayor Daley because the Daley regime had be-

come too conservative on civil rights, First Amendment rights, and public policy. Daley and his council majority refused to allow up-and-coming
politicians like Singer into positions of power within the machine or the
council. As a result, Singer ran against Daley for mayor in 1975. Retiring
to private law practice after his defeat in that election, Singer became a
successful lawyer and eventually an ally of Daley's son, Mayor Richard
M. Daley, but from 1971 to 1975 he was one of the opposition leaders in
the council building a record from which to run his mayoral campaign.

In 1971 I was elected to the city council for the first time. I was unusual
in Chicago politics in that I was elected alderman after having lived in
the city for only three years. Most aldermen had lived in Chicago their
entire lives, were considerably older, and came up through the political
machine. In contrast, I had grown up in Texas, imbued with the western
cowboy myths of heroic individualism. More importantly, I was a participant in the unpopular civil rights movement in the turbulent 1960s in
the South. I also differed from my fellow council members in profession:
I was a college professor at the University of Illinois at Chicago. Like my
ally Bill Singer and "Young Turks" Edward Vrdolyak and Edward Burke,
I was only thirty when I entered the council. Most powerful aldermen
were in their sixties, as was Mayor Daley. This age difference meant that
younger aldermen had entirely different views on how Chicago should
be governed, and we were not shy about criticizing our elders.

I moved to Chicago in 1967 to teach political science at the University
of Illinois at Chicago, my first real job after completing my Ph.D. I became politically active quickly. In a few months after arriving in Chicago,
I joined the Eugene McCarthy for president campaign, which forced
President Lyndon Johnson to resign and also forced a change in U.S. Vietnam War policies. I first became Ninth Congressional District campaign
manager and, after the primary election, state of Illinois campaign manager for McCarthy through the chaotic 1968 Democratic National Convention in Chicago. After the convention fiasco, a handful of former Mc-
Carthy campaigners and I founded the Independent Precinct
Organization, which helped elect Alderman Singer as the first Independent from the North Side of Chicago to defeat the Daley machine. After
helping elect other North Side Independent state legislators and state
Constitutional Convention delegates, I was elected as 44th Ward alderman and joined Singer in the opposition bloc in the city council in 1971.

I added some of the fervor and tactics of the civil rights and anti–Vietnam war movements to the clashes inside the council chambers. I understood confrontation politics from personal experience and could no more
be intimidated by Mayor Daley and his council supporters than I had
been intimidated by southern bigots setting off pipe bombs or yelling
racial slurs at me in my civil rights protests in Texas. The clash that Daley

and I had over the appointment of Tom Keane Jr. to the Zoning Board of Appeals was emblematic of the battles of the 1970s. Some apologists for the mayor said that his outburst came because he had been upset by his wife's health and had been working too hard. More fundamentally, however, he was protecting the machine's power base. The challenge to Tom Keane, to nepotism, and to favoritism was a challenge to the entire system of machine politics in which Daley was raised.

Only a few years earlier the 1968 Democratic Convention had been the focus for a challenge to the war in Vietnam as well as the power of the president, Democratic Party leaders, and the Chicago police. The battles on the convention floor and the "police riot" on Chicago's streets constituted a turning point in America's politics. That challenge was reenacted in 1971 on the floor of the council. Daley was angry that college students had turned against him and "the establishment." And now a college professor from very campus that he had built, over community opposition, challenged him.

Again, at a March 14, 1973, council meeting two years after the clash over Tom Keane Jr.'s appointment, I raised the issue of nepotism because the mayor gave city insurance business to the firm of Heil & Heil, which employed one of his sons. And the local circuit court, whose judges he elected, gave profitable court receiverships to another Daley son. At that meeting, I introduced an accountability resolution that "ordered" the mayor to account for his influence in granting his sons city insurance contracts and lucrative court receiverships.

My resolution proclaimed:

WHEREAS one son of the Mayor of the City of Chicago, is associated with Heil & Heil, Inc., a firm which recently received the major share of the insurance for the City of Chicago;

WHEREAS another son of the Mayor is known to have been appointed attorney for the receiver for an extraordinary number of receiverships by the Chancery Division of the Circuit Court of Cook County . . .

NOW THEREFORE BE IT RESOLVED that the Mayor be asked to account to the City Council at its next regular public meeting as to whether he has unlawfully or unwisely used his influence as mayor of Chicago and President of the City Council to award City of Chicago insurance policies to his son, without competitive bidding;

BE IT FURTHER RESOLVED that the mayor be asked to account to the City Council . . . whether he has unlawfully used his influence as Mayor and as President of the City Council to cause his son to receive undue preference in the allotment of receiverships;

AND BE IT FURTHER RESOLVED that if the Mayor of the City of Chicago shall fail to account for his actions as Mayor and as President of the

City Council . . . *or* if the Mayor shall establish that he did use his influence
as a public official unlawfully or unwisely to benefit members of his family,
the City Council shall carefully consider . . . the possibility of censure under
Rule 50 of the Rules of Order of the City Council.[65]

Alderman Claude Holman, who was chairing this meeting in Daley's
place, refused to let my resolution be presented. So I stood in silent
protest for five and a half hours trying to be recognized. Needless to say,
the effort to pass my resolution failed. The newspapers reported that at a
closed session of the Cook County Democratic Central Committee Daley
blurted out, "If a man can't put his arms around his sons, then what kind
of world are we living in? I make no apologies. If I can't help my sons,
[my critics] can kiss my ass."[66]

Despite the defeat of my accountability resolution, my battle with the
administration over nepotism and favoritism continued. At the next
meeting, in April 1973, I used a parliamentary ruse to raise the issue
again. My criticism of the mayor was contained within a resolution os-
tensibly praising city comptroller David Stahl, who had resigned his city
government post. Stahl had revealed in newspaper interviews that city
insurance had been placed with Heil & Heil on direct orders of Mayor
Daley. Not only did my resolution praising the city comptroller for
telling the truth not get debated, but Daley ordered the police and the
sergeant at arms to forcibly silence and seat me. They were too short and
weak to accomplish their task. Then the mayor ordered my microphone
turned off, but that also failed to silence me. Using a parliamentary ploy,
the mayor's allies finally sent the resolution to the Rules Committee. It
was buried there so that it could not be debated and voted on in the
council in the future. However, it did not prevent me from making future
motions to discharge the committee and from debating the issues on the
floor several more times.

On September 12, 1973, Alderman Keane tried another tactic to eliminate the continuing embarrassment of my accountability resolution. He
had the administration aldermen unanimously support my motion for
immediate consideration of the resolution. In the debate that followed I
cited Daley's repeated assurances to the press since February 27 that he
would have a statement on the insurance and receivership issues "at the
proper time." I now claimed that it was "a matter of [Daley's] word." Daley responded, "Watching your performance here, I am ashamed again
that you are in an educational institution in this state." I replied, "The
question is whether [the council can] make you accountable." Daley
again promised to make a statement on the matter at the proper time and
added, "You don't have to worry about my word. If your word were as
good as mine, you'd be all right." The council then voted 35–7 to defeat

my accountability resolution with Aldermen Despres, Cousins, Lawlor, Langford, Singer, and Hoellen voting with me.[67]

Mayor Daley never publicly answered charges about his family's conflicts of interest. Sometimes, in the early 1970s, city council battles appeared to be about narrow issues like ethics ordinances, freedom of information, or simple demands like numbering legislation and making copies available to the public. Other times larger issues about the future direction of the city and its politics were compressed into volcanic floor debates on nepotism, favoritism, corruption, and demands for greater civil rights for minority groups, women, and homosexuals.

Machine Versus Independent Reform Politics

The city council, as always in Chicago history, faithfully reflected broader city politics. Chicago politics by the 1960s was not primarily defined as Democrats versus Republicans. Between the Civil War and 1931 Republicans mostly dominated Chicago politics, but after 1931 the Democrats won all mayoral elections. Controlling the mayor's office and most of the executive positions in Cook County government, the Democratic Party thus controlled patronage jobs, which guaranteed a paid patronage army to work the precincts. Without patronage the Republican Party fell apart in Chicago. In the 1950s there had been a viable Republican Party and as many as a dozen Republican aldermen in the city council. By 1977 there were no Republicans in the council, and in the 1990s there was only one. As the number of Republicans dwindled, the factional divisions between "machine Democrats" and "Independents," who were primarily liberal Democrats, came to dominate the city's politics. Independents were liberal on national issues like the war in Vietnam and fiscally conservative on city budgets (wanting to eliminate waste and promote efficiency). They strongly favored expanded human and civil rights and also favored citizen participation and control of local government. The machine, on the other hand, was nonideological and focused on gaining and maintaining political power. It favored middle-of-the road national Democratic Party policies, the benefits of the welfare state, local economic development, and keeping political power in the hands of the mayor without undue citizen interference in policymaking.

However, the machine was changing in the 1970s. Although earlier eras had witnessed political machines that offered material exchanges (a job for precinct work, government services for a vote for the party, and government contracts for party contributors) and affective exchanges (cultural incorporation, symbolic recognition, and ethnic representatives in government for immigrant groups), by 1971 the machine was often depending on a commitment model.[68] The Democratic machine still won most elections, not because it delivered government services well to low-income voters or because the precinct captains had face-to-face contact with voters of their own ethnic group, but because the majority of voters in most wards were still convinced that "the party represents the interests of a social class, ethnic group, or a locality with which [the voters] identify."[69] Independents and reformers often seemed to be more concerned with abstract reforms or national political issues and not as interested in the nitty-gritty of local community services.

Material rewards were still key in keeping the loyalty of the party workers, primarily by providing the party precinct captains with government jobs, but the machine was forced to compete with the reformers by appealing to the *values* of the voters. Democratic Party candidates had the advantages of a patronage army to deliver their message, a still popular party label, goodwill from the party's more than forty years in power in Chicago, financial backing from businesses and organized labor, the party's reputation for invincibility to frighten off challengers, and support of regular party leaders throughout the city. But these advantages and the dwindling supply of material rewards were not enough to guarantee that machine candidates would always win. Minorities and women were not being given their fair share of power, and real economic and social issues, such as the loss of manufacturing jobs, racial segregation, and the deplorable condition of the Chicago public schools, were not being solved. The middle class was beginning to conclude that the old-fashioned machine wasn't addressing their concerns. Thus the Democratic Party was beginning to be undermined by the 1970s, even though it still seemed invincible at the beginning of the decade. Yet reformers slowly won more and more elections, undercutting the solid base of the machine.

Coffee Rebellion

While the Republican Party dwindled in Chicago and Independent Democrats became the opposition, there were some stirrings of change in the Democratic Party and among Democratic aldermen. There was even a minirevolt in December 1972 by Young Turk regular Democratic aldermen, which the press called the "Coffee Rebellion." Twenty-three of the regular Democratic aldermen led by Aldermen Ed Vrdolyak, Ed Burke, Clifford Kelly, and Chris Cohen met in a caucus similar to the regular meetings of the opposition bloc. Their stated intent was to focus on some procedural reforms of the council, but their real goal was to gain more power for themselves.

The regular Democratic aldermen in the Coffee Rebellion wanted the right (1) to submit their own legislation with some assurance that it would receive support from the city administration and (2) to have caucuses with Alderman Keane before council meetings so they would know what was going on. However, the rebellion was soon stopped by Mayor Daley and Alderman Keane. As Tom Keane would later say, "We just turned them over our knees and spanked them."[70] Although the rebellion was short-lived, it served notice that some of the younger regular Democratic aldermen were not willing to wait for decades for their chance at power.

Singer described the minimal role allowed even bright machine aldermen: "You could hardly call [the city council] a legislative body. . . . It didn't really meet the standards. When I first went there, there were three or four guys in the city council who just snored. [The mayor's floor leader, Alderman Tom] Keane used to put one of the sergeant of arms next to [Alderman] Brandt, who would fall asleep. There were times when they called his number and he said, "Aye," and went back to sleep. . . . The mayor determined all the legislation. Everything had to come from him. Some guys in the council were smart, the younger guys in particular. [49th Ward alderman and Keane's law partner] Paul Wigoda was not a dummy by any means, and some other guys had some brains, but they all were preempted. If they had an idea, they had to give it to the mayor. If they wanted to introduce it [themselves], it wouldn't go any further than if I [as an Independent alderman] introduced it."[71] As Alderman Ed Burke would later say, "In the years [Daley was mayor] we were useful to fill chairs and vote the way we were told to vote. That was the extent of it."[72]

Council Rules and Freedom of Information

During the last years of Mayor Daley's long reign (1971–1976), critical issues creating dissension and divided roll call votes in the city council fell into five major categories: (1) machine control versus participatory democracy (including council rule battles and fights over freedom of government information), (2) racial discrimination, (3) sexual discrimination, (4) good government reform (honesty, efficiency, and frugality in government including budget issues and tax policies), and (5) national and foreign policy issues like the war in Vietnam.

Commonly recurring fights in the last years of the Daley council were battles over parliamentary rules, which would make information more easily available to aldermen and the public and would let all aldermen play a role in introducing and passing legislation. In addition to the floor fight over nepotism, the issues of freedom of government information, council rules of procedure, and the proposed Home Rule Commission to recommend improvements in city governance occupied many council meetings in 1971–1972. For instance, there were nine separate votes on changing the *City Council's Rules of Procedure* and the appointment of aldermen to committees and committee chairmanships. These fights began even before the April 22, 1971, first official meeting of the new council and continued unabated throughout the year. Votes on the nine proposed rule changes and committee chairmanships ranged from as close as 39–11 to as overwhelming as 41–3.

The battle lines were drawn at the very beginning. On April 8, 1971, the new council held its informal organizing meeting. Alderman Tom Keane, the mayor's floor leader, following tradition, designated ten council members—two from each group of ten wards (wards 1–10, 11–20, 21–30, 31–40, and 41–50) and an additional three at-large members to serve as a special Committee on Committees to organize the council by proposing rules of procedure and committee appointments.[73] Alderman Despres moved to substitute two Independents for two of the at-large members, and his motion was defeated by a vote of 38–9. Freshman alderman and Catholic priest Father Francis Lawlor moved that committee memberships be chosen by lottery, only to have his proposal defeated by a voice vote. Debate then began as to whether all aldermen would be notified of this committee's meetings and allowed to testify before council rules and committee assignments were adopted. African-American alderman William Cousins challenged secret meetings of the committee: "If I'm locked out, I'll act accordingly," he said. "If I'm stepped on, I'll scream. I won't be subjected to tyranny for the next four years." He was answered by administration supporter Alderman Vito Marzullo who replied, "He can holler and scream all he wants to. We're going to run [the Council] the way we want. " Alderman Keane cited the mayoral election results as giving the "mayor a clear mandate" to run the council and the city as he wanted. I then moved that the meeting of the Committee on Committees be publicized and that all aldermen be given the chance to testify before the committee. "Move we adjourn," Alderman Keane shouted, smiling. His motion passed—and set the tone for the next four years.[74]

The Independent (or opposition) bloc of aldermen formed after this informal council session and proposed a comprehensive set of rules changes that included the following:

1. providing more funds for staff assistants for all aldermen
2. holding council meetings in the evening to allow more citizens to attend
3. extending the ten-minute limit on debate to fifteen minutes and not turning off aldermen's microphones at the mayor's orders
4. assigning legislation to committees immediately instead of burying it in Rules Committee

5. giving aldermen the right to vote on appointments individually
6. assigning no alderman to more than six committees and appointing all fifty aldermen to serve on the Finance Committee
7. allowing for minority reports to the council from committees[75]

Needless to say, all of these proposals were dismissed by the Committee on Committees and defeated at the formal council session on April 22, 1971. Throughout the Daley era, the city clerk failed to ever provide a meaningful legislative numbering system, a systematic way of analyzing aldermanic voting patterns, or copies of pending legislation to the public.[76]

Obtaining public information was even more difficult for citizens than for aldermen or the press. In a 1973 memorandum to the League of Women Voters, league officer Andrea Rozran tells a Kafkaesque story of trying to obtain copies of twenty-four ordinances and pending rule amendments on city council reform that had not received a hearing by the council's Rules Committee. After checking with the municipal reference librarian, staff of the Legislative Reference Bureau, city clerk, and staff of the city council Committee on Committees and Rules, she found that copies of this pending legislation were unobtainable. Rozran reported that one city official said, "Such proposals could be misinterpreted by the public, and . . . they are subject to amendment." These comments reflect the generally negative view city officials had of making information public except for puff press releases from the mayor's office.[77]

Racial Discrimination

Throughout Chicago's 150-year history the second most powerful political division after party and factional affiliations has been racial and ethnic identity. Put simply, in Chicago politics, race matters. In the 1971–1976 city councils the racial division that mattered beyond all others was the split between African Americans and whites. This was not so clear at first glance. First, although the percentages of African Americans in the city council always lagged behind their percentage in city population, the council was more racially integrated than the U.S. Congress, the Illinois state legislature, and most legislative bodies in America.

Second, black and white aldermen were part of both the majority and the opposition blocs. Two of the seven core Independent opposition bloc members were African Americans. The other blacks in the council loyally supported Mayor Daley, as had most African-American aldermen since his election in 1955.

A telling vote that demonstrates the role that race played in the city council was on a resolution introduced by Alderman William Cousins on

TABLE 4.2   Racial Characteristics of Chicago-Area Congressmen and
Aldermen, 1971

Racial Group	Chicago Pop. by %	% Chicago Congressman	% Chicago Aldermen
White	58.1	90	72
African American	32.8	10	28
Latino	7.4	0	0
Other Nonwhite	1.7	0	0

SOURCE: Bureau of the Census, *1970 General Social and Economic Characteristics and General Population Characteristics.*

firebombing homes. In April 1971, a black family moved into an all-white neighborhood at 67th and Wolcott on the Southwest Side. A few days later their home was firebombed. Cousins introduced a simple resolution declaring that the city council was opposed to firebombing homes. By a vote of 34–13, and with all but two black machine alderman voting with the majority, the resolution was defeated and sent to the council's Rules Committee for burial. Obviously, on this vote black machine aldermen did not represent the clear position of their African-American constituents, who opposed the racial firebombing of their homes. Of course, white machine aldermen as well as blacks were sometimes forced to vote against the interests and opinions of their constituents because the machine controlled their elections and the patronage jobs for their precinct workers.

This issue was so explosive that the black machine aldermen were fearful that it could be used to defeat them at the next election even if they had the backing of the machine. So at the next council meeting machine black aldermen, with the permission of Mayor Daley, introduced an almost identical resolution which said "that the City Council reaffirms and repledges its concept that all persons have the right to live in any section of the City without fear of violence."[78] After a private meeting in the mayor's office with loyal African-American aldermen, Mayor Daley gave them permission to introduce this resolution, which now passed unanimously with all black aldermen voting in favor.

Ten years later, in reflecting on this strange voting behavior in which firebombing homes was ignored at one council meeting and condemned by the same aldermen at the next meeting, Cousins mused,

I am convinced that many of the black aldermen [in voting against my resolution] voted against their conscience and I know that they voted against the interest of their constituents . . . because they felt compelled to do so out of party loyalty. If voting a certain way was not the party line, they would not vote that way. . . . Blacks have been castrated actually in terms of political representation . . . because they have had to swear allegiance . . . to the party. They have had to understand that even if it requires voting against the interests of their constituency at times, it was necessary that they do that in order that they remain in the good graces of the party. Since the party put them in, the party could take them out [of office].[79]

In July 1969, on another racial issue, Judge Richard B. Austin in *Gautreaux v. CHA* ordered the Chicago Housing Authority (CHA) to desegregate its public housing by building in white neighborhoods in Chicago. In the spring of 1971, CHA submitted to the Chicago City Council and the Chicago Plan Commission a list of 275 sites, which would provide approximately 1,700 units of low-income family housing. It was agreed by CHA and the city that at least 500 units of low-income CHA housing would be approved by June 15, 1971, with up to 1,700 units to be approved by December 15, 1971. In return, the U.S. Department of Housing and Urban Development was to release $55 million in federal funds to the city for model cities and urban renewal programs. The court-ordered plan for public housing sites was introduced into the council on March 10, 1971, but allowed to lie dormant until after the April 6, 1971, aldermanic elections.[80]

At the October 6, 1971, city council meeting Alderman Singer and I moved to suspend the rules to debate a resolution to direct the Planning and Housing Committee to hold "immediate hearings on new public housing sites in order to be in compliance with the agreement between the city and Department of Housing and Urban Development." As usual, we lost our motion, 6–37. However, our resolution was supported by both Democratic alderman Seymour Simon and Republican alderman Jack Sperling, who agreed that there is "great need of more quality public housing scattered on small sites throughout the city and the suburbs." Planning and Housing Committee chairman Terry Gabinski said that the dispute with Judge Austin concerned whether areas in which the city approved sites were in white or nonwhite sections of the city. He went on to say about integrated public housing in Chicago: "The people don't want it. I can assure you that I get very little mail urging such housing. Every indication I have is that people don't want it."[81]

Finally, Judge Austin ordered the CHA to select housing sites in white neighborhoods without allowing a city council veto over housing sites, which they had previously. On May 18, 1973, the U.S. Court of Appeals by a 2 to 1 decision upheld the order of Judge Austin. CHA chairman Charles Swibel declared it was "clearly a usurpation of power of the judiciary over the legislature." Republican alderman Ed Scholl (who would later be convicted on corruption charges) expressed the disappointment of his city council colleagues about the decision: "What upset me is that the courts have taken this out of the hands of the people. Their representatives in the city council should have been in the position to make a decision on this." Democratic alderman John Aiello agreed that the courts should have upheld the state law letting the city council decide the location of public housing sites: "The judicial system does not make the laws. It should carry out the laws made by the state legislature and the city council." Other members of the opposition bloc and I agreed that under different circumstances it would be better for the council to influence site selection, but the machine's support of segregation made that impossible. In the debate I argued, "Mayor Daley and the council have continually upheld a policy of racism [in regard to sites]. This [judicial] decision had to occur."[82]

The racial cleavage between blacks and whites demonstrated in these votes and council decisions slowly undermined the machine, and a reversal occurred. Mayor Richard J. Daley won his 1955 election based on electoral majorities from the black wards. Through the 1960s, with the civil rights struggles, the Democratic machine aligned itself more and more with the white ethnic groups favoring segregation. By the last year of Daley's reign, the city had lost federal lawsuits on segregation of public housing, segregation of Chicago public schools, and discriminatory hiring and promotions in the police and fire departments. The federal government withheld $195 million in federal revenue sharing funds until the city agreed to desegregate after Daley's death.

Not surprisingly, these racial issues became increasingly more divisive in the city council. Additionally, African-American voters responded by electing more and more Independent aldermen and state legislators. They used their votes to defeat segregationists like state's attorney Edward Hanrahan in the 1972 election. Nevertheless, at this stage most blacks simply withdrew from politics. They stopped registering and voting for a local Democratic Party that had betrayed them, even as they continued to vote heavily for the national party. In later decades, blacks would resume registering and voting in large numbers to elect Mayors Jane Byrne and Harold Washington to better represent their interests. These racial fights in the city council during the 1970s highlighted and publicized racial issues that led to electoral defeats for the Daley machine after the mayor's death.

Sexual Discrimination

Women were even less well represented in the council than racial and ethnic minorities. In the city councils of the 1970s women made up between 4 percent and 8 percent of the council despite being 51 percent of the population. At the beginning of the third millennium, there are still no openly homosexual men or women in the council. It was 1993 before the first openly homosexual candidates were elected to the local school councils and 1996 before the first openly homosexual candidate was elected to the state legislature.

The issue of gay rights first came up in 1971–1972 city council. Gay rights (entitled more broadly human rights) ordinances were introduced and consistently voted down in the 1970s and 1980s. It was 1988 before the first gay rights ordinance was adopted by the city council. However, women's issues were prominent in the council in the 1970s. The clearest women's rights issue was a budget amendment to provide equal pay for all janitors, male or female. The proposed budget amendment for equal pay offered by Alderman Despres received eight votes, including the two female members of the council. One alderman, Marilou Hedlund, voted for this equal pay budget amendment even though she was a Daley supporter on virtually every other council vote.

In 1972, pay toilets at O'Hare Airport became a women's issue because men could use urinals without having to pay, whereas women had to pay every time they used a toilet. The issue of pay toilets began almost as an aside in a council debate on censorship at the O'Hare Airport. Near the end of the meeting of February 24, 1972, Alderman Simon objected to the proposed renewal of contracts for the operation of the newspaper concession at O'Hare Airport because the ordinance gave the commissioner of aviation the power to censor any material he found objectionable, from lewd girlie magazines to political commentary such as Mike Royko's book *Boss*. Simon told his fellow aldermen that they would be striking a blow for liberty in denying the commissioner this power by not renewing the contract.

> Turning toward Mayor Daley, he continued, "Just as you, your Honor, would be striking a blow for liberty by removing those locks (coin-op pay toilet locks) on the toilets at the airport." Laughter—a voice is heard, "Seymour, they caught climbing over one of those doors." More laughter, another voice, "No, he climbs under them." Mayor Daley: "We're surveying the problem."
>
> [Alderman] Simon continued saying that the pay toilets were discriminatory against women (who are barred from using the men's "free" urinal). By now everyone is having a good time. Alderman Anna Langford (16th) rose and stated her concurrence with Alderman Simon's position. More laughter and applause.[83]

However, when the pay toilet issue was put to a vote, it again brought over the vote of majority bloc alderman Hedlund, who once again voted with the opposition. In 1973 she and staunch mayoral supporter Alderman Paul Wigoda offered an ordinance to ban pay toilets, gained the mayor's support, and passed the legislation in March 1973. As with African-American aldermen, sometimes pro-administration aldermen could get mayoral permission to introduce legislation that had been originally proposed by the opposition bloc in order to defuse electoral opposition to the Democratic machine.

Later in the 1970s, a resolution favoring the Equal Rights Amendment to the U.S. Constitution split the usually firm mayor's majority bloc. However, in this case, Alderman Adeline Keane, who replaced her husband on the city council when he was sent to the federal penitentiary for bribery and corruption, voted and spoke against the ERA. All of the other alderwomen spoke and voted for the ERA, along with the Independent aldermen. Thus, although they arose only rarely in the 1970s, women's issues tended to split the city council along slightly different lines than the usual pro- and anti-Daley blocs. Publicly, sexual discrimination issues further undermined the Democratic machine, but not as much as racial issues would by the end of the decade.

The City Budget

In 1971, another divisive vote, in addition to the budget amendment for equal salaries for all janitors, was the one to adopt the total city budget. It ended in a divided roll call vote of 41–6. The budget debate focused on several other issues that year, such as streamlining garbage collection, cutting council committee staffs, transferring state income tax funds to the public schools, giving the council more control over federal community development funds, and changing the city's power to issue bonds without voter approval.

Independent aldermen offered a budget amendment, which the administration defeated, to streamline garbage collection by eliminating one garbage loader on each garbage truck. In 1971 each truck had four men and a supervisor assigned to it. The elimination of the extra garbage loader would not be implemented until the 1980s, despite millions of dollars in savings that this simple change would bring, because of union pressures, the large number of patronage jobs involved, and city government inertia.

There was a heated budget debate on cutting city council committee staff members in 1971, although the proposed amendment to cut council staff also received only six favorable votes. Likewise, the parking tax on automobiles in parking garages was passed over the vigorous objections of five opposition aldermen. An attempt to transfer some of the city's share of state income tax revenue to the public schools, which were facing a financial crisis, was also defeated by the mayor's aldermen. Opposition aldermen offered an unsuccessful amendment to give the city council more control over the federal grants for programs like Model Cities, which traditionally were used more to hire patronage workers than to help the poor who lived in those communities. Altogether, the minority bloc offered over 100 budget amendments in different packages in the 1971 budget battle. All of these proposals were defeated by Mayor Daley's city council supporters regardless of their merit.

By 1972, Independent aldermen offered a complete alternative city budget with proposed amendments to many city programs. Many of our proposed reforms slowly were adopted over the next two decades as the city was forced to make cuts to balance the city budget when the federal government under Presidents Reagan and Bush cut federal funding to U.S. cities, but in the 1970s our budget amendments were defeated.

At the April 5, 1972, meeting of the council, the city administration passed an ordinance which, for the first time, allowed the city to issue bonds without voter approval. Alderman William Singer and I offered a series of amendments that would have required a special three-fourths vote of the council to approve the bonds, would have limited each bond issue to $25 million, and would have required two well-advertised public hearings before the council could approve issuing bonds. Our proposals were defeated by a vote of 29–7, with only Independent aldermen and two Republicans supporting the amendments.

In the debate on the bond ordinance, Alderman Hoellen declared that citizens are "uptight against taxes" and "losing trust in leaders all over America." Singer said that "absolutely no public consideration was given" in passing the ordinance. Despres argued that "tax levels are past the danger point and this paves the way for [a] vast increase [in taxes]." I explained, "Our principal objection is to giving total power without any checks and balances to the mayor and the rubber stamp of the majority of the city council to decide the bond issues without any real mechanism for full public participation and without any requirement to justify the expenditures—its just absolute total power, it's a kind of tyranny of money."[84] Opposition aldermen fought hard over budget issues but always lost in the final votes.

Changes in the City Council of 1975

In 1974, Alderman Michael Bilandic replaced Alderman Thomas Keane as the mayor's floor leader and Finance Committee chairman. As veteran reporter Harry Golden of the *Chicago Sun-Times* described the difference in the two aldermen's styles in running the council: "[Alderman Bilandic] cut out the charade-like debate which had prolonged budget sessions from midmorning until past mid-night. Now, city business moves with dispatch, civility and dullness . . . in a Council chamber that no longer rings, but drones."[85] Reporter Jay McMullen described Bilandic as "a voluble corporation lawyer with a flair for amassing statistics to support administration policies in long Council speeches. . . . On a clear day he can talk forever."[86]

What had changed fundamentally was that as a result of the retirement of aldermen like Despres, Hoellen, and Singer, as well as the loss of local aldermanic elections by two Independents, the opposition bloc dwindled to five. (We would decline to three by the time Bilandic became mayor in 1977.) Nonetheless, in May 1976 we decided to take a stand against the routine burial of our proposals in council committees. At a May 24, 1976, press conference we vowed to use parliamentary maneuvers and filibusters to immobilize the council if serious hearings weren't given to seven new and seven long sidetracked measures. Fifth Ward alderman Ross Lathrop, who had replaced Alderman Despres in the council, had done a study which showed that 75 percent of all substantive legislation introduced by either Independent or regular Democratic aldermen still languished in committee. In contrast, 95 percent of Mayor Daley's legislation had been passed and the rest had been held back at his direction.[87]

The May 26 council meeting lasted nine hours, the longest in eleven years, with seventy-seven roll call votes, the highest number in council history. After our fourteen proposals were buried in the Rules Committee, we demanded roll call votes on every item that came before the council and sent all other legislation to the Rules Committee. Alderman Bilandic countered by moving to discharge the Rules Committee of this legislation and had the two-thirds vote to do so. Then the majority aldermen were able to vote to approve a batch of twenty-nine routine ward matters that had gotten caught in the crossfire. After all this shouting and fury, progress was made at the next council meeting on June 9, 1976. Independent aldermen were allowed to introduce and send to substantive committees more than twenty proposed ordinances.[88]

Participatory Versus Machine Politics

By the 1970s, battles for more democracy took place in the community as well as in the council chambers. The belief that citizens should have a voice in and control over public and private decisions that most affect their lives was behind my founding of the Independent Precinct Organization (IPO) in 1969 and the 44th Ward Assembly in 1972. IPO, in opposition to the political machine, provided voters a more participatory way of determining candidates and elections. The 44th Ward Assembly gave citizens and their directly chosen community representatives a way to guide my decisions and control my vote as alderman in the city council.

Both were antithetical to the machine mentality, which sought to buy political support with government favors, contracts, and jobs. This form of
neighborhood government also differed from the traditional Republican
platform of running government more like a business. The machine centered political authority in the hands of party bosses. IPO, in contrast,
gave authority to members who contributed time and money to electoral
and issue campaigns without the inducement of material rewards.

On a grander scale the 44th Ward Assembly was composed of elected
delegates from every precinct and every community organization and
was open to participation by any citizen of the ward who chose to attend
its meetings. At those monthly meetings, after careful debate, study, and
deliberation, the Ward Assembly by a two-thirds vote determined my
vote in the city council and the projects that we undertook together in the
community. It directly challenged the machine concept of hierarchical
control and closed-door decisionmaking. And it was successful in making good decisions for the Lakeview neighborhood and in promoting
citywide legislation such as bank antiredlining laws.[89]

The challenge of participatory versus machine politics was carried not
only by IPO and the Ward Assembly but by Saul Alinsky–inspired community organizations, the Independent Voters of Illinois, and various
black and Hispanic Independent political groups. There were many vari-
eties of opposition to the Daley machine beginning to sprout in Chicago
by the 1970s.

During the 1970s the central struggle in the council chambers was also
over democratic versus autocratic control. In Chicago, since the nineteenth century, the machine had always won this battle despite some
election defeats, public officials being jailed for corruption, and the continuing cry in the media and among civic groups for reform. Like their
predecessors, Mayor Daley, his aldermen, party workers, and business
supporters believed in putting forth a balanced ticket of candidates from
various ethnic groups and factions within the party. By offering economic rewards to party voters, contributors, and precinct captains (supplied by the government in the form of services as favors, government
contracts, and government jobs), the party then won elections for the vast
majority of its candidates, especially the key executive positions that
have the most power to distribute spoils and rewards to the party faithful. It was a system subject to nepotism, patronage, favoritism, corruption, and abuse of power, but it was justified by machine supporters as
democratic because elections were held and those who won controlled
the government.

Mayor Richard J. Daley modernized the old-fashioned machine system
by appointing competent career professionals to run various city agencies and to deliver general government services efficiently and effec-

tively—that is, he took away the ward bosses' control of government services to make Chicago "the city that works." As long as the police and fire departments made wealthy and middle-class neighborhoods safe and secure, the Department of Streets and Sanitation ensured that the streets were well repaired and the garbage was picked up, the federal government provided money for social services to the poor, and property taxes were kept low, the majority of Chicagoans were prepared—despite graft, corruption, and authoritarian political control—to vote Democratic machine candidates back into office. For many Chicagoans, the machine also represented ethnic groups, interest groups, and community concerns of local voters better than many reformers had in the past.

The "growth machine," or developmental regime, that developed under Mayor Daley was built around the Democratic machine and its ties with business, institutional, labor, and ethnic leaders. Mayor Daley could "pursue a course of action only insofar as the formal decentralization [of fragmented governments and authority was] overcome by informal centralization" and that was best done through the political party machine.[90] Daley wanted to do "big things," to be a "builder mayor," and he did not necessarily care too much about which ones. He waited for businessmen and heads of major institutions to propose projects. "According to the Chicago view [at the time], a policy ought to be framed by the interests affected, not by the political head or his agents. In this view, the affected interests should work out for themselves the 'best solution' of the matter." When all the principally affected interests such as the business leaders and labor unions were satisfied with a proposed project, then Mayor Daley would adopt it as his own and implement it with the support of the business and civic sector and with his clout within the party guaranteeing the necessary government actions.[91] For developing the State Street corridor in the Loop or building expressways with federal funds, this informal system of decisionmaking was adequate for the growth machine. For handling race problems, improving public schools, or stemming the loss of manufacturing jobs, it wasn't.

There were two faces to Daley's rule—his political machine and his growth regime. Daley gave Chicagoans "jobs, stood up for their way of life against threats from all sides, and made their city work. He had built up Chicago, leaving skyscrapers, schools, highways, and a thriving downtown to proclaim his greatness for generations. But Daley would be remembered by millions of others who saw in his career the dark side of modern America. They viewed him as the master of a corrupt political system, backward-looking, power-hungry, and bigoted, who ruled in the name of some groups and at the expense of others. They saw him as someone who had built a city founded on unfairness and who was deaf to calls for change."[92]

While Daley, his machine, and his regime might hold down taxes and deliver basic city services, it was ill equipped to handle social problems, which became central in the 1960s and 1970s. The machine's response to the civil rights movements, the anti-Vietnam protests, and calls for citizen participation was to ignore the problems, to contain the issues, to use the Police Department's "Red Squad" to spy on dissenters, and to jail protesters and their spokespersons. Finding creative solutions, making accommodations, or sharing power with new political figures from radical reform movements was not the machine way. To give political power to African Americans equal to their population or their potential votes would diminish white ethnic group dominance. Just as there is no such thing as partial totalitarianism, the authoritarianism of Daley and his machine could not be weakened without an entire shift in power from tight hierarchical control toward participatory democracy.

At least since the Chicago Fire of 1871, Chicago political history has been structured around this struggle between democracy and authoritarianism, between reform and machine politics, and between those who support and those who oppose a redistribution of power and wealth. The fight for procedural democracy and the fight for substantive democracy have been intertwined. In the 1970s this continuing historical struggle was manifested in city council battles. The city council reenacted the pitched street battles of the 1960s within its chambers.

Not only participatory democracy but racial justice was denied. Chicago remained the most segregated city in North America.[93] This was not because Mayor Daley was necessarily a racist, but because white ethnics and their aldermen wanted the city segregated. Before the 1970s, the law governing public housing required that all public housing sites had to be approved by the city council. So all public housing for families was segregated in all-black neighborhoods and one or two liberal white neighborhoods. In 1955, 45 percent of the *proposed sites* would have been in white or substantially white neighborhoods, and in 1966, over 50 percent, but the council vetoed these sites. From 1955 to 1971 the Chicago Housing Authority built 10,256 apartments and *all but sixty-three were in black neighborhoods*.[94] Mayor Daley was a force for continuing segregation, but he could not have acted as he did without the support of the council.

While the federal courts and national civil rights legislation began to desegregate schools, employment, and housing, Chicago's city council attempted to maintain the racial status quo—to keep blacks in their place. The concerns of youth over the war in Vietnam were ignored. Neighborhood government never had a chance to be born despite successful experiments by community organizations and by my 44th Ward Assembly. Political change could thus be held back in Chicago, but it could not be prevented altogether. In the short run, machine politics triumphed over reform, as it did so often in Chicago's history. But Daley's successors would have much weaker control than he enjoyed. No future mayor would ever completely regain the mastery and control of Richard J. Daley's reign.

Notes

1. Harvey Molotch, "The City As a Growth Machine," *American Journal of Sociology* 82 (1976): 309–330; Edward Banfield, *Political Influence* (New York: Free Press, 1964); Andrew Jonas and David Wilson, eds., *The Urban Growth Machine* (Albany: State University of New York Press, 1999); and Gregory Squires et al., *Chicago: Race, Class, and the Response to Urban Decline* (Philadelphia: Temple University Press, 1987).

2. Roger Biles, *Richard J. Daley: Politics, Race, and the Governing of Chicago* (DeKalb: Northern Illinois University Press, 1995), pp. 5, 8, 17–18. The quote by Kennelly is taken from John Barlow Martin, "How Corrupt Is Chicago?" *Saturday Evening Post*, March 31, 1951, p. 71.

3. There are many detailed biographies of Richard J. Daley. The newest and perhaps the most balanced is Adam Cohen and Elizabeth Taylor, *American Pharaoh: Mayor Richard J. Daley* (New York: Little, Brown, 2000).

4. Eugene Kennedy, *Himself! The Life and Times of Mayor Richard J. Daley* (New York: Viking, 1978), p. 47.

5. Biles, *Daley*, pp. 35–36.

6. Bill Granger and Lori Granger, *Lords of the Last Machine: The Story of Politics in Chicago* (New York: Random House, 1987), p. 156.

7. Kennedy, *Himself*, p. 114.

8. Kennedy, *Himself*, p. 121.

9. Kennedy, *Himself*, p. 131.

10. Biles, *Daley*, p. 225.

11. Biles, *Daley*, p. 63.

12. Roman Pucinski, "7 Runoffs Won by Democrats," *Chicago Sun-Times*, April 6, 1955, pp. 1, 5. Newspaper article in Leon Despres Papers (scrapbooks on microfilm) at the Chicago Historical Society (hereafter Despres Papers).

13. George Tagge, "Wife of U. Of C. Aide Files for 5th Ward Job," *Chicago Tribune*, Despres Papers.

14. Despres ran with the endorsement of both IVI and the local Republican Party, just as I would do twenty years later in my aldermanic campaigns in the 44th Ward. It was a winning combination for both of us, but it has been very rare for Independent Democrats and Republicans to combine this way in opposition to the Democratic machine.

15. "New Council Needs a Vigorous Reform-Economy Bloc," *Chicago Sun-Times*, April 7, 1955, Despres Papers.

16. Alderman Leon Despres and Alderman Seymour Simon, interview by author, June 9, 1998.

17. "Economy Bloc Asks 4 Council Chairmanships," *Chicago Tribune*, April 12, 1955, Despres Papers.

18. "City Council Votes Approval of Makeup of Committees," *Chicago Tribune*, April 22, 1955, Despres Papers.

19. "Trouble Not New to Cullerton," *Chicago Today*, October 2, 1970.

20. Jay McMullen, "Keane Confronts His Council Critics," *Chicago Sun-Times*, December 13, 1972, Thomas Earl Keane biography, Chicago Historical Society Biography Collection.

21. "P. J. Cullerton, Former Dem Leader Here, Dies," *Chicago Tribune* (n.d.; Chicago Historical Society Biography Collection); and David S. Robinson, "Parky Cullerton Dead at 83," *Chicago Sun-Times*, January 27, 1981.

22. William Griffin, "Keane Era Ends in 31st Ward," *Chicago Tribune*, February 18, 1979, sec. 3.

23. Kennedy, *Himself,* p. 68.

24. "Keane Still at Work," *Chicago Sun-Times*, April 17, 1986.

25. Jay McMullen, "Tom Keane—A Man of Power," *Chicago Daily News*, May 14, 1969.

26. Jay McMullen, "Keane Confronts His Council Critics," Thomas E. Keane biography, Chicago Historical Society Biography Collection.

27. Despres Biography by Lois Wille, *Chicago Daily News,* May 23–24, 1970, Despres Papers.

28. Jay McMullen, "A Council Conscience Retires," *Chicago Daily News,* October 29, 1974, Despres biography, Chicago Historical Society Biography Collection.

29. Quoted in David Axelrod, *Chicago Reader*, May 16, 1975, Despres biography, Chicago Historical Society Biography Collection.

30. David Axelrod, *Chicago Reader*, May 16, 1975.

31. Edward Schreiber, "A Thorn in the Side of Daley and Alderman Keane," *Chicago Tribune*, October 29, 1967, Seymour F. Simon biography, Chicago Historical Society Biography Collection.

32. Quoted in Milton Rakove, *We Don't Want Nobody Sent* (Bloomington: Indiana University Press, 1979), p. 333.

33. Quoted in Rakove, *Nobody,* p. 342.

34. Quoted in Rakove, *Nobody,* pp. 298–299.

35. Quoted in Rakove, *Nobody,* pp. 299, 304.

36. Kennedy, *Himself,* p. 133.

37. "Aldermen Resume Calls on Mayor," Despres Papers. Newspaper article; no identification other than title.

38. "City Sales Tax Adopted, Daley Lashes Bohling," *Chicago Daily News*, July 14, 1955, Despres Papers.

39. Quote and the description of the legislative action taken from the newspaper article "Council OK's 2 Cent Levy by 42–3 Vote," Despres Papers. Newspaper article; no identification other than title.

40. Cohen and Taylor, *American Pharaoh,* p. 169.

41. William Grimshaw, *Bitter Fruit: Black Politics and the Chicago Machine, 1931–1991* (Chicago: University of Chicago Press, 1992), p. 93.

42. Jay McMullen, "Council Plans Hike in Expense Funds," *Chicago Daily News,* Despres Papers.

43. "It Costs $10,451 to Run 5th Ward Office: Despres," *Chicago Daily News*, November 26, 1955; and "Summary of Four Year Aldermanic Record of Alderman Leon M. Despres," 1959, Despres Papers, box 38, folder 5.

44. "Alderman Swindle Sheet," *Chicago Sun-Times*, November 15, 1955, Despres Papers.

45. "Aldermen Vote Selves Extra $100 a Month," *Chicago Tribune*, December 12, 1955, Despres Papers.

46. "Seek to Kill Fund for Censor Board," *Chicago Daily News*, November 15, 1955, Despres Papers.

47. "Council Oks 5% Earning Tax on City's 3 Major Utilities," Despres Papers. Newspaper article; no identification other than title.

48. "Vote 42 Million City Pay Boost," *Chicago American*, December 13, 1955, pp. 1–2.

49. "Daley Walks Out with $562,462,214 Budget," *Chicago Defender*, December 17, 1955, p. 4.

50. Notes from Len Despres attached to the *Chicago Defender* article, "Daley Walks Out with $562,462,214," Despres Papers.

51. "Driveway Revision Slips into Council," *Chicago Daily News*, January 18, 1956, Despres Papers.

52. Alderman Leon Despres, interview, June 9, 1998; and "Sain Backs Shift in Driveway Law," *Chicago Daily News*, January 26, 1956, Despres Papers.

53. "Alderman Despres Cites Need for Changes in Way of Issuing Driveway Permits," *Chicago Daily News*, February 6, 1956, p. 16.

54. "Citizens Group Backs Driveway Rule Change," *Chicago Daily News*, February 11, 1956, p. 8.

55. Despres, report of the March 13 meeting, Despres Papers.

56. See *Chicago Sun-Times* and *Tribune* articles on March 14, 1956, in Despres Papers.

57. Jay McMullen, "Driveway Business: Mayor Has Way. Aldermen Give Up Power over Permits," *Chicago Daily News*, March 29, 1956, Despres Papers.

58. McMullen, "Driveway Business."

59. Mervin Block, "Driveway Rule Shed by Council" and "Rule over Driveway Permits Surrendered by City Council," *Chicago Tribune*, March 29, 1956; and McMullen, "Driveway Business."

60. Mike Royko, *Boss: Richard J. Daley of Chicago* (New York: Dutton, 1971), pp. 13–14.

61. Kennedy, *Himself*, pp. 220–222.

62. Dan Walker, *Rights in Conflict* (Chicago: National Commission on the Causes and Prevention of Violence, 1968).

63. A Sindlinger public opinion poll quoted by Melvin Holli in the chapter entitled "Daley to Daley," in Paul Green and Melvin Holli, eds., *Restoration 1989: Chicago Elects a New Daley* (Chicago: Lyceum, 1991), p. 196.

64. Rakove, *Nobody*, p. 366.

65. Since there was no official record of proposed legislation, I began a card file system at my aldermanic office in 1971. A copy of the legislation and the card file are among the Dick Simpson Papers, Special Collections, Main Library, University of Illinois at Chicago. The accountability resolution was introduced in March 1973 and numbered ML–73–42 in this system.

66. Harry Golden Jr., "The Mayor in Crisis: He Can Take the Heat," *Chicago Sun-Times*, March 4, 1973, p. 3.

67. The description and quotations are from Harry Golden Jr., "Daley Almost Keeps His Cool Under Attacks in Council," *Chicago Sun-Times*, September 13, 1973, p. 58.

68. For a description of these exchange and commitment models of machine support, as well as a description of the findings of earlier studies such as those by Harold Gosnell, see Thomas M. Guterbock, *Machine Politics in Transition* (Chicago: University of Chicago Press, 1980), chaps. 1, 10.

69. Guterbock, *Machine Politics*, pp. 9, 226–227.

70. James Winters, "Democracy in Chicago: The Passing of the Late, Great Irish Machine," *Notre Dame Magazine*, December 1983, p. 21.

71. William Singer, quoted in Rakove, *Nobody*, pp. 368–369.

72. Cohen ad Taylor, *American Pharaoh*, p. 145.

73. Technically, there were elections by each group of ten aldermen of two members of the committees. But Alderman Keane and the mayor's allies had chosen those who would be elected from each tier before the caucuses were held.

74. Quotes and description of the council meeting are taken from Jay McMullen, "Council Majority Flexes Muscles," *Chicago Daily News*, April 8, 1971.

75. Edward Schreiber, "Eight Aldermen Seek More Staff Funds, Night Council Sessions," *Chicago Tribune*, April 17, 1971.

76. Surprisingly, before 1983, the executive branch of city government was not required to make public most information held by government departments and agencies, even though all of these records were paid for by taxpayer dollars. In May 1983, when Harold Washington became mayor, one of his first official acts was to sign the first executive order in city history, the Freedom of Information Executive Order, which has been resigned by each Chicago mayor since. A new city clerk would finally put basic city council data for citizens on the Internet in 1998. Thus the battle for public information took three decades.

77. Andrea Rozran, "Search for Proposed Ordinances, Part I" (memorandum to the League of Women Voters, July 6, 1973). See also *Northwestern University Law Review* 68, no. 2 (May–June 1973): 239.

78. For the original resolution, see *City Council Journal of Proceedings*, April 22, 1971, p. 44. For the second resolution introduced by Alderman Frost and others, see *City Council Journal of Proceedings*, May 5, 1971, p. 114.

79. Bill Cousins, interview, in Dick Simpson and William Mahin, *The Chicago City Council* (Chicago: University of Illinois at Chicago, 1982), videocassette.

80. "CHA Feud Dumped into Council's Lap," *Chicago Daily News*, March 10, 1971, pp. 1, 21.

81. Sheldon Hoffenberg, "Gabinski: No More Meetings on Housing Sites," *Lerner Booster*, October 13, 1971.

82. Steven Pratt, "Swibel Hits Court Order on CHA Sites as 'Usurpation of Power,'" *Chicago Tribune*, May 20, 1973, p. 3.

83. David Weiner, "Pay Toilets: A Pressing Problem," *Daily Planet*, March 2–16, 1972, p. 9.

84. Edward Schreiber, "City Oks Bond Issuance Without Vote," *Chicago Tribune*, April 6, 1972; and David Weiner, "The Slickest Power," *Daily Planet*, April 27–May 11, 1972, p. 4.

85. Harry Golden Jr., "Ald. Bilandic: No Cadillac, No Keane-isms, No Color," *Chicago Sun-Times*, April 11, 1976.

86. Jay McMullen, "Keane: A Major Blow to Daley," *Chicago Daily News*, October 10, 1974, p. 3.

87. Harry Golden Jr., "4 Daley Foes Threaten a 'Logjam' in Council," *Chicago Sun-Times*, May 25, 1976, pp. 1–2.

88. Fred Orehek, "Minority Aldermen Lose 9-Hour Battle with Regulars," *Chicago Tribune*, May 27, 1976, p. 3; and Greg Hinz, "Independent Bloc Wins Round Two of Council Battle," *Lerner Booster*, June 12–13, 1976.

89. See especially Greta Salem, "Citizen Participation: Opportunities and Incentives" (Ph.D. diss., University of Maryland, 1974); and Dick Simpson, "Chicago's 44th Ward: A Case Study," *South Atlantic Urban Studies* 6 (Fall 1979).

90. Banfield, *Political Influence,* p. 237.

91. Banfield, *Political Influence,* pp. 270–271.

92. Adam Cohen and Elizabeth Taylor, *American Pharaoh: Mayor Richard J. Daley* (New York: Little, Brown, 2000), p. 558.

93. See Pierre de Vise, "Chicago's Widening Color Gap" and "Chicago's 1987 Economic Report Card," in Dick Simpson, ed., *Chicago's Future: In a Time of Change* (Champaign, Ill.: Stipes, 1993), pp. 45–62, 70–76. As late as 1980 the segregation index was 90 percent. In the 1990s the segregation index finally improved slightly, dropping to 86 percent. However, this means that 86 percent of the population would have to move to create census tracts in which the number of African Americans was equal to their percentage of the overall Chicago population.

94. Ken Pierce and Lois Weisberg, "A Day in Court—Chicago Style," in Dick Simpson, ed., *Chicago's Future: An Agenda for Change* (Champaign: Stipes, 1988), pp. 496–497.

5

Michael Bilandic's Interlude, 1976–1979

After Mayor Daley died, Mayor Bilandic, a first-generation Croatian American, was selected to continue city government and the growth machine. However, he and his subservient city council were unable to cope with the silent revolution that was occurring in the late 1970s. Without the clear clash that race and party politics had created in the Daley era, the social and economic base of the city was still crumbling. During most of the 1970s and 1980s, Chicago lost about 60,000 people, 25,000 jobs, and 12,500 units of housing a year. By the 1980s, Chicago had shrunk from a population of 3.6 million people to less than 3 million. During the 1970s and 1980s, Chicago lost more than 250,000 manufacturing jobs. Unemployment and joblessness soared to 12 percent or higher. The real human costs in the hardest-hit neighborhoods included suicides, home loss, bankruptcy, mental illness, and spouse and child abuse.[1]

Although the machine could react to political demands and requests from businessmen or major institutions, plan public works, and respond to mundane citizen requests for standard city services, it could not cope well with social and economic changes. Thus Bilandic and his city council failed to respond well to the social and economic transformations of the 1970s. City government continued to support downtown development, a new South Loop residential development, and limited industrial revenue bonds as its sole strategy of economic development. Between 1978 and 1984, some 115 industrial revenue bonds were issued to allow low-interest loans to businesses that chose to stay in Chicago and expand their facilities. But a downtown development strategy and a few industrial bonds could not prevent the overall loss of a quarter of a million manufacturing jobs. Alderman William Singer, in his mayoral campaign of 1975, had revealed that the value of all property was declining and that property taxes were stagnant despite high inflation. The Bilandic administration did not respond with effective programs to combat any of these negative trends.

In the late 1970s, the most important clashes no longer occurred primarily between protestors and police on Chicago streets, as they had in the 1960s. They occurred silently as factory after factory closed, homes were abandoned, and families moved from Chicago to the suburbs or cities of the sun belt. The part of Chicago's population that was left behind was poorer, and the downtown development strategy proved inadequate to stem the tide.

Mayor Richard J. Daley's reign is usually portrayed as creating the quintessential rubber stamp city council. After all, journalists and political scientists dwell on his tenure in office in their accounts of Chicago politics. In truth, however, the brief reign of Michael Bilandic provided the purest form of rubber stamp council, although it was not created by his personal power. Daley's reelection in 1975 had brought with it the defeat or retirement of many Republican and Independent aldermen. When Daley won his sixth term of office in 1975, he elected with him an overwhelming majority of regular Democrats. Thus the pro-administration dominance in the council increased during the Bilandic interlude in 1977 so that the balance of power was 45–3, with two vacant seats. Michael Bilandic inherited this rubber stamp council.

The story of the Bilandic years begins with his being selected acting mayor by the council after Daley's death in 1976. How he was elected by the maneuvering of ethnic and power blocs and the overwhelming vote by which he was confirmed reveal the fundamental role of race and ethnicity in Chicago politics. During the crisis that occurred after Daley's death, the council reverted to primordial patterns of ethnic and racial divisions. When Mayor Daley died on December 10, 1976, he had not groomed a successor. This created a power vacuum, since he had ruled Chicago with an iron fist as mayor and chairman of the Cook County Democratic Party Central Committee since 1955. In 1976 there was no orderly legal pattern of succession to replace a mayor who died in office. Chicago had faced a similar crisis in 1933 when it replaced Mayor Cermak after his assassination with Mayor Kelly. Yet adequate laws governing succession had not been passed in the forty years since that crisis. The only firm rule in place in 1976 was that an acting mayor would be elected by the city council from among its own members. There were four key contenders in the succession battle in 1976.

Eleventh Ward alderman Michael Bilandic was a Croatian American who served as Mayor Daley's own 11th Ward alderman in the city council. He knew little about politics, which he had always left to Daley. He was generally thought of as a cold fish—haughty, aloof, and arrogant. He was not well liked by the other aldermen, but he had held the most powerful position in the council as Finance Committee chairman and floor leader. "Bilandic had the face of a basset hound with large watery blue eyes. . . . He was an amiable enough man, immersed in details, with the flat unemphatic speech of a man who finds public attention puzzling." As "a lifelong Bridgeport resident of Croatian descent, quiet, colorless, timorous, and believed to be unambitious, Bilandic had dutifully served as Daley's surrogate in the city council since 1969 and seemed the perfect caretaker for Chicago."[2]

Fourteenth Ward alderman Edward Burke was an Irish American alderman from the Southwest Side neighborhood next to Daley's. A former policeman, Burke replaced his father, who had been 14th Ward alderman and ward committeeman when he died. He was younger, brighter, and better educated than most pro-Daley aldermen. Therefore, he was often given the task of defending the administration's proposals on the floor of the council. He was ambitious but not ruthless enough to take control of the city. He had been one of the organizers of the Coffee Rebellion only a few years earlier and he would go on to become Finance Committee chairman in Harold Washington's and Richard M. Daley's administrations. "Burke . . . was raw and tough. When his father Joe Burke, died and the post of committeeman and alderman fell vacant in Canaryville, nobody gave Eddie anything. Eddie was a cop then, street-smart and cold-eyed and only twenty four years old. He never forgot his enemies who had gathered at his father's wake in 'little clusters' around the funeral parlor, 'discussing who would get what. It was almost like the Roman soldiers casting lots for the garments under the cross at crucifixion.'"[3] He had won the 14th Ward battles for alderman and committeeman seven years earlier, and now he was a contender to replace Daley as mayor.

Thirty-Fourth Ward alderman Wilson Frost served as Democratic Party ward committeeman and alderman for many years. He was the leading African-American regular organization member of the council. As a lawyer, he was smart enough to govern. Usually, however, he preferred to let others propose legislation then react to their proposals. He had created almost no legislation of his own in his years in the council. He would follow the same pattern when he became Finance Committee chairman after the mayoral battle of 1976. He was the candidate from the black community to become the first African-American mayor in the history of the city.

Tenth Ward alderman Edward Vrdolyak was another Croatian-American candidate. "Fast Eddie" was a millionaire lawyer with his own law firm specializing in personal injury cases. Although frequently investigated by grand juries, he had never been convicted of corruption or fraud. A tough street fighter who fought his way to power in the 10th Ward, he later became the chairman of the Cook County Democratic Party Central Committee, ran for mayor as a Solidarity Party candidate, and left the Democratic Party to become a Republican Party candidate for county office. By the 1990s, he would return to his lucrative private legal practice and serve as a radio talk show host.

Added to this cast of top mayoral contenders were lesser candidates like Polish-American alderman and former congressman Roman Pucinski. Also important to the succession were three administrators who had served in key positions in Richard J. Daley's cabinet: Tom Donovan, the patronage chief; William Quinlan, the corporation counsel; and Frank Sullivan, Daley's press secretary. They had run the government during Mayor Daley's "small stroke" two years earlier. They kept the government running and directed the succession process now.

As a good Greek drama begins with an omen, so does the story of Daley's succession. After recovering from the "small stroke" that he suffered two years before his death, Daley told Aldermen Vrdolyak, Frost, and Fred Roti at the aldermanic Christmas party in 1976, "'If anything happens to me, you fellows stick together.' Vrdolyak [was] startled by the comment. He [said]: 'Mayor, you're going to live to be 100.' Daley chuckle[d] but then turn[ed] serious again and [said]: 'I'm telling you— you guys stick together, or everything we've worked for together will be for nothing.'"[4] In the all-out struggle for succession, Daley's plea for unity among the regular Democratic aldermen would first go unheeded. Only later would the machine reunite around the division of the spoils.

Within hours after Daley's death on December 20, 1976, Corporation Counsel William Quinlan advised administrators at city hall that under city and state law there was no acting mayor. He and a handful of top Daley aides, including Donovan and Sullivan, decided to follow the same pattern of governing that had worked earlier during Daley's "small stroke." Deputy Mayor Kenneth Sain was to handle administrative matters and Alderman Wilson Frost, as president pro tem, should preside over the meeting of the city council that would elect an acting mayor until a formal election by the voters could be held.

These government details did not matter to most Chicagoans saddened by Daley's passing. On the local level it was akin to the death of John Kennedy, Robert Kennedy, or Martin Luther King Jr. on the national level. However, thoughts of power crowded out sadness from the heads and hearts of many politicians. On the night that Daley died, African-American politicians and community leaders held three meetings to plan how to gain more power in the succession struggles. Some even dared to hope that they might elect the first black mayor in Chicago. At the wake the next day white politicians gathered in little groups to talk about Daley's successor just as they had in the 14th Ward at the death of Ed

Burke's father. No one was sure which individuals and groups would control the city. Mayor Daley had been careful not to name an heir who might seek to overthrow him before he was ready to relinquish his power.

At City Hall, the aldermen began holding political caucuses before the mayor was buried. Nine African-American aldermen met with Wilson Frost in a show of support for his newly declared candidacy to become acting mayor. Other ethnic groups gathered similarly. A Polish bloc met in Alderman Pucinski's office. They refused to support Pucinski's candidacy, however, because they were certain he could not win. Nonetheless, they agreed that they wanted more spoils for their ethnic group in the coming power shift.

One nonethnic meeting was held between reform and machine aldermen who had some desire to reform the council itself. In this joint caucus, they discussed the process by which power was to be shifted. But there was too little cohesiveness among the pro-administration and reform aldermen and too few votes in the combined group to elect the next mayor. If all "reform-minded" aldermen had added their votes to a solid bloc of thirteen black aldermen, we might have had the necessary votes to gain control of city government. But too many of the white aldermen either didn't like Frost personally or represented conservative white constituencies that would not let them vote for him. On the other hand, too many black aldermen were so strongly controlled by their ward committeemen or were so dependent on city patronage jobs to maintain control of their ward that they could be ordered by patronage chief Tom Donovan not to support Frost. No one wanted to be on the losing side of this power struggle because jobs were at stake. Thus the nonethnic coalition in the council was doomed by racial tensions and by pro-administration aldermen's dependency on patronage.

Later in the week a seven-member Jewish bloc formed for the first time in the city council. It included both reform and machine aldermen, who agreed to push for adding a legislative assistant to aldermanic staffs. But the group was too small to demand a more significant share of power in the transition. Having watched stronger ethnic groups lobby early for power, however, they too reverted to their core support group in order to make their demands.

During Mayor Daley's wake, funeral, and memorial service, in addition to holding political caucuses, aldermen made phone calls continuously, trying to get the inside track on the power struggle, all grabbing, as they were able, for their own piece of the action. No one was sure who would emerge from the power struggle successfully. As the calls and caucuses continued, various aldermen were suggested and rejected as mayoral successors.

In the meantime the chief administrators in Daley's government, acting for the dominant Irish 11th Ward and other major power blocs of the city such as bankers and businessmen, slowly but surely moved to contain the ethnic revolts and to maintain the status quo as well as they could. The future of city government and the governing regime of Chicago was at stake.

The most important meeting called by City Hall officials was held on December 21, the day after Daley's death, in the office of Tom Donovan, Daley's patronage chief, with Aldermen Bilandic, Burke, Frost, Vrdolyak, Marzullo, and Roti. The administrators present were Donovan, Sullivan, and Quinlan. Quinlan's legal opinion, that there was no acting mayor, was read and the interim structure of government discussed. Even Alderman Frost did not dissent at the time.

The political forces that had backed Daley, especially the 11th Ward crowd and powerful businessmen, quickly settled on Bilandic as successor. Bilandic, as Finance Committee chairman, knew how the government was run and was acceptable to the 11th Ward, which he had represented as alderman. As a corporate lawyer, he was certain to follow traditional and financially conservative policies acceptable to the business community. But he wasn't well liked by the aldermen. They preferred someone like "Fast Eddie" Vrdolyak, with whom they could make political deals. Most of all, if Bilandic were elected, the 11th Ward and the Irish would still run the Democratic Party and the city. This meant that other aldermen and other ethnic groups would not gain much power in the transition. Electing someone other than Bilandic or an Irish alderman would shake up the government and open the way to quick advancement and power for less powerful aldermen and ethnic groups.

Daley's funeral was held the next day, December 22. I remember thinking at the funeral that Daley would have liked it. Unlike his divided city council, his eulogy included no dissent. His faults were buried with him, and his fame was left to live. Those who supported him and those who opposed him were brought together to bow to his remembrance. But Daley was dead and politics, like nature, abhors a vacuum.

After his funeral another summit meeting of city administrators and powerful aldermen was held in Donovan's office. This time the meeting was held without Frost. By now the phone calls and caucuses had resulted in five potential candidates for mayor: Alderman Pucinski with only his own vote, Alderman Burke with slightly more support, Alderman Vrdolyak with ten to twelve votes, Alderman Frost with a wavering thirteen black votes and those of three white reform aldermen, and Alderman Bilandic with just short of the twenty-five votes needed to be elected. In the City Hall meeting Vrdolyak told everyone that he was confident, based on phone calls from other council members, that he had enough votes to be elected acting mayor. But he was bluffing. Bilandic then said that "'the old man' [Daley] had groomed him to take on the duties of acting mayor from his base of experience as Finance Committee chairman and [as] ex-officio member of all committees." Bilandic asked the others in the room to support him, and they indicated that they would. Faced with their support for Bilandic, Vrdolyak agreed to support him as well if he could have Bilandic's current job as Finance Committee chairman.[5]

However, these behind-the-scenes decisions would not go unchallenged. On the night of December 22 more than 200 African-American leaders backed Frost for acting mayor at a unity meeting at Robert's Motel, the site of civil rights gatherings in the past. Ethnic and racial battle lines were now drawn. On December 23, Alderman Frost attempted to hold a press conference at Daley's fifth-floor office declaring himself "acting mayor," but City Hall administrators had the police bar the doors. Under state law and city council rules, Alderman Frost had a reasonable claim to be acting mayor, at least until the council could officially vote on a successor. Frost said at his press conference, "I am by virtue of the laws of the state of Illinois and legal precedents established in case law, the acting mayor of the city of Chicago and have been since the death of Richard J. Daley." He also said that Daley had been his "friend and teacher" and that Mayor Daley had called him into his office in 1974 after his illness and said, "If I had died, you'd be here now." But after Frost left, Mayor Daley's press secretary, Frank Sullivan, appeared to say: "There is no acting mayor at this time. . . . Frost is reversing himself."[6]

Frost's press conference had to be held in the city council chambers over the clatter of workmen preparing for the Daley memorial service. The fact that Frost was barred from even using the press auditorium in the mayor's office was a clear indication that he didn't have the powers of acting mayor. Nevertheless, his attempt to assume power was dramatic, and fear of potential new race riots like the ones that had racked the city after Martin Luther King's assassination in 1968 caused him to be taken seriously in the transition struggles.

On Friday, December 24, and Saturday, Christmas Day, Alderman Edward Burke acted as a go-between for Bilandic, Frost, and Vrdolyak. Frost agreed to withdraw from the race for acting mayor if he was elected Finance Committee chairman. So Vrdolyak was forced to back down from his demand to become Finance chairman, but he was then offered Frost's former position of president pro tem. City administrators and white political leaders still feared that if Frost pushed his candidacy and lost, there might be a race riot. This made compromise with Alderman Frost essential. Negotiations finally were completed on December 26. By now Tom Donovan was calling ward committeemen to tell them that they would lose their patronage jobs if their aldermen did not vote for Bilandic. As negotiations continued, a post of vice mayor was created and offered to Frost, but he turned it down. The vice mayor post, however, would be used to solve succession problems after Mayor Harold Washington's death in 1987. At the time, it was given to the Polish bloc, which accepted it as a recognition of their ethnic group's importance in the machine. Thus the turmoil and uncertainty began to abate as ethnic groups and their aldermanic representatives shared power.

On December 27 several black community delegations met with Frost, who still insisted that there was no deal and that he would be running for acting mayor if he could get the necessary twenty-five votes. The Polish bloc met on the same day and chose Alderman Casimir Laskowski as the Polish candidate for vice mayor. So by December 28 all the principal ethnic blocs had been appeased. Frost and Vrdolyak had decided they couldn't round up the necessary votes to win the mayoralty.

The *Chicago Tribune* declared the special council meeting to elect an acting mayor "the most dramatic council meeting in years, and spectators stood four deep behind the occupied seats. The glass-encased upper balcony was filled with blacks who had come to support Frost and they rapped the glass with keys and coins when a black alderman, Bennett Stewart (2nd) stood to second Bilandic's nomination. The lower gallery was filled with Bilandic loyalists who rose with cries of derision when . . . Dick Simpson (44th), characterized the election as 'nothing more than a backroom deal by three or four aldermen in a smoke-filled room.'"7

At this meeting, Vrdolyak, who had originally hoped to win the acting mayor position himself, nominated Alderman Bilandic. Alderman Ross Lathrop, who had replaced Leon Despres as 5th Ward alderman, attempted to place Frost's name in nomination and made a brief speech about the need to follow democratic processes. However, Alderman Frost, who was chairing the meeting as president pro tem, ruled that Alderman Lathrop was out of order, in effect declining the nomination. After the meeting he would tell reporters, "Why should I be the one who will take the suicide jump? . . . The only way I could sit in that [mayoral] chair is to have 25 [council] votes and I don't have them. I want to be a winner for my people."8

Fifteen aldermen hurried to second the nomination of Alderman Bilandic. Only Alderman Oberman and I spoke against his nomination. In my speech I recognized the positive qualities of Alderman Bilandic but said that he was "a product of the same 11th Ward backroom powers that have ruled the city for years. We are signing our own consent to future tyranny." This brought sharp retorts from several aldermen. Alderman Burton Natarus said, "If [Simpson] hasn't got the guts to place his own name in nomination, he ought to shut up and sit down." Alderman

Bernard Stone chimed in, "If you think you or someone else is better qualified, have the guts and stand up and be counted." Alderman Richard Mell, who had been attempting to elect Vrydolyak as acting mayor before the deals were cut, said more realistically, "There were other candidates, [but] majority rules in this city. We have settled on a man who can carry on."[9] Alderman Martin Oberman, who had replaced Bill Singer as 43rd Ward reform alderman, opposed Bilandic, declaring, "Bilandic did not campaign on the issues. What was campaigned on was the pie. The pie has been cut up." As might be expected, Oberman also got a negative response from the majority aldermen. The dean of the council [the alderman who had served for the most years], Alderman Vito Marzullo, shrieked, "That's a disgrace to the city."[10] When the debate ended, Bilandic was elected mayor by the city council and Alderman Laskowski vice mayor, with only Alderman Marty Oberman and myself voting in opposition. As expected, Alderman Frost was elected Finance Committee chairman and Alderman Vrdolyak president pro tem unanimously.

In press interviews afterward Bilandic said that he believed he was elected acting mayor "because as chairman of the Finance Committee I was able to become familiar with all the important aspects of city government—especially the city budget."[11] After he was sworn in, he pledged not to run in the special election to be held in the spring of 1977 for mayor to fill out Daley's term of office, and he resigned his position as 11th Ward alderman. In his acceptance speech he said, "It is important . . . that I announce that I am not a candidate for mayor. I am resigning as alderman of the 11th Ward and I will not be a candidate to fill that vacancy at a later date." He added that the succession crisis was over and that "the city of Chicago can face the future with confidence."[12]

In its editorial on December 28 and December 29, 1976, the local NBC television station (WMAQ) said, "The formation of ethnic and racial coalitions to bargain for slices of the power following Mayor Daley's death made Chicago look like a last bastion of an old style of backroom, horse-trading politics. . . . Picking political figures on the basis of race and nationality is wrong. It is divisive. It polarizes the city. And it is unfair to the individuals chosen. They may be the right people, but if they've been picked for the wrong reasons, they will start their new jobs with a definite lack of confidence from the public." Alderman Pucinski in his editorial reply on WMAQ-TV defended the machine's version of ethnic representation:

> WMAQ-TV says it is wrong to pick political figures on the basis of race and nationality. . . . It fails to recognize that Chicago is a beautiful mosaic—made up of citizens of different races, religions and ethnic origin—each of whom

has subliminal pride in his or her own ancestry. I was a member of the team that put this rapprochement together and I am proud that we were able to defuse what otherwise could have been a dangerous confrontation.[13]

In short, Alderman Pucinski concluded that the politics of race and ethnicity was fine. But representation is not merely a matter of making sure that our own racial or ethnic groups gets some of the power and some of the spoils. This continuing conflict over different concepts of representative democracy would become the hallmark of the Bilandic city council.

Mayor Bilandic quickly reversed his pledge and became a candidate to complete Mayor Daley's term in office. He defeated a group of candidates in the Democratic primary, including Alderman Pucinski, state senator Harold Washington (an African-American candidate from the South Side who would succeed in a second mayoral campaign in 1983), and former state's attorney Ed Hanrahan. Bilandic won with slightly more than 50 percent of the vote and carried thirty-eight of the fifty wards. He went on to defeat Republican alderman Dennis Block in the June runoff election by landslide proportions.

The Bilandic Council

Mayor Bilandic was a caretaker mayor trying to keep Daley's empire together and cope with social, economic, and political changes that Daley had contained, but he was unable to pull it off. "Bilandic put the job of mayor on—like a comfortable bathrobe." Political scientist Paul Green gave this more charitable assessment of Bilandic's performance: "Bilandic maintained a balanced city budget, kept the city's bond rating high and, until late in his term, reinforced the public service city tradition that 'Chicago was the city that worked.' Bilandic also maintained peace in the city council by using a strategy that relegated all controversies and fights behind closed doors. Years later, Bilandic refused to call the council during his term a rubber stamp. Rather he claimed it 'had the opportunity to perform its tasks . . . but they did it backstage.'"[14] However, Mayor Bilandic was able to maintain peace and control only with votes of the regular Democratic aldermen. The floor fights and the basic council voting pattern remained unchanged from the Daley years. The administration and reform blocs became more cohesive, although the reform bloc was reduced to three members within the year. Deviations in voting among administration aldermen simply was not tolerated when Bilandic was mayor and, if anything, the two blocs became more polarized. So, thanks to Daley, Bilandic had a council that was subservient in approving administration programs even though it was contentious and polarized.

Paul Peterson, in his study of voting on the Chicago School Board during the Daley era, called these voting patterns "ideological bargaining." Machine aldermen and reformers didn't just differ on separate roll call votes about separate issues. They also engaged in a more basic struggle over machine domination of Chicago, and their votes on each issue were mostly determined by whether it would advance or detract from that domination. Peterson suggested four defining characteristics of this pattern of voting: "(1) participants in the policy-making process will include groups committed to broad-gauge objectives who become involved in a range of policy questions; (2) such groups will find similar allies and similar enemies across a range of policy questions; (3) enduring and significant linkages between inclusive social groups and important political factions will occur; and (4) groups will find defeat of the opposition preferable to 'reasonable compromise.'"[15] So it was with the Daley and Bilandic councils.

The Bilandic council divided more or less along the same dimensions as the Daley council: (1) machine control versus citizen participation, (2) racial discrimination, (3) sexual discrimination, and (4) good government reform. There were no new aldermanic elections for two years after Daley's death, and thus there were no new aldermen on the council to alter the old balance of power or change the fundamental issue dimensions on which the existing council blocs were divided. However, the Bilandic council particularly was marked by three key votes that highlight the issues of democratic representation in a machine-controlled council. The first was the question of filling aldermanic vacancies in two wards, the second was the self-interest of alderman in higher salaries, and the third was the taxicab scandal, which played an important role in the next mayoral election.

Aldermanic Vacancies

Usually, legislative bodies such as the Chicago City Council do not vote directly on issues of representation. The legislative branch of government is simply assumed to be representative, at least in the formal sense of being fairly elected by the voters to represent them. But from time to time, aldermen die or resign for various reasons and aldermanic seats become vacant. As one would expect, the mayor and the council deal with these vacancies not according to abstract theories of representation but according to the opportunities that they present for political advantage.

During the Bilandic era, when special elections were required to fill vacancies and opponents to the city administration were likely to be elected, no special elections were held. This meant that constituents in those wards were left without any representation in the legislative process and without an elected aldermanic ombudsmen to ensure proper city services in their community. The most dramatic aldermanic vacancies occurred in 1977. Forty-Sixth Ward alderman Chris Cohen, a Young Turk and Coffee Rebellion member of the Daley administration voting bloc, resigned to become regional director of the Department of Health, Education, and Welfare. Forty-Eighth Ward alderman Dennis Block, a Republican who had been aligned with the reform aldermen, also resigned in 1977 after being defeated as the Republican candidate running for mayor against Bilandic. Several attempts were made by community organizations in these two North Side, lakefront wards to have the city council fill the vacancies. The reform aldermen brought to the floor of the council ordinances to hold a special election for these wards on three different occasions, but each time they were defeated by the Bilandic majority. These three council votes made it apparent that the intent of the Bilandic administration was to leave these seats vacant for two years until the regular elections in 1979. Politically, this was advantageous because these were wards in which Democratic reformers or Republicans might be elected. Their election would strengthen the small opposition bloc of anti-Bilandic aldermen and they might also raise issues embarrassing to the administration.

Citizens in the 46th and 48th Wards challenged this in court. In *Brand v. the City Council* constituents complained about their lack of representation:

> The lack of representation in the City Council deprives plaintiffs of their voting and representation rights under the equal protection clause of the Fourteenth Amendment to the Constitution. . . .
>
> Since the resignation of Alderman Cohen on November 3, 1977, the City Council has passed upon matters of substantial importance to the people of the 46th and 48th Wards, including review and approval of the City budget for 1978, which includes expenditures for all City services and projects in every ward of the City, including the 46th Ward and the 48th Ward.
>
> The deprivation of representation will continue to cause irreparable injury to plaintiffs by depriving them of any voice or representation in the important affairs which can be expected to be considered and passed upon by the City Council during the period until the vacancies in the office of Alderman are filled. For example, the City Council will review and approve the 1979 budget for the City; will act upon the annual municipal tax levy; and will allocate several hundred million dollars of grant money from the federal government to services and projects throughout the City, including services and projects in and for the 46th and 48th Wards.[16]

After hearing the evidence, federal judge John Powers Crowley issued a preliminary order requiring special elections in the 46th and 48th

Wards in the shortest period of time allowed under the election laws. Mayor Bilandic, under court order, introduced the necessary ordinance to call special elections. Although the outcome of the council vote was a forgone conclusion because of the court order, the council's debate illuminates the council's lack of concern about representation. The administration aldermen argued that the cost to the taxpayers in holding the election was too high, that the money required for the candidates to campaign was too great, and that this action represented the takeover of city council's legislative function by the federal courts.

> Alderman Edward Burke: "We all, I think, treasure the history the Founding Fathers have established and the democracy we enjoy. But we also have to confront the practicalities of the matter and that is to fill these offices by special election are a severe burden on the taxpayers of the City of Chicago."
>
> Alderman Burton Natarus: "It's a matter of principle. He [Judge Crowley] is ordering the Legislature to make a law. He's becoming a one-man Legislature. . . . I pray tell you today that this Federal District Court Judge has all but wiped out local government. That's what he has done . . . there is no local government today."
>
> Alderman Edward Vrdolyak: "I think the courts without question have become legislators. But I don't know why everyone is mad. I'm sometimes classified as an administration alderman and certainly in the 46th and 48th wards I would like to see aldermen elected . . . who should be sympathetic to the administration. I think it is very ironic to have Alderman Simpson and Alderman Oberman on the side for an immediate election when everybody knows—everybody knows—that over a short period of time that organization candidates have a distinct advantage."

The reform aldermen countered with arguments as to why representation for the constituents of the 46th and 48th Wards was so essential.

> Alderman Ross Lathrop: "Indeed, Alderman Vrdolyak, the advantage does go to the administration and the 'Machine' when such elections are conducted. And I think that underlying principle which is involved and which Alderman Simpson, Oberman and myself have been arguing about—which informed the introduction of our ordinances early on following the vacation of these seats—the underlying principle is so important that indeed the practical politics are set aside. It is more important to abide by the United States Constitution, it is more important to do those things than it is to make decisions on 'pragmatic political bases.'"
>
> Alderman Dick Simpson: "This action today is right. It's as simple as that. The principle of filling such vacancies is not a matter of whim, not a matter of legislative prerogative."[17]

Despite the administrative aldermen's public arguments about the cost to the taxpayers of holding special elections, money required for candidates to run in the elections, and the supposed necessity of preserving the separation of powers, the ordinance to conduct these special elections was adopted unanimously. Under federal court order, the city and the council had no choice but to comply. The "sound and fury" of the aldermen in the debate made no difference to the outcome.

Aldermanic Pay Raises

Just as the vote on aldermanic vacancies in the 46th and 48th Wards illustrates the clash over the right of voters to be represented in city council, the aldermanic pay raise issue illustrates another failure of aldermanic representation. In this case the aldermen were willing to ignore their constituents' views even when they were known. By the fall of 1978, inflation was high and would worsen in the months ahead. President Jimmy Carter had established the Council on Wage and Price Stability, which set a voluntary national effort limiting wage increases to no more than a 7 percent. Aldermanic salaries had increased substantially during the 1970s, from pay commensurate with a part-time job to nearly a full-time salary. When I was first elected alderman in 1971, our salary was only $8,000 a year, but by 1975, it had grown to $17,500, and most aldermen, as lawyers or insurance brokers, had other major sources of income.

By the time that the proposed aldermanic raises came up for a vote in 1978, I had decided to retire at the next election, so the salary decision would not affect me personally.[18] However, since my aldermanic colleagues had a direct financial interest in the pay raise, most of them supported the highest possible raises of 60 percent or more. Among pro-administration supporters of high pay raises, the most outspoken were Aldermen Marzullo, Burke, Vrdolyak, and Gabinski. Alderman Solomon Gutstein, a reform-minded pro-administration alderman from the 40th Ward who had replaced Alderman Simon, and Alderman Ross Lathrop, an Independent alderman from the 5th Ward who had replaced Alderman Despres, joined me in opposing high raises in aldermanic salaries. Alderman Oberman, after first being attracted by the potential pay raise, joined our opposition in trying to find a compromise pay raise within the limits established by the President's Council on Wage and Price Stability.

The pay raise issue became public on December 1, 1978, when the council's floor leader, Alderman Frost, after consulting with Mayor Bilandic, held a caucus with members of the Financial Committee. When the Finance Committee reassembled in public after the closed-door caucus, a city budget amendment was introduced to raise aldermanic salaries 60 percent, to $28,000 a year, in spite of federal wage guidelines to limit all pay raises to 7 percent. While the public might have supported a 7 percent pay raise, it was clear that the taxpayers were opposed to such massive raises for public officials. Over my dissenting vote the Finance Committee approved the raise.

Bilandic and administration aldermen stuck to their original pay raise proposal despite the opposition of President Carter's anti-inflation adviser, Alfred Kahn, who said to the press that he would "seek a rollback of 'outrageous' [city council] pay raises [which] violate [President] Carter's 7% voluntary wage guideline."[19] "Alderman Solomon Gutstein announced that he was opposed to any aldermanic raise in light of what he called the failure of most incumbents 'to take their responsibilities seriously and to concern themselves with legislation.'"[20] A few days later, as public opposition continued to grow, Alderman Oberman proposed an alternative pay raise of 7 percent a year calculated from 1975, the date of the last raise. Oberman, in defending his plan said, "I think that aldermen deserve some type of pay raise, but the citizens are right to be outraged [by the 60 percent proposal], and I have heard from many of them in the last few days."[21]

The pay raise issue was one of those rare instances when aldermen knew accurately the opinions of their constituents. The media were editorializing vigorously against the proposed pay raise and aldermen were receiving letters and phone calls from outraged constituents. As the *Chicago Tribune* reported, "City Hall switchboard operators said they have received numerous calls from Chicagoans critical of the pay increase. 'They are screaming their heads off,' an operator said. 'They want to know which aldermen are supporting these raises so they can vote against them.'"[22] These public outcries influenced neither the mayor nor the city council. Pressure from President Carter's staff did force a compromise, however. Mayor Bilandic introduced a new budget amendment at the council meeting on December 13 that increased salaries in stages, from $22,500 in 1979 to $27,600 in 1982 by additional raises of 7 percent each. This amendment was carried by a vote of 41–6. Despite the violation of the simple 7 percent raise standard, the President's Council on Wage and Price Stability "issued a finding that the pay schedule complies with anti-inflation guidelines." The President's Council reached this conclusion because the city argued that aldermen were a part of a 457-member city management group with average raises of only 4.5 percent.[23]

In the final council debate, administrative aldermen argued that the pay raise was just a public relations problem for aldermen while I maintained that it was a problem of democratic representation when constituent opinions were so well-known and aldermen ignored them. In response, Alderman Gabinski said that "the press have really done a job on us [aldermen]." For him, the loud constituent protest against aldermen receiving a 60 percent salary increase when other citizens were restricted to 7 percent was a public relations problem created by the media, not a matter of aldermen failing to represent the views of their constituents. I maintained that the salary issue was not a problem of timing or coverage by the press: "At a time when the public expected the government to look out for its best interest, government officials acted in their own self-interest."[24] In many situations aldermen do not know their constituents' views, but even in those dramatic situations like the pay raise debate, when they do know what their constituents want, they feel free to ignore them. In this case they chose to put their own self-interest in receiving more money above the broader public interest of curbing inflation in the economy. All but six aldermen voted for the pay raises despite vocal opposition by both the press and the public.

The Taxi Scandal

In January 1976, commissioner of Sales, Weights, and Measures Jane Byrne also became the commissioner of Public Vehicle Licenses in charge of the taxi franchise and licenses. The city by ordinance established taxi fares as well. At budget hearings for her department in November 1975 she announced that she would be inspecting taxicabs much more frequently to guarantee their safety after many reports in the newspapers of unsafe cabs. Jane Byrne's authority was extended at the May 4, 1977, council meeting by a 41–3 vote to require her department's approval of all independent operation of taxicabs. Then on July 13, 1977, the council approved an 11.7 percent increase in taxi fares, again by the usual 42–3 vote. In November 1977, Byrne released a memorandum describing how the taxi fare increase had been "greased" by Alderman Vrdolyak and Mayor Bilandic. She said in the memo that "the entire [city council] action was fraudulent and conspiratorial and should not have been granted." She reported a "secret" meeting at Midway Airport between Mayor Bilandic, key administrative personnel, and the owners of Yellow and Checker Cab Company. In a second meeting with the owners and the taxicab unions, Bilandic proposed getting a fare increase through the city council quickly:

> Mayor [Bilandic] began by saying, "I think it is established that to provide quality service there would have to be a rate increase." Jerry Feldman [the owner of Yellow and Checker Cabs which had 80 percent of the licensed taxicabs in Chicago] said, "How soon can we expect it?" The Mayor said, "We can have the [legislation] called up, pass it in Committee [on Local Transportation], present it to the Full Council, place it on defer and publish to avoid any discussion." Feldman answered, "That takes us into August."

The Mayor looked at him and said, "Not necessarily. I can call an emergency City Council Meeting the following week. Oh, we won't make the rate increase the reason for the Council Meeting. We'll blowup some other matter to look important and quietly tack the increase on in unfinished business." He looked at everybody and said "That's how it's done." Bilandic then asked Jerry Feldman how much of an increase he was speaking about and he said in the neighborhood of 12%. That was quickly agreed to.[25]

Commissioner Byrne in her memo further charged that the figures and "audit" supplied by the cab companies to justify the fare increase were fraudulent.

Although two newspaper reporters had copies of the memo that Byrne had asked them not to publish, because it would get her fired, her memo was made public on the 10 o'clock television news on CBS. Bilandic was in the studio to answer the charges and, like his answers a few months later on the snowstorm in 1979, the session did not go well.

[CBS News Anchor Bill] KURTIS: How would you characterize these statements, all these quotes?

MAYOR BILANDIC: It has to be incorrect.

[CBS News Anchor Walter] JACOBSON: Did she make them up?

KURTIS: Are they wild figments of her imagination? . . .

BILANDIC: Well you'll have to ask her. . . . You see, what I don't understand, Walter, is you have a self-serving document, something that somebody wrote, put down on a piece of paper, and never had it see the light of day until four months later. That very same person had an opportunity to testify at a public hearing when these matters were raised. Figures were presented, the company stands behind those figures and vouches for those figures.

Mayor Bilandic's answers may have been "all correct and lawyerlike . . . but he was in a television studio, not a courtroom." As the newspapers began to devote front-page coverage to the fight and to print Jane Byrne's memo in full, "Jane Byrne was successfully using the news media to make [Bilandic] look like a crook."[26]

Based on Byrne's memo, Aldermen Lathrop, Oberman, and I called a special council meeting on November 22, 1977, for the purpose of creating a committee to investigate and consider rescinding the July 13, 1977, taxi fare increase. At this meeting we had a surprising victory. Floor leader Wilson Frost and Alderman Oberman cosponsored a resolution, cosigned by all council members, declaring that it is "now in the public interest to re-examine the data" submitted by Checker and Yellow Cab Company that justified the fare increase.

Mayor Bilandic presided calmly over this special council meeting despite the fact that Byrne had denounced him as a conspirator in the fraudulent rate increase and he had fired her the previous day. The committee appointed to investigate the taxi fare increase and Byrne's charges included the three of us in the opposition bloc who had called the meeting and sixteen regular Democratic aldermen. None of the special committee members were from the Local Transportation Committee, which had conducted the pervious hearings and recommended the taxi fare increase. Nor was any alderman involved in the controversy, such as Alderman Vrdolyak who had arranged the secret meetings between the mayor and the cab companies. The Special Taxi Cab Investigating Committee was chaired by Alderman Frost. The resolution establishing the committee specifically called for an audit by one of the nationally recognized accounting firms known as the Big Eight, excluding both Arthur Anderson and Ernst and Ernst, which had previously worked for Checker and Yellow Cabs.

On December 7, 1977, the city budget proposed by the administration and approved by the city council provided $200,000 for the investigation. The Special Taxi Cab Investigating Committee named Arthur Young as the accounting firm to report on the financial data used in the taxi fare increase and hired well-known lawyer Jewel Lafontant as the taxi-probe counsel. Alderman Oberman charged that her selection was "greased" by Alderman Frost. In a closed-door session the committee voted 10–4 to confirm her appointment. Aldermen George Hagopian, Lathrop, and I voted for Special Attorney General Joseph Karaganis, and Alderman Oberman voted for Milton Shadur, an attorney later appointed a federal judge.[27]

Arthur Young and Company reported to the investigating committee on March 15, 1978, that "Checker Cab Co. and Yellow Cab Co. were losing money in the year before the controversial 11.38 per cent increase . . . and that 'a fare increase of some measure was justifiable.'" Since the company did not report gross fares of their leased cabs, the auditors could not conclude "that the (specific) fare adjustment granted was justified under the criteria of the code." The counsel and the auditors recommended amending the taxi ordinance to tighten future regulation of fares. Alderman Oberman asked if the council could revoke the fare increase "on grounds that the companies had not met the reporting requirements of the ordinance." Committee counsel Lafrontant declared that the ordinance was "obsolete" but that it would be "legally indefensible on that account to move to rescind the action the council had taken under it." She asserted that would violate the cab companies' rights. The fare increase, she argued was "over and done with."[28]

A week later, the Special Investigating Committee met for a final time and, unsurprisingly, voted 10–3 to recommend its dissolution and to end the investigation. In defending the action, administration stalwart 1st Ward alderman Fred Roti said that he was "satisfied that the rate increase was justifiable" and that, since a U.S. grand jury and the Internal Revenue Service were investigating the rate increase issues, further aldermanic inquiries "would only duplicate the work of the federal government and waste the taxpayers' money."

Urging that the auditors be fired and the investigation be continued, Alderman Oberman charged that the Arthur Young report was "a political, public relations statement, which is an apology for the taxi companies, and I find it unacceptable." He charged again that Arthur Young was chosen over the other audit firms because the administration "wanted a political statement," not a financial statement. Alderman Frost in later interviews with reporters said, "Based on the data reviewed by the auditors and showing that the taxi companies understated, rather than overstated, their loses in the 1977 hearings, we could draw only one conclusion that the taxi fare increase was justified." Accordingly, on April 21, 1978, the council followed the committee's recommendation and ended the taxi fare hike probe by the usual vote of 40–3. However, the "taxi-gate scandal" sparked the beginning of Byrne's run for mayor.[29]

The Silent Revolution

The Bilandic council came to an end with the elections of 1979. Bilandic had been firmly in control of the rubber stamp city council that he had inherited after the brief power struggle following Daley's death. He kept most members of Daley's cabinet and made some progress in resolving old problems. He won his interim election in 1977 with a commanding majority. On the surface, it seemed that the machine under Mike Bilandic's titular leadership would keep control without difficulty. However, those appearances were deceptive. A groundwork had been laid over the years of council debates about democracy and better citizen representation. Inefficiencies in city government had been exposed, and many Chicagoans were disgusted with political corruption and the cost of city services. Most of all, growth of the African-American and Latino populations was so great that they could no longer be considered junior partners in a minority white-controlled party machine. All these factors conspired with the peculiar personalities and circumstances of 1979 to bring change. The Bilandic interlude gave way to a different regime, but the Chicago City Council stayed pivotal to the changes.

In comparison to the 1960s, the 1970s were a quieter time. By 1972,

President Richard Nixon had begun to scale down the Vietnam War and consequently, during the Bilandic interlude from 1976 to 1979, American foreign policy was no longer a dividing issue in the council. The 1970s saw a growth in the environmental movement highlighted by the Earth Day celebration at the Chicago Civic Center and in twenty other cities across the country. However, after Mayor Daley reintroduced and passed Alderman Singer's antipollution ordinance limiting air pollution, Chicago became a leading local government in the passage of antipollution legislation. As 11th Ward alderman, Michael Bilandic had regularly introduced proenvironment legislation, and thus environmental protection was no longer a divisive issue in the council.

When Bilandic became mayor, he defused the worst of the racial issues momentarily. He settled the case of the African-American patrolman, which Mayor Daley had refused to settle. As a result, there were now official affirmative action procedures for hiring and promoting minorities and women in the Chicago Police and Fire Departments. The power to veto public housing sites had already been removed from the city council by the federal courts in 1973 by the *Gautreaux* decision, so public housing was not a central issue in the Bilandic council. By settling the racial discrimination cases against Chicago, Bilandic received $195 million in revenue sharing funds that the national government had withheld until Chicago complied with federal court desegregation rulings. Although race would be a major factor in future mayoral elections, it was not a central focus in the Bilandic council, other than in his election as interim mayor.

So the anti–Vietnam War, environmental, and civil rights movements were not providing the momentum for reform that they had during the Daley councils. As the opposition forces in the council shrank, the council simply became more of a rubber stamp. When Aldermen Singer and Hoellen had run for mayor against Mayor Daley in 1975 and lost, they gave up their council seats. Alderman Leon Despres retired after twenty years of leading the opposition in the council. African-American Independent alderman Anna Langford was defeated in her reelection bid. In 1976, African-American Independent alderman William Cousins was elected a judge. Alderman Dennis Block, the last Republican alderman to serve in the council until 1991, ran for mayor against Bilandic in 1977, lost the election, and resigned as alderman. Democratic alderman Christopher Cohen, who had begun to vote with the Independent bloc more frequently, resigned to become regional director the U.S. Department of Health, Education, and Welfare. Thus the Independent bloc dwindled to three under Mayor Bilandic. Moreover, fewer aldermen could be convinced to cross over to vote with us. During the Bilandic interlude the pro-administration and opposition blocs in the city council became more cohesive and there was no room to compromise.

Despite this rubber stamp council, Bilandic was not the powerful, domineering politician that Richard J. Daley had been. His cabinet consisted mostly of holdover Daley appointees, as most government policies he pursued were Daley's. Bilandic had not been elected on a platform of his own. When he undertook initiatives such as settling a potential taxicab strike and granting a taxicab fare increase, he created bad publicity for himself and his administration. Moreover, Bilandic was not a ward committeeman nor chairman of the Democratic Party. One of Daley's sons held the 11th Ward committeeman post and a Daley family ally, Cook County Board president George Dunne, was party chairman. So Bilandic did not have his own power base. He was not a political boss. He was supported primarily by the State Street businessmen, real estate developers, the Daley family, their political allies, and party loyalists. Given this base of support, Bilandic might make some adjustments in government and some new policy decisions, but his principal role was to continue the status quo.

Mayor Bilandic's objective in the city council was to keep control, to keep the lid on explosive issues, and to eliminate political opposition. The central focus of debate in the council continued to be procedural and substantive democracy, and thus the fight over filling aldermanic vacancies is a perfect symbol of the Bilandic council. Fairness and principles of representative democracy dictated that the vacant aldermanic seats in the 46th and 48th Wards be filled by special elections until regular elections could be held more than two years later. The mayor and his strategists thought that the political advantages of a smaller Independent bloc in the council outweighed any theoretical right to representation and services that citizens in those wards might have. In taking that stand, Bilandic undercut his credibility with the reformers without appreciably strengthening his position with the Democratic machine.

Although Richard J. Daley kept aldermanic salaries at part-time wage levels, Bilandic relented to aldermanic pressure despite President Carter's attempt to prevent wage increases in order to control rampant inflation. Consequently, in 1978, aldermen voted themselves the first in a series of pay raises that would increase aldermanic salaries to $27,600 in 1982. Bilandic caved in to aldermanic greed and ignored public opinion.

Finally, the taxi fare increase that Mayor Bilandic maneuvered through the council in 1977 may have been illegal. The resulting taxicab scandal launched Byrne's successful campaign for mayor against Bilandic in 1979. In this issue too the public's desire for safe cabs and low fares was ignored in the backroom deals.

Overall, the Bilandic council was a logical extension of the rubber stamp councils begun under party bosses like Anton Cermak and Ed Kelly, and perfected under Richard J. Daley. The fights that had begun over the repressive use of the Rules Committee to bottle up reform legislation in Daley's last year in office when Bilandic was floor leader now extended to constant battles over issues, including aldermanic vacancies, aldermanic pay raises, and taxi fares, as sustained protests by the opposition bloc publicized the faults of the Bilandic administration and his aldermanic supporters.

In political history, as in individual lives, when extremes emerge, they frequently prompt a dialectical turn to the opposite extreme, as when chaotic anarchy is replaced by autocratic dictators or when repressive tyrannies lead to democratic revolutions. Thus the extreme rubber stamp council and autocratic mayoral rule could not be maintained by the plodding, methodical, uncharismatic Mayor Bilandic. Still, it would take an unusual act of Mother Nature, bureaucratic bungling, racial insensitivity, and the revelation that the supposedly all-powerful City Hall was lying to the public to bring down this regime. Byrne, a machine maverick masquerading as a reformer, would accelerate these historic trends that social and economic forces were generating. The Daley machine would not continue unchallenged under Bilandic's weak leadership.

The Bilandic interlude was an attempt to continue the status quo—to continue the Democratic machine, the growth machine, and a rubber stamp council—under a weak mayor unable to hold together the empire that Daley had built. Inexorable forces—racial clashes, a growing minority population, a switch from manufacturing to a service economy, decay of the political machine, and a failure to modernize city government and its patronage-based delivery of city services—would soon crack the facade of omnipotence that had contributed to the success of Bilandic's predecessor. A silent revolution from machine politics and a growth machine regime was taking place below the surface of politics as usual.

Notes

1. For exact statistics, see Dick Simpson, ed., *Chicago's Future: In a Time of Change* (Champaign, Ill.: Stipes, 1993), pp. 4, 38–39, 70, 88, 103–104.

2. Bill Granger and Lori Granger, *Lords of the Last Machine: The Story of Politics in Chicago* (New York: Random House, 1987), pp. 184–185; and Roger Biles, *Richard J. Daley: Politics, Race, and the Governing of Chicago* (DeKalb: Northern Illinois University Press, 1995), p. 233.

3. Granger and Granger, *Lords of the Last Machine*, p. 185.

4. William Braden et al., "10 Days That Shook Chicago," *Chicago Sun-Times*, January 2, 1977, p. 1.

5. Braden, "10 Days," p. 1.

6. Braden, "10 Days," p. 1.

7. Neil Mehler and Robert Davis, "Alderman Frost Withdraws, Bilandic Chosen Mayor," *Chicago Tribune*, December, 29, 1976, p. 12.

8. The description of the meeting and the quotation are from Ellen Warren and Saunders Saperstein, "Pucinski Will Run in Spring," *Chicago Daily News*, December 28, 1976; and Mehler and Davis, "Alderman Frost," pp. 1, 12.

9. These quotes are from Greg Hinz, "Bilandic Is 6-Month Mayor," *Lerner Booster*, December 29, 1976, p. 1.

10. Mehler and Davis, "Alderman Frost," p. 12.

11. Mehler and Davis, "Alderman Frost," p. 12.

12. Warren and Saperstein, "Pucinski Will Run," p. 1.

13. The original editorial opposing racial and ethnic political maneuvering was broadcast by WMAQ on December 28–29, 1976. Alderman Pucinski's WMAQ editorial reply was broadcast on January 4–5, 1977. Copies of the text of both are in the Dick Simpson Papers, Special Collections, Main Library, University of Illinois at Chicago.

14. Paul Green, "Michael Bilandic (1976–1979)," in Paul Green and Melvin Holli, *The Mayors: The Chicago Political Tradition* (Carbondale: Southern Illinois University Press, 1987), p. 164.

15. Paul Peterson, *School Politics Chicago Style* (Chicago: University of Chicago Press, 1976), p. 51.

16. *Tom A. Brand vs. The City Council of the City of Chicago et al.*, Civil Action No. 78C30 in the U.S. District Court for the Northern District of Illinois, Eastern Division, "Complaint for Declaratory and Injunctive Relief," pp. 9–10.

17. The quotations from the aldermanic debate are from Dick Simpson and William Mahin, *The Chicago City Council* (Chicago: University of Illinois at Chicago, 1982), videocassette; and Harry Golden Jr., "Special Votes Called in the 46th, 48th," *Chicago Sun-Times*, February 9, 1978, p. 2.

18. An aldermanic raise wouldn't have affected me anyway. During the eight years I served as alderman, I donated my aldermanic salary entirely to running my aldermanic service office. Over the eight years this amounted to more than $100,000.

19. Harry Golden Jr., "Bilandic Sticks by 60% Pay Raise," *Chicago Sun-Times*, December 5, 1978, p. 5.

20. Golden, "Bilandic," p. 5.

21. Robert Davis and William Juneau, "Oberman: Raise Our Pay 7% a Year," *Chicago Tribune*, December 6, 1978, pp. 1, 18.

22. Davis and Juneau, "Oberman," p. 1.

23. Harry Golden Jr., "Aldermen Cut Back Pay Hikes, *Chicago Sun-Times*, December 14, 1978, pp. 5, 24.

24. Greg Hinz, "Most Local Aldermen Happy with 4-Year Pay Raise Plan," *Lerner Booster*, December 16–17, 1978, pp. 1, 6.

25. "The Full Text of Comr. Byrne's Taxi Memo," *Chicago Daily News*, November 16, 1977.

26. Bill Granger and Lori Granger, *Fighting Jane: Mayor Jane Byrne and the Chicago Machine* (New York: Dial, 1980), p. 184.

27. Martin J. Oberman, "Taxi-Rate Inquiry Greased by Choice of Its Probers," *Chicago Daily News*, January 24, 1978.

28. Harry Golden Jr., "Cab-Fare Data·Failed to Meet Law: Auditor," *Chicago Sun-Times*, March 16, 1978, p. 6.

29. Harry Golden Jr., "Council Unit Upholds Taxi Fare Hike," *Chicago Sun-Times*, March 23, 1978, pp. 5, 58; and Golden, "Aldermen Hail Push for Taxi Code Overhaul," *Chicago Sun-Times*, March 24, 1978.

6

Jane Byrne's Turmoil,
1979–1983

Jane Byrne was a protégé of Mayor Richard J. Daley. For symbolic purposes she served as the woman cochair of the Cook County Democratic Central Committee. Within city government she served as Daley's commissioner of Consumer Sales, Weights, and Measures. But Jane Byrne had no political base of her own. She was not an alderman, a state legislator, or a ward committeeman. Consequently, when Daley died, she lost her clout. Then in 1978, she accused Mayor Bilandic of "greasing" a taxicab fare increase. She charged that even if he had not been bribed, he had been influenced by the owners of the two largest taxi companies to illegally pass a city ordinance granting a taxi fare increase. Not surprisingly, Bilandic fired her. She then launched her campaign to run against him for mayor.

Because Bilandic had won his election easily in 1977 and the machine was still believed to be invincible, "Fighting Jane" Byrne was Bilandic's sole opponent in the Democratic Party primary election of 1979. However, citizen discontent with city government had been building. In addition to the taxicab scandal, African Americans were dissatisfied with city services and racial discrimination while white liberals believed government reforms were badly needed to modernize government. Yet, despite the discontents of various groups, Jane Byrne had no chance to win until the Great Snowstorm of 1979.

The blizzard began on New Year's Eve, 1978. By New Year's Day twenty-two inches of snow had fallen. On January 12–13, 1979, another twenty inches fell. The temperature dropped below zero. The city government was unprepared to cope with such a blizzard. As the snow piled higher and higher, traffic ground to a halt. Even main streets were blocked and businesses and schools closed. Cars became trapped and many streets became impassable. City services totally broke down. By the second snowfall, the CTA elevated trains had problems keeping schedules. So the decision was made to cut service to smaller stations on the South and West Sides in the African-American community. Closing them brought immediate cries of discrimination and racism. What made matters worse politically was that Mayor Bilandic appeared on television trying to tell the public that city crews were clearing the streets and towing cars to public school parking lots, and that everything would quickly return to normal. But the city snow-clearing operation failed totally—this snow was simply more than the government could handle. The city was snowed in.

> Bilandic was now frantic, his calm demeanor replaced by the crazed, wide-eyed grimace of a frightened man. He called a press conference to announce a new city plan that required residents to remove their cars from side streets and park them in newly cleared areas designated by the city, including school parking lots. . . . The *Tribune* sent around a reporter team to the various lots designated in Bilandic's plan and discovered that many had not been plowed at all. Overnight, Bilandic became a laughingstock.[1]

Byrne quickly criticized the city snow operations. She used the snow as a backdrop for her television commercials. Meanwhile, Mayor Bilandic continued to promise the impossible. He appeared as foolish as he had in the television interview when her memo on the taxicab scandal had been released. The *Chicago Tribune* covered the mayor's speech to Democratic precinct captains in which he likened "criticism of his administration to the Crucifixion of Jesus, the mass murders of Jews and the recent collapses of foreign governments," which seemed totally absurd to the voters.[2] A few weeks later these same voters clearly remembered Bilandic's promises that the snow was being removed and the CTA's method of rerouting public transportation. They voted for Byrne in protest. Reformers and blacks combined with disgusted Democratic Party voters to help Byrne narrowly win the primary with 51 percent of the vote. As the party nominee, she went on easily to win the general election.

Political scientist Paul Green analyzed the election results as follows: "The key to Byrne's win, outside of the elements, was the coalescing of existing antiorganizational forces behind her candidacy. Byrne won twenty-nine wards in three main areas of the city (the middle-class black South Side, the string of lakefront independent/liberal wards, and several wards in Chicago's Northwest Side Polish community). Her later reconciliation with the organization did not dilute the fact that potent political forces were working in the Chicago electorate and from the traditional machine's viewpoint, 'they were out of control.'"[3]

TABLE 6.1   The 1979 Democratic Mayoral Primary: Regression Estimates of Group Voting Behavior

	Bilandic	*Byrne*	*Nonvote*
Citywide[a]			
Blacks	14.2	20.3	60.4
Whites	24.7	24.2	51.0
Latino	14.0	4.2	81.6
Blacks			
Dawson Wards	14.7	20.4	64.8
Other South Side	12.1	23.7	64.0
West Side	16.0	15.1	68.8
White ethnics	28.9	24.5	46.4
Northwest side	21.9	26.4	51.6
South Side	36.9	22.3	40.4
Total citywide	18.6	19.5	61.8

[a]Entries in this table are percentages of voting-age population, and rows sum to 100 percent, except for rounding errors.

SOURCE: Paul Kleppner, *Chicago Divided: The Making of a Black Mayor* (1985).

Political scientist Paul Kleppner's method of analyzing Chicago elections allows us to pinpoint the results. In the 1979 primary, Byrne won the election because she received a majority black vote, split the white vote nearly evenly with Bilandic, and only lost the small Latino vote.[4]

Although the voter turnout rate in the African-American community was only 34.5 percent, blacks overwhelmingly voted for Byrne. "Their performance in 1979 marked the first occurrence (probably since 1943) of blacks' not giving at least a plurality to the slated [Democratic Party] candidate for mayor." Thus Kleppner concurs with Green:

Byrne's victory was not quite the fluke that it appeared to be. Her candidacy appealed to strains of discontent that existed before the snows—the ongoing antipathy to the Machine among white liberals along the Lake Shore, the resentment harbored by the Northwest Side ethnics over the leadership monopoly of the South Siders, and the growing disaffection of the city's blacks. She appealed to these groups by focusing on Bilandic and assailing him as the leader of a "cabal of evil men" who were arrogantly insensitive to the needs of the neighborhoods. At the same time, because she was not an outsider to the Machine and because she identified herself with Daley's image and evoked memories of what the city had been like when he was in charge, she reassured white ethnics that she posed no threat to their continued control of their neighborhoods and schools. Therefore, they felt free to choose between the white contenders without fear of jeopardizing their cultural dominance.[5]

This was also the first local Chicago election in which the media overwhelmed the precinct captain's ability to deliver the party vote. Byrne had no precinct captains, no endorsements from Democratic Ward committeemen, and only a handful of volunteers. Independent aldermanic campaigns provided her only poll watchers to keep the election honest and to provide her with early results when the polls closed. Yet, because Jane Byrne was running for mayor in a high visibility race, further heightened by the collapse of city services during the Great Snowfall, she was able to gain major coverage in the media. She also had sufficient funds to purchase some television ads to get her message through to the voters without precinct captains or volunteers. A political machine that could not win a party primary for its own mayoral candidate was no longer the legendary machine of the Richard J. Daley era.

The Byrne Council: Young Turks Come to Power

Jane Byrne in her four years of office had an extraordinary effect on Chicago politics. She was feisty, egocentric, and temperamental, but also insecure in her new position of power. In spite of (or because of) her personality, she undermined the political party machine that had dominated Chicago government for forty years, first by defeating it in election and then by splitting it into factions. She weakened city government by a revolving-door policy that fired experienced city department heads appointed by Daley and Bilandic and replaced them with a parade of newcomers whom she hired and fired with abandon. Finally, she broke apart the governing regime of the machine/City Hall/business leaders because she could not supply the stability and clout necessary to produce reliably probusiness, progrowth laws, and government projects.

In Chapter 5 I introduced Aldermen Frost, Vrdolyak, and Burke, who went on to control the Byrne city council. The Byrne council was defined by the clash between them and a small bloc of Independents led by Alderman Oberman. Therefore, it is important to focus on Mayor Byrne and Alderman Oberman to complete the introduction of the key political actors of this period in Chicago politics.

Jane Byrne was born Jane Burke (no relation to Alderman Burke) to a relatively wealthy Irish family in the Sauganash neighborhood on the far

Northwest Side of Chicago. She graduated from Barat College and married William Byrne, who was subsequently killed in a plane crash as a Marine pilot. The Byrnes had a daughter, Kathy, who would later hold jobs in the city government while her mother was mayor. After William Byrne's death, Jane worked briefly as a volunteer in John F. Kennedy's campaign for president in 1960. Mayor Daley met this feisty Irish-American woman in that campaign and gave her a job at City Hall. In 1968, he made her commissioner of the Department of Weights and Measures. Later, she dated and eventually married Jay McMullen, the City Hall reporter for the *Chicago Daily News* who worked as her press secretary after she became mayor. Although she was known for her role in exposing the taxicab scandal, she was still an unknown quantity when she became the first woman mayor in Chicago's history. Although she knew how City Hall worked from the inside, she had no prior experience holding elective office and made some bad mistakes in her first elected position.

Alderman Martin Oberman was elected in 1975 to replace William Singer as an Independent alderman representing the 43rd Ward in the North Side Lincoln Park neighborhood. Oberman was a lawyer who had been a volunteer in Independent politics from the first Singer campaign in 1969. When Singer ran for mayor in 1975, Oberman ran for his aldermanic seat with the endorsement of IVI, IPO, Singer, myself, and other elected Independent officials. Oberman served in the council from 1975 to 1987. He was politically ambitious but firmly committed to the principles of good government and Independent politics. He took over the leadership of the Independent bloc in the city council when I retired in 1979, twice ran unsuccessfully for attorney general of the state of Illinois, and continued to head reform organizations such as the Chicago Council of Lawyers after he retired from the council.

Byrne had many critical decisions to make upon taking over the mayor's office. As a city department head for over a decade, she knew how city government had worked under her mentor, Mayor Daley, but she couldn't operated it as effectively as he did. One of her first acts when she became mayor was to fire city department heads who had been loyal to Mayor Bilandic and might support her feared rival, Richard M. Daley, in future challenges to her. She installed her own team but, unfortunately, did not create a stable administration. Hers became a revolving-door government. She fired the head of her transition team, Northwestern University professor Louis Masotti, and threw out the team's report and recommendations without reading them. She had a half dozen different budget directors during her four-year term. In general, her administration was characterized by turmoil, constant changes in personnel, and frequent policy shifts, in contrast to the long, stable administrations of Daley.

One of the major decisions that Byrne faced in the first days of her administration was how she would work with the city council. She had not run on a ticket with aldermanic candidates; rather, they had been elected on their own without her help. Moreover, she had run for mayor on a reform platform. In her campaign she had criticized the Bilandic regime, promised a "congress of neighborhoods" to bring decisionmaking closer to the people, and consistently attacked the "evil cabal" of aldermen who were aligned with Bilandic and participated in backroom deals such as the taxi fare hike. It was logical, then, to assume that Byrne would work with a coalition of "Independent" and "machine" aldermen to reform the city council and advance her new programs. Independent alderman Oberman and regular Democratic alderman William Lipinski assembled just such a coalition to back the new Byrne administration. This is the account of Alderman Oberman's meeting with Mayor Byrne the day after the primary election:

> "Congratulations on your tremendous victory," [Alderman Oberman] said.
> . . .
>
> [Mayor Byrne replied,] "The congratulations should go to you. . . . It was really the politics that you have been preaching and that Singer and Simpson and Despres stand for, that won the election. . . . That's what the people of Chicago spoke for, that they were tired of this closed, corrupt system. They wanted that kind of politics. And so you should be congratulated."
>
> Jane Byrne was talking about the core of the problem that Friday morning with Marty Oberman. The city council had been emasculated by Daley in concert with Tom Keane. The aldermen were trained seals; the council was a rubber-stamp parliament. . . .
>
> Martin Oberman was charmed out of his socks. Not only was the lady listening to him, but she was including him. He could come in from the cold and be an insider.[6]

Thus Oberman and Lipinski began their efforts to reorganize the city council for Mayor Byrne. They relied on her flat declaration that she wanted Burke and Vrdoyak out of all positions of power in the council.

After her election, however, Byrne sought help from these two members of the "cabal of evil men" she had earlier criticized. She allowed Aldermen Vrdolyak and Burke to put together the committees and the rules for the new council. They, not Oberman and Lipinski, were to run the council. In short, she turned back to the machine of which she had been a part during the Daley era. Mayor Byrne would later say, "I can't govern this city unless I cut a deal with [Vrdolyak and Burke]. I have no constituency in the council. I don't have anything in the bureaucracy. I bark orders from the fifth floor and nobody listens. If I don't have these people with me, government won't operate."[7]

Vrdolyak and Burke had been among the Young Turks as part of the so-called Coffee Rebellion in the Daley city council. Now, under Byrne, they were to gain the power they felt they deserved. They locked up the committee chairmanships at the first council meeting and ran it for the rest of Mayor Byrne's four years in office. Even so, under Mayor Byrne, the iron-fisted reign of Daley and Bilandic over the council began to erode. It was not just the small bloc of Independent reform aldermen who revolted. African-American aldermen began to vote with the opposition as Byrne's term in office continued and the black community became more and more dissatisfied. Although Byrne was still able to pass her administration's legislation, more and more often aldermen split from supporting her.

The council's principal controversies in the Byrne years were government reform, city finances, race, labor disputes, economic development, and social issues. Of these, only labor disputes were a new agenda of the 1980s—the other issues had occurred a number of times during Chicago's political history. Despite the consistency of the issues, the machine continued to deteriorate under Byrne's often inept leadership. Yet she was able to continue the basic rubber stamp pattern that Chicago had followed since the Depression.

Council Rules

Under Mayor Byrne the city council continued many of its old patterns. The committee chairmen chosen by Burke and Vrdolyak mostly were unchanged from the Daley councils. Machine aldermen tended to serve a long time and be reelected many times, so the senior members of the council often served twenty years or more. The average age of council members was sixty, although there was a sprinkling of Young Turks and young reformers among council members.

When the council rules were adopted on April 7, 1979, all proposed reform amendments, even a simple proposal to publish quarterly reports of city council voting records, were defeated by a vote of 42–8. Thus, even at the beginning of the Byrne administration, there was a marked increase in the opposition bloc from three to eight members. Opposition to Byrne would continue to grow as she alienated more aldermen and their constituents in the later years of her term. Yet most aldermen still weren't ready for reform. Had the mayor been willing to lead the charge, enough aldermanic votes could have been swayed that procedural changes could have been adopted, but without her leadership, this council was no more willing to reform itself than the Daley or Bilandic councils had been.

Redistricting

During Mayor Byrne's reign, 1980 census data became available. It was the legal obligation of the mayor and council to redraw the boundaries of the fifty wards to guarantee equal population in each ward in keeping with Supreme Court decisions guaranteeing "one man, one vote." The ward map was drawn by Martin Murphy, head of the city's Department of Planning, with the help of former alderman Tom Keane, who had been the principal architect of the 1971 remap (even though he had since served time in federal prison for corruption). Amendments to the boundaries of individual wards were obtained by aldermen in secret negotiations with Murphy and Keane in return for their support of the overall map.

The Byrne council ended its backroom deal making and publicly voted on the new map on November 12, 1981. The intent of the map was to protect as many pro-administration aldermen as possible with safe districts for their reelection campaigns. This meant protecting white incumbent aldermen in a number of communities that had become populated by a majority of African Americans and Latinos. Although the 1970 map had provided for an average ward population of 67,400, by 1980 that had dropped to 60,100 because of the city's population loss. However, the African-American population had increased from 33 percent to 40 percent of the total population while the white population had dropped.[8]

Despite African-American population growth, the Byrne ward map proposed to create only seventeen majority black wards, even though it would have been easy to create more. For example, in the 37th Ward blacks had grown from 12.5 percent in 1971 to 76 percent before the remap. After the map was drawn, 17,000 whites were moved into the new 37th Ward boundaries, and 37,000 blacks moved out to create a ward that was 50 percent white and only 37 percent black. This gerrymandering was done to keep 37th Ward alderman Thomas Casey, chairman of the Rules Committee and a reliable ally of Mayor Byrne, in the council. A number of other black and Latino wards represented by white ethnic aldermen supporting Mayor Byrne were drawn the same way.[9]

After an extended debate about the racial inequalities of the remap, the council voted 34–15 to approve it. A lawsuit challenging the ward remap was filed in the federal courts. In 1986, the court ordered the redistricting of seven racially changing wards and mandated special elections. The court ruled that the Byrne council map clearly discriminated against both black and Hispanic voters.

Appointment of Boards and Commissions

In the last years of the Byrne council, the most common racial issues were mayoral appointments to the Chicago School Board and CHA public housing board. Byrne's nomination of whites to replace blacks on both bodies led to major conflicts with the African-American community. In May 1980, Mayor Byrne nominated eleven school board members. Only two ran into difficulties in the council: Thomas Ayers, former CEO of Commonwealth Edison electric power company, whom Byrne wanted to head the board, and Cuban-American businessman Luis Salces. Alderman Oberman objected to the appointment of Thomas Ayers, especially since Mayor Byrne had chosen only three people with children in the public school system to serve on the school board. Oberman argued, "But if there was a need for a white business leader on the board, we could have found one among the three million people of Chicago, those who haven't moved out (to the suburbs)." Oberman concluded, "Tom Ayers is a good man. But this is not the spot for him."

On behalf of the administration, Alderman Richard Mell argued that the issue was not whether Ayers lived in the city or in the suburbs. He said, "I don't have that problem. If Ayers is a good man, I'll vote for him." Regular Democratic alderman Burt Natarus added, "He came to Chicago without a dime and rose to become chairman of a multibillion-dollar corporation. Isn't that the American dream? Is there a person here who doesn't want it?" After the debate, Alderman Frost, as head of the Finance Committee, introduced a municipal code amendment to avert a court fight on whether Ayers met the state residency requirements for school board membership, using the city's home rule powers to override the state law, which requires members of local boards to reside in the municipality. Frost's resolution was approved by one of the tightest margins during the Byrne era, 28–16. Ayers appointment was then approved, 31–15.[10]

The Battle over the Transition Team Report

The fight over the transition team report did not occur in the city council but between the mayor, the news media, and the courts. It illustrates some of the key defects of the Byrne administration. Following an increasingly common practice for large governments, Mayor Byrne decided to have a transition team prepare for her administration taking office. After winning the primary in February 1979, she appointed a twenty-six-member transition team headed by Louis Masotti, on leave as director of the Urban Affairs Center at Northwestern University. I headed the section of the team that studied the operations of city government and prepared a 700-page report entitled *New Programs and Departmental Evaluations* on the details of government operations. We proposed 197 specific recommendations for government reforms.

Our report was presented to Byrne after her inauguration in April 1979, and she gave it to her aides to review. She had by that time, however, disposed of Professor Masotti because of comments he made while she was out of town about who might be hired and fired in her new administration. Since he was out of favor, the entire transition team report was shelved and never implemented. The *Chicago Lawyer*, a publication of the Chicago Council of Lawyers, learned of the report's existence and asked for a copy of it as a public document. They were turned down and took the matter to court. In December 1979, the court ordered the report released. The *Chicago Lawyer* then obtained a copy of the original report from me and in turn made it available to the newspapers in June 1980.

Mayor Byrne's reaction to the report's publication was to continue to ignore its recommendations and attack the *Chicago Tribune,* which printed much of it. Mayor Byrne charged that the *Tribune* had "engaged in innuendoes, lies, smears, character assassination and male chauvinistic tactics" since her election in April 1979. In retaliation, she banned the *Chicago Tribune* from the City Hall press room. Mayor Byrne's husband and press secretary, Jay McMullen, said that the mayor "believes the *Tribune* is damaging Chicago. The paper never wanted her to be mayor and doesn't want her to be mayor now, and they are trying to destroy her administration."[11]

The news media, of course, opposed the mayor. A CBS editorial summed up the media's view:

> The mayor got angry when the Trib published . . . the mayor's secret transition report. She was so mad, she threatened to take away the Trib's desk in the City Hall press room. Suddenly, no one was paying attention to the transition report, only the dispute. So the mayor won.
>
> She succeeded in keeping the focus off the report . . . [which] spelled out serious problems faced by the city when the mayor took office. And [the report] recommended solutions. . . . In the year she's had the report, the mayor's done very little. . . . Most of the problems—and solutions—have been ignored. The mayor can try to discredit the report, try to keep it secret, try diversionary tactics. But she can't make the problems it reveals go away . . . unless she takes action.[12]

The mayor finally relented and allowed the *Tribune* reporter to continue his work at his usual desk in the City Hall press room. After a few weeks, the furor over freedom of the press ended and business went back to usual at City Hall. However, Mayor Byrne and her administration continued to ignore the report's recommendations for reform.

It was difficult to get copies of all public records during the Byrne administration, not just the transition team report. The difficulty was so great that in 1981 Alderman Oberman had to sue the city to obtain official city documents, including Mayor Byrne's expenditure contingency funds of $178,000, a consultant's report on city personnel, the "memorandum of understanding" for a bank loan, the amount of overtime wages for city employees, damages and attorney's fees in personnel cases in federal court, the number of seasonal employees in one department, and the vacancies in another. His complaint concluded that "the Mayor has promulgated the new policy . . . intended to deny members of the public access to reports and records of the obligations, receipt and use of public funds." The media agreed with Alderman Oberman's opposition to city government secrecy, but that was not enough to bring change in the policy.[13]

Budget Votes

As often was the case in city council, many substantive issues about efficiency, taxes, and good government came in the form of amendments to the mayor's proposed budgets. Unlike city council procedural reforms, issues of raising taxes and spending money on city services directly affect the aldermen's constituencies. Therefore, aldermanic votes supporting budget amendments and opposing tax increases were among the highest in opposition during the Byrne administration. She still got her budgets through, but not without significant opposition—both among aldermen and the voters.

Mayor Byrne's first budget was blasted by nine aldermen for cutbacks in vital services, secrecy, and massive waste. In a City Hall press conference on December 11, 1979, Alderman Oberman charged, "The mayor has completely backtracked on her commitment to open up city government." The aldermen offered scores of budget amendments aimed at an "'unjustifiable increase' in spending, such as for tripling of the public relations staff, and drastic cuts in essential programs, such as day care and the work of the Human Relations Commission and the Department of Energy and Environmental Control." African-American aldermen opposed Byrne because she neglected the black community, and white reform aldermen opposed her because she had betrayed the reform agenda. In their prepared statement the aldermen declared, "She is asking for nearly $100 million in new taxes, most of which will hit poor people the hardest." They also criticized the budget hearing schedule because it continued the "conscious policy of concealment" of the Daley and Bilandic administrations. The aldermen maintained that "it is an insult to the city council and the public to give us a 428 page budget with many changes in format only one working day before the Finance Committee hearings." Finally, they charged that despite the mayor's claim that she was eliminating 1,749 jobs that were currently vacant, there had been 2,748 vacancies when she was sworn in. Thus she had actually added 1,000 employees to the city payrolls since she became mayor.[14]

The December 27, 1979, vote on an amendment to cut positions in the mayor's press office lost, 6–38; the motion to remove the fourth laborer from the garbage pickup crew lost, 8–41; and the mayor's final budget was approved by a vote of 40–7. By 1981, the vote for reform aldermen's budget amendments increased slightly to 38–10. Despite losing these votes, many of their budget reforms would be adopted gradually over the years without fanfare during later administrations when federal budget cuts forced city belt tightening.

The Firefighters Strike

One of the most controversial issues during the Byrne years was the firefighters strike. Before Byrne, private negotiations between the mayor and union leaders led to the setting of wage and working conditions but not to written labor contracts. Since the late 1970s, Alderman Oberman had proposed a comprehensive collective bargaining ordinance. Under Bilandic, the ordinance was defeated. However, since Byrne had run on a platform of creating union collective bargaining contracts for all city employees, early in her term Oberman's ordinance was adopted. Negotiations with the firefighters, however, did not go well. When the firefighters union couldn't get the city to agree to the contract they wanted, they struck. As the strike dragged on, new firefighters were hired to replace the strikers. After the strike was finally settled, both strikers and strike breakers would be kept on the payroll, but morale in the Fire Department would plummet.

At each stage of the negotiations and strike, the city council tried to become involved. Many aldermen favored the firefighters and opposed the administration. Five separate votes in the council concerned the strike. They included a resolution asking for a status report, a resolution to hold hearings on the strike, and a resolution to require firefighters and city negotiators to testify before the city council. These resolutions were offered in January and February 1980, during the strike, and were defeated by votes of 40–7 and 35–11. A resolution to reveal the strike's cost to the city was defeated on March 20, 1980, by a vote of 14–32, and the emergency firefighter appointees were given probationary career civil service status by a vote of 34–5 on May 13, 1981. After the firefighters strike was settled, a similar contract with police was approved by a vote of 38–6 on August 19, 1981. Afterward labor contracts with various unions became routine and considerably less controversial, but they were very unsettled during most of Byrne's term in office.

Economic Development

In addition to the other issues, there remained the perennial debate about how the city should develop economically. Various development proposals and schemes came before the city council for approval. One controversial proposal that recurred several times during the Byrne years was the Presidential Towers apartment building project. Land for the project was bought from Byrne confident and supporter Charles Swibel, who was a banker, real estate speculator, and chairman of the Chicago Housing Authority Board. The Presidential Towers project was put together by business partners of powerful congressional Ways and Means Committee chairman Dan Rostenkowski, who supplied the special federal tax breaks to make these politically well-connected developers rich. Although the poor were displaced by this development, the city council approved it in a series of contested and divided roll call votes.

Tearing Down the Daley Machine

Beyond the council fights, Mayor Byrne presided over a turbulent transition in machine politics. She attacked and split the party. She began by defeating Bilandic, proving that under the right conditions the machine could be defeated for high offices even in primary elections. In highly visible elections, the media could replace the party precinct captains in reaching the voters in this new TV era. Byrne proved that candidates for higher office could get their campaign messages to the voters without the traditional party foot soldiers.

Byrne continued her conquests by dividing the party into Byrne and Richard M. Daley factions. In March 1982, she engineered a coup to replace a Daley ally, county board president George Dunne, with Alderman Vrdolyak as chairman of the Cook County Democratic Party. Later she supported Alderman Burke in a race against Daley for Cook County state's attorney. As a result, votes in the Democratic Central Committee, instead of unanimously supporting a single party "boss" like Richard J. Daley, now were divided between pro-Byrne and pro-Daley factions.

At City Hall, Byrne attempted to purge Daley and Bilandic supporters. However, a federal court decision, the Shakman Decree, prevented patronage hiring and firing. Specifically, the court permanently enjoined the mayor from "conditioning, basing or knowingly prejudicing or affecting any term or aspect of government employment, with respect to one who is at the time already a government employee, upon or because of any political reason or factor."[15] So pro-Daley employees fired by Byrne got their jobs back with pay under order of the federal courts, eroding her base of loyalty in the city's bureaucracy.

The machine was more than party patronage workers. It was also a coalition of key interest and ethnic groups, and Byrne broke apart some long-time alliances. Despite having supported union bargaining for city employees during her mayoral campaign, Byrne forced the first strike by the firefighters union when she refused to meet their demands. In doing so, she drove a wedge between the unions and the Democratic Party, which had been allies for decades.

Byrne did more than simply split the party and alienate organized labor. She destroyed the foundations of the Chicago power structure. As political scientist Milton Rakove explained, the party's power under Daley "rested on a base of three major interlocking entities within the city's body politic—the ward organizations, the governmental apparatus of the city of Chicago . . . and powerful private interest groups and constituencies." It was this political/governmental/private interest group coalition that Byrne destroyed. "When Byrne cleaned out the top level of the city bureaucracy, many of the city departments were left in the hands of appointees who were unfamiliar with the dynamics, informal relationships and policies of the system that Daley had created and Bilandic had retained. In other words, what Byrne did was to bring down and disrupt the political/governmental/private interest group system that Daley had created in Chicago."[16]

Daley had revitalized the machine and restructured the regime that had governed Chicago and directed downtown redevelopment since 1955. Byrne now broke the linkages between the city bureaucracy and the business and institutional leaders who ruled the private sector. Chicago government during the Byrne years was characterized by continual crises, confrontation, vacillation, new policies, and new personnel in her revolving-door administration. Business and institutional leaders needed government stability and stable policies if they were to undertake long-term investments and major projects. They did not get it under Mayor Byrne. Altogether, Byrne was more effective at dismantling the machine and the regime from within than protestors and reformers had been with their attacks from outside.

Growing Revolt in the African-American Community

The electoral coalition that had elected Byrne consisted of a majority of African Americans who had concluded that Bilandic and the remnant of the Daley machine would not share power fairly with them. Mayor Bilandic and the Democratic machine had refused to dismantle the barriers of segregation that had existed since the city was founded, so blacks had voted for Byrne in protest. Anti-Daley liberals, on the other hand, voted for Byrne because of her reform platform and because she had exposed the taxicab scandal. White ethnic machine supporters voted for her because they were angry at Bilandic for failing to clear the streets during the Great Snowstorm of 1979 and for lying about the city's efforts. Byrne had alienated her liberal supporters almost as soon as she took office by sacking her transition team, turning the city council over to Vrdolyak and Burke, and failing to enact the reforms that she promised during her campaign. White ethnics remained split between Daley and Byrne factions of the party. Then, foolishly, Byrne pursued a series of public policies that alienated the African-American community. A partial list of Mayor Byrne's deeds that angered the black community includes the following:

1. Byrne appointed black deputy superintendent Sam Nolan as acting police superintendent only to replace him with a white insider, Richard Brzeczek.
2. She refused to appoint black deputy school superintendent Manford Byrd as school superintendent, appointing a white woman, Angeline Caruso, instead. Then she appointed a minority controlled–board of education and they selected a black, Rev. Ken Smith, as president, whereupon she refused for a time to swear in the new members.
3. The ward remap of 1981 deprived blacks of majorities in two wards and Hispanics in four. The federal courts reversed the situation in 1986 and required that special elections be held in seven wards. The federal courts held that the city willfully discriminated against blacks and Hispanics in drawing up the map.
4. In February 1981, Byrne replaced two black members of the board of education with what black activists characterized as "two racist, white women" from the Southwest and Northwest Sides of the city.
5. Byrne attempted to dump a former black ally, Alderman Allan Streeter, but he was reelected in the January 1982 special aldermanic election by 56 percent of the vote.
6. Byrne's CHA appointments in July 1982, when she was forced to replace Charles Swibel as executive director, were particularly pointed because 84 percent of CHA tenants were black. Byrne appointed her white aide, Andrew Mooney, as director and two white women to replace two black members of the CHA Board.

> In the city council nine black aldermen voted against Byrne's ap-
> pointments, a sure sign of discontent in their communities.[17]

Byrne's actions "encouraged a widespread belief among blacks that Mayor Byrne regarded them as subjects rather than citizens of their city."[18] Mayor Byrne's CHA appointments, in particular, led to a boycott of ChicagoFest, a twelve-day city government festival featuring national entertainment and ethnic food. It was one of the showcases of Byrne's government that black community organizations, under the leadership of Rev. Jesse Jackson, protested in ways that cost attendance, revenues, and acute embarrassment for the mayor. It demonstrated, as had the successful reelection of Alderman Allan Streeter, what the black community could accomplish when it was united. Her actions not only led to the ChicagoFest boycott but also to a massive black voter registration drive that provided a new constituency to oppose both the Daley and Byrne factions of the Democratic Party.

Toward the end of her reign, Mayor Byrne tried to demonstrate her concern for the African-American community. Under the protection of a large number of Chicago policemen, she moved her residence into the Cabrini-Greene CHA project. But the black community viewed her action as a public relations ploy. Just as she had weakened the machine and the governing coalition of Chicago, Byrne now unwittingly helped mobilize the black community against her into a more cohesive political force.

As these shifts occurred in the city council along the cleavage of race, another change was occurring in national politics. In 1980, Ronald Reagan was elected president of the United States. Members of Congress took his election as a mandate for major cuts to domestic social programs, aid to cities, and foreign aid. The effects of these federal budget cuts on cities were major. General programs such as revenue sharing would be eliminated along with many more specific federal grant programs. By 1983, President Reagan's proposed budgets, if they had been fully adopted by the Congress, would have meant a loss of more than $400 million a year to Chicago's local governments. Cuts in welfare benefits to individual Chicagoans created higher rates of unemployment, hunger, and homelessness with which the city now had to cope.

In the Byrne years neither the city council nor the city as a whole was able to come to a consensus on a new plan to cope with Chicago's growing social and economic problems made more difficult by dwindling federal resources. The city would become more divided by racial politics before there could be any reconciliation, consensus, or positive city planning.

Notes

1. Bill Granger and Lori Granger, *Fighting Jane: Mayor Jane Byrne and the Chicago Machine* (New York: Dial, 1980), p. 214.

2. Quoted in Granger and Granger, *Fighting Jane,* p. 214.

3. Paul M. Green, "The 1983 Chicago Democratic Mayoral Primary: Some New Players—Same Old Rules," in Melvin G. Holli and Paul M. Green, eds., *The Making of the Mayor: Chicago 1983* (Grand Rapids, Mich.: Eerdmans, 1984), p. 20.

4. Paul Kleppner, *Chicago Divided: The Making of a Black Mayor* (DeKalb: Northern University Press, 1985), p. 116.

5. Kleppner, *Chicago Divided,* pp. 116–117.

6. Granger and Granger, *Fighting Jane,* pp. 218–220.

7. Gary Rivlin, *Fire on the Prairie: Chicago's Harold Washington and the Politics of Race* (New York: Henry Holt, 1992), pp. 72–73. He is quoting Renault Robinson on what Mayor Byrne told him.

8. The demographic data is taken from Ben Joravsky, "Whites Moved In, Blacks Out in Ward Shift," *Chicago Reporter,* January 1982, pp. 4–6.

9. Joravsky, "Whites Moved In," pp. 4–6.

10. Greg Hinz, "Council Debate Evokes Dramatics," *Lerner Newspapers,* May 17–18, 1980.

11. Michael Zielenziger, "Byrne Links Tribune 'Vendetta,' Land Deal," *Chicago Sun-Times,* June 23, 1980, pp. 1, 58; and Michael Zielenziger, "Byrne Won't Enforce Ouster of Reporter," *Chicago Sun-Times,* June 24, 1980, pp. 1, 6.

12. "Byrne Disputes with Tribune," WBBM-TV editorial, July 3–4, 1980. Copy in Dick Simpson Papers, Special Collections, Main Library, University of Illinois at Chicago.

13. *Martin J. Oberman v. Jane M. Byrne et al.* Complaint and Writ of Mandamus for Injunctive Relief, p. 10. See also Lynn Sweet, "Oberman Sues Byrne, Aides over Records," *Chicago Sun-Times,* October 27, 1981, p. 1; David Axelrod, "Byrne Hiding Public Data," *Chicago Tribune,* October 27, 1981, pp. 1, 4; and "Oberman's Suit," WGN-TV editorial 81–265, November 2, 1981, Dick Simpson Papers, Special Collections, Main Library, University of Illinois at Chicago.

14. Harry Golden Jr., "Nine Aldermen Rip Byrne's Budget," *Chicago Sun-Times,* December 12, 1979, p. 5.

15. For a summary of the Shakman Decree in its various stages, see "Patronage: Shakman v. Democratic Organization of Cook County and Rutan v. Republican Party of Illinois," in Dick Simpson, ed., *Chicago's Future in a Time of Change* (Champaign, Ill.: Stipes, 1993), pp. 147–154.

16. Milton Rakove, "Jane Byrne and the New Chicago Politics," in Samuel K. Gove and Louis H. Masotti, eds., *After Daley: Chicago Politics in Transition* (Urbana: University of Illinois Press, 1982), pp. 217, 232.

17. Kleppner, *Chicago Divided,* pp. 137–143.

18. Kleppner, *Chicago Divided,* p. 143.

PART III

Council Wars and Chaos

Alderman Richard Mell demanding attention during the election of acting mayor Eugene Sawyer in 1987. (Reprinted by permission of the *Chicago Tribune*, photographer Chuck Berman, December 6, 1987.)

7

Harold Washington's Council Wars, 1983–1987

In 1979 Mayor Byrne defeated the machine because of a fluke: a snow-storm and the coalesce of antimachine forces. Once she became mayor, however, her new electoral coalition was not nurtured. Rather, she tried to govern with machine support. Instead of successfully restoring the machine, she succeeded in splintering the political and governmental system perfected by her mentor, Richard J. Daley. Even so, Harold Washington might not have won the 1983 election had Mayor Byrne and State's Attorney Richard M. Daley not split the white community. Washington won the primary in 1983 with only 36 percent of the vote based on an interracial coalition that was mostly black. Seventy-nine percent of his vote came from the African-American community, 16 percent from the Latino community, and only 4 percent from the white community.[1]

Washington's brief reign signaled three fundamental changes in Chicago politics: (1) a new balance of power between the races in which blacks achieved parity while other minorities as well as women and ho-mosexuals gained new positions of clout at City Hall; (2) a shift in the regime running Chicago from downtown businesses, developers, major institutions, and politicians to a balance between the downtown elite and grassroots community leaders; and (3) the coming to power of a "pro-gressive" administration following a progressive political agenda in the place of a machine-dominated government. The civil rights revolution, which had occurred on the streets of Chicago and the nation in the 1960s and had continued in the city council floor fights of the 1970s, would fi-nally win City Hall and elect the first black mayor of Chicago in the 1980s.

1983 Campaign

Who was Harold Washington? Washington's parents, Roy and Bertha Washington, moved to Chicago from downstate Illinois in the 1920s. Roy originally got a job in the stockyards. Harold, their fourth child, was born in Cook County Hospital in 1922. Roy went on from his job in the stockyards to become a lawyer, a minister, a Democratic Party precinct captain, and eventually an assistant corporation counsel for the City of Chicago.

After Roy and Bertha were divorced in 1930, Roy was granted custody of the four children. Two children were raised by grandparents, but Roy and his two youngest sons, Edward and Harold, moved into the home of Roy's sister. Edward and Harold went to Catholic boarding school in 1926 but returned to the Chicago public schools in 1929. Harold attended DuSable High School from 1936 to 1939 and then joined the Civilian Conservation Corps. Back in civilian life, he married Nancy Finch in 1941 and then served in the U.S. Army from 1942 to 1946. After the war he attended Roosevelt University on the G.I. Bill and graduated from Northwestern University Law School in 1952.

When Washington's father died in 1953, Alderman Ralph Metcalfe offered Harold his father's position as assistant corporation counsel and offered to make him precinct captain in the 3rd Ward on the South Side. In 1965, Washington was elected to the Illinois House of Representatives, and in 1976 he moved up to the Illinois State Senate. His biographer describes his "duplicitous role" in his years in the state legislature "as a Democratic machine hack in Chicago and a political independent on most issues in Springfield." He did not fight the party in the precincts, but he felt free to vote his conscience and to represent his African-American constituency in the legislature, even if he had to go against the Democratic Party's positions.[2]

In 1977, Washington ran for mayor in the Democratic primary against Mayor Bilandic. Although he lost the race badly, he went on to be elected congressman from the First Congressional District of Illinois to replace his former mentor, Congressman Ralph Metcalfe, after his death in 1980. Washington learned politics from inside the machine, but once he made the break in the late 1970s, he became a force for a new politics for Chicago. He was a liberal, progressive black leader who knew the machine from the inside but had left "plantation politics" behind long ago. He was a master orator able to sway crowds and television audiences with his wit and intellect. He was a deeply compassionate man, an inveterate reader, and a workaholic. His firsthand experience with racial discrimination and the dictatorial aspects of the Democratic machine made him determined to eliminate both.

"The most significant feature of Chicago's 1982 and 1983 electoral seasons was the political mobilization of the black community. After decades of control and manipulation by the city's Democratic machine, Chicago blacks awakened to their own racial interests and used the ballot box to advance them."[3] A massive voter registration campaign was mounted among African Americans under the slogan, "Come Alive, October Five." More than 200 community organizations joined forces to push voter registration. The usual political and civil rights organizations were of course involved, but black churches also backed the drive. Father George Clemens, a Catholic priest, condemned failure to register to vote as a sin and some black churches even stopped distributing free food to poor blacks without a voter card.

This grassroots organizing paid off. Between 1979 and 1983, African Americans showed a net gain of 193,000 registered voters, whereas whites showed a net gain of only 1,656. Voter turnout also doubled in the black community, from 34 percent in the 1975 primary to 65 percent in the primary of 1983.[4] In the meantime, Mayor Byrne was undermining her base of support in the white community and strengthening opposition to her reelection within the party. So when Byrne appeared before the party slate-making committee on November 23, 1982, to seek endorsement for her reelection as mayor, she faced defections.

> Byrne's endorsement has been carefully orchestrated, and Her Honor's brief speech goes well as she humbly presents herself before the committee. . . . [Then] Vrdolyak lays out the political bottom line. . . . he tells the committeemen, "Chicago needs Jane Byrne," and "if anyone wants to take us [the Democratic organization] on, they better pack a lunch because it will be an all-day job." . . . Eventually, an endorsement roll call is taken and twelve more committeemen join [George] Dunne [whom she had dumped as party chairman] in refusing to support Byrne. The mayor walks away with a battle victory, but even her most ardent backers recognize that the war has just begun. Daley and Washington Committeemen have held firm, and they are ready to challenge Byrne and the existing Democratic organization for city control.[5]

Two weeks earlier, on November 4, State's Attorney Richard M. Daley had announced his candidacy for mayor. Without mentioning Jane Byrne by name, Daley lambasted her record on raising taxes and failing to provide good city services: "People are worried about the future of Chicago because they have experienced the results of mismanagement. People are worried about the future of Chicago because they know the city has ineffective leadership."[6]

A week earlier, on November 10, in a hotel ballroom on the South Side before a crowd of hundreds of supporters and a bank of television cam-

TABLE 7.1   Estimates of Group Voting in the 1983 Democratic Mayoral Primary

	Washington	Byrne	Daley	Nonvote
Citywide[a, b]				
Blacks	54.3	7.9	1.9	35.7
Whites	2.6	30.4	31.4	35.3
Latino	2.8	12.6	8.3	76.0
Blacks				
Dawson Wards	54.1	8.2	2.5	35.1
Other South Side	57.8	7.3	1.4	33.3
West Side	46.3	8.9	1.5	43.1
White ethnics				
Northwest side	0.8	33.2	29.1	36.8
South Side	0.5	28.3	45.7	25.4
Lakeshore	5.8	30.6	25.5	37.9
Ward 5	24.3	17.3	24.3	33.9
Hispanics				
Puerto Rican[c]	3.8	31.2	15.1	49.6
Mexican[d]	2.1	10.4	7.6	78.6
Total citywide	20.2	18.5	16.4	44.4

[a]Entries in this table are percentages of voting-age population, and rows sum to 100 percent, except for rounding errors.

[b]Developed by weighting the estimate of each group's voting behavior within eight subareas of the city.

[c]Estimates of Hispanic behavior in predominantly Puerto Rican Wards 26 and 31.

[d]Estimates of Hispanic behavior in predominantly Mexican Wards 22 and 25.

SOURCE: Paul Kleppner, *Chicago Divided: The Making of a Black Mayor* (1985)

eras, Washington had entered the race with a speech I helped draft, saying, "The city that supposedly works, doesn't. . . . Chicago is a city divided where citizens are treated unequally and unfairly." Washington went on to give his vision for the city: "I see a Chicago that runs well, but in which services are provided as a right, not as political favors. I see a Chicago of education excellence and equality of treatment . . . in which jobs and contracts are dispensed fairly . . . and in which justice rains down like water. I see a Chicago in which the neighborhoods are once again the center of our city, in which businesses boom and provide neighborhood jobs, in which neighbors join together to help govern their neighborhoods and their city."[7]

The three candidates began their campaigns with less than three months until election day following very different strategies. "More so than her two rivals [Daley and Washington], Mayor Byrne's strategy from the outset was based on being able to win a significant share of the vote among whites, blacks and Hispanics. . . . Byrne's strategy was to cut into Washington's plurality and to try to win as much as 25 percent of the black vote for herself. . . . But it was for the white vote that Byrne fought most vigorously and her competitor there was Daley. . . . She raised the specter of the 11th Ward's being restored to dominance over the Machine and the city through a Daley victory."[8]

Daley had problems putting his campaign together. His hope of gathering defections in the black community and of building a major base of support in the Hispanic community did not work out. But he was a major contender for the white vote. "In the liberal areas, where distrust of the Daley name was strong, he presented himself as an independent. He attacked Byrne's misuse of patronage, her enormous campaign fund, and her deceptive television advertising. . . . In the ethnic communities . . . Daley pitched his appeal to the hard-working, taxpaying homeowners, blistering Byrne for her fiscal mismanagement, her tax increase, and her lack of leadership. . . . [And] he invoked his father's name and the memory of an earlier and better Chicago, 'the city that worked.'"[9]

Washington was neither the incumbent mayor nor the son of the legendary Richard J. Daley. When he had run against Michael Bilandic for mayor in 1977, he received only 11 percent of the vote. "Washington's plan involved solidifying his base in the black community, developing a coalition with Hispanics, and appealing for white support. His strategists publicly expressed the hope of winning up to 15 percent of the white vote."[10]

Washington needed to mobilize a crusade in the black community to build on the successful voter registration drive. His goal was to get 80 percent of African Americans to vote and at least 80 percent of them to vote for him. To do this he had to preempt the field, keep any other major black candidates from running, and reach the black voters with his campaign message. At the same time, the black vote alone was not enough to elect him. He had already made contact with the Mexican-American community through an alliance with Juan Soliz, a state legislator who would be running for alderman. I set up a meeting between Harold and key Puerto Rican leaders, especially Rev. Juan Morales from the Westtown neighborhood, to broaden his Latino support. As the campaign grew, these contacts developed into alliances with "progressive" community, religious, and political leaders from both the Mexican-American and Puerto Rican neighborhoods. These alliances produced only 16 percent of Washington's final vote in the Democratic primary, but the Hispanic community produced enough votes for Washington to ensure his narrow election in the general election in April.

But even a unified black vote and support from some Latinos was not enough. Washington's victory in the primary was made possible by white voters splitting their support between Byrne and Daley, with Washington winning some white votes. The largest part of Washington's white vote came from the liberal lakefront organized by Washington volunteers and IVI-IPO. White supporters in Uptown and on the Northwest Side were targeted by community organizers Helen Shiller, Slim Coleman, and their Fair Share Organizations. It was also whispered that powerful Ward committeeman Mike Madigan told his precinct captains not to get out Southwest Side white voters, but to let Washington win in exchange for the support of the legislative Black Caucus for his run for Speaker in the General Assembly. In any case, whites split their votes between Daley and Byrne while blacks rallied behind Washington.

The 1983 campaign was a watershed election that fundamentally changed Chicago politics. It was decided primarily on race and political ideology. Washington's campaign and his government defined a reform agenda composed of three parts:

1. good government reform (honesty and efficiency in government)
2. empowerment (affirmative action to bring minorities and women into the highest levels of government and to redistribute government jobs and contracts)
3. citizen participation and control (decentralizing government decisionmaking, empowering neighborhood organizations, and government accountability)[11]

These different agendas appealed to different constituencies. Good government appealed to the business community and civic advocates like the League of Women Voters, empowerment appealed to the African-American and Latino communities, and the promise of greater citizen control appealed to liberals who had adopted this ideal in the 1960s.

Strategists for Byrne and Daley slowly began to recognize the threat of the Washington campaign. On the Saturday before the February primary, Democratic party chairman Ed Vrdolyak spoke to white precinct workers on the Northwest Side and bluntly told them, "A vote for Daley is a vote for Washington. It's a two-person race. It would be the worst day in the history of Chicago if your candidate . . . was not elected. It's a racial thing. Don't kid yourself. I'm calling on you to save your city, to save your precinct. We're fighting to keep the city the way it is."[12] When

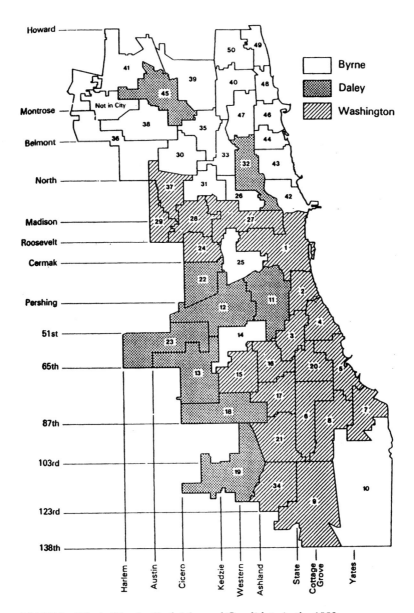

MAP 7.1   Wards Won by Each Mayoral Candidate in the 1983
Democratic Primary

Vrdolyak's quote immediately became front-page news, it rallied Washington supporters to show up and vote against Byrne and Vrdolyak, while it widened the split between Byrne and Daley supporters. It admirably summarized what the election was about—protecting the status quo politically and leaving the white power structure in control of City Hall.

After narrowly winning the 1983 primary, Washington was pitted against former Republican state legislator Bernard Epton in the general election, which Washington won with a narrow margin of only 52 percent. Once again race was pivotal. This time Washington received nearly 100 percent of the black vote and 80 percent of the Latino vote. His white vote climbed slightly to 12 percent.[13] A number of white Democratic machine ward committeemen and their precinct captains worked openly for Epton's election: better a white Republican than a black reform Democrat as mayor they concluded. Both the primary and general elections of 1983 used overtly racist language. "The open and unblushing use of racial, ethnic and religious slurs reached an all-time high in the 1983 Chicago mayoral campaign. That campaign unloosed an overload of emotional block blusters, racial code words, and slurs. Tocsin calls to action, such as 'It's our turn now. . . . We want it all, we want it now. . . . It's a racial thing don't kid yourself. . . . Ditch the bitch and vote for Rich. . . . Go get-em Jewboy. . . . Epton! Epton! He is our man. We don't want no Af-ri-can,' punctured the heady contest."[14]

Despite the racial nature of the campaign, Washington was confident that having won the primary, he would win the general election. He appointed Bill Berry and me to cochair his transition team right after the primary. Our team involved a large number of community and civic leaders in analyzing city government under Mayor Byrne and in proposing hundreds of reforms, from simple changes in personnel to reorganizing departments and creating new mechanisms of citizen participation. One result was a 400-hundred page formal report entitled *Blueprint of Chicago Government*.[15] Unlike Mayor Byrne, who refused to read the transition team report and had to be sued to make its contents public, Mayor Washington embraced the work of his transition team, released the published version at a press conference in the mayor's office, and implemented many of its reform proposals.

Council Wars

Aldermen Vrdolyak, Burke, and Oberman continued to have major roles in this new council. However, Aldermen Tim Evans and David Orr would be central players as well. From the South Side's 4th Ward, Alderman Tim Evans was an emerging young black leader whom Washington chose as his council floor leader. Born in Hot Springs, Arkansas, Evans had come to Chicago as a teenager. His mother, recently divorced, wanted to live close to her teaching job in Gary. But she couldn't find adequate housing there, and so the family moved into Chicago's South Side.

Evans studied at the University of Illinois and John Marshall Law School. Like Washington, he began as a young lawyer in the city corporation counsel's office. He caught the eye of one of the most powerful black politicians of the Richard J. Daley era, 4th Ward alderman Claude Holman. At Holman's request he moved into the ward in 1969 and began to climb his way up the black "submachine." When Alderman Holman died suddenly in 1973, Mayor Daley chose Tim Evans as both 4th Ward alderman and ward committeeman.

Alderman Evans, although an educated lawyer with liberal leanings, stayed loyal to the machine during the Daley and Bilandic mayoralties. However, he bolted from party loyalty when Mayor Byrne appointed whites instead of blacks to the Chicago Housing Authority Board. Although Harold Washington chose Evans as head of the Finance Committee and as his city council floor leader in 1983, he didn't have the votes to make it stick, but Evans became the leader of the pro-Washington minority on the council floor. In 1986, after the special aldermanic elections changed the balance of power in the council, Evans was finally elected Finance Committee chairman and served in that post until Washington died. Evans was described in the *Chicago Enterprise* magazine as "oracular, energetic and wantonly ambitious; a garrulous man whose near-naive openness can command people to forgive him for rarely showing up on time."[16]

Another political figure who emerged after Mayor Washington's death was Alderman David Orr. Just as Alderman Martin Oberman became the floor leader of the Independent aldermen and the opposition bloc under Mayor Byrne, Alderman Orr played that role during the Washington era, becoming vice mayor, acting mayor for a brief period, and then Cook County clerk in 1990, a post that he still holds.

Orr was a young, active political science professor at Mundelein College who was elected alderman of the Roger's Park neighborhood (49th Ward) in 1979. He was an Independent working with first IPO and later IVI-IPO. During the 1980s and 1990s Orr was the de facto leader of the Independent aldermen and he authored ethics reform and landlord–tenant ordinances that passed during the Washington era. After Washington's coalition in the council gained the majority in 1986, Orr was elected vice mayor. In this role, he chaired the chaotic council meeting at which Washington's successor was chosen in 1987. Later, as County clerk, he would reform an antiquated and corrupt county office and make it a model for the country. Although he had strong support from the African-

American community for his election as county clerk, he could not get their support as a white reform candidate for mayor.

There was a prelude to the organization of the council after Mayor Washington's election. Although most of the work of Mayor Harold Washington's transition team was made public, there were several private memoranda to the mayor. One memo contained a draft of an executive order (the first in Chicago's history) providing citizens with freedom of information. A second memo recommended that the mayor sign a consent decree in the Shakman case in federal court, which formally eliminated patronage in future city hiring as a matter of law. A third memo proposed a plan for a change in the mayor's cabinet to provide for deputy mayors to help coordinate the sixty agencies and government units under the mayor's control. All three of the steps recommended in these memos were accomplished in the first days of the new Washington administration.

A final private memorandum dealt with the Chicago City Council. We recommended a strategy of careful alliances and committee chairman appointments to give Mayor Washington a working majority in the council. We believed that by cultivating a handful of the white "machine" aldermen, Washington could combine his existing support among black, progressive white, and Latino aldermen to gain control. The memo listed all committee and committee chairmanship appointments to be made in the new council according to ten principles:

1. Key Washington supporters are in crucial positions (e.g., Aldermen Kelly, Davis, Bloom, Frost, Humes).
2. All Washington supporters and probable supporters are included (41 out of 50).
3. [Alderman Eddie] Vrdolyak is proposed to be removed as chairman of Building and Zoning but retains an important committee chairmanship and is thus not embarrassed.
4. Bad actors are not included (e.g., Aldermen Roti, Marzullo, Schulter, Laurino).
5. [Congressman Dan] Rostenkowski is not hurt (Alderman Terry Gabinski is kept as committee chair).
6. [State Representative Mike] Madigan is not hurt (Alderman Madrzyk is kept as committee chair).
7. [42nd Ward committeeman George] Dunne is not hurt (Alderman Natarus is kept as committee chair).
8. [State's Attorney Richard M.] Daley is not hurt (Alderman Huels is promoted to committee chair).
9. All black incumbents and Independents are committee chairmen.

10. Poles are not embarrassed (they keep five committee chairmanships).[17]

However, we did not fully anticipate, even after the racially divisive elections, that racial conflict would make compromise impossible in the city council. Mayor Washington with his long experience of racial discrimination was more realistic in this regard.

Council Wars began on April 19, 1983, when newly elected Mayor Washington let it be known that he wanted to strip the old guard aldermen from the Byrne administration of their powerful committee positions, including removing Alderman Edward Vrdolyak as chairman of the Planning and Zoning Committee. Vrdolyak took this as a declaration of war and planned a campaign to retain his position within the council.

Ten days later, in his inaugural address, Washington announced that Chicago was facing a fiscal crisis—the city general fund had a potential shortfall of $150 million, the Chicago public schools were $200 million in debt, and the city's transportation system faced a $200 million deficit. He announced a freeze of all city hiring and raises, eliminated several hundred employees added to the city payroll as the Byrne administration was going out of office, made cuts in executive salaries, and ended unnecessary city programs. He emphasized: "My election was the result of the greatest grass roots effort in the history of the city of Chicago. . . . My election was made possible by thousands and thousands of people who demanded that the burdens of mismanagement, unfairness and inequity be lifted so the city could be saved. One of the ideas that held us all together said that neighborhood involvement has to take the place of the ancient, decrepit and creaking machine."[18]

A number of the aldermen took Washington's harsh criticism of the Byrne administration as a signal that the election battles would continue in the new government. Under the leadership of Alderman Vrdolyak, who promised committee chairmanships and patronage jobs to aldermen who allied with him, the old guard mobilized a majority of the council to oppose the new mayor and his reforms. On May 2, when the council formally met for the first time, the mayor simply didn't have the votes. Alderman Vrdolyak had formed a solid bloc of twenty-nine of the fifty aldermen. Lacking the votes he needed, Washington gaveled the meeting to order and then adjourned it without recognizing aldermen from the opposition bloc seeking to speak. The mayor and his twenty-one aldermanic allies walked out of the meeting, but Alderman Vrdolyak then seized the gavel and continued the meeting with the remaining majority. They adopted rules of procedure, appointed committee chairmen as they wished, and made aldermanic appointments to council committees. In the end, the federal courts would recognize the legitimacy of the council

TABLE 7.2   Racial and Political Base of Chicago City Council Voting Blocs

	Vrdolak 29	Washington 21
Voting age population		
% white	68.8	21.9
% African American	10.8	71.7
% Latino	16.9	3.9
Support in mayoral election		
% Harold Washington	25.9	86.1
% Bernard Epton	73.7	13.6

SOURCE: Paul Kleppner, *Chicago Divided: The Making of a Black Mayor* (1985).

majority, and thus the fault lines for council wars were set. From 1983 until 1986, most controversial council votes would be divided 29–21.

One problem with the division of the council was that it not only divided along the traditional political split in Chicago, machine versus reform, but it also reflected racial divisions. Twenty-five members of the Vrdolyak twenty-nine were white aldermen, two were black, and two were Latinos. Seventeen of Washington's twenty-one supporters were black aldermen, two were white reformers, and two were Latinos. The aldermen in the two blocs represented racially different wards that had voted very differently in the 1983 elections.

This era in Chicago is not known as "Council Wars" (a play on the title of the popular *Star Wars* movies) simply because there was a split in council voting. The city council battles were portrayed as a war of good and evil, with good and bad men and women squarely arranged on either side of the fight. Chicago during this era also earned the label "Beirut on the Lake" because of the vituperative nature of the political battles and the unwillingness of the factions to compromise. At the time Beirut, Lebanon, was in the middle of a brutal Middle Eastern war involving various Arab factions and Israel, and it was being bombed to rubble.

Budget Battles

City budgets became battlegrounds for both factions, with both Mayor Washington and Alderman Burke as Finance Committee chairman and floor leader for the majority bloc offering very different budget proposals. The majority faction would vote down the mayor's budget, and the mayor would veto or threaten to veto the Burke budget. The city would teeter on the brink of financial bankruptcy until the leaders of the two factions finally negotiated a compromise budget just hours before the city would have to stop paying its bills for lack of authorization to spend money. This endangered the city's bond rating and its ability to borrow money at reasonable rates. For example, "The two factions fought a six-week battle over the 1984 budget. . . . . At first, the council majority refused to let Washington rescind a property tax cut. Washington threatened massive layoffs, including police and firemen, and refused to budge from that position. Eventually, the Vrdolyak bloc yielded."[19]

A similar fight occurred over the federal Community Development Block Grants (CDBG) funds in May and June 1985. Ten separate parliamentary and substantive roll call votes divided 26–21 over how to spend this federal money. On Tuesday, May 28, 1985, the council's Finance Committee voted to reallocate $14 million of Mayor Washington's $126 million CDBG proposal from minority poor communities, for which the funds were intended, to working and middle-class white communities. The previous year the mayor's veto of a similar majority bloc proposal ended in a last-minute compromise, with the final proposal being flown to Washington, D.C., to meet the federal deadline. Alderman Burke defended this year's majority bloc proposal to reallocate $14 million to machine white ethnic wards: "We feel that all areas of the city are entitled to funds to stop growing blight and slum conditions in their neighborhoods. . . . Fourteen million dollars is a small amount out of a total amount of $126 million and should not constitute a reason for jettisoning the entire proposal."[20]

Fifth Ward alderman Larry Bloom, a Washington supporter, led the attack on Burke's amendments to reallocate the $14 million and urged the mayor to veto the package. "This is the most sinister, irresponsible political act of the year," Bloom charged. Majority bloc alderman Roman Pucinski, who was seeking $1.3 million to repair WPA streets in his ward, replied, "One billion dollars have been spent over the last 10 years in low- and moderate-income areas. I feel the time has come that the rest of Chicago should benefit from these programs." The problem with Alderman Pucinski's argument was that the federal guidelines specified that CDBG funds had to be spent in low- and moderate-income communities, and his Northwest Side Ward was a middle-class community ineligible for these funds.[21]

As predicted, Mayor Washington once again vetoed the majority bloc amendments to the 1985 CDBG proposal, although in 1985 CDBG funds became linked with a proposed neighborhood bond issue. Before the council meeting the mayor had announced a five-year $3.1 billion master plan for rebuilding and repairing the city's infrastructure. However, Alderman Burke and the majority had also tied up a key component of that plan, a $110 million bond issue for neighborhood repairs, for the last two years. They did not want the mayor to get credit for neighborhood repairs before the next mayoral election, now only two years away.

Mayor Washington obtained an extension of the deadline from the federal government for Chicago's CDBG proposal, but the council meeting on June 12, 1985, was a madhouse.

> An Uptown community activist and supporter of Mayor Harold Washington [Slim Coleman] leaped from the press section of the council chambers, shouting obscenities and rushing menacingly toward Ald. Edward Vrdolyak [10th], leader of the mayor's opposition. . . . An unruly gallery that packed the chambers to support the Washington administration taunted the majority bloc members who narrowly passed the controversial [Burke version of the CDBG] ordinance. . . . [In response] Ald. Roman Pucinski [41st] declared, "You can hoot, you can shout, you can jeer and you can cheer, but the fact remains you are not going to change one vote here."[22]

Budget Director Sharon Gilliam insisted that changes proposed by the majority bloc violated federal guidelines that the funds be spent solely in low- and moderate-income areas, but amendments by the majority bloc still passed, 26–21.

The following council meeting on June 26 was equally raucous. At the outset, Mayor Washington vetoed the majority bloc's amended CDBG plan. Then the majority sent the administration's substitute proposal to the Finance Committee to be buried and passed another version of their own proposal by the usual factional vote. Two days later, the city administration mailed layoff notices to 1,300 city workers, whose jobs were tied to the federal community development funds being held up by the council. This finally brought a solution to the impasse. With council support, the mayor was able to submit an acceptable CDBG plan to the federal government while many projects that the majority bloc aldermen had wanted were included in the neighborhood development bond fund. Council Wars battles often led to such financial brinksmanship, but the city was able to avoid bankruptcy and improve city life despite the wars on the council floor. Both the CDBG and neighborhood bond projects were worthwhile developments that improved Chicago.

At the August 1985 city council meeting the general obligation bond issue of $185 million for neighborhood development was approved with full aldermanic participation in deciding the repairs and improvements to be made in their own wards. The Planning Department produced a series of maps showing how money from all sources (CDBG, the bonds, city and state funds) produced "the most even distribution of spending for neighborhood improvement in Chicago's history. Every ward, including the white ones hostile to Washington, shared equitably in the funds.

Some wards got more than others because the needs were greater. Some white wards also got more money than black ones. For example, the all-white 41st Ward on the far Northwest Side got $4.26 million for new street construction, residential street resurfacing and other improvements. The all-black 21st Ward on the South Side received $1.99 million for residential street resurfacing and other improvements."[23] With these compromises, both the CDBG proposal and the general obligation bonds, which had been held up for over a year, were able to obtain council approval, even in the Council Wars council.

Changes in Governance

Although these pitched council battles raised racial tensions, they were not entirely negative. Contrary to racist fears, the city did not perish because there was now a black mayor, a black police superintendent, a black school superintendent, and more minorities working in prominent positions at City Hall. African Americans proved as able as whites to run the city. The end of political control by white males (particularly the Irish) was an important change in Chicago history. Unlike Byrne, Washington brought a broader-based "rainbow coalition" to power by his appointments. He promoted progressive whites, Latinos, and women, as well as blacks, to top positions in city government. Smaller groups like Asians and homosexuals also received posts in government and had their concerns addressed. Many city agencies were more effective and more responsive to neighborhood organizations than before. Federal government funds for social services and Community Development Block Grant moneys were no longer used primarily to hire patronage workers but were turned over to churches, social service agencies, and community organizations to deliver social services more cheaply and effectively.

The Council Wars were positive to the extent that opposition aldermen were forced to offer budget reforms of their own and to make sure that white communities were not forgotten in the distribution of money for neighborhood improvements. They forced the administration to articulate clearly its goals and to rally support from among civic organizations and community groups. The mayor and his aldermanic supporters had to take their case to the "people" and mobilize massive public support to prevail.

One undesirable consequence of Council Wars was that the number of council committees grew from twenty-nine to thirty-seven, in this fifty-member council, to allow majority bloc supporters to be rewarded with committee chairmanships. The budget spent on additional council staff grew accordingly. It was an expensive war because the Chicago City Council had more committees than any other council in the country and more standing committees than the U.S. House of Representatives with 435 members.

Council Wars ended when a federal court ordered special aldermanic elections in seven wards to redress the gerrymandering and racial inequality created by the ward map adopted by the Byrne council. New elections in four Latino and three black wards were held on March 16, 1986. With pro-Washington aldermanic victories in four wards, the old 29–21 division was reconfigured into a 25–25 tie. Since by council rules Mayor Washington could then cast the tie-breaking vote, the balance of power shifted dramatically. Washington took full advantage of his new majority to reorganize the council, with his supporters taking over the committee chairmanships, approving the mayor's appointees to boards and commissions that had been blocked for three years, and passing the mayor's budget without the previous brinksmanship. On June 6, 1986, Mayor Washington used his tie-breaking vote to slash the number of committees from thirty-seven to twenty-eight and to stack the key committees with his allies. Alderman Vrdolyak lost his chairmanship when his Committee on Neighborhoods was abolished. Alderman Burke continued as head of the Finance Committee but a new committee, the Budget Committee chaired by Alderman Evans, would henceforth handle the city budget and Community Development Block Grants, thus stripping Burke of his most important powers.

After the June council meeting Mayor Washington declared, "All in all it was a good day for Chicago. We tried to keep it low key. There was no braggadocio, no flaunting of power. There was no putting of people down." Alderman Vrdolyak insisted that the council rules had been flouted. He called the action "legislative piracy" and said, "It's a sham of fairness and reform. All the phony reformers are out of the closet now for keeps. We know that phony left-wing rhetoric ain't going to get it with the people of Chicago when they say, 'We're for you, here's a higher tax bill.'"[24] The meeting took a dramatic turn when 9th Ward alderman Perry Hutchinson, a Washington ally, arrived at City Hall in an ambulance and was wheeled first into the mayor's office and then to the council floor to vote. He had been absent the previous week, which had denied the mayor's bloc his critical vote. His vote allowed the mayor to cast the tie-breaking vote to reorganize the council and also to approve appointments to the Chicago Park Board so that a new pro-Washington majority could fire Democratic Party ward committeeman Ed Kelly as Park District superintendent.

Ethics

One important issue decided in this new council continued to have consequences for Chicago politics and is emblematic of the changes during

Council Wars. Since 1985, the first ethics ordinance in Chicago's history had been languishing in committee. It had been drafted by an Ethics Commission appointed by the mayor, and some of its proposals had been enacted by executive order already. However, limits on campaign contributions and creation of a permanent Ethics Commission with investigatory powers required council action. Alderman Orr, who had served on the commission, was the council sponsor of the proposed ordinance. On the eve of the 1987 election, when aldermen were standing for reelection, Orr brought the ethics ordinance back from the Rules Committee, where it had been bottled up for two years. In January 1987, it passed unanimously, by a vote of 49–0, with even the most adamant opponents in the anti-administration bloc afraid to vote against it. They were afraid to explain an antiethics vote to the voters on election day only a month away. Although the split in the council was still only 26–24, the mayor and his reform allies frequently won by larger margins. Most aldermen prefer to be on the winning side, and a number of them were deserting the losing opposition bloc that they had been willing to support when it was the majority.

1987 Elections

Washington handily won reelection in 1987 and began to consolidate his power at City Hall. In the primary he again defeated former Mayor Byrne in a head-to-head contest, winning 54 percent of the vote. In the general election he garnered 54 percent of the vote against Alderman Vrdolyak, who received 42 percent running as a third party candidate, and Northwestern University professor Don Haider, who received 4 percent running as the Republican candidate.[25] When these results are compared to Mayor Washington's win with a mere 36 percent of the vote in the 1983 primary and a bare 52 percent in the 1983 general election, they demonstrate a shift in voter sentiment, particularly in the Democratic primary. Washington retained his support in the black wards, where he continued to receive 90 percent of the vote, and strengthened his support in the four Latino wards and among lakefront liberal voters. Whereas Washington had failed to carry any of the lakefront wards in 1983, he carried three of them in 1987.

Another important trend occurred in the 1987 election. The backlash among white ethnic voters was subsiding, which in turn eroded the racial backing for the opposition bloc in the city council. "The widespread expectation that [Washington] would create a black machine that would exact retribution from his white 'enemies' did not materialize. There was no mass firing of whites at City Hall, ward services were not rolled back and scatter-site public housing was not spread throughout the ethnic wards. . . . Washington did not increase his share of white eth-

TABLE 7.3   Aldermanic Election Results

Votes for Winner	1979	1987
100%	20	6
Greater than 60%	10	17
Greater than 50%	10	14
Less than 50%	10	13

nic votes in 1987; however, the level of opposition to him diminished significantly."[26] White ethnics turned out in smaller numbers to oppose Washington in 1987 than in 1983, but Washington was disappointed not to win more of their votes. Because the white ethnic vote was not greater for Washington in 1987, the mayor made policy and rhetorical shifts after the 1987 election to become even more of a mayor for the entire city.[27]

In addition to voter shifts occurring at the mayoral level, a profound change was occurring at the aldermanic level. In the 1979 aldermanic elections, at the height of the Democratic machine's power, twenty of the fifty aldermen were elected with 100 percent of the vote because they had no opponent on the ballot. In 1987, all but six races were contested. In 1979, less than 150 candidates ran in the fifty wards for alderman, whereas in 1987 the number topped 300. By 1991 there was an all-time high of 324 candidates, and in 1999 there were 283 candidates for the fifty seats.[28] There is a big difference between a council in which 40 percent of the members were chosen without opposition versus a council in which only 12 percent ran unopposed, as shown in Table 7.3. When the council became more competitive and the political direction of the city was in doubt, more candidates were willing to run against a machine that was no longer invincible.

From Council Wars to Rubber Stamp

The elections made a profound difference in the voting behavior in the council. Instead of 21–29, the practical division was now 39–11 in support of Mayor Washington. Alderman Vrdolyak, having run for mayor and lost, was replaced in the council by his brother, Victor Vrdolyak. Victor cast a lot of opposition votes but provided no leadership to the opposition bloc. Since Mayor Washington now had a solid majority backing him in the council and a weakened opposition bloc opposing him, he could, for the first time, freely adopt programs he had promised before but had been unable to pass through the gridlock of Council Wars.

Aldermen now voted with the Washington administration's floor leader, Alderman Evans, an average of 83 percent of the time. The opposition, which had been so cohesive during Council Wars, was now split while Mayor Washington's supporters remained unified. If aldermen during Council Wars were simply voting the will of their constituents on each issue, how was it possible that white aldermen who had formerly opposed Mayor Washington on every issue suddenly found themselves in agreement with the mayor on these same issues after the 1987 election? Because power was more important than substance. Proposals that had been blocked before the special 1986 aldermanic elections were now simply reintroduced and passed. The balance of power had changed.

The council in Washington's second term did not become as complete a rubber stamp as it had been under Mayors Daley and Bilandic. Rather, it was similar to the weak rubber-stamp council that had existed under Mayor Byrne. Viewed from the council floor, however, the differences in the councils during Mayor Washington's two terms were extraordinary.

The Brief Triumph of Progressive Politics

One discriminatory aspect of city government in prior administrations was the allocation of government contracts. Prior to 1984, less than 10 percent of the city's contracts had gone to business enterprises headed by minorities or women, even though minorities made up nearly 60 percent of the population. In April 1985, Washington issued an executive order requiring city agencies to award 25 percent of their contracts to minority business enterprises and 5 percent to women-owned businesses. By 1987, minority-owned businesses received 33 percent of the city's contract dollars while women-owned business enterprises received 6 percent. Affirmative action in government contracts was one of the major changes accomplished without aldermanic approval.[29]

The same discriminatory pattern had occurred in government hiring in the past. At the low point in affirmative action under Mayor Byrne, 28 percent of all new hires had been African-American, 6 percent Hispanic, and 26 percent women. In 1986, by contrast, the Washington administration hired 55 percent blacks and 12 percent Hispanics. Moreover, 41 percent of the new hires were women. Among department heads and major administrative positions the contrast was even more dramatic. Under Mayor Byrne only 17 percent of the major city appointments had been African-American and none had been Latino. Under Mayor Washington 42 percent were black and 3 percent Latino.[30] Despite budget and hiring limitations from a budget deficit left from the Byrne years, the employees of city government were beginning to reflect the racial balance of Chicago's multiracial population. Since Chicago was the most segregated city in North America, this was a striking achievement by the Washington administration.[31]

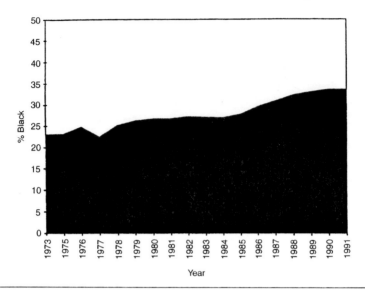

FIGURE 7.1   Percentage of City Jobs Held by Blacks in Chicago, 1973–1991
SOURCE: Patrick Joyce, "A Reversal of Fortunes: Black Empowerment, Political
Machines and City Jobs in New York City and Chicago," *Urban Affairs Review*, 32,
3 (January 1997), p. 306.

Washington and his council allies accomplished more. By signing the
Shakman Decree, Washington virtually eliminated patronage in city government. By promulgating his executive order creating freedom of information, he opened City Hall records for the first time. By signing an
ethics executive order, and then in 1987 passing the first ethics ordinance
in Chicago's history, he kept his campaign promises of good government
reforms.

Rerouting Community Development Block Grants to community organizations instead of hiring more City Hall patronage workers was another
major Washington reform. Hearings on the CDBG funds and on the city's
operating budget were held in the neighborhoods and opened the budget-
ing process to greater citizen participation. During the Washington administration, the city spent more than $300 million on neighborhood infra-
structure improvements. Economic development was no longer simply a
matter of building the Loop downtown but of creating balanced development of businesses and industries in the neighborhoods as well. The Washington administration worked with community organizations and supported neighborhood empowerment. In return, community organizations
provided the political support necessary to win Council Wars.

In a 1985 poll of historians, political scientists, and journalists of the
forty-three Chicago mayors since 1837, Harold Washington was ranked
eleventh among Chicago's top mayors. When the poll was repeated in

1994, he had risen to third place, behind Richard J. Daley (1955–1976) and Carter Harrison Jr. (1897–1905, 1911–1915). Washington was recognized as the third greatest mayor in Chicago's history "because he was the city's first African-American mayor, was an outstanding campaigner and speaker, and helped to move blacks from the periphery into the center of politics for at least two elections."[32]

Washington said in his last months in office that he planned to govern for twenty years, as Mayor Daley had before him. It is impossible to know how much more of his reform agenda might have been adopted if he had finished even his second term in office. The Council Wars era from 1983 to 1986 and the brief months from 1986 to 1987 when Mayor Washington gained control over the council were among the most dramatic periods in Chicago's history. Blacks, Hispanics, Asians, women, and homosexuals gained real power at City Hall for the first time. Opposition to Reaganomics and support for the city as a nuclear weapons–free zone were led by the mayor and his department heads, not just opposition groups. The growth machine of the old Chicago regime, which favored urban growth focused on major public works projects and development in the downtown Loop area, was replaced by a balanced program of neighborhood, as well as downtown, economic development.[33]

Chicago politics and government were permanently transformed. Washington proved that an African American could be elected mayor and govern the city as well as his white predecessors. He appointed blacks to head the most important city agencies, such as the Police Department, the Chicago public schools, and the Chicago Housing Authority, while he appointed Latinos and women to key position as well. City Hall was no longer the bastion of white males. After Mayor Washington's era, future mayors would continue to appoint more blacks and minorities to head key units of city government than previous mayors had. As his supporters maintained, the floor in city government had been raised. There were expectations about affirmative action and ending racial discrimination that could not be reversed.

Similarly, the executive order that Mayor Washington signed providing citizens, community organizations, and journalists freedom of information has been reauthorized by Mayors Sawyer and Richard M. Daley. Washington's ethics ordinance has been extended to cover campaign fund-raising and other governmental abuses of power.

Thus the racial barrier was broken in Chicago, affirmative action and political reform were installed at City Hall, and old-style machine control was a thing of the past. Of course, such a fundamental transformation did not occur without resistance. Instead, this era was marked by Council Wars.

The Washington administration also made two basic changes in the use of Community Development Block Grant funds. First, Mayor Washington redirected most of the funds away from paying patronage employees to funding community organizations to provide social services and neighborhood economic development. Second, he targeted the money to minority low-income neighborhoods. Instead of using these poverty funds to build and strengthen the machine, Mayor Washington used them to empower community groups and to weaken Democratic Party ward organizations. The council finally agreed to allocate CDBG funds in this way as long as new city bond funds were used for infrastructure improvements as the aldermen directed. The result was the largest neighborhood improvement program in the history of the city and a less powerful political machine.

Although Chicago would never be the same, it did not perpetuate Washington's progressive vision. The turbulent era that had seen his rise to power was soon replaced by a chaotic council and then by a "new machine."

Notes

1. James Lewis, Garth Taylor, and Paul Kleppner, *The MetroChicago Political Atlas '97–98* (Chicago: Chicago Urban League/Metro Chicago Information Center/Northern Illinois University, 1997).

2. My account of Harold Washington's biography is taken from Dempsey Travis, *Harold: The People's Mayor* (Chicago: Urban Research Press, 1989). The quotation is from p. 87.

3. Paul Kleppner, *Chicago Divided: The Making of a Black Mayor* (Dekalb: Northern University Press, 1985), p. 135.

4. Kleppner, *Chicago Divided*, p. 148.

5. Paul Green, "The 1983 Chicago Democratic Mayoral Primary," in Paul Green and Melvin Holli, eds., *The Making of the Mayor: Chicago 1983* (Grand Rapids, Mich.: Eerdmans, 1984), pp. 26–27.

6. Kleppner, *Chicago Divided*, p. 150.

7. Statement of candidacy by Harold Washington, candidate for mayor, November 10, 1982, Dick Simpson Papers, Special Collections, Main Library, University of Illinois at Chicago.

8. Kleppner, *Chicago Divided*, pp. 157–161.

9. Kleppner, *Chicago Divided*, pp. 156–157.

10. Kleppner, *Chicago Divided*, p. 162.

11. William Grimshaw, "Is Chicago Ready for Reform?" in *Making of the Mayor*, pp. 141–163.

12. Kleppner, *Chicago Divided*, p. 177.

13. Kleppner and Taylor, *Chicago Political Atlas*, p. 42.

14. Melvin Holli, "Daley to Daley," in Paul Green and Melvin Holli, eds., *Restoration 1989: Chicago Elects a New Daley* (Chicago: Lyceum, 1991), p. 202.

15. Dick Simpson et al., *Blueprint of Chicago Government: A Study for Mayor Harold Washington by the Agency Review Unit of the Transition Team* (Chicago: University of Illinois at Chicago/League of Women Voters, 1983).

16. The Tim Evans biography is taken from "Profile: The Long-Awaited Candidacy of Alderman Timothy C. Evans," *Chicago Enterprise*, November 1998, pp. 13–14. The quotation is on p. 14.

17. "City Council Reorganization," private memorandum to Harold Washington from the Agency Review Unit of the transition team, April 22, 1983, p. 1. A copy of the memorandum is included in the Dick Simpson Papers, Special Collections, Main Library, University of Illinois at Chicago.

18. Harold Washington, "First Inaugural Address, April 29, 1983," in Alton Miller, ed., *Climbing a Great Mountain* (Chicago: Bonus Books, 1988), p. 3.

19. David Fremon, *Chicago Politics Ward by Ward* (Bloomington: Indiana University Press, 1988), pp. 4–5.

20. James Strong and Manuel Galvan, "Majority Bloc Shifts Funds to Its Members' Wards," *Chicago Tribune*, May 29, 1985, sec. 2, p. 2.

21. John McCarron and James Strong, "'Council Wars' Threaten Funding," *Chicago Tribune*, May 30, 1985, pp. 1, 4.

22. James Strong and Manuel Galvan, "Council Chamber Turns to Madhouse," *Chicago Tribune*, June 13, 1985, pp. 1, 17.

23. Francis Ward, *The Harold Washington Years* (forthcoming). Manuscript, chap. 4, p. 97.

24. James Strong and Robert Davis, "Council Foes Stripped of Their Power," *Chicago Tribune*, June 7, 1986, pp. 1–2.

25. William Grimshaw, *Bitter Fruit: Black Politics and the Chicago Machine, 1931–1991* (Chicago: University of Chicago Press, 1991), p. 192.

26. Grimshaw, *Bitter Fruit*, p. 193.

27. Letter from Melvin Holli, February 9, 1999, Dick Simpson Papers, Special Collections, Main Library, University of Illinois at Chicago.

28. See the *Chicago Sun-Times*, December 21, 1990, p. 20; and the *Chicago Tribune*, December 15, 1998, sec. 2, p. 8.

29. Barbara Ferman, *Challenging the Growth Machine: Neighborhood Politics in Chicago and Pittsburgh* (Lawrence: University of Kansas Press, 1996), p. 114.

30. Ferman, *Challenging the Growth Machine*, p. 117.

31. Patrick Joyce, "A Reversal of Fortunes: Black Empowerment, Political Machines, and City Jobs in New York City and Chicago," *Urban Affairs Review* 32 (January 1997): 306.

32. Melvin G. Holli, "The Experts Choose Chicago's Greatest Mayors," *Public Perspective*, August-September 1995, pp. 54–56.

33. For a discussion of the change in economic development policies, see Gergory D. Squires et al., *Chicago: Race, Class, and the Response to Urban Decline* (Philadelphia: Temple University Press, 1987); Pierre Clavel and Wim Wiewel, *Harold Washington and the Neighborhoods* (New Brunswick, N.J.: Rutgers University Press, 1991); and Joel Rast, *Remaking Chicago: The Political Origins of Urban Industrial Change* (DeKalb: Northern Illinois University Press, 1999).

8

Eugene Sawyer's Chaos, 1987–1989

The 1980s were a turbulent time in Chicago's history. Before the decade had begun, Jane Byrne had been elected as the first woman mayor. She turned the city council over to the "evil cabal," which she had run against in her election campaign, presided over a revolving-door administration, and fractured the old Daley machine. Then Harold Washington was elected as the first black mayor. Council Wars, unprecedented in Chicago's history since the Civil War, had slowly given way to a rubber stamp council that supported the mayor's reform proposals. After Washington died, the council experienced a period of chaos during which it spun out of anyone's control.

Nationally, the 1980 election of Ronald Reagan had brought talk of a Republican revolution creating a permanent political realignment in which Reagan conservatives rather than Roosevelt liberals would control the dominant political party in America. The federal government scaled back the funds it provided to cities such as Chicago and the welfare recipients who lived within their boundaries. No new public housing was built. The Chicago City Council in these times of limits and financial constraints, facing a conservative mood in the country and a lack of strong mayoral leadership, retreated from the progressivism of the Washington era. The council turned inward, became factionalized, and flailed about without direction.

Sawyer's Selection

With the sudden death of Mayor Washington on November 25, 1987, the problems of mayoral succession that had previously occurred when Mayors Cermak and Daley died were repeated under new laws, with new twists, and with a clearer racial impact. In 1987, the succession process fell short of what we would expect in a representative democracy. Mayor Washington died in Northwestern Memorial Hospital of a massive heart attack, as had Mayor Daley. He collapsed at his desk in his office at City Hall. Although paramedics were summoned immediately by his press secretary, who had been meeting with him, neither they nor hospital doctors could revive him. Washington's sudden death "exposed the weak foundation of his reforms."[1] Without his charismatic leadership, the city council quickly reasserted its power. Once again, aldermen were key contenders in the succession battle because the acting mayor would be chosen from among them by vote of the council until a popular election to elect a new mayor could be held. There were four notable mayoral contenders in the battle for succession.

Alderman Larry Bloom was a white liberal reform alderman from Hyde Park (5th Ward) on the South Side, which was 75 percent black. An intelligent, articulate lawyer, Alderman Bloom represented the same liberal, Independent, integrated ward that had provided earlier reformers such as Charles Merriam, Paul Douglas, and Leon Despres (as well as Mayor Washington). He had openly criticized Mayor Byrne since being elected in 1979 and strongly supported Mayor Washington. He was made chairman of the Budget Committee by Washington in 1986. Now, in 1987, he hoped to be elected as a compromise candidate for acting mayor. He later ran as a candidate for mayor, Cook County state's attorney, and city treasurer, but he lost all three elections. Although he was a reformer in the council, his career ended in disgrace with his corruption conviction in the federal "silver shovel" investigation in 1998, in which he admitted bribery, extortion, mail fraud, and helping a legal client evade unpaid property taxes.[2]

Alderman Tim Evans, a black, was a South Side alderman who had been ward committeeman since 1971. Mayor Washington had selected him to head the Finance Committee and to serve as his floor leader. Although Evans had been a loyal supporter of Mayors Daley and Bilandic, he had broken with the political machine during the Byrne administration. Despite his new opposition role in the council, he continued as Democratic ward committeeman and as a member of the Central Committee of the Democratic Party of Cook County. Most African-American reform political leaders and community activists supported Evans's claim to be the rightful heir to continue the Washington reform legacy.

Alderman Richard Mell was a white, Northwest Side Polish-American alderman and ward committeeman. He had been born in 1938 to a working-class family in Muskegon, Michigan. Alderman Mell had remained loyal to the machine and had been a committed member of the Vrdolyak opposition bloc during the Council Wars period. He hoped to rally all the white members of the city council and to pick up support from a few black and Latino aldermen by promising them traditional political favors and power. The *Chicago Tribune* described him as "a skilled organizer and a charismatic field marshal."

> And, if at times he's skirted the edge of propriety—using a gang leader as a campaign worker, and hitting up liquor licensees for political contributions, even as he threatens to close their businesses—well you have to do what it takes to win. In return Mell has reaped the spoils of victory. Take city jobs. The aldermen has hundreds of them, for members of his political organization and his family. . . . [But] Mell is a new breed ward boss. He doesn't see himself as a cog in a machine, but as a free agent on a wide-open playing field in a game without rules. Indeed, he switches allegiances, within the party, and sometimes even outside the party at the drop of a hat. Alderman Eugene Sawyer . . . [said of him], "He's not the kind of guy who would stab you in the back; he'd stab you in the chest."[3]

Mell was the consummate wheeler-dealer who in 1987 was looking to move up—to mayor if he could make it that far but up the ladder in any case.

Alderman Eugene Sawyer was a black South Side alderman and ward committeeman. Like a number of Chicago's black aldermen, Eugene Sawyer had been born in the South. He grew up in Greensboro, Alabama, graduated in 1956 from Alabama State University, and taught chemistry at Prentiss Institute, a prep school in Prentiss, Mississippi. After he came to Chicago, he became a protégé of former 6th Ward alderman Robert Miller and went to work in the city's Water Department, first in the collection department and later as a chemist. He was elected 6th Ward committeeman in 1968 and alderman in 1971. Sawyer remained loyal to the machine until late in the Byrne administration but then supported Washington in the 1983 election and in Council Wars. He had a nearly 100 percent voting record in support of all the Chicago mayors under whom he served. He had never headed a major council committee or introduced a single major piece of city legislation as alderman. He was quiet, soft-spoken, and easy to get along with. He "was a civil-service alderman: faceless, bland, and with a record almost blank."[4]

In a dramatic turn of events, Eugene Sawyer was selected by the city council to be acting mayor. He held the post for fifteen months, only to lose the mayoral election in 1989. He was selected by the council as a compromise candidate with whom both white and black machine aldermen were comfortable. They expected him to be more of a tool that they could control than he turned out to be. But the Sawyer era is remembered primarily for its confusion and turmoil as various political leaders and groups sought to gain the power to govern the city.

This is the story of how the Sawyer era began. Even before Alderman Tim Evans returned from Northwestern Memorial Hospital, where Mayor Washington was pronounced dead, the mayoral campaign maneuvering had begun at City Hall. The *Chicago Tribune* reported:

> With one eye on the television set that was delivering the grim news to his third-floor City Hall office, [African-American West Side] Ald. William Henry (24th)—who had made no secret of his disdain for elements of [Mayor Washington's] reform agenda—began calling other aldermen into his office and started to line up their ward-organization armies.
>
> "There was an appropriate sadness," said one alderman of the gathering in Henry's office during those tense afternoon hours Wednesday. "On the other hand, it seemed like, 'Hallelujah, we're free.'"
>
> A few hours later, as Evans—Washington's council floor leader—returned from the hospital, he was grabbed by Ald. Bobby Rush (2d). "I asked him if he wanted to be mayor and he said, 'Yes,'" Rush recalled. "I told him what was going on [in Sawyer's camp]. And we started making calls that night."[5]

Evans and his supporters were too late. Alderman Henry had already lined up six black aldermen to support Sawyer and had talked to the rest. In the meantime, Mell was telling reporters that he had lined up twenty votes. He would offer spoils, power, and committee chairmanships to the other council members in an attempt to get the necessary twenty-six votes to be elected, but he couldn't break the council's racial barriers to get a majority.

Presidential candidate Rev. Jesse Jackson, learning of Mayor Washington's death, flew back from the Middle East. He met with black aldermen and community leaders to try to get unity around a single black candidate. At one point in those sessions Sawyer was asked if he really wanted to be mayor and he mumbled a reply that couldn't be heard. It was taken as an early sign of his indecision. After this first meeting, Jackson began to work out a strategy to elect Evans. On Friday and Saturday he met with Hispanic aldermen and tried to line up their support. Mexican-American alderman Jesus Garcia was delayed so long meeting with Jackson that he missed an interracial meeting with Independent aldermen that he had called at his own ward office. Thus he was unable to convince them to vote for Evans. Alderman Edwin Eisendrath, who was at the meeting, proposed supporting Larry Bloom instead.

The four Latino aldermen (two Mexican Americans and two Puerto Ricans) decided to vote as a bloc to maximize their influence. They eventually decided to vote for Evans. However, their unified support was insufficient to elect him. A year later, in the 1989 mayoral election, they split their support among a variety of candidates with one of them, Juan Soliz, running for mayor as the first Hispanic candidate. However, he failed to obtain enough voter signatures on his nominating petitions to get on the ballot and thus his effort failed.

While these various racial caucuses were occurring, two meetings were held among the twenty-four white aldermen at the Northwest Side home of Alderman Joseph Kotlarz . At these meetings, both Alderman Mell and Northwest Side Alderman Terry Gabinski attempted to get enough support to be elected mayor. Yet, even if they could get the unified support of most of the old-time white machine aldermen, they still had to get support from white lakefront reformers and a couple of Latino or black aldermen to win. When it became clear that neither Mell nor Gabinski could line up the requisite votes, Mell began meeting with Sawyer to see if a winning coalition to elect either Sawyer or Mell could be put together. Finally, in a clandestine meeting in a restaurant parking lot, Mell was convinced that Sawyer had the necessary black supporters. If Mell swung the ethnic white aldermen to him, Sawyer could be elected. Earlier attempts to elect Bloom (despite his being an Independent reform alderman) fell through because he demanded support from both black and white aldermen, wouldn't promise the necessary political rewards to potential aldermanic supporters, and simply wasn't able to get the necessary votes.

After a marathon session of the city council a few days later, attended by several thousand former Washington supporters who vocally backed Evans, Sawyer was elected acting mayor by a vote of 29–19 at 4:01 in the morning. What may have been the most raucous meeting in the city council's turbulent history began at 5:30 the evening before. The night had been filled with speeches and dramatic moments, such as Mell leaping on his desk and demanding to be recognized by the interim mayor and meeting chairman, Alderman David Orr. But the biggest drama focused on Mayor Sawyer, who was closeted in his office with aldermen and his pastor, trying to decide if he was up to taking the job. He seemed to have lost his nerve, despite having the necessary votes. The vocal opposition of thousands of citizens in the chambers unnerved him. The television cameras caught all the action on the council floor and in the galleries and sent it unedited to the tens of thousands of Chicagoans watching until the early morning hours. Alderman Mell later recounted this behind-the-scenes story:

> Sawyer told Ald. Richard F. Mell (33rd Ward), "Dick, I can't do it. I gotta pull out."
>
> "OK," Mell recalls sighing, saying he was feigning sadness. "But you should tell the people who backed you. That's the least you owe them. . . ."
>
> "It was a ruse to get him in the room with us!" Mell exults. "Once inside, I slammed the door and locked it. I thought, 'Now we gotcha, you son of a

bitch!' Then we climbed all over him. When we walked out, he was so weak he wobbled like this—whoa!—and we had to steady him. But he was ours."[6]

When he finally entered the council chambers, Alderman Sawyer's knees buckled and he nearly fainted. But at 4 A.M. the roll was called and Sawyer was elected acting mayor.

Sawyer was chosen because "he had no enemies because he had done nothing that would have created them. He had been virtually a mute during his many years in the council."[7] Also, the city's elite feared that there would be race riots if a white alderman were selected to replace the popular Harold Washington. But mostly he was chosen because the old black machine aldermen whom Washington had not purged and the white ethnic machine aldermen, who were still a powerful voting bloc, believed that Sawyer would cooperate with them as he had over his many years of loyal machine support in the council.

In 1987 the selection process was carried out by secret caucuses, just as it was ten years earlier when Mayor Bilandic was chosen to replace Mayor Daley. But ethnic politics had given way to racial groupings— white, black, and brown. Racial background was much more of a motivating force than other characteristics—Irish or Polish, Catholic or Jew, party hack or reformer. The struggle to succeed Mayor Washington was unrepresentative of politics as usual in Chicago. It was also a major setback to black empowerment. As Monroe Anderson, Sawyer's press secretary, would later write about the split in the black community and their loss of power, "No one did anything to us but us. We fell on the sword and . . . continue to complete our self-inflicted disembowelment."[8]

The Sawyer City Council

While various candidates maneuvered to run in the upcoming mayoral election, the acting mayor and city council struggled to govern the city. During the first few months, the fate of the city hung in the balance. Would Sawyer be able to achieve the control of the legendary Richard J. Daley? Or would he develop the tenacity and vision of his predecessor, Harold Washington? Would he back the machine faction represented by Alderman Burke or work with the Washington coalition represented by Aldermen Evans and Orr? Would he honor the promises he made before being selected to carry on the programs of Mayor Washington? Or would he follow the advice of supporters such as Alderman Mell?

After his inauspicious and conflict-filled selection on December 2, 1987, at one of the most turbulent council meetings on record, Mayor Sawyer tried to make a positive beginning at healing the wounds created by his selection as acting mayor. In his speech following his swearing-in he promised:

The reform movement initiated by Mayor Harold Washington shall remain intact and go forward. . . . This city government will be an open city government, open to all people all of the time. . . . There will be no cronyism or favoritism. . . . I shall continue to unite black, white and Hispanic, Slav and Jew, Christian and Asian, white ethnics and new immigrants. . . .

I will continue to support and advance the mayor's progressive reform agenda. I will continue his efforts to reform our education system . . . to provide decent affordable housing . . . the mayor's affirmative action programs in hiring, purchasing [and] contracts . . . [and] the mayor's economic development program.[9]

True to his word, in his governmental policies, Mayor Sawyer mostly continued programs of the Washington administration, much as Mayor Bilandic had continued the policies of the Daley administration. Soon the council faction that had put him in office began to oppose him. At the same time, genuine reformers in the council and reform organizations in the city did not trust him.

Aldermen who had opposed Mayor Washington, such as Burke, Vrdolyak, and Mell, had voted to elect Mayor Sawyer whereas aldermen in the pro-Washington coalition—blacks from the South and West Sides of Chicago, Latino aldermen and lakefront liberal aldermen—opposed his election. But now council voting switched as the former Washington backers supported Mayor Sawyer's council proposals adopting Washington's programs, and the very aldermen who had selected Sawyer as acting mayor now opposed his legislation.

In the first four months of Mayor Sawyer's term as acting mayor (from December 1, 1987, to March 30, 1988) there were 102 divided roll call votes. The twenty-nine aldermen who had elected Sawyer voted with him only 65 percent of the time on those roll calls. Yet the nineteen who had voted for Alderman Tim Evans now voted with the Mayor Sawyer 84 percent of the time—a 20 percent difference. Overall, Sawyer's control of the council was much weaker than any recent mayor's, except Mayor Washington during Council Wars. Sawyer lost 16 of the first 102 votes of his administration, and more than fifteen aldermen opposed him on 37 percent of all votes. Compared with other mayors since the Great Depression, Sawyer was less able to pass his legislation. A new coalition had to be put together to pass each separate proposal because, unlike most modern Chicago mayors, he did not have a majority bloc to support him.

The opposition to Mayor Sawyer was not fully united either. Aldermen simply used the uncertainty of this period to press their own agendas. They felt free to withhold their votes from the mayor in order to bargain for his support for their own pet projects. Burke voted most frequently in opposition to Mayor Sawyer. He explained his and other white ethnic aldermen's opposition to Mayor Sawyer as a "result of 'frustration and dis-appointment' that Sawyer [had] not done more for them and their wards . . . not rewarding [his supporters] with such perquisites as jobs and council committee posts. 'He turned his back on the people who sup-ported him and rejected them out of hand,' Burke said in explaining his voting record. 'It's only natural that once you've been rejected you would feel less likely to support the man.'" On the other hand, Evans contended that the white aldermen never intended to support Sawyer for the long term but had voted for him to "bifurcate the movement" that had elected Harold Washington. As for his own frequent agreement with Sawyer during council votes, Evans said that "many of the matters that have come before the council . . . were holdovers from the Washington admin-istration that deserved approval."[10]

There was also a minor party realignment. Former alderman Edward Vrdolyak became chairman of the Republican Party, although under Mayor Byrne he had been elected chairman of the Democratic Party. He recruited a former ally, North Side alderman Bernard Stone, to run as a countywide Republican candidate in 1988. Consequently his brother, 10th Ward alderman Victor Vrdolyak, who had replaced him in the council, and Alderman Stone now became a supposed Republican opposition bloc. Victor Vrdolyak was absent for many votes and voted with the mayor 52 percent of the time when he was present. Alderman Stone voted with his former ally, Mayor Sawyer, only 51 percent of the time. However, in the next election, Alderman Victor Vrdolyak would be replaced by a regular Democrat and Alderman Stone would rejoin the Democratic Party. Party labels meant very little in this confused Sawyer era.

Reorganization of the Council

Unfortunately, Sawyer did not have Washington's vision or leadership skill. So his government was one of vacillation. His "plainly diffident de-meanor" caused reporters to mock him as "Mayor Mumbles."[11] During the first months of his regime, he left the former Washington leadership in the council unchanged. Then on April 14, 1988, Mayor Sawyer's allies gave a $170,000 budget boost to three city council committees chaired by Sawyer supporters. The increase went to the Committee on Education, chaired by Alderman Patrick O'Connor, the Committee on Rules, chaired by Alderman Anna Langford, and the Committee on Traffic and Public Safety, chaired by Alderman Tony Laurino. The vote to approve these in-creases was 27–18. Alderman Evans said after the meeting, "These alloca-tions are inappropriate [because] there was sufficient money in their [committee] budgets to carry out their responsibilities. Now [the pro-Sawyer aldermen] will have to answer to the citizens of Chicago whose money they will be spending and probably wasting."[12] This maneuver allowed Sawyer to appease his council allies while at the same time forestalling their efforts to reorganize the council with them in control once again. The effort to forestall the reorganization of the council didn't work, however.

On May 25, 1988, the voting bloc that had elected Sawyer unceremoniously dumped Alderman Orr as vice mayor by a vote of 31–15. His successor as vice mayor was drawn from a hat containing the names of Sawyer backers. When the winner of the drawing turned out to be freshman Northwest Side alderman Patrick Lavar, he declined the post, accepting chairman of the Committee on Streets and Alleys instead. The post was then offered to the more senior Alderman Gabinski, who became the new vice mayor by default. Then on July 13, 1998, members of the Evans faction likely to support his mayoral campaign were dumped from their committee chairmanships, including Alderman Evans as chairman of the Finance Committee. This parliamentary coup was carried by a vote of 25–17. Mayor Sawyer claimed that he lacked control over the council to prevent these actions, yet he acquiesced. He could have used his veto to prevent these changes if he had really wanted to fight the council reorganization, but he did not.

Chaos Grows

His vacillation further weakened his stature in the council. To Mayor Sawyer's credit, he was able to eventually pass some important measures originally proposed by Mayor Washington such as the human rights ordinance, which guaranteed gays and lesbians equal rights in employment and housing. While he lost more votes than any modern mayor (other than Mayor Washington during the Council Wars), he did have the tenacity to reintroduce measures, and he eventually got them passed, including a $621 million property tax levy with a property tax increase, which finally passed on February 16, 1989. Yet factionalism among the aldermen only increased. Aldermen voted against even routine resolutions such as those congratulating couples on their fiftieth wedding anniversary if the "wrong" alderman sponsored the resolution. Name-calling, shouting, jumping on tables, generally poor manners, and mangled parliamentary procedure became the hallmark of the council. The media came to describe it as a "circus" and the aldermen as "ill-behaved children." Moreover, most council battles were not based on high principles or different conceptions of the public good. Rather, petty personal politics reigned during the Sawyer period.

The roll call votes of the council in 1987–1988 revealed six disturbing trends:

1. An incredible 387 divided roll call votes in a single year, the largest number of any council studied.
2. The lack of 100 percent support for the mayor or complete loyalty by any group of aldermen.
3. The highest number of legislative defeats for any mayor in modern times other than Mayor Washington during Council Wars.
4. An increasing number of absences by aldermen who, given the circus atmosphere, no longer thought that their votes counted.
5. The pro-Evans faction that had opposed his election voted with Mayor Sawyer more often than the pro-Sawyer aldermen who had elected him acting mayor.
6. Instead of two factions divided around ideology and political programs, there were multiple factions based on personality, race, and personal self-interest.

As the city council splintered into more and more factions, the mayor was unable to command any truly solid bloc of supporters. This was true even though he put in his ally, regular Democratic alderman Burton Natarus, as his floor leader. No alderman (not even his floor leader or his own Alderman Robertson, whom he had appointed to replace himself) supported him 100 percent of the time. Aldermen voted against measures because of petty personal reasons, race, and self-interest, or merely because they wanted to vote against proposals presented by opposing bloc aldermen. These multiple factions created unstable coalitions that changed from vote to vote. As the mayoral campaign of 1989 began to heat up, opposition by the different factions supporting Sawyer, Evans, Bloom, and State's Attorney Daley for mayor began to make these divisions deeper. Two issues are particularly illustrative of the chaotic Sawyer era: (1) the failure of aldermanic accountability legislation and (2) the original failure and eventual passage of the human rights ordinance.

Aldermanic Accountability

Mayor Sawyer, having been a creature of a machine-dominated council and a ward boss for nearly two decades, hardly was an advocate for city council reform. On January 9, 1989, the City Club of Chicago released a comprehensive city council reform program that proposed ten major reforms. This reform agenda was endorsed by a dozen good government organizations such as the League of Women Voters. The newspapers were once again filled with exposés and stories about excesses of the city council, but getting reforms adopted was as difficult as it had always been. The reforms proposed by the City Club were to disclose pending legislation, floor debate, aldermanic expense accounts expenditures, zoning conflicts of interest, and voting records in a useable form; to reduce the number of council committees and to reform the committee staff system; to promote citizen participation by publishing a regular calendar of council and council committee meetings, encouraging substantive debate and ending campaign funding loopholes; and finally to create greater citizen participation in the form of neighborhood government and little city halls in the neighborhoods. The scorecard in Figure 8.1 shows how these reforms fared by the end of the Sawyer administration and how much still needed to be accomplished if Chicago was to have a democratic and effective city council.[13]

FIGURE 8.1   City Council Reform Report Card

Reform Proposal	*Grade 5/30/89*
Disclosure of Pending Legislation and Debate	F
Aldermanic Allowance Disclosure	A–
Zoning Conflict Disclosure	B–
Voting Records Published	F
Reduces Committees/Budgets	C+
Committee Staff Reform	F
Regular Calendar of Meetings	F
Promote Substantive Debate	F
Campaign Fund Loopholes	A
Community Participation Proposals	F

SOURCE: Dick Simpson et al., *Chicago City Council Reform* (Chicago: City Club of Chicago/University of Illinois at Chicago, 1991).

Alderman Orr, on the same day he was dumped as vice mayor (May 25, 1988), introduced a series of ordinances to require aldermen to disclose spending from their aldermanic expense accounts. The timing of his legislation was inspired by a *Chicago Tribune* exposé and by the growing demand for city council accountability. In 1987, the *Tribune* in a lengthy series of articles had attacked corruption in the council, citing conflicts of interest, selective paving of streets (including those on which aldermen lived), wasteful spending of committee funds, and securing zoning changes without releasing the names of the property owners. In that series, the *Tribune* reporters revealed that "records of council expenditures show aldermen spending thousands of dollar each year on travel, gifts, office remodeling and the employment of business partners, campaign workers, family members and friends."[14] One of the many aldermen whose expenses they documented was Alderman Patrick Huels from the powerful 11th Ward:

> Alderman Patrick Huels sent his secretary to a Wabash Avenue store to pick up office supplies for his Committee on Licenses. The secretary returned with five picture frames and two pen-and-pencil sets, including a 10-karat gold-filled, green onyx Cross desk set. Taxpayers picked up the bill for $326.29. . . . In the following year, Huels used committee funds to pay for monthly car-phone bills ranging from $38.80 to $327.74; a $22-a-month beeper service; a $350 "hands free duplex" to allow him to use the phone outside his car; a $155 telephone delivered to his ward office; $100 in cab fare coupons; a $103 Polaroid camera; an oak computer cabinet, chair and hutch priced at $315 and a $621 unitemized Diners Club International charge for "office equipment."[15]

The *Tribune* detailed other aldermanic purchases such as television sets and travel that seemed to have no legislative purpose. Despite Huels's expenses, his committee had met only a few times and approved no legislation in 1985, when the expenses occurred. Aldermen, under the rules of the council, spent their aldermanic expense accounts and their committee expense funds with virtually no restrictions. Exposés such as those in the *Tribune* fueled proposed reforms in the council, but the necessary votes to pass reform legislation were just as difficult to obtain in the Sawyer council as they were in the earlier rubber stamp and Council Wars councils. Most aldermen continued to fight to protect their privileges.

In addition to Alderman Orr's proposals to require reporting on aldermanic expenditures, Alderman Henry, who was also criticized in the *Tribune* series, introduced an alternate package of aldermanic disclosure legislation on June 8, 1988. On July 13, by a vote of 31–4, both packages of legislation were sent to a special subcommittee chaired by Alderman Henry to be buried, despite Mayor Sawyer's promised support for the reforms. Then on November 30, 1988, after receiving an official opinion from the city's corporation counsel that aldermanic expense allowances could only be spent for public purposes and not pocketed as salary by the alderman, the council took another vote on aldermanic accountability. This time a watered-down version of Alderman Orr's legislation was introduced by the mayor's floor leader, Alderman Natarus, reiterating the decision of the corporation counsel. However, the Burton Natarus ordinance did not require aldermen to disclose how they spent their money. The motion to substitute the weaker ordinance prevailed by a vote of 34–11, with most of the Sawyer supporters voting for the legislation and many of the Evans supporters opposing it as too limited. After attempts to strengthen Natarus's legislation failed, the weaker ordinance passed, 40–4.

In all other areas of reform, the council refused to budge. Despite scandals and public pressure, the council adopted no other reforms during the Sawyer interim until just before the 1989 mayoral elections. Alderman Orr again offered an ordinance to require aldermen to disclose any financial interest they had in property to be rezoned. Alderman Natarus tried to block a specific amendment requiring that alderman disclose if they, their friends, or relatives realized financial gain from rezoned property within three years of any zoning change. In debating the issue, an angry Natarus accused Orr of hypocrisy in ways that illustrate how irrational and personal the council rhetoric often became in the Sawyer era:

> "McCarthy is to communism what Orr is to ethics," the red-faced Natarus shouted. Natarus said Orr needs to stump for ethics to compensate for failure to deliver ward services. "Orr needs to accuse people of falsehoods, lies and alleged crimes," Natarus went on. "There is a man who went on TV [and] accused me of taking zoning bribes. I resent the continued haranguing . . . that zoning is something bad, that land use control is bad, that it always involves chicanery." . . .
>
> Orr denied the allegation, saying that in a TV interview he accused Natarus of merely blocking reforms. Orr called Natarus's outburst a "wide-ranging, silly and immature speech."[16]

After Natarus's impassioned speech, Alderman William Krystniak moved to send the ordinance back to committee, but his motion failed, 30–16. Then the new restriction on aldermen in zoning legislation passed unanimously, 44–0, with even Alderman Natarus voting in favor despite his impassioned speech attacking the ordinance. Once again ethics legislation had passed on the eve of the 1989 election because each mayoral candidate's aldermanic supporters did not want to have their candidate accused of blocking legitimate council reform.

The Human Rights Ordinance

The human rights ordinance, the most important feature of which extended civil rights protection to gays and lesbians, had originally been defeated during the Washington administration by a vote of 30–18. Mayor Sawyer resubmitted the proposal and it was approved on June 23, 1988, by the city council Committee on Human Rights and Protection by a vote of 7–1 despite strong objections by Chicago church leaders and some aldermen. At the public hearing on the ordinance, the Roman

Catholic Archdiocese of Chicago declared, "The draft ordinance contains wording that could be interpreted by the courts or the proposed human-rights commission as providing acceptance or approval of homosexual acts or of advocacy of a lifestyle that advocates such acts. . . . For these reasons, the archdiocese, while endorsing the overall intent of the human rights ordinance, cannot support this ordinance."[17] Other church leaders testifying against the ordinance were even more adamant in their opposition. Rev. Erwin Lutzer of the Protestant Moody Church said, "We oppose the ordinance because it condones homosexual behavior and puts homosexual behavior on a par with heterosexual behavior," adding that it could force landlords and employers to "violate their own moral conscience." Finally, Alderman George Hagopian, who challenged all the witnesses in favor of the ordinance, "charged that the measure condones and promotes homosexuality and proclaimed, 'When the day comes that I vote for an ordinance that supersedes the word of the Lord, I want to be dead.'"[18]

On the other side, more than thirty organizations endorsed the ordinance, including Operation PUSH, the American Civil Liberties Union, the United Methodist Church, and IVI-IPO. Rick Garcia, speaking for the Gay and Lesbian Town Meeting, said, "We will not be denied this time around. We're increasingly vocal, we're increasingly organized, we're becoming politically mature, and we will have our rights respected and acknowledged and upheld." Mayor Sawyer argued, "Our ordinance has a wider base of support than the previous ordinance introduced in 1986. It extends coverage to a broader group of individuals [in addition to gays and lesbians] and prohibits discrimination in the areas of employment, housing and public accommodations." However, as might be expected, the white aldermen who had helped to elect Sawyer were not persuaded. In addition to the opposition by Alderman Hagopian, Alderman John Madrzyk remained adamantly opposed: "It's still the gay-rights bill under another name. I am not going out and legitimize homosexual and lesbian practices."[19]

On November 14, 1988, when Mayor Sawyer brought the human rights ordinance to the floor of the council, it failed again, by a vote of 26–21. The issue mobilized the conservative religious community—white Protestants, black Protestants, and Catholics—in opposition. The Bible, morality, and practical politics all entered into the discussion. What finally allowed the ordinance to pass was, once again, the upcoming special mayoral election in 1989. All three potential candidates—Eugene Sawyer, Tim Evans, and Richard M. Daley—wanted support from the gay community. Rich Daley (despite being an Irish Catholic whose church opposed the legislation) convinced a few of his white machine aldermanic supporters who had opposed the measure in earlier votes to change their position and support it this time. With Daley's help, the ordinance passed narrowly by a vote of 26–24 on December 14, 1988.

Chaotic Interlude

Sawyer was neither Richard J. Daley nor Harold Washington. He didn't have the power and determination of a Mayor Daley, nor the vision and leadership of a Mayor Washington. He could neither command machine support from the white ethnic wards nor hold together the progressive coalition of Washington. The tenuous reform movement that had been patched together by Mayor Washington split apart and chaos reigned.

In Washington's 1987 mayoral reelection campaign he specifically proposed an "Action Agenda for Chicago's Future, 1987–1991" with hundreds of specific goals. For example, Washington's agenda to create and retain jobs included

1. a decent job for every Chicagoan
2. a small business development program
3. a new industrial park program
4. proposals to deal with plant closings
5. further development of the central area business district
6. strengthening Chicago's manufacturing base
7. a better linkage between Chicago's poor and suburban employment growth
8. better education and job training
9. more state and federal funding for urban economic development[20]

Sawyer inherited this activist agenda, but he did not have the political clout to carry out such an ambitious program. He was thwarted by a council that spun out of his control, by a city administration that he didn't appoint and that wasn't loyal to him, and by a national administration that remained under conservative Republican control.

The best case for Mayor Sawyer's accomplishments was written by his press secretary after both left office.

Acting Mayor Sawyer . . . enacted the late Mayor Washington's 1988 budget and a needed $66 million tax increase before he had been in office a month. In January 1988, he got council approval for legislation that broke the taxi monopoly in the city, something that Mayor Washington had not been able to do. In February, Sawyer managed to round up enough aldermanic support to get a bill passed allowing lights in Wrigley Field so that the Chicago Cubs would no longer be the only team in major league baseball unable to play night games at home—a feat his five predecessors were either unwilling or unable to accomplish. Sawyer got the ball rolling for private development of land around O'Hare Airport. During the Sawyer administration, an unprecedented agreement was reached with the fireman's union, guaranteeing labor peace for four-year chunks of time. And after a number of failed attempts under Sawyer's leadership, the city council finally passed a long-overdue human rights ordinance that protected gay and handicapped citizens from discrimination in employment and housing.[21]

Crediting Mayor Sawyer with this list of accomplishments may be generous in that all of these projects had been initiated during the Washington administration, but there is no doubt that these efforts were brought to fruition on Mayor Sawyer's watch. Sawyer, however, had great difficulty in moving the city or its city council forward in new directions of his own, and he never created an agenda for the city's future like Washington's. Like Mayor Bilandic before him, he presided over a brief interim as political power changed hands once again.

The regime that had governed Chicago was in flux. The election of Mayors Byrne and Washington had greatly weakened the Democratic machine. The party was split between factions, there was no supreme party boss, patronage had been undermined by the signing of the Shakman Decree, and the party had lost several elections for higher offices. Just when the business community, leaders of major institutions, and allies such as organized labor finally had begun to be willing to deal with a progressive city administration under Harold Washington, he died. His progressive new policies, which favored balanced downtown and economic development, for instance, were in doubt. So the other regime participants waited to see if progressive forces would prevail in the current power struggle or if the old machine politics would triumph. In the meantime, business leaders, bankers, and lawyers hedged their bets and gave campaign contributions to both Sawyer and Daley.

Just as neighborhood organizers and spokespeople had begun to receive more government funds for their programs and were offered a seat at the table when city government policies were being developed, the game changed again. For the most part, the neighborhood activists backed Alderman Tim Evans in the vain hope that he could hold the Washington coalition together and continue the progressive, pro-neighborhood agenda of the Washington administration. With the split in the black community between support for Sawyer and Evans, their cause was hopeless. But in this period of turmoil and transition, no one could be sure how the power struggles would be resolved.

Throughout the brief, chaotic Sawyer interlude the major players in the old Daley regime and the newer Washington regime waited for the dust to settle. Chicago was again at a critical political crossroads. Mayor Sawyer, to his credit, carried out some of the reforms that Washington planned; however, he remained a weak mayor with no agenda of his own. His base of support in the African-American community, and in the city as a whole, was limited and he didn't have much chance to win the special election that would be held a little more than a year after he took office. So the council returned to the familiar pattern of bickering and corruption that had characterized the earlier Gray Wolves period, when every alderman was out to get his share of the spoils. Dedicated aldermen were once again overwhelmed by the hacks. Yet the chaos of the Sawyer interlude would not last long.

Notes

1. William Grimshaw, *Bitter Fruit: Black Politics and the Chicago Machine, 1931–1991* (Chicago: University of Chicago Press, 1992), p. 197.

2. Abdon M. Pallash and Robert Davis, "Bloom Joins Long, Sad List," *Chicago Tribune*, December 6, 1998, pp. 1, 16.

3. Patrick Reardon, "Lord of His Ward," *Chicago Tribune*, August 26, 1996, p. 1.

4. Thomas Roeser, "Profile: The Slow Inevitability of Mayor Eugene Sawyer," *Chicago Enterprise*, October 1988, p. 13.

5. R. Bruce Dold and Ann Marie Lapinski, "The Making of the Mayor: Sawyer Vote Arranged in Parking Lot," *Chicago Tribune*, December 6, 1987, pp. 1, 22–23.

6. Roeser, "Profile," p. 11.

7. Grimshaw, *Bitter Fruit*, pp. 198–199.

8. Monroe Anderson, "The Sawyer Saga: A Journalist Who Just Happened to Be the Mayor's Press Secretary, Speaks," in Paul Green and Melvin Holli, eds., *Restoration 1989: Chicago Elects a New Daley* (Chicago: Lyceum, 1991), p. 94.

9. Eugene Sawyer, "Speech Following His Swearing in As Acting Mayor," in Dick Simpson, ed., *Chicago's Future: In a Time of Change* (Champaign, Ill.: Stipes, 1988), pp. 590–592.

10. Ann Marie Lipinski, "Council Foes Going Sawyer's Way in Council," *Chicago Tribune*, June 29, 1988, sec. 2, pp. 1–2.

11. Grimshaw, *Bitter Fruit*, p. 201.

12. Cheryl Devall and James Strong, "Sawyer Council Allies Get Budget Hikes," *Chicago Tribune*, April 14, 1988, sec. 2, p. 1.

13. Dick Simpson with Jennifer Arneson, Lisa Dushkin, and Ann Gentile, *Chicago City Council Reform* (Chicago: University of Illinois at Chicago/City Club of Chicago, 1991). Reprinted in Dick Simpson, ed., *Chicago's Future: In a Time of Change* (Champaign, Ill.: Stipes, 1993), pp. 276–286.

14. Dean Baquet, Ann Marie Lipinski, and William Gaines, "City Council: The Spoils of Power," *Chicago Tribune*, 1987. Reprinted in Dick Simpson, ed., *Chicago's Future* (1993), pp. 290–298.

15. Baquet et al., "Spoils of Power," p. 295.

16. John Schmidt, "Bitter Council Floor Fight Is Prelude to 44–0 Vote," *Lerner Papers*, March 12, 1989, p. 2.

17. James Strong, "Sawyer Offers Revised Gay-Rights Bill," *Chicago Tribune*, June 9, 1988.

18. James Strong, "Rights Law Gets by 1st Hurdle," *Chicago Tribune*, June 24, 1988, p. 4.

19. Strong, "Sawyer Offers Revised Gay-Rights Bill."

20. Harold Washington, "Action Agenda for Chicago's Future: 1987–1991," in Dick Simpson, ed., *Chicago's Future: In a Time of Change* (Champaign, Ill.: Stipes, 1988), pp. 575–589.

21. Anderson, "Sawyer Saga," p. 107.

PART IV

Return to Mayoral Control

Alderman Edward Burke in 1998 speaking on the latest round of ethics rules. (Reprinted with special permission from the *Chicago Sun-Times,* Inc. ©2000, photographer Bob Black, December 3, 1998.)

9

Daley's Return, 1989–2003

The split within the African-American community and splits within the reform coalition that had elected Harold Washington led to the election of Richard M. Daley as mayor in 1989. But Daley also won because he ran a high-tech modern campaign that differed from the campaigns of his father and earlier machine candidates. His victories completed the unraveling of Mayor Washington's progressive coalition and brought about the creation of a new regime.

The regime that now governs Chicago, which I call the New Chicago Machine, retains some aspects of the past but has new elements. The previous Richard J. Daley progrowth machine had been composed of real estate developers, major downtown businesses, labor unions, major institutions like universities, and the Democratic Party. Although the Democratic Party, labor unions, and major institutions continue to support the new Mayor Daley, most of the older downtown commercial, real estate, and financial businesses that had supported his father are no longer central to the new regime. Of the twenty-one companies that had composed the powerful Chicago Central Area Committee in the 1950s and 1960s, only a couple contributed a total of a few thousand dollars to Richard M. Daley's multimillion-dollar 1999 campaign.[1] Daley's support, at least in terms of financial contributions, now comes more from wealthy lawyers, lobbyists, bankers, stock traders, and the construction firms and unions that depend on contracts from City Hall. In 1999, bankers, lawyers, and stock and options traders gave Richard M. Daley more than $463,000 to run a modern Clintonesque campaign with political consultants, public opinion polls, press secretaries, direct mail, and television ads to supplement the work of the old-time precinct captains. As Daley would later say, "People aren't what they used to be. People don't vote for parties. They vote for the person. It's all television money and polling now. It's not parades. It's not torchlights and songs."[2]

Don Rose and James Andrews, who served as political consultants for one of his opponents, describe the new urban political machine under Richard M. Daley:

> In the late 1980s it cost upwards of $4 million to run a rigorous campaign for mayor of Chicago. . . . The massive infusions of cash necessary for such campaigns simply cannot come from golf outings and putting the squeeze on patronage workers. . . . Such money now must come from institutions where the benefits of government run, not in the hundreds of thousands of dollars, but in the millions: law firms, financial organizations, and developers. Thus, the $50,000 or $100,000 contribution to candidates becomes the ticket to municipal . . . access for such institutions. . . . The term that emerged for this process . . . was "pinstripe patronage."
>
> This, then, is the next and higher stage of the new urban political machine, which must spend millions upon millions to feed the media monster (rather than the families of precinct captains) and utilize contemporary technologies such as computerized mailing and phone banking.
>
> The important cogs in the machine are not the ward bosses and the sewer chiefs of old, but development-businessmen . . . and lawyer-lobbyists.[3]

The regular Democratic Party has also changed. The Shakman Decree has made trading government jobs for precinct work unconstitutional.[4] Although the old machine still exists, it is weaker than it was in Richard J. Daley's heyday. Some Democratic Party precinct captains who still work city precincts got their jobs at the city, county, park district, or other local governments before the Shakman Decree took effect and remain loyal to the party. Other "volunteer" precinct captains with government jobs believe that party precinct work will bring them raises or promotions. These old-time precinct captains, however, are now linked with what has been called a new politics of candidate-oriented, media-based, synthetic, high-tech campaigns.[5] For the funding of this new media-based campaign, Daley in 1999 received only $47,000 from political figures and party organizations. The party no longer provides the finances needed for the media-based campaigns; the candidates must raise this money on their own.

The 1999 campaign finance disclosures also reveal Daley's spending habits as a candidate. Daley spent $3.41 million during the 1999 primary, whereas his campaign contributed less than $3,000 to other political campaigns. Instead, Daley's largest expenditure was for promotional material and campaign consultants, including printing, consulting fees, polling, mailing, paid advertising, printing, and other associated political services. In all, this category accounted for nearly $2.4 million of his $3.4 million in campaign expenses, or 68 percent of his total expenditures. The second largest category of Daley's expenditures, 21 percent of his campaign spending, included salaries for his campaign staff, reimbursements for staff expenses, and insurance and hospitalization for injured personnel. Another 3.55 percent was spent for office space, telephones, office equipment, and travel for campaign staff. Thus modern, high-tech, media-based mayoral campaigns require huge sums of money for consultants, media, and professional staff. The days of precinct captains delivering simple brochures and campaign promises door-to-door are gone.

Democratic Primary

How did Daley, who lost in 1983 to both Washington and Byrne, come back in 1989? His road to victory began in 1987. After the city council elected Sawyer acting mayor in the early morning hours of December 2, 1987, Alderman Evans and his supporters filed a lawsuit to force the Chicago Board of Elections to schedule a special mayoral election in 1989. They believed that an early election would give Evans a better chance to be elected before Sawyer could consolidate his power as mayor, but their lawsuit benefited State's Attorney Daley more.

Based on Evans's lawsuit, the courts subsequently ruled that the special mayoral election should be held in 1989. The Democratic primary included five candidates: State's Attorney Daley, Acting Mayor Sawyer, and Aldermen Tim Evans, Larry Bloom, and Edward Burke. Washington's victory in 1983 had made it clear that candidates who split the votes in their racial base of support couldn't win. Thus Sawyer and Evans had a major problem. If they both ran, they both would lose the primary.

Evans decided on a more chancy strategy. On December 29, 1988, he announced that he was withdrawing from the February 1989 Democratic Party primary to form a new Harold Washington Party. He would run as the Harold Washington Party candidate in the April general election instead of contesting the February Democratic Party primary. Ever since 1983, party loyalties had begun to be discarded in local election contests—particularly in mayoral campaigns. The Republican Party was so weak that candidates could form new parties to contest local elections without fear of a Republican victory.

Evans not only decided to skip the primary to run in the general election but refused to endorse Mayor Sawyer in the Democratic primary. Reverend Jesse Jackson and other black community leaders endorsed Sawyer for the primary and Evans for the general election, but the split in the black community between "progressive" and "machine" elements continued for the next decade. Evans's supporters refused to vote for

Sawyer in the primary. In turn, Mayor Sawyer, after he lost the primary, refused to endorse Evans in the general election and Sawyer's supporters refused to vote for him. The controversy between factions caused voter registration and turnout in the African-American community to drop significantly.

Only one white candidate had any potential appeal to the African-American community and that was Alderman Larry Bloom, who represented the majority black 5th Ward of Hyde Park. However, he was unable to raise sufficient funds to be competitive. Even after a televised mayoral debate, public opinion polls showed him with only 12 percent of the vote, so he withdrew in February 1989. Bloom endorsed Mayor Sawyer in the primary and Alderman Evans in the general election, but public opinion polls found that his supporters actually split between the black candidates and State's Attorney Daley instead of uniformly supporting black candidates. Liberal whites who supported Bloom refused to supply enough votes to either Sawyer or Evans to defeat Daley.[6] In general, the liberal lakefront wards would vote for Daley, who was endorsed by liberal politicians such as former Alderman Bill Singer and State Senator Dawn Clark Netsch. Daley was also endorsed and supported by Aldermen Luis Gutierrez and Juan Soliz and many of the traditional business and political leaders in the Latino community.

Richard M. Daley, the foremost potential white candidate in 1989, was the eldest son of Chicago's legendary boss. He had three brothers and three sisters, but he became the best-known politician. He was born in 1942 and grew up in the family home in the Bridgeport neighborhood, a white ethnic, working-class community on Chicago's Southwest Side. He was an average student at De La Salle High School (which his father had also attended) and graduated with a bachelor of arts and a law degree from DePaul University. He was never an academic and he required three tries to pass the bar exam. He was first elected in 1969 as a state Constitutional Convention delegate and soon afterward as a state senator. "When Richard J. [Daley] died, [his] son was a state senator, unloved and without respect from the rest of his colleagues. . . . He was considered a backbiter and a tattletale and was named by *Chicago Magazine* as one of the 10 worst legislators in the state."[7]

However, his political fortunes improved. He ran for state's attorney in 1980 despite the opposition of Mayor Byrne, Alderman Burke, and a number of the Democratic ward committeemen and won. He did a solid job as state's attorney and, although he did not prosecute corrupt public officials, generally ran the office well. In 1983, in his first race for mayor, he lost in a very bitter battle to both Harold Washington and Jane Byrne. He was, however, easily reelected as state's attorney in 1984 and 1988.

Like his father, he was not a good public speaker and frequently burst forth with malapropisms. "Daley often seems overwhelmed, desperate, and sometimes struck by stage fright and fully conscious of the public relations limitations that nervously propel him into Daleyspeak—the collection of fits, starts, unconnected monologues, clumsy parallels that become ridiculous, radio-taped non sequiturs." However, also like his father, he was a very shrewd politician: "that awkward, giggling fellow disappears in private, where he's low-key, cunning, the acknowledged master of political calculus."[8]

Because Richard M. Daley had won reelection as state's attorney in November 1988 by a 2 to 1 margin and had narrowly lost the mayoral race in 1983, he was able to force other white candidates for mayor to step aside for him. He then hired liberal, professional campaign consultant David Wilhelm as campaign manager, former *Chicago Tribune* political reporter David Axelrod as his media consultant, and a highly respected black radio reporter, Avis LaVelle, as his press spokesperson. These early decisions indicated that he was going to run a very different campaign from the traditional one run by party operatives and family members in 1983. Daley in 1989 had the money and media expertise to run a modern high-tech campaign alongside the usual party patronage precinct work. His campaign received unanimous support from traditional ward bosses in the white ethnic community, although some were personally only moderately in favor of Daley. What was new was support that State's Attorney Daley now received from bankers, lawyers, and some liberal white elected officials who had opposed him in 1983. They provided him with the financial support and endorsements that made him a front-runner.

Daley officially announced his candidacy on December 5, 1988, and immediately launched a $200,000 television ad campaign. Alderman Burke, who had been in the race, dropped out and endorsed Daley. Burke later wrote, "The formula for Rich Daley's victory was simple: play it straight and stay above the fray. . . . Rich Daley did a good job in campaign '89 of avoiding the issues that divide and focusing on the issues that unite."[9] In addition to having money and unified white political support, Daley stressed positive themes of professionalism in government and avoided the issues of race that had been so prevalent during Council Wars.

After Evans, Bloom, and Burke withdrew, the Democratic primary turned out to be a head-to-head contest between Sawyer and Daley. In this battle, Mayor Sawyer had some assets. As mayor, he had avoided any major disasters and had racked up some accomplishments. Equally impressively, he had been able to raise $2 million in campaign funds by September 1988, before Daley entered the race. Nonetheless, the Sawyer campaign was a complete flop. Mayor Sawyer's press secretary afterward wrote that the Sawyer campaign lacked "a cohesive campaign strategy. There was no theme. No vision. No position papers were published. Although the campaign was selling Sawyer as the mayor for all the people, too much time was spent securing his base [in the African-American community]."[10] Even the few black leaders who endorsed him, such as Jesse Jackson, did not believe he could win.

Disunity in the black community between the Sawyer and Evans factions caused many potential Sawyer voters to stay at home. Many vocal black community leaders, such as Congressman Gus Savage, viewed him as an "Uncle Tom" who was merely a front for white aldermen such as Mell and Burke who had elected him acting mayor. Because Mayor Sawyer focused so much campaign effort unsuccessfully trying to regain support in the black community, he totally failed to build any significant support from white ethnics, lakefront liberals, or Latino voters. His campaign manager, Reynard Rochon, was a New Orleans political consultant, "an outsider who had little interest and less appreciation for the subtleties and nuances of Chicago politics."[11] He tried to run the Sawyer campaign on television commercials and closed-to-the-media coffees with community residents. Sawyer's inability to control the city council meant that he didn't have much of a legislative record on which to run, and thus he did not have the advantages of most incumbents in this election. Finally, Sawyer failed to mount either a precinct-based campaign or a high-tech direct mail and phone campaign to reach voters. In the end, the united white vote and substantial Latino support for Daley easily overcame the divided African-American vote.

In contrast to Sawyer, Daley ran a nearly flawless campaign. He had done a solid job as state's attorney. He raised $4 million for the primary, avoided direct racial appeals, did better in the one televised debate than the low expectations of him held by the media and the voters, and obtained important endorsements from prominent white liberals and Latino leaders. To top it off, Daley held a number of successful press conferences and received strong endorsements from both major daily newspapers. His only mistake during the campaign was a mangled statement that the press recorded as "you want a *white* mayor to sit down with everybody." His campaign claimed that he had twisted his usual campaign slogan, "What you want is a mayor who can sit down with everybody," and actually said, "You want a *what* mayor who can . . ." Whatever he may have said, the Sawyer campaign was unable to exploit Daley's statement to unify the black community as Washington's campaign had been able to take advantage of Alderman Vrdolyak's clearly racist speech in 1983. Daley won the Democratic primary, 486,586 to 383,795.

Surprisingly, however, in one of the twists for which Chicago politics is famous, the Republican primary proved more interesting than expected. The party endorsed Dr. Herbert Sohn, who was opposed by former alderman Edward Vrdolyak in a last-minute write-in campaign. Vrdolyak had served as Democratic Party chairman under Mayor Jane Byrne, lost as a Solidarity Party candidate for mayor running against Washington in 1987, and lost his campaign for clerk of the Circuit Court in 1988 as a Republican candidate. He entered the 1989 race late, after Daley had announced and Burke had withdrawn. Despite the odds against it, he won his write-in campaign in the usual low-turnout Republican primary by a margin of just over 1,100 votes. The question was now, with Vrdolyak on the ballot in the April general election, would he split off enough of the white ethnic support from Daley for either Vrdolyak or Evans to win the election?

General Election

Despite Vrdolyak's presence in the three-way race, which would determine the future of Chicago politics for at least the next decade, the general election turned out to be a rerun of the primary. Once again money was a major factor. Daley raised more than $7 million while Evans raised only $1 million, most of it too late in the campaign to be used well, and Vrdolyak ran a shoestring campaign.

Like Sawyer, Evans ran a campaign that had an incoherent strategy created by competing factions within his campaign. One result of this campaign infighting was an unwise decision not to run television advertising. Rather, the campaign would rely on free media coverage and grassroots precinct work. Without a clear message to the voters and a means to deliver it, Evans was unable to persuade blacks to mobilize in his support or to persuade most whites and Latinos that they should vote for him. Evans was late to campaign events, the campaign was disorganized, some of his supporters, in contrast to Daley, raised racial issues in counterproductive ways, and the news coverage was frequently negative. The Daley campaign, which combined high-tech and old machine campaign techniques, won by a vote of 577,141 to Evans's 428,104 and Vrdolyak's 35,998. Vrdolyak's campaign just never caught fire. White ethnics refused to split their vote and lose to a black candidate twice.

The New Daley Council

How would the new Mayor Daley govern? "He [was] politically conservative, blunt, a devoted family man . . . [and] devoutly Roman Catholic. ... Trained from birth to assume the mayor's job, he enjoy[ed] the support of a business community and a bungalow belt that likes things the way they are and don't want to see a black mayor in City Hall."[12] Most of all, he knew how to govern. As his brother Bill Daley said of him, "I've never met anybody in politics who has a better gut for what normal people are thinking."[13] Most specifically, he had learned from watching his father how to bend the council to his will.

Daley took control of the city council at its meeting on April 26, 1989. At that meeting chairmen, vice chairmen, and members of city council committees were reappointed in order to give Daley control of the critical council committees and, at the same meeting, some city council reforms were adopted. Council committee chairmen who had not opposed Daley in the election mostly retained their positions. However, all critical committees, including the Finance, Zoning, and Rules Committees, were given pro-Daley chairmen who could be counted on to push the mayor's legislation. Alderman Burke (who had withdrawn from the mayoral election and backed Daley) once again became chairman of the Finance Committee. However, Alderman Patrick Huels from the mayor's own 11th Ward became the mayor's whip, or political floor leader, with the task of rounding up aldermanic votes and handling sensitive political negotiations with aldermen.

During this first meeting after the election, South Side African-American alderman Bobby Rush, who would oppose Mayor Richard M. Daley in the 1999 mayoral elections, attempted to refer the motion on committee chairmanship and membership back to the Rules Committee for further negotiations between mayoral supporters and opponents. This test vote failed, 35–12, and the die was cast. It was clear that the mayor had the votes to control the council. Another effort by African-American alderman Dorothy Tillman, who had been a vociferous supporter of Alderman Evans's mayoral campaign, proposed to incorporate aldermanic requests for committee assignments into the proposed appointments. Her motion also failed. After those amendments were defeated, the final council reorganization proposed by Mayor Daley passed, 36–14.

The mayor's opponents in the floor debate argued that this was a return to the old rubber stamp council, underrepresentation of minorities, and the continuation of waste in city council expenditures. Alderman Evans commented, "This particular [reorganization] resolution looks an awful lot like business as usual. This resolution continues the waste that has been permeating this council." Although seven black aldermen and two Latino aldermen were named to the twenty-seven committee chairmanships, those aligned to Evans's unsuccessful mayoral bid were dumped. "We're going back to the old ways," said Alderman Tillman. "We have been excluded." Among the fourteen aldermen who voted against Mayor Daley's council reorganization were nine African Americans, two Latinos, and three progressive white aldermen. The mayor's proposals also reduced the number of committees from twenty-eight to twenty-seven and reduced committee staff budgets by 20 percent because Daley wanted to signal that he was making reforms in the council.

The original City Club reform proposals had recommended cutting the number of committees from twenty-eight to nine, which would save millions of dollars. When asked why his cuts were smaller than those recommended by the City Club, Daley answered, "You know how difficult it is dealing with any member of a legislative body. I think it is a good effort on our part."[14]

Another council reform unanimously adopted (by a vote of 46–0 with four absences) when Daley took over was the "Sullivan proposals" on campaign finance reform. The proposals were a part of the City Club reform proposals as well. Tom Sullivan was a former U.S. attorney highly respected in the legal community, which had supported Daley heavily in the mayoral election. The Sullivan proposals amended the ethics ordinance passed under Washington to limit contributions to aldermanic and mayoral candidates by any "person who has done business with the City within the preceding four . . . years" to $1,500 per election. The Sullivan amendments further prevented city employees from soliciting campaign contributions and removed city employees in sensitive departments such as Purchasing from political involvement. Finally, the Sullivan amendments created an Office of Municipal Investigation to investigate corruption and improper behavior on the part of city officials, with the exception that the office could not investigate aldermen or council staff members. Reform aldermen, of course, supported these measures, and since the aldermen who supported the mayor were afraid politically to oppose them, the Sullivan amendments passed unanimously.[15]

After the first two meetings of the new Daley council, Alderman Burke claimed that "the city council is not a rubber stamp but a certain amount of cohesion in the council is important." He contrasted the Daley council to Council Wars under Mayor Washington and said that relative quiet was prevailing because a "majority of aldermen support the mayor."[16]

Maps 9.1–9.3 show how the racial voting blocs in the council evolved during the turbulent 1980s. Map 9.1 shows the divisions in Mayor Washington's Council Wars, with his support coming from aldermen who represented African-American and lakefront liberal wards. Map 9.2 shows Sawyer's ever changing base of support during his chaotic interim. In the vote to organize the council shown in Map 9.2, he had the support of some of the African-American aldermen who had helped elect him, along with most of the white ethnic aldermen. African-American aldermen loyal to Evans opposed Sawyer, along with the white lakefront liberals and several Latino aldermen. Aldermen vacillated between support and opposition. In the end, the Washington coalition aldermen provided the most backing for his administration's programs, even though they opposed Sawyer as mayor. Map 9.3 shows that Daley's council coalition of support was firmer and that it was almost the mirror image of

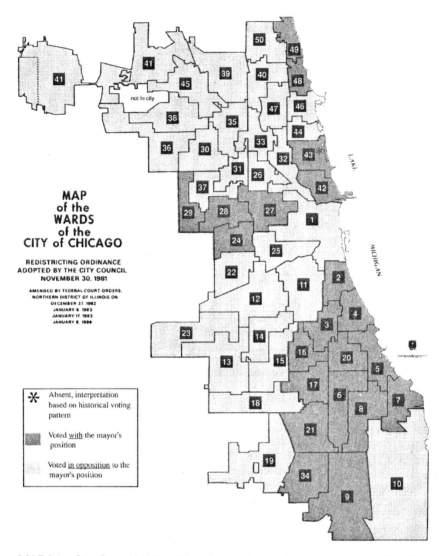

MAP 9.1 City Council Voting Blocs Supporting and Opposing Mayor Harold Washington, 1983

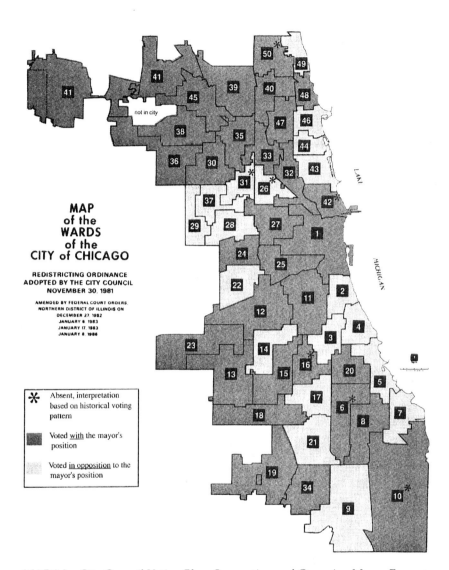

MAP 9.2   City Council Voting Blocs Supporting and Opposing Mayor Eugene
Sawyer, 1988

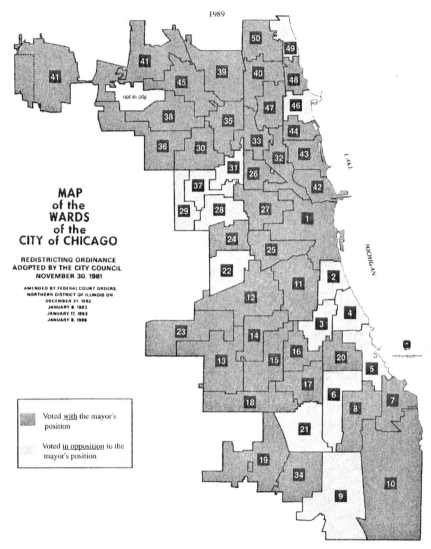

MAP 9.3 City Council Voting Blocs Supporting and Opposing Mayor Richard M. Daley, 1989

Washington's support. However, Daley gained more and more aldermanic support after his later reelections as mayor. He rallied all the white
ethnic aldermen, some of the blacks, and a majority of the Latino aldermen. Yet the most liberal members of the council in all three racial communities opposed his administration in 1989.

Mayor Washington had begun his mayoral term in 1983 by signing the
Executive Order on the Freedom of Information. Mayor Daley began his
term in 1989 by cutting the budgets of the city council committees, adopting limited campaign finance reform, agreeing to continue the patronage
hiring and firing limitations of the Shakman Decree, and setting up the
Office of Municipal Investigation. These were actions that his father,
Mayor Richard J. Daley, would not have taken and were meant to signal
that he would be a different kind of mayor. Some political scientists and
journalists have characterized the new Daley's reign as a management
regime. One wrote that "the mayor's 'orientation resembles that of the
pro-growth regime with policy substituting for patronage as a buffer for
economic elites.' Daley seems intent on service delivery as a way to keep
political allies and win votes. His regime comprises regional business interests, special interest groups fighting tax increases, large-scale investors, and city agencies which must optimize services under tightly
controlled budgets. Daley also must accommodate wealthy friends of
Chicago's Democratic party while pursuing more economical and equitable forms of development."[17] Although he abided by the Shakman Decree, which outlawed old-time patronage jobs, he rewarded his business
supporters with "pinstripe patronage" of large city contracts. This favoritism would plague his administration throughout his tenure.

Just before the Daley administration took office, I, in collaboration with
other researchers from the University of Illinois at Chicago, published
Blueprint of Chicago Government: 1989, which contained 103 reform recommendations for improving city government.[18] In a second study after Daley's first year in office, we found that the mayor had made improvements in the executive branch of city government and in ethics. On the
negative side of the balance sheet, we found a decrease in affirmative action, a continuation of archaic laws, a decrease in public participation in
city government, and a return to a rubber stamp city council. By checking
city budgets, department reports, press stories, and interviews with officials in some departments, we were able to determine that after one year
in office, Mayor Daley had implemented 33 percent of our original reform proposals in some form and partially implemented another 15 percent; 45 percent of the proposals had not been implemented; and no information was available on the other 7 percent.[19] Moreover, Daley in his
first term kept some of Washington's department heads, most importantly the chief of police.

The greatest improvements in the first year of the new Daley administration were made in departmental performance and in cost savings in the delivery of some city services. For instance:

- In the Department of Streets and Sanitation a loader was removed from the back of each garbage truck as garbage pickup was mechanized.
- In the Police Department the 911 emergency phone number was modernized and civilians were used in more departmental positions that did not require sworn personnel, which had the effect of putting additional police officers on the street.
- In the Planning Department there was a computerization of permit processing to speed up the permit review process.
- Reforms, including the use of the "Denver boot," helped collect millions of dollars in parking tickets that had gone uncollected in previous administrations.

Daley was praised as "a 'hands-on' action-oriented leader more in the CEO or city manager mold than an old-style boss-politician. His passion for management is such that a few insiders label him a 'policy nerd.' [Daley] told *Chicago Enterprise*, February 1999, that he wanted to 'get control' of the bureaucracy and achieve 'better productivity' and 'accountability of the work force.'. . . The central aim of the Daley administration was economic growth and job expansion."[20] As part of the economic growth agenda, the mayor pushed redevelopment of Navy Pier and two large projects that failed—a multibillion dollar airport to be built at Lake Calumet in the southeastern section of Chicago and a $2 billion land-based gambling casino to be constructed near the downtown central business district.[21]

One major criticism of the new Daley administration was in the area of affirmative action. Thirty-two percent of city contracts still went to minority enterprises, down only 2 percent from the Sawyer administration. However, the number of African Americans holding top policy-making jobs in the city decreased by 25 percent, despite the fact that blacks still held 31 percent and Latinos 10 percent of the top jobs.[22] Over the first two years of the Daley administration, a disparity of roughly 20 percent between the number of white policymakers and black policymakers developed. Thus some concluded that "despite his public pledges to practice fair and open government in the Washington tradition, Daley is actually pursuing a mixed course, best understood as machine politics, reform style. Government has become more centralized under Daley, and the involvement of interest groups—ranging from neighborhood organizations to women and minorities—has been reduced. The distribution of top administrative and contractual benefits

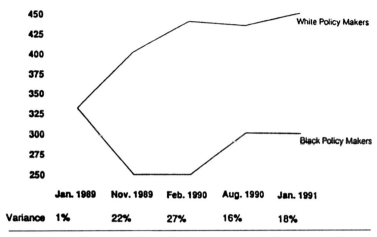

FIGURE 9.1   Black and White Policymakers in the Sawyer and Daley
Administrations
SOURCE: William Grinshor, *Bitter Fruit* (1992). Original data from
Chicago Sun-Times August 9, 1990 and January 31, 1991.

also has largely reverted to the machine style of rewarding friends and
punishing enemies."[23]

Still, Daley's regime differed substantially from his father's because
some reforms were implemented and a number of managerial improvements were made.

While Daley made managerial reforms and improvements in the executive branch, the city council settled back into a voting pattern typical of
rubber stamp councils. Daley solidified his control by filling aldermanic
vacancies through appointment. Daley's council contrasted sharply with
Council Wars under Mayor Washington and the fragmented council under Mayor Sawyer.

Originally, Daley's aldermanic supporters were nearly all white. There
were only two African-American and two Latino aldermen among the his
strongest supporters in his first two years in office. Conversely, only three
of the nineteen Daley opponents were white and they were the lakefront
liberal, Independent aldermen Bloom, Helen Shiller, and Orr. Although
Daley prevailed in most votes, his rubber stamp council remained volatile
and a number of key city council votes were closely divided.

These city council votes that engendered the most dissent in 1989–1990
indicate the lines of cleavage and the issues on which the mayor was
most vulnerable:

1.   a proposal to spend $6.3 million of the city's budget to provide
      increased police protection and full-time nurses at public
      schools (defeated December 13, 1989, 25–22)

2. a vote to require United Airlines to share the $3 million in expenses for a sewer and water hookup for their new reservation center at O'Hare Airport (defeated December 6, 1989, 23–22)
3. a procedural motion to divide the vote on budget amendments (sent to committee December 13, 1989, by a 23–22 vote)
4. appointment of commissioners to the Home Equity Program (passed July 19, 1989, 25–12)
5. a motion to require the deputy mayor for education to respond to concern about her statements on the public schools (defeated April 6, 1990, 15–24)
6. a motion to discharge from the Committee on Health consideration of a proposed ordinance to create an office of Local Drug Control Policy (defeated September 13, 1989, 19–22)
7. a motion to suspend the rules to adopt a resolution to urge the Department of Health to postpone negotiations for privatization of City of Chicago Public Health Service facilities (defeated October 25, 1989, 17–22)
8. a motion to discharge from the Committee on Housing an ordinance on parcels of land to be developed by Kenwood Academy in Alderman Tim Evan's ward (defeated October 4, 1989, by a 17–20 recount vote following an initial 19–19 tie)

These issues of budget, improved health and safety at public schools, developments at O'Hare Field, the Home Equity Program, a deputy mayor's statements about schools, and various health and economic issues (including a Kenwood Academy development in opposition leader Evans's ward) did the most to rally both the African-American and reform aldermen in the opposition. But no single issue was popular enough among all the aldermen for the opposition to defeat Mayor Daley. Unlike his predecessor, Mayor Sawyer, Daley lost no votes, had less opposition, and had much more unified support. There were nearly 300 fewer divided roll call votes in Daley's first year of office than there were in Mayor Sawyer's controversial reign.

Daley's Budget Battles

In 1991, most of the aldermen who had served in the previous council were reelected, and therefore the voting pattern in the council remained much the same as it was in 1989–1990. Yet with his successful reelection, Daley gained greater control and dissent began to decline. The number of divided roll call votes decreased to seventy-four in 1991–1992, down from the ninety-nine in Daley's first year as mayor. He had managed to quiet racial tensions, although black aldermen still voted against him on some key racial issues. Jumping on tables and incivility in the council were eliminated.

Daley, like his father before him, had to confront a brief and ineffective rebellion. In the early 1970s, the council's Young Turks had created the so-called Coffee Rebellion; during Mayor Bilandic's reign, a small group called the Reluctant Rebels under the leadership of Alderman Jeremiah Joyce staged a similar low-key rebellion. Again on May 6, 1992, nine pro-administration aldermen held a press conference "to announce an agenda of relatively mundane legislation as a symbol that Mayor Richard M. Daley's administration must pay attention to them."

Three pieces of legislation introduced by the aldermen illustrated their vow of increased participation in council legislation. They called for (1) private businesses given $50,000-plus contracts to "endeavor" to hire Chicago residents for at least half of their jobs, (2) a "whistle-blower protection" ordinance to provide protection to city employees "who reported malfeasance on the part of their superiors," and (3) a redefinition of the duties of the city council Building Committee to give it authority over the city's infrastructure. Their proposed legislation wasn't adopted, but this minirebellion was an indication of discontent in Daley's council even among his supporters.[24]

Their discontent grew with the proposed 1993 budget the following fall. Chicago's city budget had to be cut because of a stagnant Chicago economy and reduced aid from state and federal governments. Mayor Daley had called his 1992 city budget the previous year a "bad news" budget with its $84 million in new taxes and the layoff of 840 city workers. While the 1992 budget raised new taxes, only $25 million of the increase was in new property taxes. Yet this relatively small property tax increase was approved only by a close 28–20 vote. Mayor Daley's 1993 budget proposals were even worse news for the aldermen and the public. In his budget message, Mayor Daley told a stunned council that he was proposing $47.7 million in new property taxes and that the city government would be laying off an additional 740 city employees.

Mayor Daley explained that he opted for the property tax because "there's no other magic formula around." There were cuts in all departments and city services other than public safety, including cutbacks in library hours. The mayor said, "Where there was waste, we cut. Where there was duplication, we merged. Where there was red tape and bureaucracy, we restructured."[25] The aldermen were unhappy with the proposed budget. One reporter described them as "howling" over the property tax increase. They were afraid of their constituents' reaction if they voted for the budget with its increased property taxes and decreased services. Loyal administration Southwest Side alderman Thomas Murphy said, "I can't support another tax increase, and I don't know anyone who

can. The people in the city and county are being property-taxed to death.
It's crazy. This is like loading a gun for your aldermanic opponent and
saying, 'Here, use it on me in 1995.'" Daley supporters who said they
couldn't vote for the budget when Daley introduced it to the council included Aldermen Madrzyk, Laski, Bialczak, Wojcik, and Banks.[26]

When the budget hearings began in November, there was a true rebellion among the aldermen.

> Something truly historic happened last week when the Chicago City Coun-
> cil held its annual week long series of budget hearings. Right in the middle
> of it, a budget hearing broke out.
>
> Chicago aldermen shucked at least for the moment their longtime image
> as the pinky-ringed hand that holds the rubber stamp, and stood up to the
> mayor saying they could not accept a big property-tax increase. By fits and
> starts, the aldermen crafted an alternative plan that would at least cut in half
> Mayor Richard Daley's proposed $48.7 million property-tax hike and shift
> some of the tax burden to pop drinkers, sports fans and horse betters. They
> also challenged Daley's public pronouncement that the Chicago Police De-
> partment could not be touched in a budget that slashes everything else. . . .
> The City Council acted more like a legislative body than it has in years.
>
> Aldermen, many acting on their own, raised ideas, gathered supporters,
> huddled with administrative floor leaders and openly dissented. . . . The
> biggest message coming out of the lively [budget] session was that Daley
> could not count on getting the 26 votes out of the 50-member council that he
> needed to pass his budget and tax increase as proposed.[27]

Finally, a compromise was reached and thirty-four of the fifty aldermen reluctantly approved a 1993 budget with a $28.7 million property
tax increase. They succeeded in cutting the property tax increase by $20
million, but then in January 1993 the process had to begin all over again
because an outside arbitrator granted larger salaries and fringe benefits
to the city's 12,500 police officers. So Daley returned to the council with a
request for another $11.6 million increase in the property tax to pay for
the raises. Once again pro-administration aldermen protested. "You can't
just keep going back to the same well time and time again," said Alderman Eugene Schulter.[28]

Contrast these budget revolts with the vote on the proposed 1995 budget two years later. In 1994, Daley's $3.578 billion budget passed 44–4,
when many of Daley's most frequent aldermanic critics even voted with
the mayor. The difference was brought about by two factors. A new city
budget director met separately with the aldermen and took their suggestions about budget improvements instead of fighting it out in budget
hearings and on the council floor. In addition, economic conditions in

Chicago improved so there was more money. Thus the proposed 1995 budget froze property taxes, cut business taxes, and provided more street repair and more police for Chicago neighborhoods. As Alderman Ed Smith, who often voted against the administration on other issues, said, "he would 'have to be a buffoon' to vote against a budget that promises 475 additional police officers."[29]

There is no doubt that city council voting on the budget, as well as on many issues during the Richard M. Daley era, had a racial cleavage. A study undertaken by the expert witness in the federal ward remap lawsuit, *Barnett v. Daley,* analyzed aldermanic voting on issues of critical importance to minorities communities from 1989 to 1994. His report shows more extreme differences in the aldermanic voting patterns on racially charged issues than their votes on nonracial issues. In the same study he demonstrated that the difference in public opinion among different racial groups in Chicago's general population correspond to these differences in voting by aldermen representing different racial constituencies. The most racially charged issues divided the council politically in a more extreme manner than votes on other issues.[30]

Ward Remap

The most fundamental voting cleavage during Daley's 1991–1999 city councils was over the ward redistricting under which later elections in the 1990s would be run. Unsatisfied with Alderman Burke's proposed ward map, minority aldermen and community leaders sued the city administration after losing a series of votes in the council and a referendum among the voters. The resulting lawsuits, *Barnett v. Daley, Smith v. City of Chicago,* and *Bonilla v. City Council,* took a decade to resolve. The plaintiffs in one lawsuit were twenty African-American and liberal white aldermen opposing the map. Thirty pro-administration aldermen then became defendant-intervenors supporting the mayor's map. The voting pattern between the plaintiffs and defendant-intervenors reflected the political and racial divisions of the council. In 1989–1990 the plaintiffs voted with Mayor Daley and his floor leaders an average of only 48 percent of the time, while the pro-administration intervenors supported him on 95 percent of the divided roll call votes. This pattern continued in 1991–1992, when the plaintiffs supported the mayor only on average 46 percent of the time in divided roll call votes while the pro-administration bloc supported him 94 percent of the time. Thus there was a difference of nearly 50 percent in the voting patterns of the two city council blocs.

The racial and political battles of remapping Chicago wards after the U.S. Census for the last four decades mirrored the divisions in Chicago political life. Whereas the ward maps in the nineteenth century used "natural geographic boundaries" such as major streets and branches of the Chicago River, later redistricting ordinances, such as the ones in 1931, 1947, and 1961, recognized "changes in ethnic concentrations and rising minority populations." This was true for the Irish, Germans, Italians, and later the growing African-American populations. The 1931 ward map had two black wards (2nd and 3rd) while the 1947 map added a third (20th). More and more white wards became black as the African-American population grew in Chicago, but the ward maps were slow to recognize these changes because of the effect that they would have on the distribution of political power.[31]

A legal challenge to the 1961 ward map proved that it deviated significantly from the actual African-American population in the city. Consequently, the federal district court ordered a new map based on the 1970 U.S. Census figures to correct the imbalance. After that map was drawn in 1971, the next remap federal lawsuit, *Cousins v. City Council*, proved that Mayor Daley's floor leader, Alderman Keane, had targeted five key wards, including his own, and drawn a map to "intentionally create a white majority where a black [or Hispanic] majority was present." Keane also failed to disclose a "secret" map drawn with the help of Alderman Paul Wigoda before the council officially considered the map.[32]

Despite the proof of racial discrimination in the 1970s remapping effort, the process was repeated under Mayor Byrne in 1980, when Rules Committee chairman Thomas Casey privately retained former alderman Keane, who had completed his jail sentence by this time, to help draw the new map. Without public input, Keane and city planning commissioner Martin Murphy prepared a ward map by May 1981. Aldermen complained of being prevented from seeing the citywide map and only being allowed to propose changes affecting their own wards. In return for ward boundaries favorable to their own reelection, they pledged their support of the new map without having any knowledge of the demographic data on which the map was based. The federal lawsuit *Ketchum v. Byrne,* which challenged the 1981 map, was not decided until Harold Washington became mayor. Then the federal courts required a change in seven of the fifty wards. Three were to be additional African-American majority wards and four, Latino majority wards. The court-ordered special elections in March 1986 reversed the Council Wars split of 29–21 to 25–25, with Mayor Washington casting the tie-breaking vote. After a runoff election in the seventh remapped ward, the pro-Washington balance became 26–24, changing the balance of power in the council.

After the 1990 U.S. Census, the council, now under Mayor Richard M. Daley's direction, once again had to remap the wards. The resulting map, drafted by Alderman Burke and Finance Committee staffer Lisa Ruble, was adopted in a very divisive council fight. It created twenty-four white wards, nineteen black wards, and seven Latino wards. Although the mayor's map was approved by the voters in a referendum, aldermanic map opponents again filed a federal lawsuit, *Smith v. City of Chicago*, and activist political and community organizations filed a parallel suit, *Barnett v. Daley*. The charges of racial discrimination were the same as the ones in the previous cases. The *Smith* plaintiffs claimed that the 1992 map "maximizes the political power of Caucasians by fracturing African American communities and drawing majority white wards that 'borrow' population from other groups." The *Barnett* plaintiffs claimed that the map "packs" blacks into supermajority wards without similarly packing whites.[33] An additional lawsuit, *Bonilla v. City Council*, charged that Latino voters were similarly shortchanged in the redistricting.

The three combined lawsuits were dismissed on December 21, 1992, by federal Judge Brian Duff, "who ruled African American plaintiffs failed to show redistricting resulted in discrimination or that actual 'intent' to discriminate was present." In a second opinion on October 8, 1993, Judge Duff ruled that the requirements of the federal Voting Rights Act were satisfied by the map. In August 1994, the court of appeals reinstated the case and remanded it for trial. The court unanimously held that the "mayor and his codefendants have, on racial grounds, created fewer black wards than a racially unbiased redistricting authority. The consequences are to give one racial group more voting power than it would have under a plan carefully drafted to give all ethnic groups voting power proportional to their population." Judge Duff ruled in June 1997 that "the plaintiffs failed to show the city's [ward] map resulted from discriminatory intent. Duff called Chicago's remap process 'the most open process of reapportionment that I have ever heard of in any case in any city.'" In his written ruling, Duff said "that the map was a product of a 'prudent political compromise' and that Alderman Ed Burke did not take control of the remap process. Opponents of the Duff ruling contend that the district court failed to consider the 'effect' of the Daley ward map, which created five more white wards than black in a city where black population exceeds the white population."[34]

Once again, in April 1998, the appeals court overruled Judge Duff, who retired as federal magistrate amid charges of incompetence and senility. The appeals court now ruled that at least one new majority black ward had to be created in time for the 1999 aldermanic elections. The appeals court said that Judge Duff "used 'deeply flawed' reasoning . . . in approving a remap that created [only] 19 wards with predominantly black populations. . . . Criticizing the protracted length of the litigation as 'absurd,' the panel gave the district court a 90-day deadline to make changes to the ward map so that it's in place in time for the aldermanic elections [in 1999]."[35]

In the original lawsuits, the expert witness for the plaintiffs prepared a report entitled *Public Preferences, Race, and Policy in Chicago,* which concluded: "Survey research reports [show] significant differences between blacks and whites in opinions and conditions related to important public policy matters such as employment, discrimination, education, and housing. Analysis of votes in the Chicago City Council [shows] that on important legislative matters . . . aldermanic votes divided along racial lines. . . . Race is often a determining factor in the outcomes of public policy and is a condition that in many cases plays a significant role in defining individual interests in public policy outcomes." In short, the number of black, white, and Latino aldermen serving in the city council has a profound effect on the policies adopted that affect Chicago and those particular racial communities.[36]

In the parallel *Smith v. Chicago* lawsuit to force the city to pay the legal fees of the opposition aldermen, my expert witness report on racial and political polarization in the city council came to similar conclusions:

1. Voting in the city council on critical issues affecting the citizens of Chicago follows racial and political patterns that are clear, distinctive, and incontrovertible.
2. These patterns are not new but have a long history of development.
3. The defendants in the case, by defending the current ward map and the validity of the elections of the current seated aldermen, preserve until at least 1999, and perhaps until 2003, the current political distribution of power in the city council, which favors the city administration and the control of the city by whites.
4. Not paying the legal fees of the plaintiffs is meant to make overturning the current balance of power more difficult.[37]

I argued in my depositions that virtually all studies of council voting come to the same conclusions. There are clear political and racial patterns of voting in the council, and these voting patterns have a long history. Therefore, the shape of the ward maps and the racial makeup that is likely to be created in the council would affect the pattern of council voting for at least a decade.

The 1992 remap lawsuits were finally settled on August 10, 1998, when attorneys for the anti-administration aldermen and the city agreed to new ward boundaries for the 18th Ward on the Southwest Side of Chicago. Under the new configuration, the ward would change from 54 percent to 72 percent black, and it was assumed that its white alderman, Thomas Murphy, would be replaced by a black alderman in this new "supermajority ward" in the 1999 aldermanic elections. In fact, however,

Alderman Murphy won reelection despite the black majority in his ward and so the racial balance in the council remained unchanged throughout the 1990s.

1995 Elections

In the first election after the 1992 ward remap, the aldermen who were elected were overwhelming pro-Daley. This election, like many elections, was decided by incumbency and campaign spending. "In Chicago city council elections incumbents have won reelection more than 60 percent of the time in the last three aldermanic elections (1987, 1991, and 1995). Not only are incumbents winning at very high rates, they also have enjoyed a fairly steady increase in average vote margin over the five elections held from 1979 to 1995." This incumbency advantage is a function of Democratic Party backing, media support, and superior campaign spending. During the 1995 election cycle, for example, incumbents spent nearly three times as much as challengers. The only major countervailing factor was the increase in the number of African-American wards that had been mobilized effectively by the elections of Jane Byrne and Harold Washington. The extension of the number of minority wards by the ward remaps in 1986 and 1992 meant that more opposition bloc aldermen were elected in these African American wards than in any other wards in the city.[38]

In the 1995 election, 138 aldermanic candidates raised $8.5 million and spent just under $6 million. The average aldermanic campaign spent $43,000, with successful candidates in the most contentious races spending on average upward of $93,000. By 1995, campaign expenditures and the incumbency advantages were more predictive of an aldermanic candidate's vote share than partisan affiliation or newspaper endorsements. About 80 percent of the cash received was evenly contributed by businesses and individuals. No other sources came close. Although the mayoral candidates received most of their business contributions from downtown businesses, aldermanic candidates, especially incumbents, received their business contributions from businesses in their individual wards. However, there is a big difference in fund-raising between black, white, and Latino candidates. When race is taken into account, white aldermanic candidates raised about four times the amount of money generated by black or Latino candidates. Donors in wealthier, and whiter, neighborhoods gave more money to candidates than did poorer, minority residents.[39]

Using regression equations, Gierzynski, Kleppner, and Lewis calculated that greater spending by incumbents and well-financed candidates increased their vote: "[in 1995] every 1 percent increase in spending

TABLE 9.1   Expenditures of the 1995 Chicago Aldermanic Candidates

Expenditures	No. of Candidates	Percentage	Cumulative %
$0–25,000	72	52.2	52.2
$25,001–50,000	25	18.1	70.3
$50,001–75,000	14	10.1	80.4
$75,001–100,000	9	6.5	87.0
$100,001–200,000	16	11.6	98.6
$200,000+	2	1.4	100

SOURCE: Gierzynski, Kleppner, and Lewis. "The Price of Democracy: Financing Chicago's 1995 City Council Elections."

boosted the candidate's vote by an average of 7.7 percent." Moreover, 80 percent of the funds raised by aldermanic candidates came from businesses or individuals (and many of the individuals were businessmen or professionals, as some 39 percent of contributions from individuals were for amounts over $750).[40]

Because of the incumbency advantages and the increasing dominance of Mayor Daley in Chicago politics, the number of candidates running for the fifty seats declined from 1991, dropping from 170 to 138. The number of uncontested seats climbed from a low of six during the Harold Washington reelection in 1987 to fourteen, or 28 percent of the aldermen, in 1995.

During the 1995 elections, Mayor Daley dominated the fund-raising in the mayoral race, which also helped the aldermanic candidates that he endorsed. He raised 93 percent of all the funds raised by mayoral candidates. He had $7.4 million available and spent $5.6 million on his campaign. "His two Democratic challengers, Joseph Gardner in the primary and Roland Burris running as an Independent in the general election, [both of whom were African Americans] together raised only $528,468, barely 7 percent of Daley's total."[41]

Mayor Daley, incumbent aldermen, and aldermen backed by Daley won the election for the most part. As a result, the city council became even more supportive of the mayor than it had been from 1989 to 1994 and Daley began to consolidate his power. The average level of mayoral support among the aldermen on thirty key issues in 1995 reached 87 percent. "Much of the mayor's success . . . is due to strong support from former members of the Vrdolyak 29 [who opposed Mayor Washington during Council Wars], freshmen who received political support from the mayor during the 1995 municipal election, and a decline in the number of contentious issues facing the Council."[42] There were fewer racially divisive votes between 1995 and 1999, but the issue of using city tax funds to pay lawyers defending the ward remap case continued to be very controversial.

The key vote reorganizing the newly elected council, which assigned chairmanships and membership on council committees in May 1995, was 35–12. "Opponents criticized the plan because minorities have only 12 committee chairmanships even though they have a majority of [26 seats on the council after the first election under the 1992 ward map]." This critical vote organizing the council set the balance of power for the next four years, except for votes on the remap case, which continued to divide the council sharply. The plaintiffs and defendant-intervenors voted consistently with their positions in the case itself. On February 17, 1996, a group of twenty aldermen led by Latino alderman Ricardo Munoz proposed an order asking the city corporation counsel to withdraw its legal brief in *Barnett v. Daley* because it embraced a U.S. Supreme Court ruling, *Miller v. Johnson,* that prevents the creation of additional supermajority minority districts. The vote on Munoz's proposed order was 27–16. In November 1995 Alderman Joe Moore, who had replaced David Orr as the 49th Ward alderman representing the North Side Rogers Park community and a leader of the Independent aldermen, proposed an amendment to delete a $500,000 allocation to prevent continuing to use taxpayer money to pay city attorney fees in the remap case. His amendment was defeated, 41–7. However, when the issue was reintroduced by a group of eighteen aldermen led by South Side black Independent alderman Toni Preckwinkle on April 16, 1996, the number of supporters had grown. The Preckwinkle ordinance failed 21–18, with eleven aldermen absent or not voting. When Alderman Joe Moore then introduced a resolution to demand accounting for remap legal fees, it received a similar vote of 24–16, with ten aldermen absent or not voting.[43]

Overall, during the 1995–1999 period, the council evolved into a stronger rubber stamp council with a pro-administration bloc of thirty, a strong Independent anti-administration bloc of seven, and thirteen other aldermen mostly voting with the administration but voting with the opposition on a few key issues. According to Alderman Moore, the opposition bloc during this period consisted of seven reliable members: Aldermen Toni Preckwinkle, Barbara Holt, Freddrenna Lyle, Robert Shaw, Rick Munoz, Helen Shiller, and Moore.[44] In fifty-nine key divided roll call votes between 1995 and 1999 only two aldermen, Shiller and Shaw, voted less than 50 percent of the time with Mayor Daley's floor leader; overall, all aldermen voted with the mayor's administration an average of 84 percent of the time.[45]

Alderman Moore characterized the city council during this period as a "pliant council" without many defining issues other than the remap votes, a proposed living wage ordinance, and a gang loitering resolution backing an unconstitutional city ordinance the U.S. Supreme Court would overturn in 1999. The council was pliant due to a variety of causes. As Alderman Moore explained,

> It is the current climate of the times. There is a lack of any cutting edge issues such as the Vietnam War or Civil Rights. And there are no egregious actions on the part of the Daley administration as there had been in Richard J. Daley's time. Today there is less patronage, less blatant abuses in city hall, less ghost payrolling (except in the city council itself). And Mayor Richard M. Daley has coopted traditional good government issues. Each time there is an abuse [such as corruption], Mayor Daley offers a new round of ethics ordinances to combat it. Therefore, [liberal] Lakefront voters think the city is run efficiently with no egregious corruption or waste.[46]

During the 1990s the political machine and the governing regime running the city evolved. "The machine is different. Money has replaced patronage as the fuel for the machine's engine. Daley can still bring out the patronage workers for some races like some aldermanic races. But, more importantly, he can drop a ton of money to fund an aldermanic candidate he favors. In [Moore's] aldermanic election in 1991, [Alderman Moore] spent $120,000 and [his] opponent, machine candidate Robert Clark, spent maybe as much as $170,000 with the in-kind contributions he received. At least $100,000 of those funds were raised for him by Mayor Daley."[47]

However, even in a pliant council gay rights and aldermanic scandals divided the council along fault lines different from the general pro-administration and anti-administration voting patterns.

Gay Rights Return.   The human rights ordinance had originally passed in 1988 by a narrow vote of 26–21. The margin was larger on March 19, 1997, on a proposal to provide health coverage to partners of homosexual city workers that passed, 32–18. The issue was not only about the morality of providing homosexuals benefits equal to those offered to heterosexual married couples, it was also a matter of politics and reelection. Alderman Ricardo Munoz said, "You know some people are going to use this issue out in the neighborhood. They'll use it on the street, in the bars, in front of the churches [against those aldermen who support this legislation]." Despite his heavily Hispanic, Catholic ward in which gay rights were not popular, Munoz voted for the ordinance. What made this vote different from many other contentious votes in the new Daley council was that Aldermen Huels and Burke, the mayor's floor leaders, also voted for this ordinance because the mayor supported it. The *Tribune* concluded, "Some aldermen voted their consciences, others voted their political futures, some negotiated amenities for their wards, some strayed [from their normal voting blocs]." It is the type of social issue that rearranged the voting patterns more typical of the Daley rubber stamp council of the 1990s.[48]

Aldermanic Scandals. For more than a century and a half, political corruption has occurred in the city council. Unfortunately, corruption persists in the Daley council today. Federal probe Operation Haunted Hall found aldermen all too ready to take bribes and to hire family members and politicos as "ghost payrollers." Ghost payrollers are paid salaries and benefits at taxpayer expense for government work they do not do. They never show up for work but draw their governmental salaries as if they did. The federal investigation of ghost payrollers in 1997 and 1998 resulted in the convictions of thirty-five people who had illegally earned more than $2.5 million in wages and benefits. A large number of these ghosts worked on Northwest Side alderman Anthony Laurino's Traffic Committee in the city council. He had a number of relatives employed by the city who did no work. He was so elderly and ill that he avoided trial, although he was indicted. Other aldermen didn't.

A parallel federal investigation, Operation Silver Shovel, focused on aldermen taking bribes from FBI moles who wanted to dump construction material in aldermen's wards. Most of those aldermen convicted were minority aldermen representing minority wards, although some white city administration officials were also convicted of taking bribes. Between 1997 and 2000, eighteen public officials, including six aldermen, were convicted of graft and corruption in this investigation.

Charged with accepting $37,000 in bribes over two and a half years, African-American alderman Allan Streeter agreed to tape-record his conversations with other aldermen and to cooperate in introducing FBI agents posing as businessmen to other public officials. This allowed the FBI to expand its sting operations. Thus, when Alderman Streeter was convicted, he was sentenced to only eight months in prison and $10,000 in restitution in return for his cooperation with federal agents. At his sentencing hearing Streeter said, "I made a serious mistake. It doesn't depict what my life is all about. I did my best to serve the people." But on the tape recordings with FBI agents he told a different story: "Rules are meant to be broken as are laws," he told one FBI agent posing as a crooked businessman.[49]

White Southwest Side alderman John Madrzyk was convicted for placing ghost payrollers on his council committee staff and for pocketing kickbacks from them. He hired his daughter-in-law and several political cronies between 1991 and 1993, paying them more than $133,000 in city funds for work they did not do. He also put his political consultant Gregory Swan on the payroll, Swan's girlfriend, and Swan's teenage son, at a cost to the city of $102,500.[50]

As part of the ever widening scandals, African-American alderman Jesse Evans was convicted of taking $7,300 in cash payments from an FBI agent who posed as a corrupt businessman "for arranging to have a city street sweeper clean the area around a construction site, a responsibility that normally falls to the site operator." He was charged as well with taking a $10,000 bribe "to drop his opposition to a rock-crushing operation in his ward." Jesse Evans was sentenced to forty-one months in prison, 200 hours of community service, and restitution and fines totaling $11,700.[51]

African-American alderman Percy Giles, first appointed to the council by Mayor Harold Washington in 1986, was also sentenced to thirty-nine months in jail for "pocketing $91,000 in bribes . . . [for] wholesale abuse, and selling his public office."[52]

Reformers were caught up in the scandals as well. Former Independent alderman and mayoral candidate Larry Bloom was indicted on fourteen counts, including "taking $16,000 in bribes, but also with bilking city and county taxpayers through two fraud schemes unrelated to Silver Shovel. . . . helping the operators of a South Side medical center dodge $238,000 in overdue property taxes and using $50,000 in city money to pay wages to members of his law office and campaign staffs."[53] Bloom originally argued that he "was mugged, not by a petty thief or street tough, but by agents of my own government." He declared that he had committed no crimes. The bribes he was charged with accepting included $6,000 in 1994 and $10,000 in campaign contributions for his race for city treasurer in 1995. In December 1998, however, Bloom admitted his guilt and plead guilty to one count of misreporting $6,000 in cash that he had received from the federal mole in 1994 as deductible income on his tax return.[54]

An even greater political controversy erupted with the conviction of former Latino Northwest Side alderman Joseph Martinez, who received $90,000 over several years as a ghost payroller doing no work. After he was defeated in his aldermanic reelection campaign, Martinez worked for Burke at his law firm while receiving pay as a ghost payroller at City Hall. In his trial, Martinez's lawyer said that Alderman Burke "had placed Martinez with three committees—finance, traffic and land acquisition—so that Martinez could receive health benefits. Martinez 'did not actively pursue those positions. . . . He was appointed to them . . . by his employer [Alderman Burke].'" Martinez was sentenced to ten months confinement, two years of probation, and 100 hours of community service, as well as being fined $15,000. After Martinez's sentencing, Alderman Burke in a written statement declared, "A memorandum filed in Mr Martinez's case [has] asserted that I participated in a scheme that gave rise to these charges. This allegation is untrue. I have done nothing wrong in connection with this matter."[55]

The *Chicago Tribune* in an editorial on June 13, 1997, called for Alderman Burke's resignation as Finance Committee chairman because of his conflicts of interest: "Ghost workers haunted the Finance Committee, and a former alderman admitted he had a no-show job at Finance while he worked for Burke's law firm." The *Tribune* also faulted Burke for crafting and voting to approve city budgets, and then afterward filing lawsuits claiming those budgets were illegal. He also "quietly changed his voting record on several matters pertaining to his law clients, erasing 'yes' votes and recording himself as abstaining."[56] Burke did not resign but continued as head of the Finance Committee despite the media's rebuke.

The following year, Burke became the subject of another scandal disclosed by a *Sun-Times* investigation. This time Burke helped a developer client obtain a $1.2 million city subsidy without revealing that he and his wife, Judge Anne Burke, received more than $300,000 in legal fees from the developer.[57] Mayor Daley joined in criticizing Burke for voting on city budgets and then filing lawsuits against the budgets for clients: "It's a very difficult position he's placing everyone in. If you are passing the budget, working on the budget, then in turn filing a lawsuit, this is very questionable." If Burke had legal questions about the budget process, Daley maintained that he had an obligation "to the tax-paying voters who elected him to raise them immediately, and not wait to use the argument on behalf of his fee-paying clients."[58] Yet Burke continued in his post and was reelected by the voters of the 14th Ward in 1999.

In October 1997, *Chicago Sun-Times* investigators revealed that Mayor Daley's own 11th Ward alderman and political floor leader, Alderman Patrick Huels, along with Alderman Burke, paid $633,731 from their council committees to an attorney who was helping run a security firm that Huels co-owned and for which Burke served as secretary. The city money was paid as legal consultant fees to Michael Pedicone, president of SDI Security, which was owned by Huels, his wife, his brother, and Pedicone. In addition, SDI Security owed two federal tax liens totaling $1,324,333 and was bailed out of its financial crisis by a $1.25 million loan from a company created by major city contractor, Michael Tadin, a longtime friend of Huels and Daley. Alderman Huels had helped Tadin win a $1.1 million city redevelopment subsidy and local government real estate tax cuts of $80,000 a year over eight years.[59]

When this new scandal broke, Mayor Daley demanded that Huels repay the loan to Tadin. Daley said, "I'm very upset and mad and disappointed in the revelations and the facts. . . . I don't think someone's business decisions should interfere with government or politics. This deals with a . . . bad business judgment. . . . He has to pay it back. That's one thing he has to do." On October 21, 1997, as public pressure continued, Huels apologized for his questionable business deals and resigned as 11th Ward alderman and the mayor's council floor leader. He acknowledged in a statement that accompanied his resignation that he had been "lax in the oversight of my business affairs. . . . Although I am certain that I broke no laws, I am equally certain that I exercised poor judgment. . . . And in so doing, I've let many people down."[60]

In response to the 1995 ghost payroll scandals, the city council, in one of its rare unanimous votes on a controversial issue, adopted by a vote of 48–0 an ordinance requiring committee chairmen to maintain a daily attendance report on each city council committee employee and to make those records available for public inspection. Then in the summer of 1997 the city council tightened the ethics ordinance again—but only after heated debate. On June 20, 1997, the council's Rules and Ethics Committee passed an amendment that gave the city's board of ethics subpoena power and the authority to punish wrongdoing by aldermen with fines up to $1,000. However, the ethics board could only investigate signed, not anonymous, complaints against aldermen.

In the debate Alderman John Buchanan declared, "Not everybody in the city council is dishonest and crooked as one would have you believe by way of inference and new kinds of controls brought forth in dictatorial decree from the [Daley] administration. . . . We are not crooks. Jam the amendment and jam your ordinance." Alderman Dorothy Tillman concurred: "I don't think $75,000 a year [an alderman's annual salary at the time] is worth being held hostage. . . . I feel sorry for my colleagues. They think they have to vote for this." On the other side, Alderman Joe Moore implored his colleagues to pass the ethics package, which included some of his amendments. "Citing the long history of aldermanic criminal convictions, [Alderman Moore] said that some citizens 'think this council is a joke. There is conduct here that would not be tolerated in any other city,' he said. 'We have to send a message to people that we are not going to tolerate any more of these shenanigans.'"[61] With Mayor Daley's strong arm-twisting, the ordinance passed the city council on July 30, 1997, by a vote of 40–9. "Council members who voted for the measure are 'nothing more than a capons-castrated rooster' who lack the 'guts' to preserve the powers of the co-equal legislative branch, said Ald. Robert Shaw (9th). They didn't send you here to reverse the clock and go back on the plantation. . . . Many people here have a snowball for a backbone. . . . They just melt and fall into line. That what's wrong with this Council."[62]

After another scandal of Alderman Burke helping a developer get a $1.2 million subsidy for which he collected over $300,000 in legal fees, the city council amended the ethics ordinance again. On December 2, 1998, by a 40–3 vote, the city council adopted rules that

> make it a crime for aldermen to "contact, either orally or in writing, any other city official or employee with respect to matters" in which that alderman has a "business relationship."
>
> Require aldermen to notify the Board of Ethics of a potential conflict upon introduction of legislation, instead of at the time of Council votes. Lists of aldermanic conflicts to be made public.
>
> Require contractors who hire aldermen to represent them on any matter to file annual affidavits with the city.
>
> Allow contracts obtained through behind-the-scenes aldermanic lobbying to be canceled.[63]

Neither the mayor's executive order nor the amendments to the ethics ordinance can hide the fact that in the twenty-five years between 1973 and 2000, twenty-six aldermen were convicted of corruption.[64] The *Chicago Tribune* continued to characterize the city council as "a government of the politicians, by the politicians, and for the politicians—and for their friends."[65]

As corruption in the city council was being brought to light, the Daley administration was also rocked by its own series of scandals. Windy City Maintenance, a janitorial firm with ties to organized crime and a contributor of volunteers and money to Daley's mayoral campaigns, "won millions of dollars in business under a city affirmative-action program [because it] falsely portrayed itself as being operated by a woman." Another firm, G. F. Structures, which had made contributions to Daley's mayoral campaigns, purchased its commercial insurance from John Daley, the mayor's brother. The owner of G. F. Structures, a friend of the city's purchasing agent, had been selected to provide wrought iron fences around city property, schools, and parks but then "charged prices far higher than stipulated in its contract."[66] In another scandal, a close Daley friend, Oscar D'Angelo, provided interest-free loans to Mayor Daley's aides and lobbied for city contracts for businesses at the airport without registering as a lobbyist.[67] These scandals led to Windy City Maintenance losing $1 million in existing city business, its false woman-owned designation, and a major future contract, since such contracts were now put out for bid. The city purchasing officer was fired and yet another amendment was made to the ethics ordinance imposing fines of $500 for lobbyists who fail to register and fines of $2,000 a day and risk of forfeiture of city contracts for companies that employ lobbyists who fail to register.[68]

The 1999 Elections

The 1999 elections brought another triumph for Mayor Daley. He was re-elected over his challenger, African-American congressman (and former 2nd Ward alderman) Bobby Rush, by 73 percent of the vote in one of the largest landslide elections in Chicago history. He and his father had now surpassed even the long-serving Mayor Carter Harrisons a hundred years earlier. In the same election ten aldermen won their elections with no opponent on the ballot, thirty won reelection with over 60 percent of the vote, and ten contests had to be decided in runoff elections.

Because of a 1998 change in state law, the 1999 election was the first mayoralty run as a "nonpartisan election" without party primaries preceding a general election. In addition to his landslide majority, Daley won thirty-three of the fifty wards and made major gains in the African-American community. Overall, he won 44 percent of the vote in the twenty black wards, up from the 28 percent he had received in 1995. The great divide in the past decades had been race, but race as a factor seemed to diminish in this election. Voting patterns seemed to reflect instead the division between middle- and upper-middle-class voters (including blacks) supporting Daley and lower-income voters supporting Congressman Rush. Daley was able to expand his support from his original base in the white working- and middle-class wards to all gentrifying areas, including black gentrifying neighborhoods. Daley was, of course, aided by facing a weak opponent in 1999, by using his incumbency to his advantage, and by avoiding falling into racial traps such as the one that defeated Mayor Byrne in 1983.[69]

Comparing Daley's campaign contributions with those of Mayor Washington provides a clear picture of differences in their base of support. Washington began his run for mayor in 1982 with financial support from a handful of affluent benefactors. He received $54,000 in donations from Johnson Publishing, a Chicago-based firm producing magazines targeting African-American readership. He received multiple loans that were cosigned by a group of political supporters, including his campaign treasurer, Odell Hicks, and Washington's successor to the U.S. House of Representatives, Charles Hayes. Altogether, Washington's campaign reported receiving more than $4 million in contributions and loans between January and June 1983. A number of the largest contributors to Washington's first successful mayoral elections were black businesses that did not benefit directly from city contracts and were not a part of the "growth machine" that had supported Mayor Richard J. Daley. In addition to the $54,000 from Johnson Publishing, Washington's largest contributions included more than $20,000 from a firm called the Stellar Group and nearly $10,000 from the makers of Soft Sheen, a cosmetic company that markets cosmetic products to African Americans.

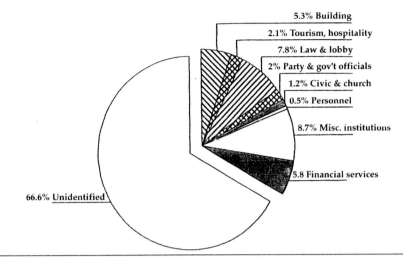

5.3% Building
2.1% Tourism, hospitality
7.8% Law & lobby
2% Party & gov't officials
1.2% Civic & church
0.5% Personnel
8.7% Misc. institutions
5.8 Financial services
66.6% Unidentified

FIGURE 9.2   Campaign Contributions to Harold Washington's 1987 Campaign

The second largest source of Washington's initial support came in the "political" category, which accounted for 2.7 percent of his revenues. Many of his contributions came from contacts he made as a congressman in the nation's capital. Speaker of the House Thomas O'Neill offered $1,000. The Democratic National Committee gave him $10,000 after he won the primary. The regular Democratic organization in the African-American 24th Ward gave him $10,000. After the primary, Washington's future nemesis, 10th Ward Alderman Edward Vrdolyak, also made a $1,000 peace offering. In all, Washington received slightly less than $100,000 from "political" sources.

The third largest category of support for Washington in 1983 came from the banking and financial services industry, which had already replaced real estate developers and State Street businesses as financial contributors to mayoral campaigns. About $98,000 came from bankers, insurance companies, and investment brokerage firms. Local civic groups and churches, often credited with serving as a base of electoral support, were not huge financial contributors, although they would contribute more to his reelection efforts in 1987. Only 0.6 percent of Washington's financial support could be traced to this civic sector in 1983.

Upon Washington's reelection, his financial base of support changed noticeably. By the 1987 primary, the construction industry became a much more important source of campaign revenue, accounting for more than 5 percent of his $5 million, although construction firms and trade unions had provided Washington's campaign with less than 1 percent of his contributions in 1983. Lawyers, who contributed less than 1.5 percent

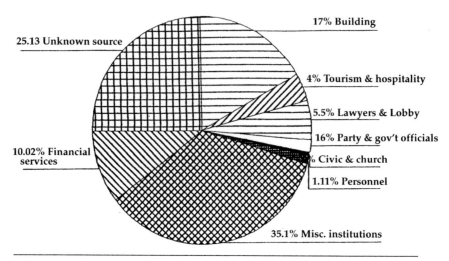

FIGURE 9.3   Campaign Contributions to Richard M. Daley's 1999 Campaign

in 1983, now gave Washington an impressive 7.6 percent of his financial support in 1987. Meanwhile, party organizations and government officials, which had been his single largest source of revenue in 1983, had dropped to third on the list, at 1.9 percent. Financial services, which had accounted for more than 10 percent in 1983, decreased to slightly more than 8 percent of Washington's 1987 revenue but were still very important. The balance of his campaign funds came from individuals and political action committees.

Washington's death in 1987 precipitated Richard M. Daley's ascension to the mayoralty in the spring of 1989. According to newspaper accounts of his mayoral campaign, Daley relied heavily on large donations "from corporate officials and leading business establishments" to raise a record $7.1 million. In the general election in 1989, "the [Alderman Tim] Evan's [mayoral] campaign released a report contending that . . . 40 percent [of Daley's donations] came from lawyers, large law firms, and real estate developers."[70]

A decade later, in his 1999 election campaign, Daley received more than $3 million in cash and in-kind donations. What is most notable is the change in the types of contributors making donations to Mayors Washington and Daley. In 1999, the construction industry provided nearly 17 percent of Daley's total revenue. The financial services industry contributed roughly 10 percent of Daley's income and the legal community produced 5.5 percent. As it was for Washington, the miscellaneous category was largest for Daley, at 35 percent, but that is because I have not been able to categorize the business sectors represented by individual contributors.

Much of Daley's strength in raising money from the construction industry is the support he receives from the carpenters and electricians unions. The Brotherhood of Carpenters PAC gave Daley $56,000 while various locals supplied additional support. The plumbing industry and associated unions gave over $65,000. A developers' PAC, by contrast, gave only $5,000. However, many individual construction firms gave Daley $10,000 each, since in Illinois business corporations can give campaign contributions directly and do not have to use PACs.

Lobbyists and lawyers produced 5.5 percent of Daley's reelection finances. Two law firms were especially lucrative sources of revenue for Daley's most recent reelection: Bell, Boyd & Lloyd and Schiff & Hardin. The tourism and hospitality industry, whose support for Washington was anemic, was quite helpful to Daley. Roughly 4 percent of his revenue came from this sector, including a $10,000 gift from the owner of the Chicago Blackhawks hockey team and another $10,000 from a livery firm from Frankfort, Illinois. The union representing hotel employees also gave Daley's campaign $30,000.

The financial base for mayoral campaigns—or at least Mayor Daley's campaigns—seems to have shifted to the service sector (bankers, insurance, and lawyers), construction (both contractors and unions), and tourism. An even more extensive study of financial contributors to Washington and Daley by John Pelissero and Timothy Krebs concludes, "Washington's [financial contributor] coalition is true to his populist and progressive regime label. His coalition consists of a significant number of retail, political, religious, and public union partners. . . . Daley's [financial contributor] coalition [by contrast] has a significant level of participation from corporate and management professionals. Specifically, his key partners are development, financial, professional, manufacturing, private sector union and retail, and are based largely in Chicago's downtown."[71] The financial base for Richard M. Daley differs from the downtown business progrowth regime that supported his father and the more progressive contributors of Harold Washington. He depends on the service or global industries, corporate lawyers, and construction firms and their unions that benefit directly from city contracts and private developments aided by City Hall.

Crossing the Bridge to the Twenty-First Century

Alderman Burke argued that the new Daley-controlled rubber stamp council elected in 1999 was legitimate because the voters had given Daley and his aldermen a mandate. Burke maintained that Chicago was "looking good" with flowers, trees, snow removal, public works, and improved city services in this affluent period. As in the previous four years, seven of the fifty aldermen remained hard-core Independent, or reform, aldermen. The rubber stamp council produced almost no divided roll call votes from the April election until November 1999. Alderman Joe Moore attributed this lack of conflict to an administration that was conflict adverse. "The administration and the mayor attempt to solve problems and defuse opposition in the council before [formal] votes are taken in order to win [over any possible opponents so as to win] all votes as close to unanimously as possible. Thus, they will change, amend, or hold legislation until they have gotten as much aldermanic support as they can. They solve problems before the vote is taken."[72]

Judson Miner, corporation counsel under Mayor Washington and the lead attorney in two decades of remap lawsuits, characterized the council beginning the third millennium differently: "With few exceptions, the current aldermen are a bunch of puppets [of the mayor] doing what they are told. According to reports, the mayor is vindictive to anyone who opposes him. There is no thoughtful debate or discussion."[73] As to his remembering past enemies, the mayor himself has said, "you don't forget who was with you and who was against you. Me? I don't forget."[74]

Alderman Moore provides a rationale for the ineffectiveness of the opposition compared with previous councils. "This Mayor Daley is not his dad. Times have changed. Now, no mayor can give short shrift [in city services and public works] to major areas of the city like the African-American [neighborhoods]. No mayor can just cut off [an alderman's] mike [to silence them] like Mayor Richard J. Daley did to his opponents." In a time of economic affluence, the mayor is able to give out more services and public works. It is likely that there will be greater dissent when future administrations are again forced to make harder decisions about raising taxes or cutting services in bad economic times.[75]

Only two issues at the beginning of the third millennium raised much protest from the aldermen. Daley's 2000 budget proposed raising property taxes, fees, and fines by $76 million in order to improve the city's infrastructure. The mayor argued that if these repairs were not made now, "some future generation will be burdened with the cost of bringing our public facilities into the twenty-first century and the cost to the taxpayer will only rise with time." Alderman Burke defended the mayor's budget, arguing that it "shows a great deal of political courage to lay out the needs that confront the city. Things are very good [in the economy]. I think we all realize that and should take advantage of that opportunity now." Northwest Side alderman Thomas Allen, who had opposed some earlier budgets with proposed tax increases, said that at least his neighborhood would get its share. "If this money were going downtown and we weren't getting anything, I wouldn't even consider supporting this. But we are getting a good return on our investment." Opposing the tax increase, Northwest Side Republican alderman Brian Doherty said his constituents already paid too much property tax. Independent Latino alderman Ricardo Munoz and four other aldermen proposed to set aside 10 percent (or $80 million) of the total $800 million in the mayor's budget for infrastructure improvements for the Chicago Transit Authority. "My concern is that the CTA is nowhere to be found in the plan. . . . The Blue [elevated and subway] Line [from the West Side to O'Hare Field] is falling apart. Other lines need reconstruction, and our buses need to be updated." However, their proposed amendment was defeated. Altogether, the disputes about the 2000 budget were much milder than the minirevolt that had been occasioned by Daley's 1992 proposed budget, when pro-administration aldermen revolted. In the end, after mild aldermanic protests and debate, Daley's budget was approved unanimously.[76]

The second controversial issue was reminiscent of my earlier opposition to the appointment of Tom Keane Jr. to the Zoning Board of Appeals, which provoked Richard J. Daley's outburst. On December 15, 1999, Richard M. Daley proposed the appointment of James Joyce as Chicago's new fire commissioner. His appointment was opposed by five reform aldermen who feared that Joyce would not be able to lead the organization in a "non-racially segregated" manner because he was a third-generation white firefighter who had spent thirty-four years in a department that had consistently been shown to discriminate against African Americans in hiring and promotions. South Side alderman Toni Preckwinkle declared, "The Chicago Fire Department has had a history of insularity and intolerance. It concerns me that our new fire commissioner has been part of that department [and the number 2 man] for such a long time."[77]

The 42–5 vote confirming the commissioner's appointment and the refusal of the five aldermen to join in a standing ovation for Joyce after the vote was taken caused Mayor Richard M. Daley to rant, "He'll lead the department, with or without your support, and that's why I selected him! This will be a vote we'll remember and I think you will apologize some day!" When they didn't stand up and applaud the new commissioner, Daley snapped, "I'd say my good mother and father always taught me respect. Even though you vote no, you should stand up and clap. Number one, that is something that I think our parents and church leaders have taught us. Please stand up!"[78] The *Chicago Sun-Times* editorialized that Daley must have known "that his angry and indignant response to the fact that five aldermen chose to vote 'no' this week to the confirmation of James Joyce as Chicago's new fire commissioner was out of order. The mayor cannot expect to win 50–0, as he did in the case of his budget this year, on everything he presents to the aldermen."[79]

Opening the Council to the Public

Two final case studies provide examples of incremental positive civic improvements during the Daley years in spite of opposition by the aldermen and the city administration. Beginning in 1971, there was a demand in the council that the public have better access to information on pending legislation, city council and council committee meeting schedules, and the voting records of aldermen. For many years city council legislation was not numbered, and when numbers finally were assigned by the city clerk, they were changed from the numbers assigned legislation when it was introduced to new numbers after it passed. Moreover, the numbers given by the city clerk were not published in the *Journal of Proceedings of the Chicago City Council* and were thus useless for tracking legislation. A similar problem existed with notice of council meetings. Dates of council and committee meetings were officially publicized by being posted on an obscure bulletin board near aldermanic offices on the second floor at City Hall. It was hard for citizens to discover the date of the next council meeting or what issues likely were to be voted on at a committee meeting. Finally, although it was possible to use the *Journal* to tabulate aldermanic voting records buried there, going through the more than 1,000 pages of a single year's *Journal* and pulling out the divided roll call votes could take up to 100 hours. They were not available to an alderman's constituents in an easily accessible form.

From the 1970s through the 1990s, I have been meeting with aldermen and various city clerks to try to improve the information available to citizens about their city council. All these efforts ended with no significant improvement. Legislation introduced in the city council by various aldermen to improve citizen information over the last two and a half decades has been routinely defeated. In 1997, city clerk James Laski promised to make more city council information available on his new homepage on the Internet, which was launched in May 1998. It provided background information on the fifty aldermen, a map of the wards, various licenses and fees payable at the clerk's office, city council and council committee meeting schedules and agendas, copies of pending and passed legislation, and a record of aldermanic voting on divided roll call votes.

In launching his Web site, Laski said, "Information is power. I want to help empower citizens who want to learn more about the business of city government. There is an easy way of doing this and a hard way. . . . I would like cooperation from [the mayor and the aldermen]. If that doesn't work, I would pursue legislation."[80] Predictably, there was resistance from members of the city council, particularly in posting agendas for meetings twenty-four hours in advance and giving notice of legislation aldermen planned to introduce twenty-four hours before council meet-

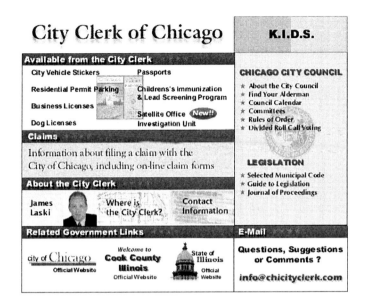

FIGURE 9.4   City Clerk's Internet Homepage

ings. Alderman Thomas Allen, chairman of the Transportation Committee, said, "We have alley and street vacations. There are appraisals. The Law Department has to meet with attorneys. Oftentimes, we don't get all the pieces put together until the night before." And as to telling citizens what legislation individual aldermen planned to introduce, Alderman Bernard Stone, a thirty-year council veteran said, "We don't even give [notice of legislation we plan to introduce] to the mayor's office. You think we're going to give it to the city clerk. It's nonsensical. What, is he kidding?"[81]

Although making city council information available on the Web is still in its infancy, it is a major step forward. Interested groups can now use this information. However, posting city council data on the Web has not continued long enough to become a custom and the requirement that this information be made public is not written into law by city council ordinance or even codified by the city council's own rules of procedure. This means that with the election of a new city clerk, or with the application of enough political pressure against Clerk Laski, the practice could be discontinued. Nonetheless, partly because of making his office more efficient and providing more city council information than ever before,

Clerk Laski was unanimously reelected without an opponent in 1999. The Democratic Party did not dare oppose him.

In addition to information posted on the Internet, the council chambers themselves have been opened and made more accessible to the public. In 1997, civic and labor organizations supporting the "living wage ordinance" had been kept out of a city council meeting considering the ordinance. In response they sued the city in *Chicago Acorn et al. v. City of Chicago* to guarantee the rights of the public to admission to the city council chamber in future meetings.[82]

The city council galleries provide 343 seats for the public, 238 of which are downstairs immediately behind the aldermen and 105 in a glassed-in section on the second floor removed from the aldermen. For years the city government packed the galleries with city employees and blocked civic and community organizations from bringing supporters into the galleries to pressure the aldermen to vote against legislation that the administration favored or to pressure aldermen to vote for legislation that the administration opposed. This practice was also followed during the 1968 Democratic National Convention, when Mayor Richard J. Daley packed the galleries with his employees and party workers to shout down and intimidate his opponents.

In her deposition for the *Chicago Acorn* lawsuit, Patricia D. Feeley, the sergeant at arms and a city council employee since 1979, testified that there were no written rules of procedures about who got seats on the main floor and in the balcony.[83] In the past, city administrations had simply filled the chamber with supporters and employees because they could. The sergeant at arms maintained that other lobbying groups were not allowed equal access as a matter of policy. It was her general practice to reserve seats for schoolchildren and tourists, but not for partisan groups. The following exchange took place between Feeley and the attorney for the plaintiffs:

Q. Well, for instance, let's say that one of my clients, the Service Employees International Union Local 88, wanted to reserve seats for a meeting involving the living wage ordinance and they wanted to reserve 80 seats for their members to come and be present during that meeting. Could they do that?

A. Well, 80 seats would be a little too much. . . . But normally, I would not reserve seats for that, no.

Q. And why is that?

A. Because I don't know . . . what people are coming to lobby for. . . .

Q. Could they reserve 10 seats for that or is it that you don't allow groups?

A. *I usually don't allow groups that are, you know, partisan . . . to reserve seats.*

Q. So it's your general practice to not allow partisan groups to reserve seats?

A. Uh-huh. . . .

Q. But it's not a questions of numbers, so much as this distinction between people there for tourism, people there for lobbying, right?

A. For lobbying right, whether it's for or against. [Emphasis added.][84]

After her damning testimony, the city decided to settle the lawsuit with a new set of written rules that opened up the city council to the general public. The new rules of procedure guaranteed (1) that the city council would no longer "discriminate in admission to public seating on the basis of any person's political viewpoint," (2) that nonreserved seating would be on a first-come, first-served basis, with the line for admission forming no sooner than one hour prior to the scheduled commencement of the meeting, and (3) that no more that one hundred seats on the main floor and sixty seats in the upstairs gallery would be reserved for groups. According to the new rules, any group may reserve up to twenty seats for a council meeting no more than two weeks and no less than twenty-four hours before the scheduled meeting date.[85]

The Chicago City Council had never had clear rules on the public's admission, which has enabled admissions to be controlled by the discretion of city employees. As a result, at a number of council meetings seats were packed with city employees and City Hall supporters in order to keep those with opposing viewpoints from being present. Limiting the number of seats that can be reserved for city employees, staff, and guests in conjunction with the first-come, first-served provisions, both for same-day seating and for reservations, ensures that the city council cannot be packed by City Hall employees and administrative supporters in the future as it had been in the past.[86]

The New Daley Machine

Richard M. Daley governs in an era that is different from his father's. Although boosterism and bossism may have served his father well, these qualities are not enough for his son to govern. Although Richard M. Daley is more enlightened and modern than his father in his attitudes and policies, he has not completely abandoned the machine politics that brought his father and him to power.

Richard M. Daley was elected mayor after Council Wars, a time of pronounced racial and political polarization in the city and the city council. He had to defuse those tensions if he was to be effective. He could not resurrect the patronage army and tyrannical control of the old Daley machine, neither could he roll back the clock on affirmative action and minority empowerment. Daley avoided most political reforms but has cast himself as a civic or good government reformer streamlining city government, improving the city bureaucracy, keeping taxes low, and limiting waste if not corruption at City Hall.

Daley quickly tamed the city council, which had been chaotic under Mayor Sawyer. His power over the council was strengthened by the fact that between 1989 and 1998, he appointed seventeen of the fifty aldermen to the seats they held. When an alderman resigned or died, the mayor appointed a successor until the next election, and the appointee most often won reelection. Needless to say, these appointed aldermen were grateful for the mayor's help, felt a debt of gratitude, and usually sided with the administration on major votes.[87] Daley also gained more power because the Independent or opposition bloc in the council was divided. Only racial issues, property tax increases, and some environmental legislation motivated significant levels of opposition in the council. The rest of the time the vast majority of the aldermen were willing to support the mayor. Further undercutting the opposition, the mayor implemented a number of managerial and budget reforms, including the unusual step for a Democratic mayor of privatizing some city positions.

Citizens' job performance ratings for Mayor Daley have been high. They were highest just after he won primary elections (60 percent of the voters said that he was doing a good or an excellent job after the 1989 primary and 62 percent after the 1991 primary). They dropped to below 50 percent in 1990 and 1992, but in comparison to Mayor Sawyer, who had only 38–41 percent approval, Daley's positive ratings remained solid. However, there is a major racial bias in the ratings. Only 18–35 percent of African Americans in the early 1990s said the mayor was doing a good or an outstanding job. Daley has not yet become the mayor of all the city and all its diverse racial groups, but he is gaining more of the black vote in each election.[88]

Chicago in the 1990s clearly was different from the Chicago of earlier years. Perhaps most emblematic of the change was the 1996 Democratic National Convention. For the 1996 convention, Chicago was spruced up with newly paved streets, flower boxes, banners, and signs along the routes to the new United Center, where the convention would be held. In 1968, the clash between protestors and police in the streets and pro- and anti-Vietnam delegates in the convention hall defined the event. Although in 1996 there were incidents in which the police were sued for harassing dissidents, the convention was marked by only a few orderly, regulated, peaceful protests. In contrast, Democrats made a gigantic show of unity as they joined together to renominate Bill Clinton and Al Gore as their presidential and vice presidential candidates. By every standard the convention was successful, including the all-important test of a unified Democratic Party triumphing in the November elections two and a half months later. Chicago handled the 1996 Democratic National Convention effectively and got positive publicity from this well-reported event. Many of the news programs made explicit contrasts with the 1968 convention and praised the new Chicago under the new Mayor Daley.

The new Daley regime and the public policies that it produces are an amalgam that William Grimshaw has called "Machine politics, reform style."[89] While keeping the support of the old machine organization, Richard M. Daley has run slick, modern campaigns. Unlike his father, he has not become a party "boss." He holds no official position in the Democratic Party, but he does maintain his own loyal army of precinct workers and political operatives. On the other side of the ledger, he has kept, to a certain degree, the affirmative action and good government reforms such as freedom of information, instituted under Mayor Washington. He has extended the ethics ordinance and has undertaken antimachine and antiunion government actions such as the privatization of janitorial services, only to indulge in "pinstriped patronage" in letting those contracts. He has been a "builder mayor" supporting big government projects, office building in the downtown, and upscale housing projects in the neighborhoods adjacent to the Loop. At the same time, following Washington's job retention strategy of preserving manufacturing jobs, he has supported zoning policies to protect manufacturing plants and to create new high-tech industries in the other neighborhoods.[90] In response to the desires of the new service and global economy business elite, he has provided for better amenities and beautified the city, especially the downtown, with more parks, flowers in street medians, and wrought iron ornamental fences around parks and schools. The greatest image of the new Chicago is no longer State Street but Millennium Park, being constructed across from Michigan Avenue, and Navy Pier on the lakefront as a playground and tourist attraction.

The old "city of the big shoulders" is being remade into the global city capital of the Midwest. Although the new regime that surrounds Daley includes some party hacks and wheeler-dealers from the past, more prominent are wealthy lawyers, bankers, and investors who make up the new business elite of the city. Meanwhile, down on the second floor of city hall, Mayor Richard M. Daley rules over a rubber stamp city council, as his father did fifty years ago.

However, this new machine is very unstable. In March 2000, Daley had a health scare that appeared at first to be a heart attack or stroke (which killed his father and Mayor Washington). We are told by the media that he only has high blood pressure, which is treatable with standard medication. But, as this scare reminds us, Richard M. Daley will not rule forever; and, like his father and Mayor Washington, he has groomed no successor.

Second, the economy that supports Mayor Daley is fragile—some call it a bubble economy based on high-tech stocks that cannot maintain their inflated values. In an economic recession, the legal and financial sectors that underpin the new global service economy will be hard hit. A government of retrenchment like the government under Mayor Ed Kelly in the 1930s will require very different allies and policies.

Most of all, there is a steady racial change in Chicago, and whites are already a minority. The 2000 census will probably show a 40 percent black population, a 35 percent white population, and a better than 25 percent Latino population. As the fastest growing population, Latinos will inevitably play a more important role in Chicago politics. They may not be willing to continue as a junior partner, as they have in the reigns of Mayors Washington and Richard M. Daley.

Notes

1. The Chicago Central Area Committee included Sears, Roebuck, First Federal Savings and Loan, Carson Pirie Scott, Commonwealth Edison, Peoples Gas, First National Bank, Hart Schaffner & Marx, Standard Oil, Skidmore, Owings & Merrill, Hilton Hotels, Illinois Central Industries, Chicago Title and Trust, Harris Bank, CNA Financial, Continental Bank, Inland Steel, Scribner, Marshall Fields, Northern Trust, and Real Estate Research Corporation. Joel Rast, *Remaking Chicago* (DeKalb: Northern Illinois University Press, 1999), p. 173 n. 2.

2. John Kass, "The New Mayor Daley," *Chicago Tribune Magazine,* August 25, 1996, p. 18.

3. Don Rose and James Andrews, "How Evans Lost the Race," in Paul Green and Melvin Holli, eds., *Restoration 1989: Chicago Elects a New Daley* (Chicago: Lyceum, 1991), p. 134.

4. "Patronage: Shakman v. Democratic Organization of Cook County and Rutan v. Republican Party of Illinois" in Dick Simpson, ed., *Chicago's Future: In a Time of Change* (Champaign, Ill.: Stipes, 1993), pp. 147–154.

5. See Dick Simpson, *Who Rules: Introduction to the Study of Politics* (Chicago: Swallow, 1970); and Simpson, *Winning Elections: A Handbook of Modern Participatory Politics* (New York: HarperCollins, 1996).

6. Richard Day, Jeff Andersen, and John Ross, "Polling in the 1989 Chicago Mayoral Election," in *Restoration 1989*, pp. 176–177.

7. Kass, "New Mayor Daley," p. 19. For more biographical background, see James Atlas, "The Daleys of Chicago," *New York Times Magazine,* August 25, 1996, pp. 37–39, 52, 56–58.

8. Kass, "New Mayor Daley," p. 15.

9. Alderman Edward M. Burke, "Voting Blocs in the 1989 Election: Ethnics," in *Restoration*, p. 69.

10. Monroe Anderson, "The Sawyer Saga: A Journalist, Who Just Happened to Be the Mayor's Press Secretary, Speaks," in *Restoration*, p. 112.

11. Anderson, "Sawyer Saga," p. 109.

12. Kass, "New Mayor Daley," pp. 15–16.

13. Atlas, "Daleys of Chicago," p. 57.

14. James Strong and Joel Kaplan, "Daley's 1st Proposals Breeze Through," *Chicago Tribune*, April 27, 1989, Chicagoland, pp. 1, 6.

15. *City Council Journal of Proceedings*, May 5, 1989, pp. 905–907.

16. Author's notes, speech by Alderman Edward Burke at the University of Illinois at Chicago, May 22, 1990.

17. Kevin Michael DeBell, "Greening the City: Explaining Chicago's Environmental Policy, 1970–1996" (paper presented at the annual meeting of the Midwest Political Science Association, Chicago, April 1997), p. 18. He quotes Barbara Ferman, *Challenging the Growth Machine* (Lawrence: University of Kansas Press, 1991), p. 61.

18. Dick Simpson, ed., *Blueprint of Chicago Government: 1989* (Chicago: University of Illinois at Chicago, 1989).

19. Dick Simpson et al., *The Second Richard Daley and His Un-Council: The First Year of the New Daley Administration* (Chicago: University of Illinois at Chicago, 1990), p. 1.

20. Melvin G. Holli, "Richard Daley (1989-)," in Paul Green and Melvin G. Holli, *The Mayors: The Chicago Political Tradition,* rev. ed. (Carbondale: Southern Illinois University Press, 1995), pp. 229–230.

21. William Grimshaw, *Bitter Fruit: Black Politics and the Chicago Machine, 1931–1991* (Chicago: University of Chicago Press, 1992), pp. 216–220. Original data taken from *Chicago Sun-Times*, August 9, 1990; January 31, 1991.

22. Simpson, "Second Richard Daley," pp. 2–3. Original data from Ray Hanania and Fran Spielman, "Blacks Losing Top City Jobs," *Chicago Sun-Times*, April 11, 1990, p. 1.

23. Grimshaw, *Bitter Fruit*, p. 219.

24. Robert Davis, "Council Rebels Fire Shot Heard 'Round the Hall,'" *Chicago Tribune*, May 7, 1992, 1.

25. Robert Davis, "Another City Budget Bomb," *Chicago Tribune*, November 11, 1992, 1, 12.

26. John Kass, "Daley, City Council Are Heading for Showdown on Property Taxes, *Chicago Tribune*, November 11, 1992, sec. 2, p. 8.

27. Robert Davis, *Chicago Tribune*, November 22, 1992, pp. 1, 6.

28. Robert Davis, "Not All Aldermen Buying Daley Tax," *Chicago Tribune*, January 1993, Dick Simpson Papers, Special Collections, Main Library, University of Illinois at Chicago.

29. Fran Spielman and Mary Johnson, "Budget Breezes in Council," *Chicago Sun-Times*, November 17, 1994, p. 5.

30. James Lewis, "Public Preferences, Race, and Policy in Chicago," expert witness report for *Barnett v. Daley*, October 25, 1995, p. 5, Dick Simpson Papers, Special Collections, Main Library, University of Illinois at Chicago.

31. Much of the story of the remap cases is taken from Karen A. Nagel and Victor M. Crown, "The Chicago Ward Map," *Illinois Politics*, July-August 1996, pp. 1, 3–8, 18–19.

32. Nagel and Crown, "Chicago Ward Map," p. 3.

33. Nagel and Crown, "Chicago Ward Map," p. 8.

34. See Nagel and Crown, "Chicago Ward Map," p. 18; Fran Spielman and Gilbert Jimenez, "Judge Upholds City's 1992 Ward Remap, *Chicago Sun-Times,* June 10, 1997, p. 12; and Nagel and Crown, "Schmidt Linked to Daley Ward Map," *Illinois Politics,* March 1998, p. 10.

35. Matt O'Connor and Gary Washburn, *Chicago Tribune,* April 3, 1998, MetroChicago, pp. 1–2.

36. Lewis, "Public Preferences," p. 1.

37. Dick Simpson, "Report on the Political and Racial Polarization of the Chicago City Council," expert witness report for *Smith v. City,* 94 C 920, January 1997. Dick Simpson Papers, Special Collections, Main Library, University of Illinois at Chicago.

38. Timothy B. Krebs, "The Advantage of Incumbency and Candidate Emergence: Chicago City Council Elections, 1979–1995" (paper presented at a meeting of the Midwest Political Science Association, April 11, 1997), p. 12. For a more detailed statistical analysis of these aldermanic elections, see Timothy B. Krebs, "The Determinants of Candidates' Vote Share and the Advantages of Incumbency in City Council Elections," *American Journal of Political Science,* July 1998, pp. 921–935.

39. The data on campaign spending in the 1995 election is taken from Anthony Gierzynski, Paul Kleppner, and James Lewis, *The Price of Democracy: Financing Chicago's 1995 City Elections* (Chicago: Chicago Urban League/Office for Social Policy Research/Northern Illinois University, 1996), p. 36. Information on the patterns of business contributions is from James Lewis, Garth Taylor, and Paul Kleppner, *MetroChicago Political Atlas '97–'98* (Chicago: Chicago Urban League/Metro Chicago Information Center/Northern Illinois University, 1997), pp. 149–150.

40. Gierzynski, Kleppner, and Lewis, *Price of Democracy,* p. 3.

41. Gierzynski, Kleppner, and Lewis, *Price of Democracy,* p. 26.

42. Victor M. Crown and Karen A. Nagel, "Daley Solidifies Council Control," *Illinois Politics,* June 1996, p. 1.

43. Crown and Nagel, "Daley Solidifies Council Control," pp. 7, 18.

44. Forty-ninth Ward Alderman Joe Moore, interview by author, August 6, 1998.

45. Victor Crown and Karen Nagel, "Daley Expands Power in Council, *Illinois Politics* 8, no. 2 (1999): 1–14, 20.

46. Alderman Moore, interview by author, August 6, 1998.

47. Alderman Moore, interview by author, August 6, 1998.

48. John Kass and Nancy Ryan, *Chicago Tribune,* March 20, 1987, pp. 1, 15.

49. Matt O'Connor, "Silver Shovel 'Judas' Sentenced to 8 Months," *Chicago Tribune,* sec. 2, pp. 1, 8.

50. Matt O'Connor, "Ghost-job Trial Ends in Aide's Conviction," *Chicago Tribune,* May 20, 1998, p. 1. See also *Tribune* stories of May 1 and May 9.

51. Mark Brown, "Weeping Evans Says Money Wasn't Bribe," *Chicago Sun-Times,* June 10, 1997, p. 9; and Michael Gillis, "Evans Sentenced to 41 Months in Bribery Case," *Chicago Sun-Times,* October, 17, 1997, p. 3.

52. Cam Simpson, "Giles Gets 39 Months," *Chicago Sun-Times,* May 27, 2000, pp. 1, 6.

53. Michael Gillis and Mark Brown, "Bloom Indicted," *Chicago Sun-Times*, July 9, 1997, pp. 1–2.

54. Gillis and Brown, "Bloom Indicted," p. 2; and Abdon Pallasch and Robert Davis, "Bloom Joins Long, Sad List," *Chicago Tribune*, December 6, 1998, pp. 1, 16.

55. Cam Simpson and Fran Spielman, "City 'Ghost' Gets 10-Month Term," *Chicago Sun-Times*, January 29, 1998, p. 10.

56. "Time for Burke to Step Aside," *Chicago Tribune*, June 13, 1997, p. 22. For the story on the original scandal, see Chuck Neubauer, "Burke's Double Deal," *Chicago Sun-Times*, May 22, 1997, pp. 1–2.

57. Chuck Neubauer and Charles Nicodemus, "Burke, Client Cash in As Chicago Loses Out," *Chicago Sun-Times*, November 15, 1998, pp. 1–2; and Neubauer and Nicodemus, "Burke, Developer Enjoyed a Rewarding Relationship," *Chicago Sun-Times*, November 15, 1998, pp. 28A–29A.

58. Fran Spielman, "Daley Blasts Burke," *Chicago Sun-Times*, May 23, 1997, pp. 1–2.

59. Charles Nicodemus and Chuck Neubauer, "Huels, Burke Paid City Cash to Colleague," *Chicago Sun-Times*, October 17, 1997, pp. 1–2.

60. Gary Washburn and Andrew Martin, "Daley Says He 'Did Right Thing,'" *Chicago Tribune*, October 22, 1997, pp. 1, 19.

61. Fran Spielman, "Aldermen in Rush on Reform," *Chicago Sun-Times*, June 17, 1997, p. 3; and Gary Washburn, "Grudgingly, Council Backs Ethics Reform," *Chicago Tribune*, June 21, 1997, pp. 1, 15.

62. Fran Spielman, "Council Approves Ethics Reform," *Chicago Tribune*, July 31, 1997, pp. 1–2.

63. Fran Spielman, "Council Oks Ethics Rules," *Chicago Sun-Times*, December 3, 1998, p. 8. This list of rules is quoted from the article.

64. A list of the convictions is provided by Patrick T. Reardon, "Aldermen's Past Legal Troubles: Zoning Played a Role," *Chicago Tribune*, November 4, 1997; and Cam Simpson, "Aldermen's Corruption Convictions," *Chicago Sun-Times,* May 27, 2000, p. 6.

65. Ray Gibson and Laurie Cohen, "King Richard's Buried Treasure," *Chicago Tribune*, November 2, 1997, p. 14.

66. Gary Washburn, "Contracts Boss Out in Shake-up by Daley," *Chicago Tribune*, February 18, 2000, pp. 1, 18. See also Gary Washburn and Laurie Cohen, "Fencing Audit Fails to Answer All Questions," *Chicago Tribune,* June 9, 2000, MetroChicago, pp. 1–2.

67. Andrew Martin and Gary Washburn, "Doors of City Hall Open to Mayor of Little Italy," *Chicago Tribune,* March 26, 2000, pp. 1, 14.

68. Gary Washburn, "Lobbying Law Gains Support After Changes," *Chicago Tribune,* May 15, 2000, MetroChicago, pp. 1–2.

69. The forgoing analysis of the 1999 Daley election is taken from a talk given by Professor Paul Green at the Illinois Political Science Association meeting, October 1999, and the short review article by Alysia Tate, "Blacks Throw Support to White Candidates," *Chicago Reporter,* January 2000, p. 4.

70. Thomas Hardy and Jorge Casuso, "Evans Assails Daley's Contributions," *Chicago Tribune*, March 17, 1989, p. 3. Cited in Rast, *Remaking Chicago*, p. 135.

71. John Pelissero and Timothy Krebs, "Electoral Coalitions, Campaign Finance, and Governing Regimes: The Case of Chicago," *Urban Affairs Review*, forthcoming.

72. Alderman Moore, interview by author, October 14, 1999.

73. Judson Miner, interview on the *848* program, WBEZ Radio, September 17, 1999.

74. Kass, "New Mayor Daley," p. 19.

75. Alderman Moore, interview by author, October 14, 1999.

76. Gary Washburn, "Daley Sells Tax Increase As Necessary Risk," *Chicago Tribune*, MetroChicago, pp. 1–2.

77. Fran Spielman, "Fire Chief Approved, but Protest Votes Rile Daley," *Chicago Sun-Times*, December 16, 1999, p. 22.

78. Cate Plys, "No Dissent in Daley's Empire," *Chicago Sun-Times*, December 17, 1999, p. 65.

79. "Begging to Differ," *Chicago Sun-Times*, December 17, 1999, p. 65.

80. Fran Spielman, "City Clerk Seeks Council Candor for His Web Site," *Chicago Sun-Times*, May 5, 1998, p. 12.

81. Spielman, "City Clerk Seeks Candor," p. 12.

82. *Chicago Acorn et al. v. City of Chicago*, 97 C 6397, November 1997.

83. Feeley deposition, *Chicago Acorn et al. v. City of Chicago*, November 21, 1997, p. 47.

84. Feeley deposition, *Chicago Acorn*, pp. 49–51.

85. Rules set forth by Patrick Johnson, assistant corporation counsel, in the consent decree in *Chicago Acorn*.

86. See Dick Simpson deposition in *Chicago Acorn et al. v. City of Chicago*, June 23, 1998, pp. 1–2, Dick Simpson Papers, Special Collection, Main Library, University of Illinois at Chicago.

87. Tom McNamee, "Daley Fills Vacancies, Builds Power," *Chicago Sun-Times*, October 23, 1997.

88. Barry Rundquist and Gerald Strom, "Citizen Evaluations of Chicago City Government," in Dick Simpson, ed., *Chicago's Future: In a Time of Change* (Champaign, Ill.: Stipes, 1993), pp. 263–264.

89. Grimshaw, *Bitter Fruit*, chap. 9.

90. Rast, *Remaking Chicago*, pp. 156–157.

PART V

History from
the Council Chambers

The overflowing city council chambers at the inauguration of Mayor Big Bill Thompson and the Chicago City Council, April 26, 1915. (Used by special permission of the Chicago Historical Society, Photo ICHI–30912.)

10

Changing Patterns in Mayor–Council Relations

In telling the history of Chicago from the perspective of the council, I have drawn on my direct personal knowledge of, participation in, and observation of the Chicago City Council, as well as on newspaper accounts, historical records, and the council's *Journal of Proceedings* too. Ultimately, however, my work is grounded in a careful analysis of the divided roll call votes in each historical era.

I examined the roll call voting of Chicago aldermen to uncover the basic nature of the political struggle that characterized each political regime. Congressional scholars have long made use of roll call votes to explain coalition formation and the role of political parties in Congress.[1] My study of the city council has utilized similar techniques in focusing on divided roll call votes, but I have analyzed these voting patterns differently than most congressional scholars. Reviewing the considerable literature on congressional and state legislative studies is beyond the scope of this book. However, the similarities between studies of Congress and my study of the Chicago City Council can easily be seen in a recent book on the U.S. Congress, *Legislative Leviathan: Party Government in the House,* by G. W. Cox and M. McCubbins. In it the authors summarize two theories of "committee government" and "party government" to explain voting in the U.S. House of Representatives since its founding in the eighteenth century.[2] As I have done, they use election statistics and roll call votes as the touchstone of their analysis, and they configure their study of congressional voting to focus on individual members' loyalty to party leaders—that is, voting with or against the position of the party leadership in the House of Representatives. Over time, they find different degrees of centralization and support for party leadership. For instance, in the Congress under Speaker Sam Rayburn, committee government was stronger. But in modern times, they conclude that "there is a system of 'conditional party government' in operation throughout the postwar era."[3] Today congressional parties, not committees, govern the House of Representatives. Cox and McCubbins refine and develop the analysis of roll call votes as the means of determining changes in governance over time, using primarily statistics of voting agreement with party leaders.

In a similar way, I focus on election results and particularly on the voting behavior of aldermen relative to the policy preferences of the mayor. I identify the policy preferences of the mayor by observing the voting behavior of the mayor's floor leader or leaders.[4] By showing who votes with and against the floor leader, I demonstrate which aldermen generally support or oppose the mayor and his or her policies. In addition, I illustrate the relative influence a mayor has within the city council by showing the size and cohesiveness of the voting coalitions that support and oppose him or her.

Although the statistical techniques I use are not precisely the same as Cox and McCubbins's, the underlying assumptions of my study of city councils are very similar to their study, and many other studies, of congressional voting behavior. In my study of city council divided roll call votes, I include procedural and budget votes as well as all substantive votes, including proposed amendments and substitute motions. Instead of selecting out only a few key votes to study, I analyze all divided roll call votes in any year studied—the universe of all divided roll call votes in statistical terms. Even if minority factions in the council are frustrated in attempts to push legislation through committees, they can often force procedural votes on their issues on the council floor. Thus any real divisions in the council are noted by studying all divided roll call votes.

It is sometimes worthwhile to study certain key votes, as when an expert witness in the ward remap lawsuit selected twenty-four votes that were racially important in the Richard M. Daley councils to illustrate the impact that race had on council voting under the 1992 ward remap.[5] However, to determine the nature of mayor–council relations and all dimensions of council voting, it is necessary to include all divided roll call votes in a particular time period rather than a smaller sample, no matter how the sample is selected. Altogether, I study more than 1,500 divided roll calls and more than 75,000 individual aldermanic votes in sample years between 1863 and 1994. I also report on other studies of city council voting that have been done—especially in the later Richard M. Daley years after I stopped collecting data.

In my work, I have defined a divided vote as one in which at least one alderman votes in opposition to the majority. Why select only divided roll call votes instead of all council votes—including unanimous ones? In the fourteen time periods covering eighteen years of council voting that I studied, the number of divided roll call votes ranged from a low of thirty-eight divided votes in 1939 (if the unusual votes of Alderman Crowe at two meetings are excluded) to an extraordinary high of 387 divided votes in 1987–1988. Usually there are from fifty to one hundred divided roll call votes in a given year. In these same years several thousand pieces of legislation are introduced and as many as a thousand routine orders, resolutions, and ordinances are passed unanimously without dissent. These include traffic signs, one-way streets, permits for activities, and congratulatory resolutions on anniversaries. For some council periods, such as the Civil War years, I have investigated the routine legislation to demonstrate the segmented pattern of city service delivery. In other times, such as the modern period, I have discussed important issues reported in the media, for example, the frequently unanimous votes on the Ethics Ordinance of 1987 and its various amendments. In such cases, I have gone beyond the formal unanimous votes to disclose the underlying political struggles. For the purpose of quantitative analysis, however, divided roll call votes disclose the nature of different mayor–council regimes most accurately. They also identify critical votes in which there is conflict and dissention which can then be studied in depth.

I have sampled at least one year of roll call voting in each mayoral administration on which I have written. In longer reigns, like those of Richard J. Daley and Richard M. Daley, I have studied two or three different years. I studied two different years under the administration of Harold Washington because the council voting patterns changed dramatically.[6] Since aldermanic and mayoral elections are held in April, a council year often runs from April or May of the year in which aldermen were first elected until March or April of the next calendar year. I usually restrict the roll call votes studied to a single year because the way in which council votes are recorded in the *Journal of Proceedings* means that it can take up to 100 person hours to go through the several thousand journal pages to record the data necessary to analyze a single year's votes. For this reason, it is impossible to study the complete voting record for the more than 150 years of council history. In fact, I would not have been able to study as many years as I have without the help of dozens of students in collecting the data during the last twenty years. If the city clerk continues to tabulate and electronically record divided council votes—and if other cities do so as well—future comparative studies of city councils will be vastly easier. Nevertheless, under the constraints of this study I have selected eighteen years of roll call data over fourteen different time periods. I have studied at least one year of data in every administration since Richard J. Daley became mayor in 1955. For earlier eras, I selected years known to be historically significant in Chicago—1863 during the Civil War, 1907 during the council of the Gray Wolves, when the struggle for Progressive reform was greatest, 1928 on the eve of the Great Depression, and 1939 on the eve of World War II. These were also years in which major historical sources were available that interpret the council behavior, such as the memoirs of Charles Merriam and Paul Douglas and at least one major Chicago history book about each period.

Roll Call Vote Analysis

For each year of roll call vote data, I develop a histogram reporting the frequency of aldermanic voting for the mayor's proposals and conduct a principal components factor analysis, using varimax rotation to uncover the number and size of stable voting blocs within each council.[7] Histograms present the number of aldermen supporting the mayor for different deciles of percentages—such as voting with the mayor 10 percent, 20 percent, or 30 percent of the time. They provide a visual way to distinguish councils. I then compare the histograms to a factor analysis of the same voting patterns. Using both histograms and factor analysis, I am able to compare two different statistical methods of calculating the roll call votes, which helps to ensure that the differences reported are real and not an artifact of particular statistical methods.

Factor analysis also allows me to describe each council in terms of the number of specific voting blocs (factors) that can be distinguished, the number of aldermen in each bloc, which bloc includes the mayor's floor leader, and the percentage of variance in council voting that is explained by each factor. Beyond both histograms and factors analysis, I use roll call votes to help locate key clashes in the city council. Then using newspaper accounts, histories, memoirs, and participant observation, I reconstruct fundamental battles in each council era, recreating the scene, describing the key actors, and recording the reasons which they gave for their actions. The resulting narrative allows us to understand what was at stake in titanic council battles in ways that a merely statistical analysis cannot reveal. From this montage of characters, struggles, and votes emerges the story of the council and the meaning of its history.

Types of Councils

In my research from the Civil War to the present, I have found empirically three types of councils: Fragmented, Rubber Stamp, and Council Wars. There are five examples of fragmented councils: 1863–1864, 1906, 1907, 1928, and 1987–1988. The first four are in the era between the Civil War and the Great Depression and *no councils studied in that era manifested any different pattern of voting.* On the other hand, of the councils I studied, only the Sawyer council in 1987–1988 has manifested this pattern since the Great Depression. It is possible that the Kennelly council from 1947 to 1955, which reverted back to the pattern of the Gray Wolves, was also fragmented, but I have not yet been able to collect the roll call vote data from that council to test the qualitative judgments that journalists have rendered on Kennelly's relations with the council.

The five histograms in Figures 10.1A–E share common characteristics. They display more or less uniform levels of support for the mayor in different deciles of the histogram. In 1863–1864 aldermen supported Mayor Sherman's floor leader, Alderman Comisky, an average of 62.7 percent of the time, but only Alderman Comisky voted his own position 100 percent of the time. No aldermen joined him even 90 percent of the time, only four 80 percent of the time, and the largest group—twelve—clustered in the 70–79 percent range of support. An equally large group of Republican aldermen and war Democrat alderman Peter Shimp were divided between 30 and 69 percent support. This level of support for Mayor Sherman's policies allowed his administration to prevail on most votes, but there was a high level of opposition and many close votes during the Civil War. The fragmented pattern of the Civil War council was duplicated in the other fragmented council histograms.

The councils under Mayors Dunne and Busse, shown in Figures 10.1B and 10.1C, were virtually identical, despite the fact that the two mayors were very different. Both of these histograms display an average level of support varying from 70 to 73 percent but ranging all the way from 20 percent to 100 percent aldermanic support of these mayors' floor leaders. Frequently Dunne and Busse were defeated in important council votes such as those on immediate municipal ownership of the traction system. Twenty years later, before the Great Depression, when Big Bill Thompson had become an "absentee mayor," there was an average of 80 percent support for the mayor's floor leader, but aldermen were still strung out more or less evenly between 20 and 99 percent support, as shown in Figure 10.1D.

The Sawyer council in 1987–1988 provides an almost perfect histogram of a fragmented council with no supporters (even the floor leader and the mayor's own alderman) able to agree 100 percent of the time. However, there were more of less even bands of 50–99 percent support for the mayor, as shown in Figure 10.1E.

In none of these councils was there a guaranteed bloc of mayoral supporters who could ensure that the mayor's programs would always be adopted. This contrasts starkly with the pattern of rubber stamp councils that followed the Great Depression, when strong mayors and party bosses could affect aldermanic elections and could control the patronage jobs given to each ward. Most often in fragmented councils, there are very many divided roll call votes. For instance, during the Civil War there were 174 divided roll call votes and during Sawyer's reign there

Histograms of Fragmented Councils

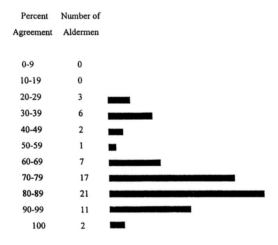

Percent Agreement	Number of Aldermen	
0-9	0	
10-19	0	
20-29	0	
30-39	5	
40-49	6	
50-59	1	
60-69	3	
70-79	12	
80-89	4	
90-99	0	
100	1	

n=32; mean=62.7; median=71; standard deviation=18.7

FIGURE 10.1A   Aldermanic Agreement with Floor Leader for 174 Divided Roll-Call Votes in the Chicago City Council, April 30, 1863–April 30, 1864, Mayor Francis Sherman

Percent Agreement	Number of Aldermen	
0-9	0	
10-19	0	
20-29	3	
30-39	6	
40-49	2	
50-59	1	
60-69	7	
70-79	17	
80-89	21	
90-99	11	
100	2	

n=70; mean=73.24; median=79; standard deviation=19.39

FIGURE 10.1B   Aldermanic Agreement with Floor Leader for 52 Divided Roll Call Votes in the Chicago City Council, January 2, 1907–April 4, 1907, Mayor Edward Dunne

Histograms of Fragmented Councils

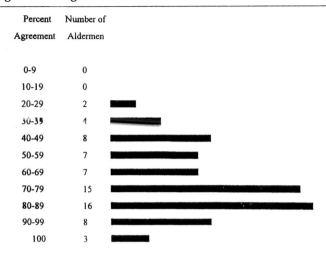

Percent Agreement	Number of Aldermen
0-9	0
10-19	0
20-29	2
30-39	1
40-49	8
50-59	7
60-69	7
70-79	15
80-89	16
90-99	8
100	3

n=70; mean=70.17; median=75.5; standard deviation=20.05

FIGURE 10.1C   Aldermanic Agreement with Floor Leader for 80 Divided Roll-Call Votes in the Chicago City Council, May 6, 1907–December 31, 1907, Mayor Fred Busse

Percent Agreement	Number of Aldermen
0-9	0
10-19	0
20-29	1
30-39	2
40-49	4
50-59	0
60-69	1
70-79	5
80-89	20
90-99	16
100	1

n=50; mean=80.56; median=87; standard deviation=18.39

FIGURE 10.1D   Aldermanic Agreement with Floor Leader for 80 Divided Roll-Call Votes in the Chicago City Council, May 1928–April 1929, Mayor William H. Thompson

Histograms of Fragmented Councils

Percent Agreement	Number of Aldermen
0-9	0
10-19	0
20-29	0
30-39	0
40-49	0
50-59	4
60-69	6
70-79	16
80-89	14
90-99	10
100	0

n=50; mean=78.20; median=78.50; standard deviation=12.02

FIGURE 10.1E   Aldermanic Agreement with Floor Leader for 287 Divided Roll-Call Votes in the Chicago City Council, December 1, 1987–November 30, 1988, Mayor Eugene Sawyer

was an all-time high of 387. Aldermen were divided in their opinions and votes about everything from simple city services to greater issues such as supporting or opposing the national government in the Civil War.

Figure 10.2A–D displays the pattern for the strongest Rubber Stamp Councils. The first four, 1939–1940, 1955–1956, 1971–1972, and 1977–1978, are examples of rubber stamp councils under Mayors Kelly, Richard J. Daley, and Bilandic. In these councils aldermen average from 83 to 92 percent support for the mayor. Kelly had a majority of twenty-seven aldermen supporting him more than 90 percent of the time; Daley had thirty-four in 1955, which increased to thirty-eight by 1971; and Bilandic, ruling over a council that had been elected with Daley in 1975, had an incredible forty-five aldermen voting with his floor leader more than 90 percent of the time. There were fewer divided roll call votes in most of the these councils, ranging from thirty-eight to sixty-one, except for 1971–1972, when opposition to Daley brought 114 divided roll call votes. The mayors who ruled over these strongest rubber stamp councils lost none of these contested votes. As Mike Royko wrote of Daley's reign, "In all the years [Daley was mayor, the council] never defied him as a body."[8]

The five councils shown in Figure 10.3A–E have the basic rubber stamp council pattern but are less extreme than the Kelly/Daley/Bilandic versions. Mayor Byrne had only twenty-four aldermen voting for her programs 90 percent of the time; Mayor Washington after his 1987 reelection

Histograms of Rubber Stamp Councils

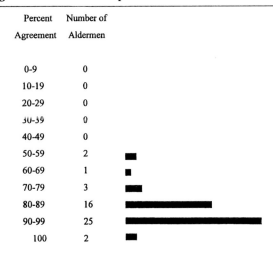

Percent Agreement	Number of Aldermen
0-9	0
10-19	0
20-29	0
30-39	0
40-49	0
50-59	2
60-69	1
70-79	3
80-89	16
90-99	25
100	2

n=49; mean=88.27; median=90; standard deviation=9.203

FIGURE 10.2A   Aldermanic Agreement with Floor Leader (excluding Alderman Crowe's dissent at two meetings) for 38 Divided Roll-Call Votes in the Chicago City Council, April 21, 1939–April 20, 1940, Mayor Edward J. Kelly

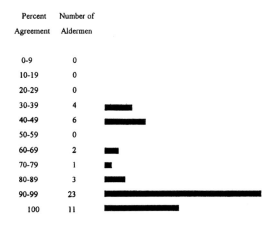

Percent Agreement	Number of Aldermen
0-9	0
10-19	0
20-29	0
30-39	4
40-49	6
50-59	0
60-69	2
70-79	1
80-89	3
90-99	23
100	11

n=50; mean=82.54; median=94; standard deviation=22.90

FIGURE 10.2B   Aldermanic Agreement with Floor Leader for 114 Roll-Call Votes in the Chicago City Council, April 22, 1955–April 5, 1956, Mayor Richard J. Daley

Histograms of Rubber Stamp Councils

Percent Agreement	Number of Aldermen	
0-9	0	
10-19	2	▮
20-29	4	▬
30-39	1	▪
40-49	0	
50-59	2	▮
60-69	2	▮
70-79	1	▪
80-89	0	
90-99	10	▬▬▬
100	28	▬▬▬▬▬▬▬

n=50; mean=84.84; median=100; standard deviation=28.18

FIGURE 10.2C   Aldermanic Agreement with Floor Leader for 114 Divided Roll-Call Votes in the Chicago City Council, April 22, 1971–April 5, 1972, Mayor Richard J. Daley

Percent Agreement	Number of Aldermen	
0-9	2	▮
10-19	1	▪
20-29	0	
30-39	0	
40-49	1	▪
50-59	0	
60-69	0	
70-79	0	
80-89	1	▪
90-99	19	▬▬▬▬▬
100	26	▬▬▬▬▬▬

N = 50; mean = 91.74; median = 100; standard deviation = 22.50

FIGURE 10.2D   Aldermanic Agreement with Floor Leader for 61 Divided Roll-Call Votes in the Chicago City Council, March 21, 1977–December 28, 1977, Mayor Michael A. Bilandic

Histograms of Weaker Rubber Stamp Councils

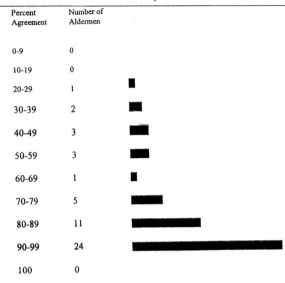

Percent Agreement	Number of Aldermen
0-9	0
10-19	0
20-29	1
30-39	2
40-49	3
50-59	3
60-69	1
70-79	5
80-89	11
90-99	24
100	0

n=50; mean=81.1; median=89; standard deviation=20.22

FIGURE 10.3A   Aldermanic Agreement with Floor Leader for 178 Divided Roll-Call Votes in the Chicago City Council, April 7, 1979–March 19, 1982, Mayor Jane Byrne

Percent Agreement	Number of Aldermen
0-9	0
10-19	0
20-29	3
30-39	1
40-49	3
50-59	1
60-69	3
70-79	3
80-89	5
90-99	11
100	20

N=50; mean=83.3; median= 96.5; standard deviation=23.9

FIGURE 10.3B   Aldermanic Agreement with Floor Leader for 32 Divided Roll-Call Votes in the Chicago City Council, April 15, 1987–September 30, 1987, Mayor Harold Washington

Histograms of Weaker Rubber Stamp Councils

Percent Agreement	Number of Aldermen	
0-9	0	
10-19	0	
20-29	0	
30-39	8	▬▬▬▬
40-49	5	▬▬▬
50-59	3	▬▬
60-69	1	▪
70-79	4	▬▬
80-89	1	▪
90-99	26	▬▬▬▬▬▬▬▬▬▬▬▬▬
100	2	▬

n=50; mean=75.40; median=92.00; standard deviation=23.35

FIGURE 10.3C   Aldermanic Agreement with Floor Leader for 99 Divided Roll-Call Votes in the Chicago City Council, April 1989–March 1990

Percent Agreement	Number of Aldermen	
0-9	0	
10-19	0	
20-29	0	
30-39	6	▬▬▬
40-49	5	▬▬▬
50-59	6	▬▬▬
60-69	2	▪
70-79	1	▪
80-89	5	▬▬
90-99	23	▬▬▬▬▬▬▬▬▬▬▬▬
100	2	▬

n=50; mean=75.70; median=90.00; standard deviation=23.70

FIGURE 10.3D   Aldermanic Agreement with Floor Leader for All Divided Roll-Call Votes in the Chicago City Council, May 9, 1991–March 24, 1992, Mayor Richard M. Daley

Histograms of Weaker Rubber Stamp Councils

Percent Agreement	Number of Aldermen	
0-9	0	
10-19	0	
20-29	0	
30 39	0	
40-49	0	
50-59	6	▬▬▬▬
60-69	4	▬▬▬
70-79	4	▬▬▬
80-89	6	▬▬▬▬
90-99	17	▬▬▬▬▬▬▬▬▬
100	13	▬▬▬▬▬▬

n=50; mean=86.44; median=94.00; standard deviation=15.57

FIGURE 10.3E   Aldermanic Agreement with Floor Leader for 71 Divided
Roll-Call Votes in the Chicago City Council, June 9, 1993–May 3, 1994,
Mayor Richard M. Daley

had thirty-one; and Mayor Richard M. Daley began with twenty-eight,
which grew to thirty nearly unanimous supporters by 1994. The average
level of aldermanic support of the mayor's floor leaders in the weaker
rubber stamp councils of Byrne, Washington, and Richard M. Daley still
ranged from 76 to 86 percent—easily enough to control the outcome of
city council decisions most of the time. But there was a stronger opposition bloc to these mayors' councils under Mayors Kelly, Richard J. Daley,
and Bilandic.

Council Wars Councils are the reverse of Rubber Stamp Councils. There
is a lot more conflict in such councils, as indicated by the relatively high
number of divided and divisive roll call votes. The divisions in the Harold
Washington council had an ideological and a racial basis. Harold Washington's Council Wars council was similar to the gridlock in Washington,
D.C., under Democratic president Bill Clinton and the more conservative
Republican Congress. These conflicts in Council Wars was not altogether
bad because some good policies resulted from these council battles, but to
the extent that they reinforced the racial divisions in Chicago and led to
governmental gridlock, they made governing difficult.

In the histogram of aldermanic agreement with Mayor Harold Washington in 1985 shown in Figure 10.4, twenty-nine aldermen voted with the
mayor from 20 to 39 percent of the time while a minority of twenty-one al-

Histograms of Weaker Rubber Stamp Councils

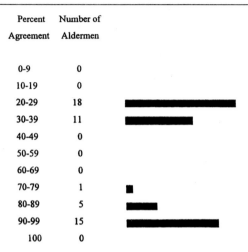

Percent Agreement	Number of Aldermen
0-9	0
10-19	0
20-29	18
30-39	11
40-49	0
50-59	0
60-69	0
70-79	1
80-89	5
90-99	15
100	0

n=50; mean=54.90; median=32; standard deviation=32.29

FIGURE 10.4   Aldermanic Agreement with Floor Leader for 111 Divided Roll-Call Votes in the Chicago City Council, January–December 1985, Mayor Harold Washington

dermen supported him from 70 to 99 percent of the time. There were no aldermen in the middle between these two highly polarized blocs, and there was a difference of more than 30 percent support between them.

Factor Analysis

Figure 10.5 provides a summary table of statistics of the factor analyses of all councils I have studied. Altogether, nine councils were rubber stamp councils, five followed the fragmented council pattern, and only one reflected a Council Wars conflict. Whereas the histograms were created by comparing the vote of individual aldermen to the floor leader, factor analysis compares aldermanic voting patterns with each other without regard for who is floor leader. The similarities between these factor analyses and histograms for various councils indicates that the patterns which I report are not due simply to particularities of the statistics used.

Fragmented councils, which held sway from the Civil War until the Great Depression, had between seven and fourteen factors, with three out of five fragmented councils having at least ten factors. There were as few as eleven and only as many as twenty-three aldermen in the first factor while the first factor explained from only 22 to 40 percent of the variance

Year	Number of Factors	Cumulative Percent of Variance Explained by Each Factor			Number of Aldermen in Each Factor			Number of Divided Votes
		Factor 1	Factor 2	Factor 3	Factor 1	Factor 2	Factor 3	
Rubber Stamp								
1977-78ᵃ	4	78	82	84	43*	3	3	61
1971-72ᵇ	3	81	86	89	41*	6	3	114
1955-56	4	69	82	8/	30*	9	9	57
1979-83ᶜ	5	56	64	69	38*	6	3	178
1993-94ᵈ	6	53	68	72	34*	7	4	71
1989-90	6	47	63	69	29*	12	4	99
1991-92	8	43	61	66	23*	14	5	74
1939	14	42	52	60	35*	5	2	38
Fragmented Councils								
1987-88	8	33	53	62	20	11	11*	387
1907	10	40	57	65	23	19	16*	80
1906ᶠ	14	31	43	52	16	13*	13	53
1928ᵍʰ	13	22	37	47	19	7	6	44
1863-64	7	34	47	55	11*	7	6	174
Council Wars								
1985	4	53	68	72	26	19*	3	111

FIGURE 10.5   Factor Analysis of the Divided Roll Call Votes in the Chicago City Council, Selected Years

in these fragmented councils. The 1907 council, which had twenty-three aldermen in the first factor, had a total of seventy aldermen in the city council, so that only a little more than one-third of the aldermen were in the first factor of any of these councils. Moreover, only in the Civil War council of 1863 was the mayor's floor leader even in the first factor. Fragmented councils, most often under the leadership of the Gray Wolves, were strongly divided and uncontrolled by the mayors. They were characterized by numerous small, loosely structured voting blocs. The mayor's floor leader was usually not a part of the largest bloc, and no voting bloc approached a majority of the aldermen. The idiosyncratic voting behavior in fragmented councils caused less of the variance in voting to be explained by coalitions. Passage of mayoral programs under fragmented councils was uncertain, since voting majorities were unstable and had to be reassembled for each issue. Fragmented councils occurred when the mayor was relatively weak and when there were factions within the political parties rather than a single, unified, dominant machine.

Rubber Stamp Councils created from three to six factors, with the first factor containing from a near majority of twenty-three to a super majority of forty-three out of fifty aldermen. (The two exceptions to this pattern were 1991–1992 and 1939, which had eight and fourteen factors respectively.) The first factor in these Rubber Stamp Councils explains from 43 percent to an amazing 81 percent of the total variance, and the floor leader is in this first factor in all Rubber Stamp Councils. These Rubber Stamp councils had from as few as 38 to a maximum of 114 divided roll call votes a year.[9] Rubber Stamp Councils had one large voting bloc, consisting of a clear majority of aldermen, that supported the mayor. That single voting coalition accounted for most of the variance in council voting behavior. There was an overwhelming pattern of cohesion among the substantial majority of aldermen who voted with the mayor. Because of this, rubber stamp councils did not serve as an effective check and balance on the executive branch of city government.

Weaker rubber stamp councils differed only in having a larger number of voting blocs than stronger rubber stamp councils. The mayor's floor leader remained in the largest coalition, which often approached a majority. In the weaker rubber stamp councils, there was not a single large voting bloc in opposition to the mayor, but often several opposition blocs. The mayor's smaller and looser voting coalition accounted for less than half of the variance in council voting. Still, even in weaker rubber stamp councils, mayors remained influential by directing the largest bloc of votes and passing the bulk of their proposed legislation. Rubber stamp councils mostly occurred only when there were strong mayors backed by a dominant political party machine. City councils tended to become rubber stamp councils the longer a single mayor stayed in power.

The Council Wars council under Mayor Harold Washington was more or less the mirror image of the strongest rubber stamp councils with only four factors, twenty-six aldermen in the first factor, and the first factor explaining 53 percent of the variance. This council differed from the rubber stamp councils in that there were many divided roll call votes in 1985, the mayor's floor leader was in the second factor, and the first two factors combined explain 68 percent of the variance. This was a highly polarized, disciplined, but contentious council. The council was dominated by two large factions—one supporting the mayor and one opposing. Yet neither bloc completely controlled the council's policy decisions. There was a lot more conflict in this council than in rubber stamp councils, as indicated by the relatively high number of divisive roll call votes and the fact that divisions in this Council Wars council had an ideological and a racial basis. The only Council Wars council that occurred in the years studied came about because a reformer defeated the machine candidates for mayor but did not carry with him a majority of aldermen into the council.

Not only are the factor analysis statistics distinctive, but each type of council appears differently when their factors are plotted in Figures 10.6A–D. The 1977 Bilandic rubber stamp council is the most extreme example of autocratic control, with its very large majority bloc of forty-five aldermen clustered around the mayor's floor leader in the upper right-hand corner, a very small minority bloc of three aldermen in the lower left, and two aldermen literally in the middle between the two polarized voting blocs. Next, the weaker 1991–1992 rubber stamp council under Richard M. Daley tends toward the same polarized voting pattern as the Bilandic council, with a pro-administration bloc clustered around the mayor's floor leader in the lower right-hand corner and an opposition bloc in the upper left. There is, however, a much larger and more diffuse opposition in this council than those under Mayors Kelly, Richard J. Daley, or Bilandic.

The 1985 Council Wars council under Mayor Washington shows the same divided structure as the rubber stamp councils, but council voting blocs are much more equal in size, being divided between twenty-one of the mayor's supporters in the lower right and twenty-nine of his opponents in the upper left corner. Finally, the 1987–1988 Sawyer fragmented council has aldermen scattered all over the diagram without any cohesive structure. These factor plots provide a visual image to complement the factor analysis statistics presented in Figure 10.5.

Ideal Types

From these statistics and from eyewitness accounts, it seems clear that very different types of councils have governed Chicago during different historical periods and under different mayoral regimes. One standard technique in social science is to see if this behavior can be organized under ideal types. Are there certain fundamental differences and dimensions to the behavior?

We can visualize the underlying forces creating these city council voting patterns, as shown in Figure 10.7.[10] The poles represent the tensions between conflict and acquiescence; control and participation and the intersection of these forces create four ideal types. To consider just one dimension, in some councils there has been mayoral dominance and tight

Factor Plots for Four City Councils

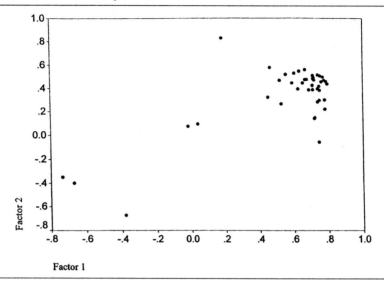

FIGURE 10.6A   Factor Plot in Rotated Space for the Chicago City Council, 1977, Mayor Michael A. Bilandic

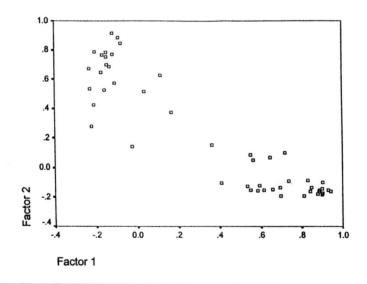

FIGURE 10.6B   Factor Plot in Rotated Space for the Chicago City Council, 1991-1992, Mayor Richard M. Daley

Factor Plots for Four City Councils

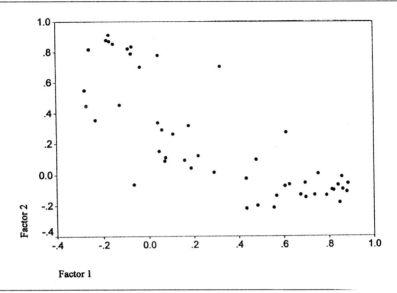

FIGURE 10.6C   Factor Plot in Rotated Space for the Chicago City Council, 1987–1988, Mayor Eugene Sawyer

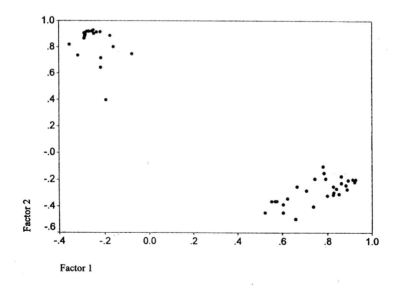

FIGURE 10.6D   Factor Plot in Rotated Space for the Chicago City Council, 1985, Mayor Harold Washington

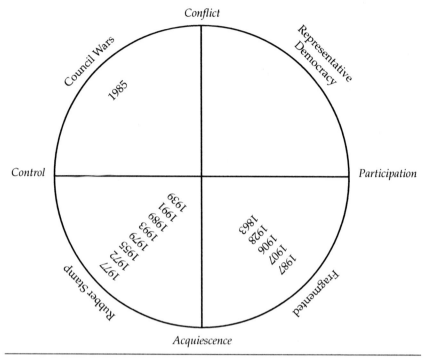

FIGURE 10.7   Types of City Councils

control over both the council and the public. Under Mayor Richard J. Daley, for instance, ideological conformity and allegiance to the "boss" were required. By contrast, in other eras there has been greater openness and the opportunity for both aldermen and citizens to participate in policy-making. Along the other dimension, there has been considerable difference between eras of polarized political conflict in both the council and the society as opposed to laissez-faire eras in which conflicts were less momentous. In these laissez-faire eras, there were many factional groups, public policy was created out of a myriad of lesser conflicts, and the public mostly acquiesced to the decisions of the city government.

These fundamental tensions between conflict, acquiescence, control, and participation create four archetypal city councils. First, there are the by now three familiar types of council: fragmented, rubber stamp, and Council Wars. However, the fourth ideal type, which I maintain has not been realized in Chicago, is representative democracy. In this model, examples of this type of council should appear in the fourth quadrant, but none of the fourteen city councils I have studied fit either the quantitative or qualitative requirements of a representative democracy.

Not only can the councils be put into the different quadrants, but they can be roughly plotted. I have plotted them in accordance with the aggregate statistics from the factor analysis of each council year, as listed in Figure 10.5. More research will be needed to determine if any one statistical measure can allow us to plot these councils more exactly, but these rough calculations serve to illustrate how city councils from Chicago and other cities can be measured.

If the underlying forces that create the different types of councils are the tension between control and participation and the tension between conflict and acquiescence, we can begin to understand the underlying political dynamics involved. Council Wars councils in the upper left-hand quadrant are created when the attempt of each faction to gain dominance and control is evenly balanced. In such a council, conflict between the factions reaches a fevered pitch. In 1862 and the beginning of 1863, the war between council factions was so great that the council was prevented from even meeting because of the split between the Democratic and Republican aldermen during the Civil War. Although there was not a physical war occurring, the Council Wars period during Mayor Washington's first three years in office resulted in a stalemate that brought the city to the edge of bankruptcy before a compromise between the Washington and Burke/Vrdolyak forces could be reached. The level of conflict is very high in this quadrant.

At the other extreme, in the lower left-hand quadrant are rubber stamp city councils in which mayoral dominance brings acquiescence from the vast majority of aldermen and opposition from a small minority, ranging from three to a dozen council members. There are, of course, advantages to having a boss run the city. Those who have access to the boss can get things done efficiently. The disadvantages are less citizen participation, less governmental accountability, and major blunders, since there is no effective check on the actions of the chief executive.

In the right-hand lower quadrant are fragmented councils. They can lead to chaos and anarchy, but in Chicago they more commonly led to the Council of the Gray Wolves. Fragmented councils are characterized by a high level of corruption and an inability to get major projects done, such as the failure of municipal ownership of private transportation systems and the failure to adopt a new city charter in 1906–1907. Fragmented councils, and the weaker political regimes of these periods, provide multiple access points for citizens to participate by influencing a single alderman or a single faction. Fluid factions in these councils shift from issue to issue and from coalition to coalition without the serious schisms of a Council War, but, generally, the city is poorly run in these weak mayor–strong council eras.

The upper right-hand quadrant, representative democracy, allows for real conflict between individuals and groups and requires that their viewpoints be heard and actively considered in council decisions. Representative democracy, according to democratic theory, leads to justice in the distribution of the goods and services of government. It balances conflict and participation in a positive way. It can be characterized by either trustee or delegate forms of voting. That is, aldermen in a representative democracy either represent the economic interests of their communities and the good of all Chicago or they represent the views of their constituents in the council.[11] Although there are individual aldermen who have been trustees and delegates in the course of Chicago history, no mayor–council regime has been characterized by this type of voting. If there were, the statistics would show a voting pattern similar to fragmented councils, and an inspection of particular votes would demonstrate that the reasons for the shifting council divisions were the merits of the issues and the different interests or opinions of different sectors of the city. Of course, representative democracies are not perfect. They can make bad policies such as imperialistic wars, slavery, and racial discrimination, but, in principle, representative democracy is the best possible political system.

So why has representative democracy not been tried in the Chicago City Council? Because citizen participation and legitimate representation of the voters have not been seen as necessary. Certain structures of representative democracy, such as elections, have been put in place, but the practice of democracy in the city council has not. Instead, attempts to create a representative city council have been perverted into producing rubber stamp or fragmented councils throughout Chicago's history.

Studying Other Cities

Histograms and factor analyses provide the empirical criteria that have guided my classification of Chicago city councils. I have supplemented this quantitative data with a careful account of the words and actions of Chicago mayors, aldermen, and other political actors. From this quantitative and qualitative analysis, I have developed the three ideal types of mayoral-council regimes that have existed in the city since 1833 as well as one ideal type, representative democracy, that has not been achieved.

I have provided an account of this particular political history in Chicago and the effects of these political patterns on the city's governance. I have, with the study of elections, city council voting, and major political actions outside the council walls, enlarged the usual classification of modern Chicago as simply a progrowth regime centered around a political machine with a brief progressive regime interlude under Mayor

Washington. Over time, by studying political conflicts and their outcomes, we are able to see larger patterns in elections and policymaking and the coalitions, traditions, and institutions that shape both.

The next step in this research on city councils and their role in urban political regimes is to discover to what extent the patterns that I have discovered in Chicago's political history occur in other American cities. I have provided new analytical tools to measure the types of councils. This methodology allows for the systematic comparison of city council behavior in different communities. Other studies will determine whether the four ideal types I have discovered are universal or peculiar to Chicago. The study of additional cities will allow an exploration of how such factors as city size, absence or presence of a city manager, single-member versus at-large council districts, different local political histories, and different demographic patterns influence council voting behavior. By comparing the governing experience in different cities over time, we should be better able to determine the impact of structural constraints, political history, and political institutions on urban governance in America in the nineteenth and twentieth centuries.

Notes

1. See M. P. Fiorina, *Representatives, Roll Calls, and Constituencies* (Lexington, Mass.: Lexington Books, 1974); H. F. Weisberg, "Evaluating Theories of Congressional Roll Call Voting," *American Journal of Political Science* 22 (1978): 554–577; C. S. Bullock and D. W. Brady, "Party Constituency and Roll Call Voting in the U.S. Senate," *Legislative Studies Quarterly* 8 (1983): 29–43; M. P. Collie, "Voting Behavior in Legislatures," in S. C. Patterson and M. E. Jewell, eds., *Handbook of Legislative Research* (Cambridge: Harvard University Press, 1985); and J. M. Snyder Jr. and T. Groseclose, "Estimating Party Influence in Congressional Roll-Call Voting," *American Journal of Political Science* 44 (2000): 193–211.

2. G. W. Cox and M. McCubbins, *Legislative Leviathan: Party Government in the House* (Berkeley: University of California Press, 1993).

3. Cox and McCubbins, *Legislative Leviathan*, pp. 155, 278.

4. In most cases the floor leader of the council has been the chairman of the all-important Finance Committee. So I have compared the votes of individual aldermen to the Finance Committee chairman's vote to develop statistics like those shown in the histograms in this chapter. However, there are exceptions. For instance, in the Harold Washington council of 1985, Alderman Evans was Washington's floor leader, even though Alderman Burke was Finance Committee chairman. Likewise, to accurately determine Mayor Sawyer's policy positions in the 1987–1988 council, I found it necessary to consider the votes of the floor leader, Alderman Natarus, Mayor Sawyer's own 6th Ward Alderman Robinson, and the mayor's public policy pronouncements. Finally, in the Richard M. Daley councils it was necessary to compare the votes of both Finance Committee chairman

Burke and the mayor's own 11th Ward alderman and political floor leader, Patrick Huels, to be sure of the mayor's policy positions. However, they were almost always in agreement.

5. James Lewis, "Public Preferences, Race, and Policy in Chicago," expert witness report, *Smith v. City of Chicago*, Dick Simpson Papers, Special Collections, Main Library, University of Illinois at Chicago.

6. The data collected over the last twenty years has recently been reconfigured into a common format for analysis. Despite experiencing some difficulties in untangling the data, I found that all but three sets of data are uniformly one year in length, with the following exceptions: All four years from 1979 to 1983 under Mayor Jane Byrne are included as one data set; 1987 includes only seven months of data between Mayor Harold Washington's reelection and his death; and 1993–1994 includes eighteen months of the latest data I have collected on Richard M. Daley's reign.

7. Each factor analysis is based on all divided roll call votes within the city council during a specific period. Aldermen are given a score of 1 if they voted for a proposal and a score of 0 if they voted against it. For some votes, aldermen abstained or were absent. In order to avoid losing cases due to missing data in the factor analysis, I compute scores for aldermen for those proposals upon which they did not vote as follows: I replace nonvoting with a measure that combines the voting behavior of the mayor's floor leader with the frequency with which the alderman in question voted with the mayor's floor leader when they voted. For each alderman, I calculate the percentage of the votes cast by the alderman that are in agreement with the mayor's floor leader. Dividing that percentage by 100 produces a simple measure of the probability that an alderman would vote with the mayor's floor leader, ranging from 0 to 1. For each missing vote, I estimate the alderman's voting behavior by setting it equal to the probability of supporting the mayor's floor leader if the floor leader voted for the proposal, or one minus the probability of supporting the mayor's floor leader if the floor leader voted against the proposal.

For example, if an alderman agrees with the floor leader 70 percent of the time but fails to vote on a particular proposal, I give that alderman a score of 0.7 if the floor leader voted for the proposal. If the floor leader voted against the proposal, the alderman would be given a score of 1 minus 0.7, or 0.3. In essence, I replace nonvotes with estimates of the probability of voting for a given proposal. In total, I recoded 13.8 percent of the votes in this manner for the factor analyses.

8. Mike Royko, *Boss: Richard J. Daley of Chicago* (New York: Dutton, 1971), p. 18.

9. The data for the Jane Byrne council covers all four years of her term, so the 178 divided roll call votes average only forty-five divided roll call votes a year. The Kelly council in 1939–1940 also has an anomaly. At two meetings Alderman Dorsey Crowe voted no on the omnibus vote at the end of those meetings and thus is recorded as voting against the administration and all other aldermen some sixty times. Because of these special circumstances in 1939, the total of ninety-eight divided roll call votes misrepresents the true levels of support and opposition. If we exclude Alderman Crowe's sixty protest votes at the June 12 and August 8 meetings, we are left with thirty-eight genuinely divided roll call votes. Histograms and factor analyses for all ninety-eight divided roll call votes

cast in 1939–1940 show exactly the same patterns as the analysis of the thirty-eight votes.

10. I was inspired to do this mandala form of the four-way chart by the work of C. J. Jung and more directly by the work of John Giannini. For a more detailed discussion of this type of chart and its personality analogue, see John Giannini, *The Compass of the Soul: Typology's Four Archetypal Directions As Guides to a Fuller Life* (Gainesville, Florida: Center for the Applications of Psychological Type, 2001).

11. For a discussion of the elements of representative democracy, see Hanna Pitkin, *The Concept of Representation* (Berkeley: University of California Press, 1967), especially her discussion of the philosophy of Edmund Burke.

11

Democracy's Endless Struggle

One of my principal arguments in this book is that the Chicago City Council is an extreme example of American politics that magnifies its virtues and defects in ways that help us understand its positive and negative features more easily. The story of the city council from the Civil War to the present is a tale of a continuing struggle to obtain the American Dream—democracy and justice. As such, this story is filled with larger-than-life heroes and colorful scoundrels. It is a story of rogues, rebels, and rubber stamps.

Chicago politics has followed a particular historical pattern, with most fragmented city councils occurring before the Great Depression and all rubber stamp city councils occurring since the Great Depression. Before the Great Depression, there was no single unified machine able to control the mayor's office and a large majority of the aldermen; rather, there were many little machines and factions within both political parties, as well as reformers seeking to defeat the machines. Since the Great Depression, other than the brief six years under Mayors Washington and Sawyer, the pattern has changed to rule by a single dominant political machine, a rubber stamp council, and a progrowth regime. Despite the differences between fragmented councils, rubber-stamp councils, and Council Wars, what is most striking about Chicago political history is that representative democracy has never flourished within the city council.

Chicago at the beginning of the third millennium remains guided by a "where's mine" politics.[1] In spite of its dominant machine and progrowth politics, Chicago remains a city of contrasts. Mayors Big Bill Thompson, Ed Kelly, and Richard J. Daley were "builder mayors," whereas Mayors Michael Bilandic and Eugene Sawyer only served as transitions to very different regimes. Although there have been famous corrupt Chicago political figures such as Bathhouse John Coughlin,

Hinky Dink Kenna, and Paddy Bauler, there have also been famous political reformers such as Abraham Lincoln, Adlai Stevenson, Charles Merriam, Edward Dunne, Paul Douglas, and Leon Despres. Chicago bosses such as Daley, Nash, Kelly, Lorimer, and McDonald have always been challenged by grassroots reformers like Jane Addams, Saul Alinsky, Gail Cincotta, and Jesse Jackson. These countervailing trends are encompassed within Chicago politics. Although the strength of the Chicago machine increased the vitality and creativity of the Chicago reform movement, in the end bosses triumphed more often than reformers. But new reformers have always emerged to tame the worst aspects of machine politics.

In this book I have asked why neither democracy nor justice has been fully achieved in this most American of cities. Thus, at heart, this is not the tale of a single city, much less a single politician or a particular social movement, but an exploration of American society. It is our history viewed over generations as seen in the microcosm of the Chicago City Council. Although there has been progress during this 150 years—economic, social, and political—there has not been ethical or moral progress. Democratic alderman John Comisky and Republican alderman Charles Holden from Chicago's Civil War council would have no difficulty serving in today's city council. In fact, they would be less corrupt and more public-spirited than the majority of Mayor Richard M. Daley's rubber stamp aldermen, far too many of whom have been convicted of corruption and sent to serve jail sentences.

In Chicago, the fight between racial groups, machine politicians and reformers, cops and demonstrators is waged in the open, with gloves off, in contrast to suburbs and small towns in which people hide behind euphemisms of polite society. Because of Chicago's raw honesty, America's past is revealed and its future foretold in the struggles in Chicago's city council chambers. This is why its galleries have often been filled with mobs of citizens shouting advice and encouragement to the aldermanic gladiators. It is why the media covers what happens within the council chambers.

Sociologists, historians, and political scientists have studied American urban politics intensively since the 1950s. They first discovered elites governing American cities; later they found pluralistic elites clashing in the public arena; and lately they uncovered governing regimes marrying business leaders and politicians—the private and public faces of power. While building on previous research, I have sought to provide a new focus and a new methodology for classifying urban politics by focusing on city councils that mirror and determine broader political developments in America.

Enlarging Regime Studies

By using quantitative and qualitative analysis, we can determine how the struggle for democracy and justice goes—whether the council is controlled by a unified wealthy elite, party factions, or machine factions under the control of ward bosses we can see whether it is best characterized as a fragmented council war or a rubber stamp council. Election battles, coalitions aligned behind different candidates, financial campaign contributions that make waging campaigns possible, and final election outcomes provide us with additional information about the key issues and voting blocs in different historical periods. Both election and city council battles are a window into the political component of the larger governing regime of the city. Campaign issues and campaign contributions often indicate who comprises the private sector of the regime which creates regime policies that distinguish, for instance, between a progrowth developmental regime and a progressive regime.

By studying roll call votes in depth and using histograms and factor analysis, we lay bare the patterns of the city council, like the DNA of urban politics. By paying close attention to what the mayors and aldermen say as they argue and vote, we learn what is at stake in their struggles. Although the Chicago City Council has been the stage for many grandiloquent gestures and much foolishness, it has also revealed what is happening to our American political experiment at different periods in our history.

Thus election and city council studies round out any analysis of the influentials in a community power structure and any decisionmaking analysis of larger brick and mortar projects in a city. This focus on electoral politics and city council battles allows us to balance the overemphasis that some studies have given business leadership, progrowth policies, and business-dominated regimes.[2] These patterns of power and politics revealed in Chicago in turn reflect the ongoing struggle for democracy and justice in America.

Chicago's Story

As I have recounted, Chicago was incorporated as a town in 1833 and as a city in 1837. Chicago government in the early nineteenth century was small, clubby, and consensual for the most part. Generally, the mayor and the aldermen were lawyers, real estate speculators, and businessmen— often displaced Yankees who had come west to make their fortunes. They led a booster regime governed by Chicago businessmen themselves who wanted the city to grow, expand, and make them rich. There was almost no corruption in city government because there were very few government jobs to give out and city services were provided segmentally. Property owners would sign a petition to pave a street or put in sidewalks, and their alderman would present it to the council. It would pass and city government would do the job but would levy a tax or an assessment on the owners of the adjacent property to pay for it. The downside of this limited, segmented government was that some tasks requiring a strong general government did not get done.

For instance, the Chicago River was polluted by the meatpacking firms along its banks. The residents of the poor neighborhoods near the stockyards wanted clean drinking water, an end to the stench, and an elimination of health hazards. But the meat packers would not agree to pay to clean up the river. It took the city decades to reverse the flow of the river and build tunnels two miles out into Lake Michigan to obtain fresh drinking water and bring an end to cholera epidemics. Thus the early nineteenth century was a time of very limited local government under a booster regime that was adequate for the birth of a city but inadequate to govern a more modern metropolis.

The second period of Chicago politics came when the Civil War created civic wars within Chicago and a partisan regime. Chicago had rallied to elect Lincoln, the first Republican president, and most Chicagoans supported the war in the early years. During the Civil War era, Chicago became the major metropolis of the West as the hub of river and rail traffic in the nation. Doubling its population every decade, Chicago included not only Yankee adventurers but displaced Southerners and large ethnic populations from Ireland and Germany. Politically, Chicago was divided between Republicans and two factions of the Democratic Party—War Democrats and Peace Democrats.

The city council, which by now contained aldermen representing the growing ethnic populations, was a strange amalgam. On some war issues like the "patriotic resolutions" the council was divided bitterly between the Democratic and Republican Parties. Whereas on other war issues such as providing funds to pay a bounty for volunteers for the Union army or providing fuel and money for widows and orphans of soldiers, the council was united. Moreover, on providing ordinary city services, such as building the lake tunnels to obtain fresh drinking water, the council was divided, not according to party lines but according to aldermen's views on the merits of the proposals. The amazing thing, given the difficulties of the war, the strong passions it aroused, the invocation of martial law, and the uncertainty of the future of the nation, was that this fragmented and divided city council with its weak mayor managed to govern as well as it did and that the city continued to grow and develop as the greatest city of the West.

The third great period of Chicago history, machine politics, was more corrupt than the first two. By now, the ethnic groups had taken control of the city council and often the mayor's chair. After the Civil War, the Great Chicago Fire of 1871, and the famous Columbian Exposition of 1893, Chicago was governed by fragmented political parties and the "Council of the Gray Wolves." After the Chicago Fire, Mike McDonald, a saloon keeper and politician, introduced the politicians and the saloon and brothel keepers to each other and pointed out their mutual self-interest. The saloon keepers would provide men with free beer and food to vote for certain favored politicians—especially those in the Levee District, the red-light, wide-open district along the South Branch of the Chicago River. They would also provide money for campaigns and bribes for the aldermen. In return, the aldermen would make sure that the police did not raid their establishments. Each Chicago ward organization was headed by a boss, and the bosses joined together into rings that controlled the city council and frequently the outcome of higher elections. The city was still divided into Republicans and Democrats, but there were several factions within each party.

The Council of the Gray Wolves was named not only because of the silver hair of the elder aldermen but also because of the rapacity with which they divided the spoils. The mayors varied during the sixty-year period in which the Council of the Gray Wolves was dominant. Mayors Carter Harrison I, his son Carter Harrison II, and Big Bill Thompson tolerated corrupt aldermen as long as they supported mayoral programs. Conversely, reformers like Mayors Edward Dunne and William Dever opposed them and tried to force major reform programs through the council. For instance, Mayor Dunne attempted to bring about immediate municipal ownership of utilities and the transportation systems. Because of opposition in the council paid for by large bribes by the traction owners, Dunne failed and Chicago would not get a genuine public transportation system until the Chicago Transit Authority was created in 1947, some forty years later. Thus the corrupt and fragmented Council of the Gray Wolves frequently was unable to solve the city's major problems. This machine politics era created a regime in which some businessmen supported petty party bosses and corrupt aldermen and others sponsored progressive reformers. Nonetheless, it was a progrowth regime, especially under "builder mayors" like Big Bill Thompson, although progress was frequently impeded by social, political, and governmental fragmentation.

After the Great Depression and World War II, a fourth political system emerged. It was the classic urban growth machine discussed in so much of the urban politics literature. In this period, the political parties became more centralized. The Chicago Democratic machine in its modern form was created by Mayor Anton Cermak in 1931 and perfected by Mayor Richard J. Daley after 1955. Daley particularly combined the role of party boss with his control of the party precinct captains and the role of mayor with his control of city services and patronage jobs. He ruled with an iron fist and gradually subdued the Council of the Gray Wolves. Daley transformed it into a council that would rubber stamp his proposals. Yet within this rubber stamp council there was spirited opposition. Reformers opposed the mayor and offered alternatives. When the opposition bloc grew strong enough, it offered an alternative government. Even though reformers such as Despres, Oberman, Orr, and myself did not come to power, many of our ideas and programs were enacted in the next Chicago regime.

Following Richard J. Daley's death, the city experienced a radical political transformation into its fifth and briefest era, the progressive regime. After a two-year caretaker government led by Daley's successor, Michael Bilandic, the first woman mayor, Jane Byrne, was elected. She was followed four years later by the first black mayor, Harold Washington. Washington ran on a progressive reform platform and created a progressive government. The white ethnic machine aldermen in the council vigorously disagreed. So began Council Wars, the greatest battles in the council since the Civil War. The council was divided 29–21, with the majority being the mayor's opponents. It was difficult to pass even city budgets to keep the city afloat and the city teetered on the edge of bankruptcy more than once. From this Council Wars period and the progressive regime under Mayor Washington came extended programs of affirmative action, freedom of government information for citizens, the signing of a court decree ending patronage, and the largest neighborhood infrastructure improvement program in Chicago's history.

The current stage in Chicago's political evolution is the sixth regime, the New Chicago Machine. Washington, like Mayor Richard J. Daley before him, died in office. Like Mayor Bilandic, Washington's successor, Eugene Sawyer, was in power for only two years. Mayor Sawyer presided over the most fragmented and chaotic council in the city's history. When the dust settled, Richard M. Daley, Richard J. Daley's son, was the mayor leading Chicago into the third millennium. A rubber stamp council mostly agreed to his proposals for a managerial government with steady improvements for the city like a downtown and neighborhood building boom, a repopulation of the city with the middle class, the new Millennium Park, school and public housing reforms, and flowers and trees planted in the parkways.

Whereas Richard J. Daley had depended on State Street businessmen and developers for campaign contributions and for support of his progrowth policies, Richard M. Daley depends more on the construction industry, lawyers, bankers, and members of the emerging global economy for campaign contributions and his programs of tourism, amenities, and downtown and neighborhood economic and housing development. Although both Daleys had rubber stamp city councils, the current mayor has less absolute control than his father, although his dominance over the council has grown each year.

Categories like machine, developmental, progressive, and managerial regimes do not adequately describe the New Chicago Machine evolving under Richard M. Daley. Although his regime resembles the urban growth machine perfected under Richard J. Daley, this Mayor Daley was originally elected by white and Latino voters and opposed by black voters. As his power increased, he has gradually won over more support from African-American community leaders and voters, but he does not yet have majority support in that community. Only in his last election did the racial composition of the voters who elected him begin to resemble the electoral coalition that elected his father. The New Chicago Machine depends on a mixture of the old-fashioned machine of patronage precinct workers and modern media, candidate-based, political campaigns; financial support from the progrowth construction industry and new business allies from the global sector of the economy; and a rubber stamp council alongside a modern government continuing programs of affirmative action, privatization, and more balanced downtown and neighborhood economic development.

City Council Reform

Throughout its 150-year history and all six regimes, the Chicago City Council has seen continued reform efforts. Since Washington's reign from 1983 to 1987, there has been some progress. The first ethics ordinance passed in 1987, as did the requirements that aldermen disclose how they spend their expense accounts and that only public expenditures are allowable. Additional rule changes require aldermen to disclose when they have a vested interest in land that they propose to rezone.

When Mayor Richard M. Daley was first elected in 1989, he added to the ethics reforms the Sullivan proposals on campaign contributions, which limited the amount of money a city contractor may contribute to aldermanic and mayoral campaigns. Although Daley cut the number of aldermanic committees only by one, he cut committee budgets by $1 million at his first council meeting. Even with a slight reduction in the number of committees in future Daley administrations, council committees are still too numerous and reform aldermen are still not provided committee staff, unlike staffing for the two parties in Congress and state legislatures. Thus the functioning of council committees has been only marginally improved under Daley.

Mayor Daley also passed three sets of amendments to the ethics ordinance to prevent the conflicts of interest that so many aldermen have experienced. As of June 2000, twenty-six aldermen have gone to jail since the 1970s for corruption. Although conflict of interest rules are stronger now, they have not solved the problem of aldermanic corruption.

Another reform has been the city clerk's disclosure of pending legislation, council and council committee meeting dates, as well as voting by aldermen on divided roll call votes. The City Hall official Web site also provides copies of the speeches and pronouncements of the mayor on public issues. Since this information appears only on the Internet, which is not universally accessible, most of the public is still unaware of the actions and the pending decisions of their mayor and city council. Nonetheless, this is a positive step in providing better citizen information.

Finally, a successful lawsuit against the city now requires that seats in the council chamber be available for citizens and citizen organizations who favor and oppose pending legislation, instead of allowing the city administration to pack the galleries with city employees and administration supporters. However, a neighborhood government or a regular method of citizen participation through public meetings, cable television, and the Internet has not been developed. Neither the mayor nor the machine aldermen in the council are interested in promoting citizen participation.

These incremental procedural reforms have proven insufficient to reform the city council. A fundamental political change in Chicago to overcome its long history of corruption and machine politics is still required. Until then the New Chicago Machine with its rubber stamp council will reign.

The Meaning for America

Perhaps the American experiment in democracy and justice will succeed only modestly, as it has in Chicago, where machine politics and outlawing overt forms of racial discrimination are the best we have managed. Maybe the goals of the American experiment are too lofty to be achieved by human beings subject to such frailties as greed, anger, ambition, and jealousy. Perhaps our history of rule by elites, a political culture of corruption and citizen indifference, and political institutions that are formally democratic but promote oligarchy are too strong to be overcome by ideals of representative democracy.

Although Chicago has produced tyrannical mayors like Richard J. Daley and demagogues like Big Bill Thompson, each generation has also produced reformers to correct the flaws in our government. From time to time, Chicagoans have elected reform mayors like Edward Dunne, William Dever, and Harold Washington and reform aldermen like Merriam, Douglas, Despres, Cousins, Rayner, Oberman, and Orr. But reform forces have never been able to gain the upper hand for long enough to re-structure the political process sufficiently to prevent a return to the Councils of the Gray Wolves or the Rubber Stamp Councils that have been the norm throughout Chicago history.

Our struggle for a better future still rages. It is restaged every other week in the Chicago council chambers and every few years at the ballot box. Although Alderman Paddy Bauler was right in 1955, when he said, "Chicago ain't ready for reform," Chicago has nevertheless improved. Of course, public influence over city policies has been limited because the council has either been ruled over by petty party bosses in the councils of the Gray Wolves or by a supreme party boss in the rubber stamp councils. Now a new machine of money, media, and technology married with the old machine of patronage precinct workers, insider contracts, and political favoritism rules Chicago.

To break the vicious cycle of either old or new machine politics takes more than a single election or a technological innovation, such as the introduction of the city clerk's homepage on the Internet. Deep social, economic, and cultural changes are needed to transform Chicago's politics and the city council that reflects them. Whether changes in the racial composition of the city, the switch to the service economy, or Chicago's new role in the global economy can fundamentally change the city's politics and government remains in doubt. For now, rogues and rubber stamp aldermen continue to outnumber rebels and reformers in the city council and in broader American politics.

However, if Chicago and American history teach anything, it is that the forces of reform, although frequently defeated, are never permanently vanquished. Under the pressure of events, new reformers always rise up and demand more democracy and justice in some new crusade. Whether the Chicago City Council will ever be converted into a representative democracy remains uncertain. Perhaps our children, or our children's children, will create a government that is truly of, by, and for the people.

Notes

1. The phrase was coined by Mike Royko in his book *Boss: Richard J. Daley of Chicago* (New York: Dutton, 1971).

2. For a critique of these studies, see especially Terry Nichols Clark and Edward Goetz, "The Antigrowth Machine: Can City Government Control, Limit, or Manage Growth?" in Terry Nichols Clark, ed., *Urban Innovation: Creative Strategies for Turbulent Times* (Thousand Oaks, Calif.: Sage, 1994), pp. 107–108.

Postscript and Acknowledgments

Originally, I had planned to append the entire record of the more than 1,500 divided roll call votes on which this book is based. However, all that detail would double its size while being of no interest to the general reader. Researchers who want the data may obtain a copy of these roll call votes in machine-readable form from Special Collections, Main Library, University of Illinois at Chicago.

I cut several hundred pages from a longer version of the original manuscript and several hundred footnotes from the final version of this book. The analysis of a number of additional roll call votes, as well as general historical materials, had to be deleted. Interested scholars will find copies of the original manuscript at the Main Library (UIC), the Chicago Historical Society, and the Harold Washington Public Library in Chicago.

Many people made this book possible. My original compilation of city council votes was begun by my aldermanic staff, especially legislative aides Sandye Wexler and Judy Stevens. This data collection was continued by a legion of undergraduate and graduate students who worked with me for a decade and a half to assemble and analyze council votes. Among the students who worked on this project and earlier publications are Jennifer Arneson, Duane Bean, Lisa Dushkin, Ann Gentile, Geneva Jackson, Lillian Larsen, Connie Mixon, Lesia Okruch, Jean Peterman, Jennifer Rexroat, Uma Sharma, and Wayne Slaughter.

Professor Tom Carsey, my colleague and journal article coauthor, helped me develop the factor analysis used to analyze the roll call votes. The histograms and factor plots used in this book were then produced by two graduate student research assistants, Sean Hogan and David Zehner, under the supervision of Professor Carsey and myself. Sean Hogan also carefully edited a draft of the entire manuscript, correcting many of my errors and making numerous suggestions for improvements. Sean also provided much of the data on financial contributors to mayoral campaigns.

My research on the city council was made possible by a series of grants by the Office of Social Science Research, the Campus Research Board, the Great Cities Institute, and the Humanities Institute at the University of Illinois at Chicago. Additional funds were provided by the Woods Charitable Fund, the Joyce Foundation, the Amoco Foundation, and the MacArthur Foundation for studies of the city council and Chicago government incorporated here. All these grants have provided me the time to do the research and to pay for the research assistants necessary for such an undertaking.

In my city council research I used especially five library archives: Chicago Historical Society, Illinois Regional Archives at Northeastern Illinois University, Municipal Reference Library Archives at the Harold Washington Public Library, Special Collections at the Main Library of the University of Illinois at Chicago, and the John and Mary Jane Hoellen Chicago History Collection at the Conrad Sulzer Regional Public Library. All the librarians who preserve these collections and assist researchers have my thanks. Without these resources such historical research would be impossible and history as a source of inspiration, warning, and insight would be lost.

I benefited from comments by four thoughtful anonymous reviewers selected by Westview Press. They helped me shorten the manuscript, rearrange the chapter order, and shorten the quotations that had made reading the book more difficult. I benefited from additional reviews of particular chapters by John Giannini, Tom Gradel, Melvin Holli, and my wife, Sarajane Avidon.

I am pleased to be working once again with Westview's senior editor, Leo Wiegman. His support and his faith in my work made publishing this book possible. The series editor, Professor Terry Clark at the University of Chicago, was very supportive and provided a careful final critique of the manuscript that improved it immensely. Both Leo and Terry value my approach to the study of politics and share my goals of justice and democracy. Copy editor Chrisona Schmidt contributed to improving the text and production editor Michelle Trader guided book production, making it swift and efficient. After all this assistance, any errors that remain in this volume are mine and are not to be attributed to the researchers, grant agencies, librarians, reviewers, and editors who helped make this book possible.

Finally, I thank my wife, Sarajane Avidon, for putting up with all the difficulties of researching and writing. I only hope that this volume sells as well as the Morgan Taylor mystery series, which she coauthors with Sue Sussman.

Index

Printed in the United States
23927LVS00004B/16-39

9 780813 397634